THE HISTORY OF THE
VIII KING'S ROYAL IRISH HUSSARS

THE HISTORY OF THE VIII KING'S ROYAL IRISH HUSSARS 1693–1927

VOLUME ONE

BY

THE REV. ROBERT H. MURRAY, LITT.D

WITH A FOREWORD BY
GENERAL THE RIGHT HON. SIR BRYAN T. MAHON
K.C.B., K.C.V.O., D.S.O.

The Naval & Military Press Ltd

Reproduced by kind permission of the Central Library,
Royal Military Academy, Sandhurst

Published by

The Naval & Military Press Ltd

Unit 10, Ridgewood Industrial Park,

Uckfield, East Sussex,

TN22 5QE England

Tel: +44 (0) 1825 749494

Fax: +44 (0) 1825 765701

www.naval-military-press.com

In reprinting in facsimile from the original, any imperfections are inevitably reproduced and the quality may fall short of modern type and cartographic standards.

Printed and bound by Antony Rowe Ltd, Eastbourne

Preface

THIS history has been written in the firm conviction that the past of the Regiment moulds the present to an incalculable degree. According to that great Irishman, Edmund Burke, "no cold relation is a zealous citizen." "To be attached to the sub-division, to love the little platoon we belong to" is the first step in the growth of civic duty. To love the regiment we belong to is the first step in the growth of soldierlike duty. That such a love animates the VIII King's Royal Irish Hussars is well known to all who have the good fortune to be acquainted with its officers and men. Nor would the writing of this history have been possible without their hearty co-operation. Major Henderson, D.S.O., O.B.E., gathered lists of early officers and transcribed documents, and these have been of inestimable service. Indeed, as the originals have been burnt in the Record Office, Dublin, it is difficult to understand how the history from 1693 to 1745 could have been written had it not been for his foresight. He, Colonel Van der Byl, D.S.O., Colonel Mussenden and Colonel Thoyts have been good enough to read my proof sheets, which owe much to the care and attention that they bestowed upon them, and I thank them cordially for their efficient assistance. Colonel Curell and Major Blakiston Houston have also helped me in many ways, and I feel most grateful to them. I owe much to Major Becke, R.A., for the untiring help he so willingly gave me. Sir Charles Oman, K.B.E., and the Hon. Sir John Fortescue, K.C.V.O., have always most courteously answered the questions which my researches prompted me to send them. Mr. Baldry, of the War Office Library, proved extremely helpful to me. The Imperial War Museum has been good enough to allow the reproduction of official photographs in Chapters XIV and XV.

The publishers of my *Revolutionary Ireland and its Settlement*, Messrs. Macmillan & Co., Ltd., kindly gave me permission to make quotations from it.

ROBERT H. MURRAY.

BROUGHTON RECTORY,
HUNTINGDON.
August 24th, 1927.

Contents

VOLUME I

VOLUME II

Contents

APPENDICES

List of Illustrations

VOLUME I

VOLUME II

List of Illustrations

MAPS

**THE COLOURED PLATES IN THIS REPRINT
ARE PLACED AFTER THE FOREWORD**

Foreword

THE VIII Hussars have hitherto been unfortunate in possessing no adequate history of the Regiment. The official record edited by Cannon, whilst meagre and not always accurate, ceases at the year 1843. The account written by Smet, the Regimental doctor, only covers the 18th century. There remains, therefore, nearly a century, and a very eventful century, during which the doings of the Regiment are hidden in the military archives.

It had long been felt that it was due, not only to those who have gone before, but to those who may come hereafter, that a complete history of the Regiment, to the present day, should be printed. The desire to carry this out was universal amongst all who were connected with the Regiment, but the difficulties in the way were great. However, in July 1925, owing to the generosity of some of the retired officers, the undertaking was made possible.

The satisfactory compilation of a regimental history is a task of peculiar difficulty. It is true that the writer may confine himself to recording the actual doings of the regiment, looking neither to the right nor to the left, but that method, though simple, can only result in an amplified journal which can have little interest for anyone unconnected with the regiment. On the other hand, he may take a larger outlook where active operations are concerned and, whilst giving due prominence to the actions of the regiment, may discuss incidentally the causes of the war, the general strategy of the campaign and any tactical considerations affecting the part taken in it by the regiment. This course will, no doubt, produce a more intelligible and readable book, but it demands a just sense of proportion in resisting the temptation to devote too much space to recent campaigns, in comparison with earlier ones, and nice judgment in knowing what to omit and when to stop, for the record of a regiment on active service could often be expanded into a history of the campaign.

These points having been considered, it was resolved to entrust the work to an experienced military historian, and the regiment was fortunate in securing the services of Dr. Murray.

The task has been, in many respects, a most laborious one. To follow the thread of the Regiment's career in ten reigns, in four centuries and in three continents has involved a great amount of research. Apart from all other references, masses of documents, often badly written, badly spelt and badly indexed, have required examination on the mere chance of their revealing some fact or detail which, though trifling in itself, might prove to be an important link in the chain of events; for the record of a regiment cannot be treated on the broad lines of an ordinary history. Much of its interest must necessarily be of a personal character.

The grateful thanks of the Regiment are due to Dr. Murray, not only for the great care and pains he has bestowed upon the work, but also for his keen sympathy with the subject.

" Pristinae Virtutis Memores," the motto granted to the Regiment a hundred and fifty years ago, speaks not only of pride for the past, but of faith and hope for the future, faith in the ever-living honour of the regiment and hope that those who come after may prove worthy of the glory and the traditions bequeathed to them. In whatever capacity a man may have served, let him feel that it is no mean thing to have belonged to the VIII Hussars.

BRYAN MAHON,
General and Colonel,
VIII (K.R.I.) Hussars.

May 21st, 1927.

General John Severne

1742

BOUSBECQUE, MAY 18, 1794.

1804

Major-General Sir Robert Rollo Gillespie. K.C.B.

LIEUT.-COLONEL THE HONBLE. HENRY WESTENRA.

1825

1844

1852

Introductory

THE RAISING OF THE REGIMENT

The VIII King's Royal Irish Hussars proudly displays, on its list of battle honours, such names of the World War of 1914–18, as Givenchy, 1914; the Somme, 1916–18; Bazentin, Flers-Courcelette, Cambrai, 1917–18; St. Quentin, Bapaume, Rosières, Amiens, Albert, 1918; the Hindenburg Line, St. Quentin Canal, Beaurevoir, the pursuit to Mons, and France and Flanders, 1914–1918. These distinctions were gained against an enemy whose sovereign had broken his word, an enemy too who threatened the very existence of the British Empire. This is entirely in keeping with the tradition of the Regiment, which was raised against an enemy whose sovereign had broken his word, an enemy too who threatened the existence of the beginnings of the British Empire. For the part that William II of Germany aspired to play at the beginning of the twentieth century had already been played by Louis XIV of France at the close of the seventeenth century. As Flanders was the seat of an international struggle in the twentieth century, so was Ireland in the closing decades of the seventeenth century.

There have been many great duels in history. There was that rivalry between man and man which was witnessed between Charles of Burgundy and Louis XI, between Charles V and Francis I, and between Philip II and the Prince of Orange. Perhaps the greatest of all was the duel between Louis XIV and William III, which, for a time at least, was fought in Ireland. The course of Irish history was powerfully affected by these two great rivals. Each of these players on the international chess-board regarded Ireland as a pawn in the game, and the thoughtful spectator must always remember that each played or attacked it from an European, not from an Irish, point of view.

The fortunes of Ireland for the last two decades of the seventeenth century depended upon the attempt of the Grand Monarch to dominate Europe, and upon the counter efforts of his rival to checkmate him. Here the custom of treating the history of Ireland apart from that of other nations has done much to obscure the course of the game. The player on his international side is hidden. No doubt from the latter point of view it is difficult to understand the progress of the game, for the play seems puzzling, and at times the moves are bewildering. Yet if the reader does not try to see the larger motives in the mind of the player, he inevitably makes mistakes, and his limited outlook blinds him to the inner significance of the events. On him who surveys Irish history from the European standpoint the highest rewards are bestowed, for he finds clues to many a move of the piece which we may call Dublin.

The House of Stewart fell in 1649, was restored in 1660, and finally crashed to the ground in 1688.[1] The historian can now write "finally," but to the men of the Restoration it was not at all clear that this time the fall was irremediable. For sixty years after the flight of James II efforts were made to restore the exiled dynasty. The ill-planned expeditions to Ireland in 1689 and 1690, and the "Fifteen" and the "Forty-Five," are specially notable. Yet a careful reading of the secret history of the time discloses other plans that seemed destined to succeed.

In spite of the efforts of Charles II and James II, the heart of England remained decisively Protestant. The English saw the tyranny of Louis XIV both at home and abroad, and this tyranny became connected in their minds with Roman Catholicism. Their own king at home, James II, convinced them that a Roman Catholic monarch and a tyrant were synonymous terms. The form of Roman Catholicism that James II and his ally, Louis XIV, professed, deserves attention. Despite the devotion of both to their communion, they regarded it as the State department of religion. The French Church in 1682 seemed on the verge

---

[1] James II fled to France, December 22–25, 1688, and landed at Ambleteuse. He afterwards set out for Ireland, and landed at Kinsale on March 12, 1689.

of separation from Rome. That noble Pontiff, Innocent XI, regarded with intense disfavour the Gallicanism of the French and the English kings, and his attitude left an abiding mark on the history of Ireland. For he swung round to the side of the Dutch king, and uttered prayers for the success of his expedition to our shores.

To ensure the success of the French moves against William of Orange it was of vital importance to gain and to hold control of the sea. Richelieu saw the worth of such control, but this insight was denied to the successor of Mazarin. For Louis XIV did not understand the force of Berkeley's pregnant line:

Westward the course of empire takes its way.

He turned his gaze east when he ought to have turned it west, and, as his gaze was steadily removed from sea to land, his fleet became in the course of time so insignificant that at last the English fleet proved supreme. In truth, neither William III nor Louis XIV properly grasped the right method of handling a navy. Besides, the French king forgot that on the ruins of Spain two other maritime nations were growing up—Holland and England. He was not fully alive to the significance of the place where his land and theirs met—the English Channel. In any struggle at sea the importance of these waters was signal, for a contest there must prove the prelude to struggles elsewhere. Tyrconnel in Ireland and Frontenac in Canada tried hard to turn the gaze of Louis westward past his own shore, but they utterly failed.

The death of Charles II in 1685 had altered the situation in some degree. Charles could—and the biting phrase neatly marks off the difference between the two brothers—if he would, and James would if he could. William in Holland saw how much depended on the friendly attitude of the new King, and he tried to secure it. James for the moment desired the friendship of Holland, for he wanted peace to complete the work of his brother. He had resolved to imitate Charles in his remarkably successful attempts to gain absolute power, for with the silencing of the opposition of the towns by the writs *quo warranto* came the subservience of Parliament. James thought that with the silencing of the two ancient universities there would surely come the subservience of the clergy. With an obedient Parliament and an obsequious clergy, what had his policy of Romanising the nation to fear? Moreover, had not his cousin of France proved that the conversion of heretics was a feasible, nay, an easy, task? Did not even Bossuet assure his sovereign that the revocation of the Edict of Nantes in 1685 was a tremendous success? No doubt James's English subjects might be affrighted at the form the conversion assumed, but much might be put down to the belief that the reports were as exaggerated as those of the 1641 Rebellion undoubtedly were. His absolute power should be shown as effectively in matters ecclesiastical as his brother's had been in the sphere of civil affairs. But—it was a grave "but"—in order to convert England to Roman Catholicism the need of French succour was apparent.

The Revolution of 1688 united Holland and England under one head, giving William the control of the three territories divided by the two pieces of water. Between his native land and England lay the English Channel, and between England and Ireland the Irish Channel. On the control of these two narrow straits the success of the combination against Louis depended, for whoever held these seas must ultimately prove master of Europe. If William succeeded in retaining it, the ascendency of France must become a thing of the past, and England, or rather William, must take its place. The silver circle of the sea preserved England from all danger of an invasion by land, though Holland lay open to a land attack through Belgium. In order to make his position impregnable it was as necessary for William to secure the safety of Belgium as it was to hold the narrow seas. "The Republic," held William, "cannot lose Belgium, its proper bulwark."

From 1689 to 1697 the struggle between England and France goes on. Nominally the King of France is supporting the exiled monarch in his attempt to regain his crown and to drive the usurper away. Really there is a life-and-death struggle proceeding between William and Louis, and on its results depends the answer to the all-important question, Is Europe to be ruled by the tyrant or is it to be allowed to develop freely? If Louis gained control of the Channel, despotism confronted Europe; while if William secured it, freedom would have every opportunity of asserting itself. The theatrical scene of farewell at St. Germain when James set out for Ireland imposes on the hasty reader who has not studied the secret history of the time. When he has, however, consulted the documents, now yellow with age, which reveal that secret history, he at once revises his estimate of the generosity of the French king. For then it becomes patent that the seeming generosity of Louis was in reality the outcome of studied ostentation and calculating selfishness, and that in the soul of the great Bourbon, with all his brilliance, there shone none of that pure zeal for liberty which gleamed so persistently in the breast of his less showy rival.

Louis in 1688 rearranged the pieces in the game he was playing. If James went to England, he might succeed at once, or he might fail; the expedition of Monmouth had enjoyed but a brief career. If, on the other hand, he went to Ireland, France in 1689 still had control of the sea. If William could be persuaded to go there, supplies to him could be blocked on the initiative of France. Let James set out for Dublin, and William must follow him. The French king resolved on an expedition to Ireland, not with the desire of seating James on his throne, but with the desire of making the wearing of the crown as uncomfortable as possible to his rival. France would best be served by a long-continued and desultory warfare, rendering William incapable of action in Europe and making the Channel still a cipher.

Discerning Dutchmen wrote near the time of the birth of William Henry, Prince of Orange and Count of Nassau: "All the world knows well enough how the French seek to become masters of all Europe, as is seen from Cassan's treatise . . . we have seen on their cannon the words *Ratio Ultima Regum.*"[1] Louis might well be credited with saying, "L'Etat, c'est moi," for he reflected the spirit of the men over whom he ruled. He states his position clearly; "When Charlemagne by his victories had brought this dignity into our House, it meant the rule over France, the Netherlands,

---

[1] Meiern, *Acta Pacis Westphalia,* I, p. 243.

Germany, Italy, and most of Spain."[1]   To him, as to his people, the frontier of the Rhine, the claims on the Spanish Netherlands, supremacy in Italy and Spain, were matters of vital moment never to be lost sight of.   Might not the sickly Charles II of Spain expire at any moment?   Who should succeed him?   None but a Bourbon, Louis was firmly persuaded.   The death of the Spanish king was momentarily expected, though he lingered on for thirty-five years.   To Spain, therefore, the eyes of Louis were always turning, for at any hour a messenger might arrive with a despatch announcing that all was over.   The question of succession to the throne of Spain formed "the pivot on which turned almost all the policy of Louis XIV; it occupied the diplomatists and the arms of France for fifty years and more; it formed the grandeur of the earlier days of his reign, and caused the misery of its end."[2] James II never understood that all his plans for his restoration to his kingdom must bend before this dominant thought in the mind of his powerful patron.   Ireland or England was to be in the front or in the background of French policy, according as each helped or hindered the solution of the intricate Spanish problem.   Interests in Spain henceforth provide the motive, conscious and sub-conscious, of French diplomacy, and determine the direction of Louis's whole policy.[3]

The thoughts of the French king were long thoughts.   In 1648 Sir Nicholas Plunkett had offered to confer the protectorship of Ireland upon him.   In 1666 he received the offer of the submission of Ireland, if the Irish were aided in their attempt to throw off the yoke of England.   Tyrconnel approached him with a similar offer.   Since June, 1686, Tyrconnel had been practically supreme ruler in Ireland, and, like Strafford, he made preparations for the contest which he foresaw.   He remodelled the Privy Council, adding eighteen Roman Catholics and two Protestants to it.   The Lord Chancellor, Sir Charles Porter, did not take a

---

[1] *Œuvres de Louis XIV*, I, pp. 72–4.

[2] Mignet, *Négociations relatives à la succession d'Espagne*, I, p. iii.

[3] On the attitude of France to Ireland, *cf.* my *Revolutionary Ireland and its Settlement*, Chap. I.

lax enough view of his functions, and he was replaced by a convert from Protestantism, Alexander Fitton. The new Baron of the Exchequer, Stephen Rice, and his colleague, Sir Henry Lynch, announced that Protestants should have nothing from them but the least the law could give them. Rice indeed declared his intention of driving a coach-and-six through the Act of Settlement of 1662, a measure he hated as cordially as Tyrconnel himself. With the Privy Council and the bench of judges remodelled, the next step was to control the sheriffs and the justices of the peace. Tyrconnel was nothing if he was not thorough. In 1686 there was only one Protestant sheriff in the whole country, and his name appeared by a mistake.

The towns were the stronghold of Protestantism, and it was vital to Tyrconnel to get rid of the householders in the hundred towns that existed. It was an easy process. Had not Charles II shown the way? The Roman Catholic Viceroy required the surrender of the charters of the towns, and in a short time all the corporations had to yield. For the future two-thirds of all the members of the corporations must be Roman Catholic. Take an instance of the thoroughness of the change. In Derry there had been sixty-five aldermen and burgesses, and all of them were Protestant. Now at one fell swoop no less than forty-five of them were Roman Catholics. There are methods of redressing grievances but such a drastic one was sure to provoke immediate trouble.

In Queen Elizabeth's day, by an Act passed in the eleventh year of her reign, Ulster was declared to be "the most perilous place in all the isle." Nor is this statement surprising, for the northern province was then the most distinctively Irish portion of the country. The native race in it was purer than in the other three provinces. Of course the term purity can only be applied relatively to any portion of Ireland, as Huxley's famous essay clearly demonstrated. The variety of races which constitute Ulster nationality is truly astonishing. "Saxon and Norman and Dane are we," sang Tennyson. Doubtless considerations of space and metre prevented him from giving an exhaustive list. For the men of the northern province not only are Saxons, Normans, and Danes; they are also Irish, Scots, French, and German.   Nor can we ignore the fact that the name Scotland is ultimately derivable from the Scoti, an Ulster tribe that colonised Scotland.   At one point there are no more than twenty miles of sea separating County Antrim from Argyll.

In the severe school of adversity the character of the Ulsterman was shaped.   He felt the heavy hand of Strafford, the Richelieu of Ireland, who loved Presbyterianism as little as his colleague Laud.   He endured the terrible days of the 1641 Rebellion, when some ten thousand Protestants were massacred.   His confidence in his own powers, however, never deserted him.   When Tyrconnel oppressed him, he at once rebelled against the authority of James II. Nor can we avoid discerning in the men of the front rank that Ulster has produced the same sturdy spirit of independence. Among ambassadors and statesmen there stand the Cannings of English, Indian, and Turkish fame, Lord Dorchester of Canada, a proconsul in the same rank as Robert Clive and Warren Hastings, Lord Castlereagh, Sir Robert Hart, Lord Bryce, Lord Dufferin, and the great figure of Lord Lawrence, who, more than any other single man, saved India in the crisis of the Mutiny of 1857.   In the ranks of the judges there stand Lord Cairns, the greatest judge of the Victorian era, and probably of the nineteenth century, and Lord Macnaghten.   Among metaphysicians there are such men as Francis Hutcheson and William James, and among writers the Brontës, William Hazlitt, Henry James, and Sir Samuel Ferguson, the real precursor of the Celtic Revival.   Among scientists there stand Sir Hans Sloane, the founder of the British Museum, Joseph Black, the discoverer of carbon dioxide, and Lord Kelvin, the Napoleon of science in the nineteenth century.   Among soldiers there are such men as Robert Rollo Gillespie, the fearless, John Nicholson, a Bayard of India, and Sir George White of Ladysmith.

The yeomen of the north realised in 1689 that the time had come for defence, if not for defiance.   The Enniskilleners announced the spirit of the whole race in their declaration that "We stand upon our guard and do resolve by the blessing of God rather to meet our danger than to expect it."[1]   The rebellion of 1689 was racial, for the moving cause was the opposition between the men of Ulster and those of the rest of Ireland.   It is a mere accident that the boundaries of race coincided with those of religion.   The Ulstermen felt towards the natives much as a Southern planter felt towards his slaves.   Contemporary writers noted in them something of the Castilian haughtiness of manner, founded upon the conscious superiority of a dominant people.[2]

In Ulster many threatening signs were to be observed early in 1689.   The farmer experienced delay and difficulty in getting his horses shod, for the blacksmith was busily engaged in the manufacture of skenes and pikes.   We hear of a friar who preached a sermon to soldiers, and the burden of his discourse was the grievous sin of Saul in not slaying the Amalekites.   Masses were said in public for an object that remained undisclosed, and the average yeoman conceived the idea that he understood the secret design.   The details of the massacre of St. Bartholomew were conned with a new and horrible interest, for some such fate seemed hanging over the readers thereof.   To come nearer home, the doings of Sir Phelim Roe in 1641 were discussed by the flickering light of turf fires, where the rising anger of many a father kindled the smouldering passions of his son.

It may be that Tyrconnel imagined that the rumours current would produce no other effect than that of terrifying the yeoman into acquiescence in his plans.   This method had been tried before, and tried with conspicuous success.   The worst of it was that the Irish enthusiasm might be inadvertently stimulated too far.   That might be awkward.   There are evil spirits which it is easier, as German legend tells us, to raise than to lay, and the spirit of ascendency is of them.   That there was no foundation for the rumour of the intended massacre of the Protestants is beyond all doubt.   Tyrconnel exercised complete control over the Government, and he had little reason to think that he would be unable to

---

[1] Hamilton, *Actions of the Enniskillen Men*, p. 58; MacCarmick, *Further Impartial Account*, p. 13.
[2] *The Character of the Protestants of Ireland* (1689) ; *The Interest of England in the Preservation of Ireland* (1689) ; two anonymous tracts.

overpower the settlers in Ulster if they dared to rise. The fact remains that his policy had been so ill-advised in its inception and so hasty in its execution that it left no hope in the mind of the settler. While he was thus agitated, the hints of the coming danger took a definite form in the shape of a letter found in the streets of Comber, County Down, addressed to Lord Mount Alexander. The anonymous note was dated the 3rd of December, 1688, and ran as follows: "I have written to you to let you know that all our Irishmen through Ireland is sworn: that on the ninth day of this month they are all to fall on to kill and murder man, wife and child; and I desire your lordship to take care of yourself and all others that are to be judged by our men to be heads, for who soever of them can kill any of you, they are to have a Captain's place; so my desire to your honour is, to look to yourself and give any other nobleman warning, and go not out either night or day without a good guard with you, and let no Irishman come near you whatsoever he be; so this is all from him who was your father's friend and is your friend and will be, though I dare not be known, as yet, for fear of my life."[1]

The letter was a hoax, but a hoax that produced grave consequences.[2] When carburetted hydrogen and air in certain proportions exist in a mine, no great harm ensues so long as they remain undisturbed. If a miner, however, enters with a lighted candle, an explosion at once takes place. This is what happened in Ulster when the letter was read. In the excited state of feeling its authenticity was never suspected, and it spread with a celerity akin to that of the notorious chupatties of 1857. In the north a spirit of active resistance was forthwith displayed, for both Enniskillen and Derry closed their gates. It is strange to reflect that the writing of this letter was the first link in the chain of events leading up to the informal gathering of the yeomen, some of whom in 1693 became incorporated into the regiment then known as Conyngham's Dragoons.

---

[1] Mackenzie, *Narrative of the Siege of Londonderry*, Chap. I; King, *State of the Protestants in Ireland*, App. No. 12.

[2] *Cf.* Leslie, *Answer to a Book intituled The State of the Protestants in Ireland*, p. 78.

A copy of the anonymous letter to Lord Mount Alexander arrived at Enniskillen on the 7th of December, 1688, and gave rise to much excitement among the inhabitants. On the 11th came a letter from Dublin, stating that two companies of infantry were to be quartered in the town. The policy of Louvois was known to the people, and whispers of the dragonnades were bruited abroad. Five men, William Browning, Robert Clarke, William MacCarmick, James Ewart, and Allen Cathcart resolved to deny the soldiers entrance to their town.[1] It is difficult to restrain a smile at this resolution when one learns that all the means of resistance in Enniskillen was ten pounds of powder, twenty firelocks, and eighty men. Yet the little town was to demonstrate that after all a spirit of undaunted resolution counts for more than material resources. "Moral force," maintains Napoleon, "is to the physical three to one." MacCarmick consulted Gustavus Hamilton, who advised resistance. The inhabitants elected Hamilton as Governor and Colonel in command, and appointed Thomas Lloyd Lieutenant-Colonel, and a small body of two hundred foot and one hundred and fifty horse was formed.[2] All the Roman Catholic residents were sent away, and the neighbouring Protestants were asked to assist in the defence. Cathcart and MacCarmick were despatched to Derry in order to secure arms and ammunition, and to acquaint the people of the maiden city of their determination to defend their town. They delivered a letter to Mountjoy, who was a nobleman with wide influence in Ulster, from the inhabitants of Enniskillen, stating, "Our resolutions are firm and fully fixed to preserve this place as a refuge for many souls to fly if any massacre should be attempted, which we daily fear and tremble to think of . . . we will demean ourselves with all sobriety imaginable ; neither did it ever enter into our thoughts to spill one drop of blood, unless we be thereunto forced in our own defence, or to take from any man the value of a farthing."[3]

[1] Paul Dane's letter to W. MacCarmick, December 13, 1688.

[2] Cf. *The Cavalry Journal*, III, p. 60, for "Tactics and Training of Cavalry, 1640–1760," by Lieut. H. C. Malet, 8th Hussars.

[3] MacCarmick, *Further Impartial Account of the Actions of the Inniskilling Men*, p. 11. On Mountjoy, cf. Avaux to Louis, April 23, 1689.

Though the town of Enniskillen had no walls, still it was protected by the waters of Lough Erne.[1]   This natural fortification was, however, impaired by the freezing of the lake, whereupon the men, like the Russians at the passage of the Beresina in 1812, resorted to the device of breaking the ice around the town.   Their spirit was such that when the supply of swords and pikes failed them, the smiths were ordered to fasten the blades of the scythes to the ends of poles.   Derry men could not send arms and ammunition, for they were all wanted at home.   Hugh Hamilton and Cathcart were ordered to go to England to procure these necessaries, and to assure the Prince of Orange of their adherence to his cause.[2]   They were to show how important was their town as being the "only inlet from Connaught to Ulster."[3]   It was in fact the key to Ulster from the side of Connaught, and, if it were captured, Derry could not hold out long.   On the 11th of March, 1689, in the market-place of Enniskillen, William and Mary were proclaimed King and Queen amidst a scene of keen enthusiasm.   Lundy tried to persuade the zealous inhabitants of both Enniskillen and Cavan that they ought to retire to Derry.   He was unsuccessful in his appeal, but the appearance of the army of Lord Galmoy at Cavan compelled the inhabitants to withdraw to Enniskillen in most piteous plight.

Galmoy advanced to Belturbet and began the siege of Crom.[4]   Much of his success depended upon the old Chinese policy of scaring the enemy by an imposing appearance before the fight began.   He employed a curious device to conceal his lack of cannon.   Two cannon were constructed of tin, bound with whip-cord and covered with buckram.   These were drawn by sixteen horses as if they were real guns, and with these he threatened to batter down the castle.   A volley of firearms was the sole answer the tiny garrison vouchsafed to give.   Meanwhile Hamilton

[1] *Macariae Excidium*, pp. 311–2, 313.

[2] Their commission from Enniskillen bears the date of January 16, $168\frac{8}{9}$.

[3] Hamilton, *Actions of the Enniskillen Men*, p. 58 ; MacCarmick, p. 13.

[4] Wolseley's despatch to Schomberg, *London Gazette*, $\frac{\text{Feb. 27}}{\text{Mar. 3}}$, $16\frac{89}{90}$; Letter from an officer at Belturbet, March, 1690.   Contrast *Macariae Excidium*, p. 314.

hurried two hundred men to their relief, and the united forces routed the Jacobite general.[1]   He retreated to Belturbet, where he stained his name by an act of gross treachery.   One of his captains, Brian Maguire, had been captured at Crom, and Galmoy offered to exchange Captain Dixie for him.   The proposal was accepted, and Maguire released.   When the prisoner came to Belturbet Galmoy tried Dixie and another prisoner, Charleton, on the charge of high treason.   The two were offered life and liberty if they turned Roman Catholics and followed the Jacobite banner.   They scornfully rejected these infamous terms, and were hanged from a signpost in Belturbet.   Maguire, to his lasting honour, was so indignant with Galmoy that he resigned his commission.   This faithless deed left a marked impression in Ireland, for the tale speedily scattered abroad.[2]   It embittered the whole contest, and made men determined neither to give nor to receive quarter from a Jacobite.[3]

Emboldened by their success at Crom, the Enniskilleners sallied forth and attacked the enemy wherever and whenever an opportunity presented itself.   Lundy renewed his efforts to persuade them to retire on Derry.   In this he was again unsuccessful, though he persuaded the men of Dungannon and Sligo to withdraw.   The misfortune of the latter town proved of good service to Enniskillen, for two troops of horse and six companies of foot arrived from it. Hamilton at last returned from England and brought with him supplies, but of these Lundy allowed merely six barrels of powder and sixty old musket-barrels to be forwarded to Governor Gustavus Hamilton.   The new troops and the fresh supplies, slight as they were, encouraged Colonel Lloyd to pursue the enemy at Trillick and Augher, and he routed them at Belleek, returning with horses, cattle, sheep, and provisions.[4]   At the end of May, 1689, he had

---

[1] Hamilton, p. 11 ; MacCarmick, p. 31.

[2] *Cf.* the repeated references in the Clarke Correspondence (Trinity College, Dublin).

[3] MacCarmick, p. 32 ; Hamilton, p. 12 ; *Ireland's Lamentation, etc., written by an English Protestant that lately narrowly escaped with his Life from thence*, p. 32 ; Story, *A True and Impartial History*, p. 7 ; Harris, *History of the Life and Reign of William III*, p. 215 ; *Narrative of the Murders perpetrated on the Protestants in Ireland by the late King James's Agents*, p. 25.

[4] Hamilton, p. 19 ; MacCarmick, pp. 40–1.

cleared the enemy out of the county of Cavan, and proceeded to Kells, within thirty miles of the capital. Hamilton marched to Omagh to make an attempt to relieve Derry, but the advance of a large force under Clancarty compelled his retreat.[1] As a result of this enterprising policy the men of Enniskillen never lacked anything. During the war Hamilton proudly informs us that in his market-place a good milch cow cost no more than eighteenpence, and a cow not giving milk sold for one-third of that price.[2]

While the men of Enniskillen were winning these triumphs, matters were not so prosperous in Derry, though one piece of notable good fortune befell the northern city in the temporary removal of its garrison. The place had been garrisoned by Lord Mountjoy's regiment, and, as he and his men were for the most part Protestants, the citizens were satisfied with them. In his desire to aid his master, Tyrconnel had ordered troops to move to Hounslow Heath, and to fill their place Mountjoy was commanded to march to Dublin at the end of November, 1688. The Earl of Antrim had lately raised a regiment, consisting largely of Roman Catholics, and it was sent to Derry. As the men had recently been enlisted, they were not in a position to take up quarters immediately, and for a fortnight the town was without a garrison. The blunder was criminal. Avaux remarked that "the man who would have served the King of France, his master, as Tyrconnel served James in taking away Mountjoy's regiment, would have lost his head." In another sense the Lord Deputy did lose his head, for his fatal mistake rendered the siege possible.

News came on the 7th of December, 1688, from Mr. George Phillips of Newtown Limavady, that Antrim's force was approaching, and the same day Mr. George Canning sent to Derry a copy of the notorious anonymous letter of the 3rd of December, 1688. Men remembered that another such letter had saved Parliament from the consequences of the Gunpowder Plot, and that the capture of Dublin in 1641 was prevented by as improbable a discovery as

---

[1] *Cf. Wars in Ireland between their Majesties' Army and the Forces of the late King James* (London, 1690).

[2] Hamilton, p. 17 ; MacCarmick, pp. 37-9.

this letter.   To people in this frame of mind the sight of Antrim's red shanks was enough.   They heard the soldiers were coming "without any arms beside skeans, clubs, and such other weapons as kearns and tories used."[1]   The authorities, however, shrank from the extreme step of refusing entry to the king's troops, but the matter was taken out of their hands by the action of the people.   As the officers and men drew near the Ferry quay entrance, some apprentices rushed out, drew up the drawbridge, and locked the gate, when the soldiers were but some sixty yards distant.[2] Thus on this eventful 7th of December did the citizens of Derry cross the Rubicon, though with grave misgivings.   Imbued with the doctrine of the divine right of kings, the Deputy Master, Buchan, and the Bishop, Hopkins, counselled submission.   "My Lord," replied Irwin, one of the apprentice boys, "your doctrine's very good, but we can't now hear you out."[3]   Arms and ammunition were taken from the magazines, and a guard was mounted.

Haunted still by a dread of the massacre, the Protestants ordered the Roman Catholics out of the city.   Fearing for the consequences of the shutting of the gates, some responsible citizens wrote to Mountjoy explaining the action of "the rabble," and trusting "your lordship will represent our danger to His Excellency, the necessity we are under, and obtain from him his allowance and countenance for securing ourselves from these Ulster enemies."[4] One may shrewdly conjecture that the real purpose of this communication was to gain time until the writers saw the squadron sail into Lough Foyle.   It was on that fateful day, Sunday the 9th of December, that the expected massacre was to take place, but the 9th came and went, and not a single Protestant lost his life.[5]   It was then argued that the day of revenge was only put off,

[1] King, p. 115.

[2] Their names are H. Campsie, W. Crookshanks, R. Sherrard, F. Sherrard, A. Irwin, J. Steward, R. Morison, A. Cunningham, S. Hunt, J. Spike, J. Conningham, W. Cairns, and S. Harvey.   The VIII Hussars notes the names of J. Steward, A. Cunningham, and J. Conningham, particularly.   Conyngham is, of course, the modern spelling.

[3] *An Apology for the Failures charged on the Rev. Mr. George Walker's Printed Account*, p. 13.

[4] The date of this letter is December 9, 1688, Mackenzie, *Narrative of the Siege of Londonderry.* App., pp. 47, 254.

[5] Story, p. 3.

and that therefore it behoved all to be on their guard. Moreover, William had entered London, and it was certain that Tyrconnel would not yield to him without a contest. These considerations were placed before the citizens by David Cairns, and they determined to persist in their defensive attitude. He organised them into a regular force of six companies, over each of which he placed a captain, a lieutenant, and an ensign.[1] Like the Enniskilleners, they resolved to send a deputation to London, and accordingly Cairns was despatched to pray for speedy succour, especially from the Irish Society, their landlords and their friends.[2]

Tyrconnel ordered Mountjoy north again with six companies of his regiment. So far the citizens remained loyal to James, though they were resolute in admitting no papists into their city.[3] Mountjoy secured admission for two of his companies, all Protestants, but, as the other four included Roman Catholics, they were quartered at Strabane, Newtownstewart, and Raphoe.[4] The people, however, insisted on the condition that their companies should mount guard in turn with the trained soldiers. Having arranged matters in the north, Mountjoy was called to Dublin in January, 1689, and his second in command, Lieutenant-Colonel Robert Lundy, became Governor. Before his recall the people of Enniskillen sent Mountjoy a deputation asking, like the Derrymen, for a favourable consideration of their case.[5] "My advice to you is," he replied, "to submit to the King's authority." "What, my lord," remarked one of the amazed deputies, "are we to sit still and let ourselves be butchered?" "The King," answered Mountjoy, "will protect you." "If all that we hear be true," retorted the delegate, "his Majesty will find it hard enough to protect himself." Before New Year's Day the flight of James to France proved that he was unable to defend himself, much less his subjects.

[1] *Apology*, p. 4 ; Mackenzie, Chap. I. ; *Reflections on a Paper pretending to be an Apology or the Failures of Walker*, p. 6.

[2] The letter to the Society at London, sent from Derry by Cairns, December 10, 1688 ; Mackenzie, pp. 160–7, 256.

[3] The Declaration (of the Mayor, Sheriffs, and Citizens of Londonderry).

[4] Mackenzie, 169.

[5] The Lord Mountjoy's Articles with the city of Derry, December 12, 1688 ; Walker, *Diary*.

As the Jacobites afterwards crowded to Limerick, so now on all sides men hurried to the maiden city. They came from Antrim, Down, Armagh, Monaghan, Tyrone, and Donegal.[1] A sober estimate puts the number of fugitives at 30,000, and of these some 7,000 were declared fit for military service.[2] The city of refuge is picturesquely situated on the left bank of the river Foyle, some four miles above the point where the river empties its waters into the Lough. On the north and west lie low hills, on the east and north flows the river, which at the city is over forty feet in depth and more than a thousand feet in breadth. The site gently ascends from the water to the Cathedral, and the houses are evidently at the mercy of men-at-war anchored in the river. In 1689 there were no houses on the right bank, and no bridge spanned the broad waters of the Foyle. The shape of the city was an ellipse, and its four principal streets formed a cross, the arms of which met in a square called the Diamond. Where each of these streets touched the wall a gate was pierced. On the north was Ship's Gate, on the south Bishop's Gate, on the east New Gate, and on the west Butcher's Gate.[3] The fortifications had originally been erected by the colonists to repel the attacks of the dispossessed Celts. The encircling wall, a mile in circumference, built of earth and stone, was over twenty feet high, from six to twelve feet thick, strengthened by nine bastions at the corners and sides, and by two half bastions. For the defence of these the London Companies had provided eight sakers and twelve demiculverins. Near the wall on the south side lay a strong fort on Windmill Hill.

The scanty store of supplies had been on the 21st of March, 1689, augmented by Captain James Hamilton, who brought with him from England 480 barrels of powder, arms for 10,000 men, and £595 in money.[4] The amount of provisions on hand was lamentably inadequate, especially when account is taken of the number within the walls. In the city were 7500 trained soldiers,

[1] Aickin, *Londerias*, II, p. 5 ; Bennet, p. 18.
[2] Avaux, April $\frac{4}{14}$, 1689 ; *cf. Macariae Excidium*, pp. 320–1.
[3] Ordnance Survey of County Londonderry, p. 99.
[4] Kempton, *Siege and History of Londonderry*, p. 393 ; Bennet, p. 16.

and the volunteers increased their ranks to 10,000 or 12,000. The weakness of Derry lay not in its men but in their commander, and in the bad condition into which the wall had been allowed to fall. Lundy was actually holding secret communications with James. His motives are not easily read, but a certain lack of physical courage, combined with a want of public spirit, marked him out as unfitted to discharge his duty in the strenuous times into which his lot had been cast. He endeavoured first to induce the Ulster garrisons to retreat to Derry, then to bring about the surrender of his own city. His tone was so despairing that many officers left the city, and more prepared to follow their example.

On his return from London, Cairns, who had gone as a member of the deputation seeking succour, carried with him a letter from William, informing Lundy that "his Majesty's greatest concern hath been for Ireland, and particularly for the province of Ulster, which he looks upon as most capable to defend itself against the common enemy. And that they might be the better enabled to do so, there are two regiments already at the sea-side ready to embark . . . with which will be sent a good quantity of arms and ammunition, and they will be so speedily followed by so considerable a body, as (by the blessing of God) may be able to rescue the whole kingdom and re-settle the Protestant interest there."[1] In penning so confident a despatch William had not bargained for the unhappy duplicity of the Governor.

In the meantime the chief command of the Irish was entrusted to the experienced Count of Rosen. Under him were Maumont, a lieutenant-general, and Pusignan, a brigadier. For the work of training and organising the Irish army about 400 French captains, lieutenants, cadets, and gunners were carefully selected. When the Jacobites crossed the Bann, they advanced steadily and reached the waterside of Derry on the 13th of April. Lundy did not strengthen the men employed to guard the fords of the Finn. Major Stroud counselled that harrows should be sunk at the fords in order to impede the movements of the cavalry. His advice

[1] Shrewsbury to Lundy, March 8, 168$\frac{8}{9}$; *C.S.P., Dom.*, 1689–90, pp. 16–17.

was disregarded, and in the sequel it proved an easy matter for Rosen to cross at Cladyford.[1]

The same day that Rosen forded the Finn, Colonels Conyngham and Richards brought 1600 troops from England.[2] Lundy conferred with these officers, and persuaded them that it was useless to land their men, for the place must fall into the hands of the enemy within a short time, as there were not provisions for 30,000 men for ten days.[3] Colonel Richards put the case for holding out most forcibly, when he said that "in quitting the town they were quitting the kingdom,"[4] but his warning passed unheeded. The Governor told the officers that he was going to withdraw secretly. The man-of-war and the nine transports sailed away with the contingent they had brought, and also took away with them the principal gentry of Derry, and the chief officers of the garrison.[5]

When James drew near Derry he sent Lundy a letter, calling upon him to surrender the town.[6] The Governor held another meeting, at which some sympathisers with his policy were present. For the surrender of the town James offered them their horses, their arms, and liberty to live in peace—terms which did not arouse enthusiastic support. The doings of the two Councils leaked out. It dawned on the townsmen that their Governor had arranged the surrender of the town, and this news, together with that of the advancing Jacobite army, spread from one to another, and aroused them to the highest pitch of excitement. Meanwhile James drew near the doomed city and felt much as Napoleon felt when he approached Malta.[7] In each case the friend inside could materially

---

[1] Hempton, p. 395. [2] *C.S.P., Dom.*, 1689–90, p. 29.

[3] *Cf.* the instructions issued to Colonel Cunningham, February 22, 1688, and to Governor Lundy, March 12, 168$\frac{8}{9}$.

[4] *Cf. The Journals of the House of Commons*, August 12, 1689.

[5] Hempton, pp. 397–400; Walker, *True Account*, April 15 and 17; A True Account.

[6] Melfort's letter, April 14, 1689. It was not received till the 17th.

[7] Duc de Berwick, *Mémoires*. James "expected to make himself master of Londonderry by means of Colonel Lundy, the Governor of that place, who, lying under several obligations to the Duke of Berwick, promised to deliver it to him" (*Life of the Duke of Berwick*, London, 1738). A lieutenant in James's army wrote a letter from Dublin, May 7, 1689: "The King hath such an interest within the place (i.e. Derry) as to keep out two regiments sent from England" (*Ireland's Lamentation*, p. 34). Yet see Avaux to Louis, $\frac{\text{April 26}}{\text{May 6}}$, 1689; *Jacobite Narrative*, (1688–91), p. 41.

facilitate the capture.   Unluckily for James, the action of his friend
was suspected.   The citizens cried out that they had been bought
and sold by another Judas, that he had sent away the English
succour for their relief, and had delivered them into the power of
their deadliest enemy.   While this heated dispute was proceeding
the sentries announced that the advance guard was in sight.
Lundy had commanded that no shot should be fired; but his
authority was over.   Captain Adam Murray was at once acclaimed
leader by the citizens and soldiers alike.   He called upon all that
were determined to fight to the last to wear white, which was,
curiously enough, the Bourbon colour, on their left arm.   Murray
and Major Henry Baker now summoned the people to arms.
Their efforts were ably seconded by the fiery words of an old
clergyman, George Walker, rector of Donaghmore.

The walls in front of the advancing army were lined with
defenders and the guns manned.   James, sure of success, came
close to Bishop's Gate, only to be greeted with the cry of "No
surrender" and the roar of cannon.   He retired as despondently
as he had advanced confidently.   The execrated Lundy hid
himself from the fury of the people, and, with the assistance of
Murray and Baker, escaped by night in the disguise of a private
soldier.[1]   In this or some other humble capacity he might have
served his country worthily.   His conduct as Governor, however,
proved his unfitness for responsibility, and illustrated once again
the applicability of the caustic phrase of Tacitus, *omnium consensu
capax imperii nisi imperasset*.   "Who," inquires Bacon, "can see
worse days than he that, yet living, doth follow the funeral of his
own reputation?"[2]   In the north of Ireland he has achieved an
unenviable form of immortality, for there, year by year, they
burn "the traitor" in effigy, much as in England, though with less
justice, they burn the effigy of Guy Fawkes.[3]

The citizens were so pleased with the conduct of Murray that

[1] Walker, p. 20.   After his escape he did not join the Irish army of James.

[2] See the penultimate paragraph in the essay on " Death."

[3] Ash, *Diary*, April 18–20, July 2 ; Mackenzie, April 18 ; Walker, April 17 ; Hempton, p. 388.

they wanted to elect him as Governor.[1] He refused the office, and his refusal does him credit, for his gifts qualified him for service in the field rather than in the council room. Major Baker was therefore elected, and when he required a colleague he named Walker. To the soldier was committed the care of the military supplies, while the clergyman was placed over the provisions, and the governance of the city was also allotted to him.[2] To Colonel Murray was assigned the care of the cavalry. When a thousand old men, women, and children retired, there were not less than twenty thousand inside the walls.[3] The men were placed under eight colonels. Many of their officers had slipped away with Conyngham, and each company whose officer had deserted it was allowed to choose its captain. The strength of the city most emphatically lay in the courage and determination of those who guarded its ramparts. The spirit of Cromwell's Ironsides lived on in these dour and resolute men. Men and women alike were penetrated by a vivid sense of the omnipresence of their Maker. They felt that they were "for ever in the Great Taskmaster's eye," and this feeling rendered them earnest and determined.[4] Their detachment from the world made them cultivate the spirit of austerity at home, and their aloofness from all forms of amusement, even the most innocent, developed a certain sternness of demeanour abroad. Puritanism constituted the great tower of strength. The Puritans of the Revolution imitated with conspicuous success the methods of their fathers in the great Civil War. Praying and preaching proved as potent a means of defence as bullet and ball. The eighteen clergy of the Church of Ireland and the seven or eight Nonconformist ministers exerted themselves to the utmost to comfort and sustain their people. "Put your trust in God, and keep your powder dry," is a remark ascribed to the practical Oliver Cromwell. The appearance of the cathedral during the

[1] *Londerias* likens him to Hamilcar and Regulus.

[2] Boyse, *A Vindication*, pp. 2, 24 ; Mr. John Mackenzie's *Narrative of the Siege of Londonderry, a False Libel*; in defence of Dr. George Walker. Written by his Friend in his Absence, pp. 5, 6.

[3] *Macariae Excidium*, pp. 318–22.

[4] *Londerias* describes John Mackenzie as having "taught the army to fear God's great name." Colonel Henderson notes the effects of Puritanism on Stonewall Jackson's character.

siege illustrated the twofold aspect of his saying. Every morning the liturgy of the Irish Church was used, while every afternoon the Dissenters employed their form of worship. On the tower of the cathedral cannon were erected, and in its vaults ammunition was stored. The defender of Derry was confident that whether he prayed or fought he was equally fulfilling the will of God.[1]

James made a last appeal to the citizens of the maiden city. On the 20th of April the Earl of Abercorn came to confer with Murray. His terms were more liberal than those offered previously. He was authorised to extend a free pardon to the garrisons, to restore their estates, and to allow the public exercise of their religion. Murray was to receive a colonel's commission and a thousand pounds. "The men of Londonderry," answered Murray, "have done nothing that requires a pardon, and own no sovereign but King William and Queen Mary. It will not be safe for your Lordship to stay longer, or to return on the same errand."[2]

According to the Duke of Berwick, the besiegers amounted to about 6000, and their headquarters lay at Carrigans and Saint Johnstown.[3] They lacked heavy siege guns, but with mortars and cannon they kept up a brisk fire both by night and day. Roofs and chimneys crashed in, and bombs tore up the streets. The besieged promptly pulled up the pavements,[4] thus leaving a soft bed of clay or sand, upon which the shells fell with comparatively little effect. The efficient Pointis effectively alarmed the garrison by his explosive shells. When he rectified the faults of his material he set to work to bombard the city vigorously. In eighty-nine days he threw 587 bombs, of which 326 were small and 261 large. We can judge of the formidable nature of the shells of those days when we hear that the largest, weighing 273 pounds, carried a charge of sixteen pounds of powder.[5] The grave danger to the

---

[1] Mackenzie, pp. 222–4.

[2] Mackenzie, April 19 and 20 ; Walker, April 20 ; Bennet, p. 20.

[3] Berwick, *Memoirs*, I, pp. 340–5.

[4] Bennet, p. 23.

[5] *Hist. MSS. Com.*, xii. 7, pp. 264–5 ; "One bum slew 17 persons. I was in the next room one night at my supper—which was but mean—and 7 men were thrown out of the third room next to that we were in, and some of them in pieces."

besieged was that some of these shells might explode their precious powder magazine. As they had neither bombs nor mortars, it was out of their power to reply to Lord Louth and his men. Incessantly the bombs came, and wrought desperate havoc among the non-combatants. So little daunted, however, were the besieged, that on the 21st of April a party sallied out under Murray, and in a cavalry encounter that ensued Maumont was slain, and his aide-de-camp, Montmejan, seriously wounded.[1]

As Rosen was in Dublin, Richard Hamilton became generalissimo of the Jacobite army, a post for which he was utterly unsuited.[1] Pusignan might have helped his inexperience and incapacity, but in a skirmish at Pennyburn he was fatally wounded.[2] Under cover of darkness the gallant Brigadier-General Ramsay, in the endeavour to secure a closer position on which to mount his gun, assaulted the Windmill fort and drove in the outposts. The Governor assailed him so vigorously that the enemy found it necessary to withdraw. Ramsay and two hundred men were slain and five hundred wounded. The besieged lamented the loss of three killed and twenty wounded.[3] Among the prisoners were Lord Netterville, Sir George Aylmer, and Colonel Talbot, Tyrconnel's brother. The captured banners were proudly hung in the cathedral, and worshippers were inspired to renewed exertions by the sight of these trophies. They also seized drums, arms, ammunition, and "good store of spades, shovels, and pickaxes." For the rest of May there was no more fighting, due, according to Walker, "to the enemy's want of courage and our want of horse."[4] The Jacobites, however, advanced more closely to the town, and the siege turned to a blockade. Letters could no longer pass freely from the besieged to their friends in the country. The Jacobite headquarters moved from Saint Johnstown to Ballougry Hill, and the troops at Brookhall came to Pennyburn. They

[1] Mackenzie, April 21 ; Aickin, iii, p. 3 ; *cf.* Avaux to Louvois, $\frac{\text{April 26}}{\text{May 6}}$, 1689.

[2] On the state of Hamilton's army *cf.* Avaux to Louvois, May $\frac{4}{14}$; Louvois to Avaux, June $\frac{3}{13}$, 1689.

[3] *Cf.* Berwick, *Memoirs*, i, pp. 115, 220, 281–2 ; Avaux, $\frac{\text{April 26}}{\text{May 6}}$, 1689.

[4] *Diary*, p. 117.

successfully assaulted Culmore, thereby diminishing the probability of relief coming by sea.   Near this place a boom had been stretched across the river, protected at each side by a strong fort; and the Frenchman who designed it wrote to Louis, assuring him that he intended to make another boom higher up the river, and then what he desired was that the English would come, so that he should have the pleasure of defeating them.[1]

The cannonade continued briskly during June, but no strong attack on the town was made till the 4th of that month.   The Jacobites then renewed their assault on Windmill Hill, near Bishop's Gate.   Their horse under Captain Butler, son of Lord Mountgarret, came on, each rider carrying a bundle of faggots in order to fill up the trench.   A heavy fire met them, but it made little impression till directed at the horses, as the men wore armour under their dress.   On the walls the yeomen were drawn up in three ranks, and acted as if they were veterans.   The two ranks behind being thus always ready to fire in their turn, the Jacobites received a continuous shower of bullets.   The women of Derry, even under the heavy fire of the enemy, fetched water, bread, and ammunition to their husbands and brothers.   When the grenadiers pressed their kinsmen sorely they hurled stones at them with considerable effect.   This was the most important attempt to storm the town, and it cost the Jacobites about four hundred men, while the citizens lost seven.[2]   The defence had been so stout that the assailants resolved to starve the garrison out.   The number in the city was vast, and the supply of food scanty.   Every care was exercised to prevent relief being brought from outside.   All the land approaches were closely watched, while the boom and the fort at Culmore prevented aid coming from the sea.   Captain Guillam in the *Greyhound* was unable to pass the fort.   On the 11th of June General Kirke, with thirty vessels, reached Lough Foyle, and on the 15th he was joined by Captain Leake in the

---

[1] *C.S.P., Dom.*, 1689–90, pp. 147–8; June 17, pp. 154, 161; Dr. John Wallis's letter to the Earl of Nottingham, August 10; Walker, p. 136; *Jacobite Narrative*, p. 64; Avaux, $\frac{\text{August 4}}{\text{August 14}}$.

[2] Ash, June 4; Mackenzie, June 4; Walker, June 4.

Dartmouth.[1] The fleet carried large provisions for the needy garrison, and a bold messenger informed them of this welcome news.

Kirke was afraid of the guns of Culmore, and thought the boom too strong to be passed. His arrival, therefore, within sight of the city was but as the cup of Tantalus to the half-starved citizens. Horseflesh was practically the only meat which could be bought, and of that the supply was not enough to meet the demand. They were compelled to eke out the deficiency with tallow, exactly measured out in small quantities. In their dire need, towards the end of the siege, weeds and herbs were greedily consumed. A mouse sold for sixpence, a rat for a shilling, a cat for four-and-sixpence, and a dog for six shillings. Butter was six-and-fourpence a pound; a peck of meal fetched six shillings.[2] The price of a small fish was precious handfuls of oatmeal; even the blood of the horse fetched twopence a quart.[3] A certain corpulent citizen imagined he saw his fellow-citizens surveying him carefully, as if they intended to eat him, and he thought it prudent to hide himself for three days. In the earlier stages of the siege thirty soldiers died daily, and towards the end the number rose to forty. The death-rate among the old men, women and children was probably higher.[4] Indirectly this heavy mortality assisted in prolonging the siege, by making the provisions last longer.[5] Plague made deadly havoc, and in one day fifteen officers died of fever.[6] The Governor, Major Baker, fell a victim, and named as his successor Colonel John Mitchelburne.[7] Not only did food supplies fail and pestilence prevail, but the war material began to give out. The supply of cannon-balls became exhausted, and their place was supplied by brickbats and stones. And all the time the garrison could see friendly vessels in the Lough, and knew that on board ample supplies were stored. A more intolerable situation it is

---

[1] *C.S.P., Dom.,* 1689–90, pp. 48, 74, 78, 80–1, 101–2, 107–8, 138, 142, 168, 199.

[2] Walker, 148 ; *Hist. MSS. Com.,* xi. 6, pp. 185–6 ; *Hamilton MSS.,* July 16, 1689.

[3] *Hist. MSS. Com.,* xii. 7, pp. 250, 265.

[4] *Cf.* the grimly fascinating narrative in Graham, *Ireland Preserved,* p. 365.

[5] *Cf.* Walker, *Diary,* pp. 111–4.

[6] *A True Account,* p. 12.

[7] Mitchelburne lost his wife and all his family—seven children—during the siege.

difficult to conceive. The stout hearts of the citizens began to fail them, and the necessity of yielding was discussed.[1]

In order to hasten the fall James sent Rosen once more to assume command. He was an officer of a coarse and strong type, determined to crush the city. There came with him ill-armed troops, and his presence restored the spirit of the besiegers.[2] He brought his lines nearer the walls, which he attempted to mine. Richard Hamilton offered fresh terms on the 27th of June. These were a free pardon, public exercise of their religion, and restoration of their goods, especially of their cattle. Rosen gave them to the 1st of July to consider these proposals : after this date no hope of grace could be entertained. When he reduced the town his army would receive orders to give no quarter, and to spare neither age nor sex. Moreover, he would gather all the Protestants from Innishowen to Charlemont under the walls to be admitted by their friends or starve outside. Remembering to what fearful straits those already within the walls were reduced, one can imagine the significance of Rosen's threat. Yet the spirit of the Puritans remained unconquered; they were resolved, in the judgment of Walker, to eat their prisoners and then one another rather than to surrender to any one but King William.[3]

On the 2nd of July Rosen kept his word. Hundreds of old men, women, and children were assembled under the ramparts to the dismay of their relatives. With a spirit worthy of Regulus, they begged the citizens not to surrender out of pity to them. For forty-eight hours the inhuman commander kept them there.[4] The garrison erected a gallows and informed Rosen that his friends, who were prisoners, required a confessor to prepare them for instant death. Then he relented. It is to the credit of James that when he heard of this barbarity he censured Rosen and recalled him, leaving Richard Hamilton in supreme command.[5]

---

[1] *Nairne Papers*, D.N., i, fol. No. 20–1.

[2] Avaux to Louis, from Dublin, June $\frac{16}{26}$.   [3] Clarke, ii, p. 367 ; King, pp. 488–91.

[4] Ash, June 26, July 3, 4; Aickin, iv, 9 ; Mackenzie, June 30 ; Walker, June 30, July 2 ; Leslie, p. 138 ; *C.S.P., Dom.*, 1689, p. 185 ; *Jacobite Narrative*, pp. 79–80 ; Dangeau, ii, p. 154 ; Clarke, ii, p. 388.

[5] Macpherson, i, pp. 210–3, 310 ; Avaux, pp. 257, 309 ; Clarke, ii, p. 366.

As July advanced the plight of the garrison became more and more desperate, by reason of the shortage of food and the insidious inroads of pestilence. The survivors gazed wistfully at the vessels anchored in the Lough, yet no help came. It appeared at length as if the proud spirit of the citizens had been laid low, for they parleyed with the enemy. They would surrender on the 26th, if still unrelieved, provided they were allowed to march out with arms, and that they received hostages for the due fulfilment of the conditions agreed upon.[1] These terms Hamilton could not grant. While the Council was deliberating, a letter came to Walker from Kirke, announcing that he was about to attempt the relief of the garrison. Schomberg had sent him a peremptory despatch, ordering the immediate relief of the town.[2]

The spirit of the sluggish Kirke was at last roused to action, and on the 28th of July he issued his commands. Three small vessels laden with provisions under the protection of the *Dartmouth* frigate were to try the passage of the Foyle. The *Dartmouth* was commanded by Captain Leake; the victuallers were the *Mountjoy* of Derry, under Captain Micaiah Browning, a native of the city; the *Jerusalem*, under Captain Reynell; and the *Phoenix* of Coleraine, under Captain Andrew Douglas. At about seven in the evening the eager watchers on the walls saw three ships sail near the fort of Culmore. The frigate was to engage the fort, and the *Mountjoy* and the *Phoenix* were to attempt the boom. Taking advantage of the wind and the rising tide, the vessels moved steadily forward. Leake covered the advance of the ships with his frigate, and they passed the fort. Then came the formidable obstacle of the boom. The *Mountjoy* broke it, recoiled, and ran aground; and the Jacobites were delighted, and redoubled their fire. The sailors fired a broadside, and this time the recoil sent the vessel into deep water. The *Phoenix* crashed against the broken boom and passed through, followed by the *Mountjoy*, whose gallant master, like Nelson, was struck down in the hour of triumph by a shot from the battery.[3]

[1] *Proposals of Articles*, July 11, 1689.
[2] *The Nairne MSS.* (Bodleian Library) contains a copy of it. *Cf. Jacobite Narrative*, p. 84.
[3] *Hist. MSS. Com.*, xii. 7, p. 255.

The two ships sailed slowly up the Foyle, and at ten they reached the quay on that memorable Sunday evening.[1]   Laughing and weeping are closely akin, and the cheers of the citizens mingled with the tears of the women, as they raised their grateful faces to Almighty God, who had delivered them in their hour of sore distress.   The days of hunger and hardship were over.   The walls blazed with bonfires, and the bells of the cathedral rang a joyful peal.

For three days more the cannonade of the enemy continued, but the morning of the 1st of August brought deliverance to the beleaguered town, which awoke to a strange silence, for during the night the investing army had disappeared, and by dawn was well on its way to Dublin.[2]   It was not a day too soon.   For one hundred and five days the struggle between Saxon and Celt had lasted. The garrison had been reduced by death and disease from about 7000 to 4000.[3]   The death-roll of the besiegers was naturally a more extensive one, and probably some 8000 of them perished before the maiden city.[4]   It is difficult to overestimate the importance of this heroic struggle.   With the raising of the siege James saw the fall of his prospects.   It was no longer possible for him to go to Scotland or even to promise to send men to Dundee, and it was just as impossible to prolong the contest in England.[5] One of Louis's aims was accomplished.   The struggle was to be confined to Ireland.   The determined stand of Ulster made possible the landing of William, though in the dark days of uncertainty it had looked as if all the designs of Louis would be successful.   Had Derry fallen before Rosen, Enniskillen must have surrendered.   If these two towns belonged to James, no foothold was left for William.   One skilled to look below the surface may perceive from the walls of Derry the ultimate defeat of Louis.   For, little as he realised it, the French king received a fatal blow from the citizens of a petty town in the north of Ireland,

---

[1] Story, *Continuation*, pp. 4–5 ; *Macariae Excidium*, pp. 318–22.

[2] Mackenzie ; Walker ; Ashe ; Buchan's letter in the *Nairne MSS.* (Bodleian Library) ; Story, pp. 4–5 ; *Macariae Excidium*, pp. 318–22.

[3] Hamill, *Danger and Folly*, p. 11 ; *Hist. MSS. Com.*, xii. 7, p. 258.

[4] *Cf. Life of the Duke of Berwick*, p. 38 ; Berwick, *Memoirs*, i, pp. 340–5.

[5] *Hist. MSS. Com.*, xi, 6, pp. 178, 184.

and among these citizens we may reckon some destined to serve in the 8th Dragoons.[1] The soldiers of Acre stood between Napoleon and universal empire, and the men of Derry stood between Louis and ascendancy in Europe. Their conduct during the siege proved to the world that they were willing to sacrifice themselves to the uttermost for the cause they held dear. Like their king, they felt that there was one way never to be defeated, and that was to die in the last ditch.

Space has been spent on the actions of the men of Enniskillen and of Derry, because some of them were the men to constitute the 8th Dragoons when formed in 1693. If we want to know what the men of 1693 were like, the readiest method is to note their characteristics in 1689, and indeed the siege of Derry is too glorious an episode to leave out in the annals of the Eighth. There is a pedigree to tradition as to everything else. Thring of Uppingham was asked when the preparation of a boy for his school should begin. Was eight or ten the proper age? Reflecting for a moment, he replied, "I think I should begin with the boy's father." In this spirit we have chronicled the doings of the yeomen who formed the rank and file of our regiment. The exploits at Enniskillen and Derry are largely theirs and theirs only, and we note them at length. When we come to the Battle of the Boyne, the sieges of Limerick, and the Battle of Aughrim, we come to actions in which they played their part, yet they are actions in which they must share the glory with other regiments.

The position of affairs in Ulster justly entitled the supporters of William to rejoice. The raising of the siege of Derry and the triumphal issue of Enniskillen from its assault were unmistakable victories. The natives of the latter town had made a gallant, though unsuccessful, attempt in June to relieve the former.[2] During the last six weeks of the siege of Derry, the Duke of Berwick was placed in charge of a flying division in order to check the raids of the men of Enniskillen, and on the 13th of July, in a skirmish with them, fifty of his men were killed and twenty taken prisoners.[3]

---

[1] *Hist. MSS. Com.*, xii. 7, p. 259.   [2] Hamilton, pp. 23–5 ; MacCarmick, pp. 45–7.

[3] On Berwick, *cf.* Burnet, iii, p. 1280 ; Avaux, October $\frac{15}{25}$, 1689 ; *C.S.P., Dom.*, 1689–90, pp. 217–9.

The Enniskilleners sent a deputation to Kirke, who gave them six hundred firelocks for dragoons, a thousand muskets for footmen, twenty additional barrels of powder, and eight small cannon.[1] Besides, he sent seven of his best officers under Colonel Wolseley, whom he appointed their commander. By a curious coincidence, the day that saw them welcomed in Enniskillen witnessed the relief of Derry: it was indeed a memorable Sunday for both towns.

The activity of Enniskillen on behalf of William was noted in Dublin, and it was resolved to make a united effort to crush it. The townsmen, acting in the spirit of their Governor, made up their minds not to wait to be attacked. When Macarthy, who had been created Viscount Mountcashel for his services in Munster, undertook to invest the castle of Crom, Colonel Wolseley ordered Lieutenant-Colonel Berry to raise the siege.[2] The latter, on the 31st of July, 1689, encountered his adversaries near Lisnaskea, but, seeing their strength, he retreated, and effected a conjunction with Colonel Wolseley's forces.[3] The brilliant Anthony Hamilton —as daring a soldier as he was a clever writer—attacked them, and was repulsed. Macarthy joined him, and the united Jacobite forces amounted to some six thousand men.[4] Wolseley had no more than two thousand under his command. As he advanced, his opponents retreated through the village of Newtown-Butler, and halted a mile beyond it. Macarthy drew up his men on a hill with a bog covering their front. When the foot had silenced the cannon commanding the path across the bog, the Enniskillen horse rode swiftly to meet the foe on the right. Macarthy therefore ordered the regiment on the left to move to the right. In the confusion of the fight the officer commanded the men not to face to the right, but to face right about and march.[5] Remembering how a hasty "Retire" almost brought about a panic among soldiers

---

[1] Cf. Clarke Correspondence, i, f. 10 (T.C.D.).

[2] On Macarthy, cf. Avaux to Louvois, $\frac{Nov. 26}{Dec. 6}$, 1689.

[3] Macariae Excidium, p. 314.

[4] Avaux to Louvois, August $\frac{4}{14}$, 1689.

[5] Story, Impartial History, p. 5; History of the Most Material Occurrences in the Kingdom of Ireland during the Last Two Years: By an Eye-Witness (London, 1691); Light to the Blind, p. 624; Macariae Excidium, p. 315.

on the Alma, it is easy to imagine the ensuing confusion. When the troops saw their comrades facing them, they concluded they were retreating. The panic-stricken Irish dragoons fled in the direction of Wattle-bridge, and the cavalry soon followed them.[1] The foot remained firm for a time, but they too finally gave way. With the recollection of the treacherous conduct of Galmoy fresh in their minds, the Enniskilleners gave little quarter. Of the six thousand soldiers that marched in the morning two thousand had been killed, five hundred drowned in Lough Erne, and four hundred captured, including Macarthy, the commander. Seven guns, fourteen barrels of powder, and all the flags and drums had also been taken.[2] Almost the whole of Ulster remained now in the hands of the Williamites. The brilliant Sarsfield at once retired from Bundoran to Sligo. The battle of Newtown-Butler was the greatest triumph won so far by the Williamites in the field.[3] The amazing fact stands out that two thousand amateur soldiers had beaten six thousand professionals.

On the 13th of August, 1689, the Duke of Schomberg, the ablest of the Williamite generals, disembarked his twenty thousand men at Bangor in County Down. He had arrived "avec le plus beau tems et le meilleur vent qu'on eut pu souhaiter."[4] The conflict was no longer local, but became outwardly the great international struggle it had long been inwardly. For the newly-landed General prospects seemed fairly favourable. With Derry relieved, Enniskillen victorious, Mountcashel's army destroyed, and Ballyshannon still holding out, it seemed as if the whole north-west of Ireland remained in the hands of his allies, while in the north-east the Jacobites merely held Carrickfergus, Newry and Charlemont. The Duke of Berwick, with sixteen hundred men, lay beyond Newry, his duty being to prevent the enemy marching

[1] *Macariae Excidium*, pp. 310–6.

[2] Avaux to Louis, August $\frac{4}{14}$, 1689.

[3] *London Gazette*, August 22, 1689; Clarke, ii, pp. 368–9; Avaux to Louis, August $\frac{4}{14}$; Avaux to Louvois, August $\frac{4}{14}$; Macpherson, i, p. 219; Wolseley's despatch, Enniskillen, August 4, 1689. *Cf.* Klopp, *Der Fall des Hauses Stuart*, v, p. 50.

[4] Kazner, *Leben Friedrich von Schomberg oder Schoenburg*, II, p. 290.

towards Dublin.[1] Schomberg ordered twelve regiments to invest
Carrickfergus, and for a week the town held out.   On surrendering,
its garrison was allowed to retire to Newry.[2]   The Enniskilleners,
remembering Galmoy's atrocious deed, argued that it was positively
wrong to permit men guilty of many excesses to depart unharmed.
As the defeated men were leaving, there arose cries of, "There is
my Sunday gown!"   "Look at that woman in my best smock!"
and "Zounds, but that's my grey pony again!" and they proceeded
to seize their property.[3]   It was with difficulty that Schomberg
saved the lives of the Jacobites, the Enniskilleners feeling intensely
furious with them.

On the fall of Carrickfergus the English marched to the village
of Belfast, and on the 2nd of September they proceeded to Newry
with the Derry and Enniskillen horse and the 5th and 6th Inniskilling Dragoons as advance guard.[4]   Both Story and Bonivert
record the eagerness with which their English comrades surveyed
these troops.   Story, the chaplain to Lord Drogheda's regiment,
writes: "I wondered much to see their horses and equipage, hearing
before what feats had been done by them.   They were three
regiments in all, and most of the troopers and dragoons had their
waiting men, mounted on garrons [these are small Irish horses, but
very hardy]; some of them had in their holsters and others their
pistols hung at their swordbelts.   They showed me the enemy's scouts
upon a hill before us; I wished them to go and beat them off, and
they answered, 'With all their hearts, but they had orders to go no
farther than where they saw the enemy's scouts,' adding in dissatisfied tones, 'They should never thrive so long as they were
under orders.'"[5]   The soldier-like Bonivert watched them with
professional eyes,[2] and writes: "The Inniskilling Dragoons came
there [Newry, 1690] to us.   They are but middle-sized men, but
they are, nevertheless, brave fellows.   I have seen 'em like masty

---

[1] He records laconically in his *Memoirs* that he had retired according to orders.

[2] Kazner, ii, pp. 297–9.

[3] Story, *Great News from Duke Schomberg's Army*, Chester, August 31, 1689 (London, 1689, Thorpe); Nihell's *Journal*.

[4] *C.S.P., Dom.*, 1689–90, pp. 256–8.   [5] Kazner, i, p. 306; ii, p. 296.

[*i.e.* mastiff] dogs run against bullets."[1] Mackay observed their promptitude in planning an expedition, and their rapidity in executing it. Captain de Bostaquet tersely describes them as serving well, "s'ils n'étaient point si picoreurs sur lesquels on pourrait faire fonds."[2] The Commander-in-Chief formed as high an opinion of them as these eye-witnesses, relying on them more than on the newly-raised English regulars.[3]

Nothing lay between Schomberg and Dublin except the river Boyne and the Pass of Duleek.[4] A well-executed diversion in the west might have compelled the English to retreat and might have gained a marked advantage in the campaign. Schomberg foresaw this, and despatched Colonel Lloyd with five hundred Inniskillings to Sligo.[5] Colonel O'Kelly was also sent west with the intent of surprising Sligo, but he was himself surprised. For the Inniskillings crossed the Curlew Mountains and astonished the outposts by their vigorous attack at the dawn of a foggy autumnal morning. Over two hundred and fifty were killed, three hundred captured, including Colonel O'Kelly, and eight thousand head of cattle taken.[6] The Inniskillings lost no more than fourteen men. Schomberg was so delighted with this success that he paraded the Inniskillings at Dundalk, and praised them for their soldier-like qualities, the veteran riding along the whole line with head uncovered.[7] The compliment was gratifying to the men, for all knew that a former Marshal of France was before them. Had the rest of the army shown the same spirit in action, Schomberg might now have marched on Dublin, but he knew that they were unfit, and he determined to remain on the defensive for the short time that remained of the military season.

John Stevens notes in his *Journal* on Saturday, the 25th of August: "A flux in Schomberg's camp and vast numbers died daily. The weather continued very various, sometimes great

---

[1] *Cf.* my edition of Bonivert, *Journey to Ireland.*   [2] *Add. MSS.*, 33264 (Brit. Mus.).

[3] *Mémoires de Dumont de Bostaquet.*

[4] Schomberg to William, September 20.   Contrast Kazner, i, p. 305.

[5] *C.S.P., Dom.*, 1689, October 8, 1689 ; Schomberg to William, pp. 287–8, 313–4, 320.

[6] Lloyd's Despatch, September, 1689.   [7] Kazner, i, p. 306 ; ii, p. 310.

rain, then very sharp weather, then foggy and mirling."[1]   The
Derry and Enniskillen men and the Jacobites, accustomed to the
climate, and the Dutchmen, inured to dampness, survived, but the
peasants of Yorkshire and Derbyshire were unable to resist the
combination of evils.[2]   There were few doctors, and their medicines
were for the care of wounds, not for the removal of pestilence.[3]
Schomberg did all that one man could do to avert the dangers
with which his army was threatened, but he received scanty support
from his staff.   Nor were James's men in a much better plight.
Both armies contended no more for the honour of victory, but for
the reputation of which could with greater steadfastness look the
angel of death—who was encamped with them—in the face.
When Schomberg had pitched his tents at Dundalk, he had fourteen
thousand men, and only seven thousand seven hundred survived
to strike them.[4]

With the landing of William at Carrickfergus on the 14th of
June, 1690, the new campaign opened.[5]   On the 22nd he reviewed
his thirty-six thousand men at Loughbrickland.[6]   English, Irish,
French, German, Dutch, and Danish soldiers passed before him.
On the 29th of June William followed James towards the Boyne,
and on the last day of that month the two armies stood face to face,
the Williamites on the north bank and the Jacobites on the south
bank of the river.   James and Lauzun had chosen their position
well.   On July 1, 1690, William met their men on the banks of
the Boyne, the famous dividing line which has witnessed so many
of the great Irish conflicts from the days of Cuchulain.   The strong
position of the Irish atoned for their deficiency in men.   The
Jacobite cavalry fought well, but the Jacobite infantry did nothing
of the sort.

[1] *Cf.* my edition of this *Journal.*

[2] Schomberg's report, January 9, 1690 ; Kazner, i, pp. 313, 321 ; *C.S.P., Dom.*, 1689–90,
p. 401.

[3] Kazner, i, p. 310.

[4] Story ; Kane ; *London Gazette*, December, 1689, and January, 1690.   *Cf.* Kazner, i,
p. 321 ; *C.S.P., Dom.*, 1689, September 26 and October 1, 1689, pp. 273, 283, 457 ; *Clarke
Correspondence*, i, f. 25.

[5] *Clarke Correspondence*, i, f. 19 ; Klopp, v, p. 138.

[6] *C.S.P., Dom.*, 1690–1, July 1, pp. 44–5, 52, 54 ; *Macariae Excidium*, pp. 186–7 ; *Clarke
Correspondence*, i, f. 21.

As soon as William had ascertained from Douglas that his right wing had passed the river he gave the signal to Schomberg, with the remaining body, to storm the fords at Oldbridge. The great guns ceased the cannonade upon the Irish horse and works, and an ominous quietness—the hushed stillness of intense expectation—succeeded. Upon the peace of that summer day there fell the stirring sounds of fife and drum, as the Blue Dutch Guards stepped out. Closely following these Guards came the two Huguenot regiments, the two Inniskilling regiments, Sir John Hanmer's Brigade, and the Danes. The whole river was covered with red and blue coats. The Dutchmen, under the Count of Solmes, climbed the breastworks in face of a heavy fire of musketry. The lack of artillery here proved of fatal import to the Irish. Berwick's horse charged the gallant Dutch, but were met with a well-sustained fire. The Derry men bravely supported their comrades, and in the end the fierce onset was repelled.

While the Dutch and the citizens of Derry were thus occupied at Oldbridge, Richard Hamilton made strenuous attempts to check the advance of the other regiments, notably the Danes. He could not put his own spirit into the Irish infantry, for Antrim's men ignominiously fled.[1] The Irish horse, under the spirited Captain Parker, charged fiercely through the French soldiers, who had no pikes to receive cavalry. William now began to put into effect his own movement against the right flank of the enemy. With his left wing he passed the Boyne between Oldbridge and Drogheda, and was now moving to Donore. Placing himself at the head of the grey Inniskillings he said: "Gentlemen, you shall be my Guards to-day. I have heard much of you. Let me see something of you," and thus charged the Jacobites, but was repulsed with loss. His English stood firm, and the onset of the Irish cavalry broke in vain against the bristling wall of seventeen-foot pikes. This fine stand of the Irish cavalry near Platin House gave their infantry time to reach Duleek. Hamilton was resolved

---

[1] La Hoguette to Louvois, Kinsale, July $\frac{4}{14}$, 1690; Desrigny to Louvois, Limerick, July $\frac{11}{21}$, 1690; Boisseleau to his wife, July $\frac{9}{19}$, 1690; and Boisseleau to Louvois, July $\frac{16}{26}$, 1690, Ministère de la Guerre; Kazner, i, p. 338.

to gain time, and he stoutly assailed the Inniskillings and the Danes, though they were much superior in numbers. Ten times did the brave cavalry charge, and ten times they were repelled.[1]

The behaviour of the Irish horse merits a comparison with the devotion of the Austrian cavalry at Königgrätz. Parker's and Tyrconnel's troops suffered the severest losses. Berwick had his horse shot under him, and Hamilton was captured.[2] This great half hour's struggle saved James's army from complete destruction.[3] The defeat could not be turned into a rout, which might have ended the war at a single blow. Had the Irish foot shown the same grim determination as the cavalry, the issue of the day might have been different.

From the old church at Donore Hill James could see that the Battle of the Boyne had been fought and lost. There he remained, till he saw his own soldiers in full retreat. He then withdrew to Dublin, reaching the capital at ten that night. To Lady Tyrconnel he announced that her countrymen had run away, and she retorted that James had won the race. In Dublin he learned that on land the French had won the Battle of Fleurus, while at sea they had triumphed over the English and the Dutch at Beachy Head. These two victories did not compensate Louis for the serious check given to his plans by his defeat at the Battle of the Boyne. He had reckoned on a war lasting perhaps ten years, and now he heard to his horror that as the result of one fight the King had fled.

The military triumph of William was slight, but the escape of James to France converted it into a victory of the first magnitude. The French rightly refused to give the contest the name of a battle; to them it was a mere skirmish.[4] The immense political importance of the flight of James was, however, obscured by a succession of war scenes in Europe. The Battle of Fleurus proved incomparably more murderous than the Battle of the Boyne. Yet after a few days the importance of this victory was gone. The effects of the

[1] " Nous ne laissâmes pas de charger et recharger dix fois," writes the Duke of Berwick.
[2] *Mémoires du Maréchal de Berwick*, i, pp. 72–5.
[3] *Jacobite Narrative*, p. 102.
[4] Rousset, iv, p. 422 ; Klopp, v, p. 150.

Battle of the Boyne are deeply graven on the history of the world. For it decided first the fate of one kingdom, and then strengthened the other and greater one.   On Irish soil William was fighting not merely for the kingdom of England, but also for his fatherland as well as for his allies.   Above all, he was fighting for the principle of liberty in the life of nations, the principle that the Grand Alliance had called into vigorous existence.   On Irish soil James was in reality fighting, not his own cause, but that of his master, the King of France.   William and James did not, as men have often said, represent the principles of Protestantism and Roman Catholicism[1]; they rather represented the eternal struggle between liberty and tyranny.   The Boyne proved to the despotic power of Louis what Austerlitz was to Austria and Jena to Prussia.   It would have been well for the French monarch if the results of that skirmish had not been half hidden from his view by the victories of Beachy Head, Fleurus and Staffarda.   The Holy Roman Emperor and the Pope both rejoiced to hear the good news from Ireland, for Gallicanism had at last received a severe blow.[2]   While State religion had thus been checked, liberty had been allowed to develop more freely than before, and both these priceless blessings are the issue of that memorable July day.

After the first unsuccessful siege of Limerick, William set out for London.   His successor, Ginkell, set before him the effective occupation of the south-west.   Despite the strong position of the Irish at Athlone, he opened the season of 1691, to the amazement of St. Ruth, by its remarkable capture.   St. Ruth expressed his wonder that so experienced a commander as Ginkell should persist in his design to take this town.   "His master," exclaimed St. Ruth, "should hang him for trying to take Athlone, and mine ought to hang me if I lose it."   Nevertheless, taken it was, and nothing remained for St. Ruth save to retreat.   He occupied the ridge of a hill, extending for about two miles on the far side of Aughrim. A mile south of Aughrim stands Kilcommodon Church, and a hill slopes gently from it; about half-way between Aughrim and

---

[1] Klopp, v, p. 142.
[2] Klopp, v, p. 167 ; *Clarke Correspondence*, July 20, 1690, i, f. 55.

Kilcommodon it reaches its greatest height of about four hundred feet, descending more abruptly at the Kilcommodon end.   Nearest the highest part of the hill lie two ancient Danish forts.   On this hill St. Ruth made his last stand, and his selection was not unwise. To the north of it stretched a red bog for a mile, so covering the Irish left as to preclude any possibility of attack on that side.   At this side also stood the castle of Aughrim, commanding the road from Ballinasloe; the castle, like so many Irish castles, was an old ruin with walls and ditches around it.   In front extended another bog, quite impassable, except at each end of the ridge.   Beyond it rose the hill of Urrachree, running almost parallel to the hill of Aughrim.   Between the two hills a stream, meandering through the valley, left the ground too soft for cavalry to use, and even infantry could only use the foot-tracks.   These tracks resembled that road of historic fame in Virginia on which the Federal officer, reconnoitring it, observed that the road was there, but he "guessed the bottom had fallen out."   To the south side of the hill of Aughrim lay the Irish right.   Here, however, the troops were somewhat exposed, as the bogs were more firm and of less extent.   St. Ruth's left then rested on the Castle of Aughrim, his right at Urrachree road, and his centre on Kilcommodon hill.[1]   The only parts suitable for cavalry were the Ballinasloe road and the Urrachree road.

When Ginkell saw the strength of the Irish position he hesitated for a time.[2]   "If," said Frederick the Great, "we had exact information of our enemy's dispositions, we should beat him every time"; but such information is never available.   Accordingly, the commander called a council of war; the rash Talmash and the cautious Mackay both encouraged him to proceed.   At six o'clock on Sunday morning, July 12, 1691, the troops marched out of Ballinasloe—the infantry over the bridge, the Williamite and French cavalry by the ford above the town, and the Dutch and Danish cavalry by that below the town.   So far as the uneven ground permitted the men formed into a double line of battle.

[1] Story, pp. 121-2 ; *Macariae Excidium*, pp. 439-41.
[2] Klopp, v, p. 304.

The strength of the two armies was fairly even.[1] Ginkell possessed some slight numerical advantage, though this was counterbalanced by the circumstance that he was the attacking party.

St. Ruth, having staked his future on the issue of the day, had done all in his power to ensure a favourable result ; for down among the bogs of Aughrim he might retrieve the errors of Athlone, and thus hope to sun himself in the favouring smile of his gracious sovereign. He was harsh and imperious by nature, but now he bent his haughty will to win the hearts of the Irish. His right wing was under de Tessé, the second in command ; at the centre the infantry were under Dorrington and Hamilton, and the cavalry under Galmoy ; and the left was under Shelden.[2] Two guns were placed at the castle of Aughrim, and three on the slope of the hill at the left centre. Behind the hill Sarsfield was stationed, with the cavalry reserves, with strict injunctions not to move without orders. The post given him shows how the judgment of St. Ruth was warped by his jealous feelings towards his subordinate—and his rival.

It was a misty morning, and the fog did not clear away till noon. When it lifted, the two armies were face to face, one on the hill of Aughrim, the other on the hill of Urrachree. Ginkell ordered

---

[1] The list of the English army gives the following numbers, reckoning the cavalry regiments at 300 and the infantry at 550, their effective strength, and allowing for two regiments of English and two of foreigners for the protection of the camp :

English : Horse	6 regts. at	300 = 2700		
Dragoons	3 „ „			
Foot	15 „ „	550 = 8250		
			10,950	
Foreigners : Horse	12 „ „	300 = 3600		
Dragoons				
Foot	8 „ „	550 = 4400		
			8,000	

19,000 (circa)

Story says Ginkell had only 17,000. He thinks that the Irish had the advantage of 1000 men, but, possibly, he means the strength of their position was as good as 1000 men extra. Elsewhere he writes that they had 20,000 foot and 5000 horse. According to *Macariae Excidium* they had 10,000 foot and 4000 horse. "The truth is," writes Colonel Henderson (i, p. 259), "that in war, accurate intelligence, especially when two armies are in close contact, is exceedingly difficult to obtain."

[2] *Jacobite Narrative*, p. 274, gives the order of battle.

some Danes, about three or four in the afternoon, to take possession of Urrachree, but the Irish repelled them. Two hundred of the 6th Inniskillings and Eppinger's Dragoons dismounted and went to their assistance. The Irish cavalry behaved as gallantly as at the Battle of the Boyne, and the fight became fast and furious. The Irish right wing reinforced their cavalry, and Portland's Horse and two of the Duke of Wurtemberg's battalions reinforced the English. The outpost fight now assumed the dimensions of a miniature battle.[1] Both sides held their own ground, and then for a time the fighting ceased. The real key to the Irish position lay on the left, as the far-sighted Mackay perceived.[2]

At five the battle was resumed.[3] The English left wing advanced by the pass of Urrachree against the Irish right. The Irish as stoutly defended as the English vigorously assailed. For two hours the fight raged between them; volley after volley was fired, and the Irish moved slowly back. They refused to retreat till the muzzles of the Williamite muskets touched their breasts. During this time the English right and centre were mere spectators. St. Ruth, seeing the fierce assault upon Urrachree, ordered men to leave Aughrim for it. Mackay had been waiting for this opportunity, and it had been given him. Discerning the weakened left and the weakened centre, he ordered his infantry to cross the bog. At half-past six the attack on the centre was delivered.[4] The 12th, 19th, 23rd, and Creighton's regiments, supported by the 9th and Ffoulks', marched thigh deep in soft bog, which they were not to pass until the infantry to the right were over the wide part and until the cavalry had forced the road to Aughrim Castle. Mackay meant these men to hinder the enemy from using their cavalry on the right wing. Despite the galling fire they drove the marksmen from the hedges, and, in their eagerness, forgetting their orders, they hotly pursued the Irish till they reached their main line. The Irish cavalry rushed down the slope and their fierce

---

[1] *Macariae Excidium*, pp. 132, 442–4; Story, pp. 134–5; Clarke, ii, p. 457.
[2] *Add. MSS.*, 33264 (Brit. Mus.).
[3] *Macariae Excidium*, pp. 444–9.
[4] *Macariae Excidium*, p. 445.

charge drove the foe into the bog; the loss was so great that to this day the spot where the English broke is known as "the bloody hollow."[1]

The 27th Inniskillings, the 18th, St. John's Derry men, Lord George Hamilton's, and the French advanced along the right. Not a shot was fired till they were within twenty yards of the hedge. A sudden blaze of matches and the click of the firelocks revealed the Irish, and huge gaps in the ranks bore eloquent testimony to the effectiveness of their fire. The cavalry rode down, and the regiments were forced to retreat. The results, so far, were that the English left was checked, the centre repulsed, and the right had done nothing. "The day is ours, my boys," St. Ruth exulted, "we will drive them before us to the walls of Dublin."[2] But he spoke too soon. Once when Napoleon seemed to be in the predicament of Ginkell he muttered that, though he had lost one battle, there was time to gain another. Though the shades of evening were falling fast, still Ginkell, too, had time to win another.

The right English wing made a determined onset on Aughrim Castle in order to gain it, and to help their infantry of the right centre. The road to this ruin was narrow, for but two horses could ride abreast. The Blues struggled through the slippery soil under a deadly fire. The glass fell from St. Ruth's eye as he saw their advance. "What on earth could they mean by it?" he asked in amazement.[3] As he watched their struggles he exclaimed, "By Heaven, they are gallant fellows; and it is quite a pity that they should thus court death." When he saw them lay down hurdles on the morass he repeated the saying ascribed to the Maréchal de Créqui, "Que plus il en passerait, plus il en battrait."[4] Ruvigny's French Horse, the 6th Dragoon Guards, and Langston's Horse followed the gallant Blues. The British infantry on the right renewed their efforts to hold their ground when they saw this splendid cavalry advance. The advantage was at last seen of Mackay's plan. The Irish cavalry had to meet the British infantry of the right centre and the British cavalry of the right wing, and

[1] Story.   [2] *Light to the Blind*, p. 689.   [3] Story.   [4] Berwick.

the combined effort proved too much for them. Ruvigny's cavalry delivered a magnificent charge, and swept the enemy away.[1] St. Ruth, even at this critical moment, did not lay aside his jealousy of Sarsfield. This general was ordered to send half his cavalry, but to remain with the other half. They were to meet the English squadron that had just passed the morass. St. Ruth hastened to put himself at their head. Turning to give the gunner an order, a cannon ball struck him, and he fell dead.[2] He died almost in the hour of victory, almost with the shout of triumph ringing in his ears. The fortunes of war, long trembling in the balance, at last fell decisively to the British. With the death of St. Ruth died many of the hopes of the French monarch. For had the general won, many of the plans of his master might have been executed. Sarsfield stopped in ignorance behind the hill till the fight was practically over. Galmoy tried to make a stand, but another charge of Ruvigny's cavalry proved irresistible. Mackay saw the left Irish wing completely broken, and the centre giving way. The bloodiest and most fiercely contested battle of the war was almost over. The English horse and dragoons pursued the flying foe, and turned their flight into a disastrous rout. The darkness of the night saved some of the fugitives, but many perished.[3] The English were enraged at hearing that an Irish officer had ordered all prisoners to be massacred, and that Colonel Herbert and other officers had thus died. The victory was crushing, and decided that the campaign must soon be finished. The English captured nine cannon, all the tents, baggage, and field equipage of the enemy, also eleven standards and thirty-two colours, which were presented to Queen Mary. That Sunday's work had been bloody, for between three o'clock and dusk some eight or ten thousand men were laid low. The loss on the English side amounted to at least one thousand killed and twelve hundred wounded.[4] The Irish probably lost

---

[1] *Macariae Excidium*, pp. 452–3.

[2] Mackay ; *Macariae Excidium*, p. 453.

[3] *Macariae Excidium*, pp. 132–3, 442–61 ; Story, pp. 123–7.

[4] Parker gives 3000 killed and wounded as Ginkell's loss, Kane gives 4000, while the official lists (*Clarke Correspondence*) give 2200.

seven thousand, for, as Ginkell wrote to William, the fight "was very obstinate."[1]

Three days after the battle, when many of the slain had been buried, and the remainder plundered by the camp-followers and peasants, Story surveyed the ground. Looking from the top of a hill he could see the naked bodies of the men, and they seemed to him like sheep dotted over the pastures and bogs.[2] This historian makes an interesting survey of the fighting qualities of English soldiers compared with those of other nations. Of course he possessed ample opportunities for making such a comparison, as his army was remarkably cosmopolitan. Just as Stevens censures the Irish officers, so he blames the English. He notes their helpless indolence in the most essential points of campaigning, their insular self-satisfaction, and unreadiness to learn from their more experienced allies. On the whole, however, he bestows hearty praise upon the English soldier. In this battle he mentions that the Londoners of the 1st, 2nd, and 3rd Dragoon Guards, the Gloucester men of the 9th, the Suffolk men of the 12th, and the Devon and Cornwall men of the 19th and 20th, the Cheshire men of the 22nd, Lisburn's Hertfordshire men, the Welshmen of the 23rd, Lord George Hamilton's Scotsmen, St. John's Derry men, the Inniskillings of the 27th, and the 5th and 6th Dragoons were all present. "They marched boldly up to their old ground again from whence they had been lately beaten : which is only natural to Englishmen : for it is observable that they are commonly fiercer and bolder after being repulsed than before : and what blunts the courage of all other nations commonly whets theirs, I mean the killing of their fellow-soldiers before their faces."[3]

Courageously as the English had attacked the hill, the Irish had defended it as perhaps they had never defended a position

---

[1] Story, pp. 138–41, reckons the Irish lost 7000 killed, Parker reckons 4000 killed and 2000 captured, and Kane reckons 17,000. *Cf. Macariae Excidium*, pp. 545–7 ; *C.S.P., Dom.*, 1690–91, pp. 444–5.

[2] *Cf.* Clarke, ii, pp. 456–8.

[3] Story ; *Add. MSS.*, 36296 (Brit. Mus.). Curiously enough, Stevens's *Journal* breaks off in the middle of a description of the Battle of Aughrim.

before.[1] Their cavalry performed as wonderful deeds as at the field of the Boyne a twelvemonth before. But Mackay's clever plan and Ruvigny's splendid charge had been too much for them. Mackay notes that if the Derry and Inniskilling regiments, who attacked the castle, had not kept firm until the Blues had time to pass the defile to join them in the attack, the English centre, then beaten, could not have recovered its ground, and the battle would have been lost. The battle of Aughrim shows what so many other contests prove, that a battle is never won till the last shot is fired.

The last stand of the Jacobites was to take place at Limerick, and accordingly on the 14th of August, 1691, the army reached Cahirconlish, four miles from Limerick. Much water had flowed under the bridge since the British had gazed on its walls eleven months before. The taking of Cork and Kinsale by Marlborough, the storming of Athlone, the Battle of Aughrim, and the surrender of Galway, might all have been inscribed upon their banners and drums. Yet a hard task lay before their victorious arms.[2] Ireton's fort had been repaired, a new fort had been built to the right, on the site of an old churchyard near it, and a third had been commenced in order to complete the line of communication between them. The star-fort on King's Island had been restored, and covered ways united it with the town. Within the old walls of Irish Town earthworks had been raised. Sarsfield and Wauchope inspired the soldiers to make a brave stand, hoping against hope that assistance might arrive from France. The undaunted Irishman commanded the cavalry, with Shelden as his lieutenant. De Tessé acted as Governor of the city.

The Commissariat had not learnt many of the lessons taught it by past mistakes, but Ginkell had mastered some of them. Large escorts under Major-General La Forest met the train of artillery coming from the Athlone depot under Colonel Lloyd's charge. This train was composed of nine 24-pounders, nine 18-pounders, and three mortars, with a corresponding allowance of ammunition.

---

[1] I. 6, 10 (*Southwell Correspondence*, T.C.D.). *Cf.* the letter of October 8, 1691, from the Right Hon. Richard Cox, Governor of Cork, giving an account of the campaign.

[2] Klopp, v, p. 304; *Jacobite Narrative*, pp. 282–98.

As at the first siege, it began to rain in such torrents that for a week it seemed the besiegers would be obliged to abandon the investment. What a rôle weather can play in fortress warfare is shown by the history of winter sieges, among which those of Belfort and Sebastopol stand out prominently. Fortunately, however, on the 22nd of August the weather cleared up, and on the 25th active operations commenced. In order to put an end to pillaging on the part of both officers and men, Ginkell forbade any one to purchase cattle from them. In truly medieval spirit he attempted to fix the price of provisions, arranging that ale from Dublin should be sixpence a quart, loaves threepence a pound, and brandy twelve shillings a gallon. The sutlers, in spite of his attempt, so manipulated the law of supply and demand that at the end of the siege ale cost fourteenpence a quart.

The English General directed his early efforts to getting possession of the external forts and earthworks. Mackay attacked Ireton's Fort, and Count Nassau Cromwell's Fort, and, after a slight defence both surrendered. The soldiers set to work vigorously, strengthening the forts, digging trenches and planting batteries; the lines of investment were so extensive that even the horse and dragoons were asked to furnish four men from each troop for spade-work in the trenches. The outworks deserted by the Irish were improved and connected by lines of communication. On the 8th of September five batteries, with the total of sixty guns, began a simultaneous cannonade upon the city; bomb and bullet, ball and fireball, fell ceaselessly within its streets. The effects of the heavy fire were visible on the 9th,[1] and on the 11th, despite the Irish fire, the breach was at least forty yards wide. Ginkell perceived that unless the town were invested from the Clare side there was little hope of a speedy reduction. In order to conceal the attempt to pass the Shannon the British pretended to raise the siege as they had done the preceding year. Two or three large guns were openly withdrawn and placed on board the fleet. Floats and tin boats were all the time being skilfully prepared. On the evening of the 15th of September the 2nd Foot, four hundred grenadiers, and six hundred

---

[1] Story, pp. 118–216.

workmen were ready to cross the Shannon about a mile above St. Thomas's Island. They were supported by Talmash with five regiments of infantry, and by Schravemoer with cavalry and six field-pieces. At midnight began the building of the bridge to the island ; from the island to the shore was fordable. When the morning dawned the grenadiers possessed the island, and the dragoons marched over the completed bridge.[1] Clifford's Irish Brigade could not dispute the passage and fled.[2] The Shannon had been definitely passed, and the fate of Limerick had been as definitely sealed.

On the 22nd the council of war determined on the crossing of the Shannon. Leaving Talmash and Mackay in command of the camp, Ginkell, Wurtemberg, Schravemoer, and Ruvigny, accompanied by practically all the cavalry, ten regiments of infantry, and fourteen field-guns, passed the river into County Clare. The grenadiers under Colonel Tiffin advanced to attack Thomond Bridge which joined County Clare to King's Island. This bridge was guarded by two forts and near it eight hundred men were posted in stone quarries and gravel pits. The grenadiers tramped on amidst the shot of the cannon, the shell of the mortar, and the bullet of the musket. Behind them came the 2nd, the 27th Inniskillings, Lord George Hamilton's, and St. John's Derry regiments. The grenadiers emptied the pits and the Irish retreated. So closely did they pursue the Jacobites that the French Major in charge of the bridge grew afraid that the besiegers might enter as well as the besieged. He therefore pulled up the drawbridge too hastily, leaving some six hundred of his allies outside it. Some of these were drowned and others slain. The result was that the city was completely cut off from all communication with its cavalry near Sixmilebridge ; this hindered the Irish from making any concentrated attack on their assailants. The English possessed the forts and earthworks on the Clare side. Close on a thousand Irish lay dead, twenty officers and a hundred men were taken prisoners of war, three brass guns and five colours were also proofs of victory.

[1] Story, pp. 216–7 ; *Macariae Excidium*, pp. 149, 480–2.
[2] Story, p. 216. *Cf.* Clarke, ii, pp. 460–1.

The besiegers lost no more than twenty-five killed and sixty wounded. As resistance was useless, the city surrendered on the 28th.

The Irish had raised the standard of rebellion against Oliver Cromwell, and the price they paid was the Cromwellian Plantation. Their land was taken from them. They had raised the standard of rebellion against William III, and the price they paid was the Penal Laws. Their political position was taken from them. The truth is that the yeomen of Enniskillen and Derry, in common with all their race, dreaded the power of the Pope, for they perceived its might in the sword and pike of the Irishman fighting the Englishman on the Continent. The French monarch was the trusted ally of their adversaries, the French monarch was a Roman Catholic. Was it not self-evident that every Roman Catholic was their enemy? The yeomen remembered that in 1646 Cardinal Pamphili, the Papal Secretary of State, had refused approval of any member of his communion swearing allegiance to Charles I. They also remembered that in 1662 the Nuncio at Brussels, De Vecchiis, had stated that a proposed address by the Roman Catholic clergy of Ireland, emphasising their loyalty to their new sovereign, constituted a violation of their faith.

The monks were, then as ever, the Pope's militia, and the militia of a man who was the Head of a State as well as the Head of a Church. The loyalty they owed the Pope came before the loyalty they owed the King. Alas! no man can serve two masters. Hegel has well said that the most intensely tragic situation results, not from a conflict of right against wrong, but from a conflict of right against right, and William III, as the repressor of ecclesiastical power and the defender of civil power, is as deserving of our respect as Innocent XII. The subjects of William must be either King's men or powerless men. This was a question on which there could be no compromise, and there could be no more a question of a subject qualifying his oath of allegiance by a reference to Innocent XII than of a soldier in the army trying to qualify his allegiance.

CHAPTER I

The Formation of the Regiment

THE second siege of Limerick terminated the Civil War in Ireland. The plans of Louis XIV had been foiled, and in this defeat the men of Derry and Enniskillen had taken no mean part. In 1689 Sir Albert Conyngham had raised at Enniskillen the regiment that is now the 6th Dragoons, and was then Conyngham's Horse. After the signing of the Treaty of Limerick, William determined to raise another regiment of Dragoons composed of the Ulstermen who had served him so faithfully. The command of this corps was given to Colonel Henry Conyngham, the only surviving son of Sir Albert. Of Colonel Conyngham's previous career it is sufficient to state that he served as captain in Lord Mountjoy's Regiment of Foot, taking part with his father's regiment at the Battles of the Boyne and Aughrim. He was promoted to the lieutenant-colonelcy on the 31st of December, 1691. That he was regarded as a trustworthy and distinguished officer is clear from the following order of the 28th of January, N.S.,[1] 1693 :—

WILLIAM R.

Right trusty and well beloved Cousin and Councillor Wee greet you well. Whereas We thought it necessary for Our Service that One Regiment of Foot with one Regiment of Dragoons be raised within Our Kingdom of Ireland to consist of the numbers menčoned in the Estabt. hereunto annext and to be commanded by our Right Trusty and Right Wellbeloved Cousin Arthur Earl of Donegall and Coll. Henry Cunninghame whom we have directed to propose to you for Your approbation such Officers as they shall think fitly qualified to serve Us in their respective Regiments with particular regard to be had to the Londonderry and Inniskilling Officers now out of Service.

---

[1] N.S. means New Style. Between the Old Style (O.S.) and the New Style there is a difference of about ten days. The year then began on March 25, the Annunciation of the Virgin Mary. All dates to March 25 were then reckoned to belong to the preceding year.

Our Will and Pleasure is that you forthwith give the necessary Orders for raising the said Regiments to be compleated by the Twentieth of March next. And for the better enabling the Officers to perform the Same We are pleased to allow Twenty Shillings a man for each Private Souldier of Foot and Five Pounds for each Dragoon his Horse and Accoutrements, And as Twenty five Private Souldiers in each Company of Foot, and 25 in each Troope of Dragoons with Horses fitt for Service Shall be produced to muster they are with the Non Commissioned Officers of such Troops and Company to be mustered and to enter into one Pay accordingly and so as anymore Shall afterwards be raised they are in like manner to be mustered untill the Numbers shall be fully compleated in each Regiment and then they are to march to and rendezvous at Kilkenny and Clonmell or such other places as you shall think fitt there to be mustred again and to be ready for Service Especiall care being to be had that all the sd. Soldrs. be known Protestants. And you are further to take notice that We have already given Orders for the timely providing and sending from hence such Cloaths and Arms as are necessary for each of the said Regimts. And so We bid you very heartily Farewell. Given at Our Court at Whitehall the 18th day of Janry. 169⅔ in the fourth year of Our Reigne.

By His Majties. Command

William Blathwayt.[1]

A supplementary warrant was issued on the 31st of January, 1693 :—

William R.

Whereas Wee have Ordered to be Raised for Our Service in Ireland One Regiment of Dragoones consisting of Eight Companys Each Compā. of Sixty Private Soldiers, two Serjeants, three Corporalls and two Drums as also one Regiment of Foot. . . . And one Company of Granadiers. . . . Likewise two Regiments of Foot to be Raised in Scotland. . . . Our Will and Pleasure Therefore is That Out of the Stores remayning within the Office of Our Ordnance You Cause the said Regiments to be supplied with such Arms and Appurtenances as are Usually Delivered to the Like Regiments Causing the same to be sent by Land Carra. to Chester, and from thence to be Transported to

---

[1] *S.P.*, *Ireland*, Bundle 366, Ormonde's letter of August 1, 1704, confirms the date of January 18, 1693. According to Dalton, this date is not in the Commission books.

Dublin and upon their Arrivall there the said Arms, etc., be Delivered to Our Right Trusty and Wellbeloved Cousin and Counceller Henry Viscount Sydney, Lieut. Genll. and Generall Governr. of Our Kingdom of Ireland or to whom he shall Appoint to Receive the same Taking the usual Indents And for so doing this shall be Your sufficient Warrt. Given att Our Court att Whitehall the 31st Day of January, 1692., In the Fourth Year of Our Reigne.

By his Majts. Comand

NOTTINGHAM.[1]

To Sir. Henry Goodricke, etc.

The names of the colonels given in the margin are Conyngham,[2] the Earl of Donegal, Sir James Moncrieff, and Earl Strathnaver.

The uniform was scarlet, lined and turned up with yellow; with yellow waistcoats and breeches; round hats with broad brims, turned up on both sides and behind; boots reaching above the knee; and yellow horse furniture. The men were armed with swords and pistols, also with long muskets and bayonets, in order that they might act either as cavalry or infantry, according to the demands of the service required. Their colonel, Henry Conyngham, was anxious that they should be in all respects properly equipped, and accordingly on the 22nd of April, 1693, he wrote from Dublin to the Lords of the Treasury, pointing out

That is is Absolutely Necessary for their Maties. Service to bring Two hundred and Fifty horses out of England for the new raised Regiment of Dragoons under his Command in Ireland, Most of wch. horses are now ready to be shipt in Chester Water and at Holly-Head, and Therefore Humbly Prays yor. Lordships' Order to the Officers on that Coast, to permitt the shiping Them Custom Free, as alsoe an Order to ye. Commissioners of the Revenue in Ireland to admitt the said Horses to be Landed at Dublin, or any other port free of all Duty There.[3]

---

[1] *War Office Warrants*, W.O. 55/401.

[2] Was Piero Strozzi the father of dragoons in 1543? The first English regiment of dragoons dates from 1672. See Fortescue, *History of the British Army*, I, p. 102. I want, once for all, to acknowledge my vast indebtedness to this work of outstanding importance. No other army has an historian so profound and so readable as Sir John W. Fortescue. His *magnum opus* ought to be in every mess and indeed in every officer's library.

[3] *Treasury Papers*, Vol. 22, T. 1/22, No. 16.

From the camp on Dighem William Blathwayt wrote on the 25th of May, 1693, that "My Lord Galway having presented the inclosed Memorial to the King, His Majesty is Pleased to order that the necessary Directions be given accordingly."[1] The memorial related to the 250 horses for which Conyngham was still agitating, and it is pleasing to remember that Lord Galway was the Ruvigny of the Irish Wars, a man who had often come into contact with the men of Derry and Enniskillen.

In order to ensure the loyalty of the regiment Roman Catholics were excluded from it, and on the 26th of June, 1693, the following oath was taken by officers and soldiers alike:

> I swear to be true to Our Soveraigne Lord and Lady King William and Queen Mary and to serve them honestly and faithfully in the defence of their persons, Crowne, and dignity against all their enemys and opposers whatsoever and to observe and obey their Matys. orders and ye. orders of the Generals and Officers set over me by their Matys.
>
> So help me God.[2]

With the spirit of the men of Derry and Enniskillen to constitute the beginnings of regimental tradition and with the due equipment of arms and of horses, Henry Conyngham had a comparatively easy task lying before him. For his officers and men had gained their experience in the best of all schools, the actual battlefield. With the free hand given to the Commanding Officers of his day, Conyngham served his regiment faithfully. In small matters, as in large, he occupied himself with all that concerned his command. On the 9th of June, 1697, he granted long leave to Lieutenant Thomas Knox, that is "a Lycense . . . to be absent for two months from this date," so the formal seventeenth century put it.[3] On the 23rd of the same month he issued an order,

> directing Capt. Breholt in the Loesdyke yacht to saile to Chester Water and receive on board the Coll. wth. his Lady and Servts. and the first opportunity of wind, and water, to bring them to His Porte, and to attend for further orders.[4]

[1] *Ibid.*, T. 1/22, No. 16.

[2] *S.P.*, *Ir.*, *Entry Book*, 1, pp. 356 and especially 360. *Cf.* Fortescue, I, p. 304.: "The Buffs had been the earliest English volunteers in the cause of liberty and protestantism; the Royal Scots had rolled back papistry under the Lion of the North."

[3] *Bk. E. Mil.*, 1697–8, p. 2.   [4] *Ibid.*, p. 5.

We learn that on the 15th of June, 1697, part of a troop quartered at Blessington marched to new quarters at Baltinglass.[1]   On the 13th of September the troop, commanded by Captain Alexander Stewart, marched to Newry and Dundalk, sending detachments from thence to Four Mile House and to Castle Roche, and they were to remain there till further orders.[2]   In 1697 the Nine Years' War with France came to an end, and the regiment was reduced to a peace establishment.   Five men out of each troop were disbanded.[3]

In 1698 an abstract was issued to Colonel Conyngham, and in it he was informed of the numbers of officers and soldiers allowed in a regiment of horse to one troop.   The numbers are:

Field Staff Officer	Quartermaster
Colonel	One Sergeant
Lieutenant Colonel	Two Corporals
Major : one troop	One Drummer
Chaplain	One Hautboy
Lieutenant	Forty Dragoons.[5]
Cornet[4]	

With the settlement of the numbers to be in a troop, there came up another question on the pay of the soldier.   In this question the matter of stoppages loomed large.   We read in 1698 that:

Whereas it appears there has bin a stop from each Dragoon in the Regiment cõmanded by Coll. Henry Conynghame one pound four in order to provide them Pistolls, wch. Arms his Maty. having not thought fit should be given them Each Dragoon hath received a broad sword value 12 shill. ; and the Collonel designing to employ the remaining 12 shill. so stopt towards the Better arming that Regiment wth. Fuzees, Wee do hereby direct that such stoppage hath been made shall be daily accounted wth. for the sd. 12 shill. on or before the first day of May next by wh. time that money is to be expend for the use aforesaid, and

---

[1] *Bk. of Entries*, 1697–8, p. 2.

[2] September 13, 1697, *Bk. of Entries*, 1697–8, p. 25.

[3] *Martial Affairs*, 1 E, 3.1, p. 161.

[4] He comes from the horn-shaped flag borne in the retinue of Cardinal Wolsey, the cornette. *Cf.* Fortescue, I, p. 118.

[5] *Mart. Aff.*, 1698, 1 E, 3.1, p. 63.

such as are not now in the Regiment from whence such stoppages hath been made are to receive each one pound four shill. if they have not already recd. the same.

By his Excs. Command.

H. MAY.[1]

For the moment we postpone the whole question of pay till the end of this chapter, simply noting the share taken by the soldier in providing for his own equipment.

The Treaty of Ryswick, 1697, brought about a reduction in the size of a troop, and on the 11th of March, 1698, elaborate instructions on the consequent disbandment were issued to Major General Levisson. It was particularly required under the second head that the soldiers be

satisfyed all their just ptentions[2] from their officers, and to let them know they shall be paid what is due to them from the King to the day of their discharge, of which you are to give them a certificate under your hand.

3ly, The Accts. of all Non Commd. Officers that come within these Rules are to be stated and adjusted and given to them And his Majy. of his Royall bounty being gratiously pleased to allow each Non Commned. Officer and Private Man Ten Days Subce.[3] from the time of his Discharge You are to advance the sume to him and returne a Certificate thereof to the Muster Master Genll. or his Deputy at Dublin with the names of the Officers and Soldiers you shall discharge in pursuance hereof and the day of their discharge, and thereupon ye. Rec. Genll. will give you Creditt for the money so advanced.

4ly, The Armes delivered out of the Stores to the Non Commnd. Officers and Private Men are to be returned into the next Store and Receipts taken for the same of which you are to send us an Acct. and if any Officers have a pretence to such Armes, upon Applycation to us they shall have right done them.

5ly, You are to pmitt. each Non Commnd. Officer and Private Soldier to carry away his Cloakes, Cloathes, Sword and other necessarys and accoutrements, and you are to give them Passes, and therein to signifie that they are not to continue together above Six in number after they are disbanded upon any Acct.

---

[1] *Mart. Aff.*, 1698, 1 E, 3.1, p. 63.   [2] Pretentions.   [3] Subsistence.

Naturally these instructions are only intelligible upon the assumption of the seventeenth century that the soldier equipped himself. This is also quite evident when we come to the manner of disposal of the horses. Here disbandment was to be carried out in the following fashion :

1st, When any Non Commnd. Officer or Private Soldier hath served a whole year, the Horse which his Majtie. Paid for by ye. Leavy money is to be given him which his Majtie. is gratiously pleased to allow but where such Person hath not served one whole year his Horse is to be sold by you, and an Acct. kept of the money to be disposed of as Wee shall direct.

2ly, Where any private Man dischargd. is to have his Horse and the same is better than some other Horses belonging to the Troope, the best Horse is to be kept, and one less serviceable or not of so much Value is to be given to the disbanded Horse man in lieu of the other.

3ly, In case any Officer hath furnished a Horse to a private Trooper the Officer is to be satisfied, such part of the Value thereof upon sale as has not bin already paid by deduction or otherwise from the Troope.

4ly, If any difference shall arise between the Trooper and his Officer, you are to adjust and determine the same, or if that cannot be done remitt the matter to the Court of Genll. Officers to be by them settled and adjusted, all which Wee desire you to see carefully and effectually perform'd and for so doing this shall be your Warrant.[1]

Major General Leveson issued this order to Brigadier Langston, Colonel Ross, Colonel Echlin, and Colonel Conyngham.[2] Fortescue's comment is that this disbandment "was an act of criminal imbecility, the most mischievous work of the most mischievous Parliament that has ever sat at Westminster."[3] Within fifteen months of this disbandment Ireland lost fifteen battalions out of twenty-one.

On the 11th of February Conyngham had already received an order for the payment of eighteen months' off-reckonings, the remainder of the daily pay of the soldier when he had paid his subsistence, due to his regiment. These off-reckonings were to

[1] *Mart. Aff.*, 1 E, 3.4, p. 18. *Cf. H.O. Mil. Entry Book*, iii, pp. 374–86.
[2] *Mart. Aff.*, 1 E, 3.4, p. 18.   [3] Fortescue, I, p. 389.

commence from the time the last off-reckonings were determined and cleared off, and the off-reckonings were to be made payable to James Leathly, Benjamin Taylor, and James Dugan, undertakers.[1]

It is quite clear that the question of off-reckonings was not settled, for on the 2nd of September, 1698, the Receivers and Paymasters General had sent to them the following:

> You will herewith receive stated Accots. of the arrears due on the present Establishment to severall Serjts. Corplls. and Drummers late of the Regimt. of Dragoons under the command of Coll. Henry Conyngham amounting in the whole to one hundred thirty four pounds, eight shillings and five pence three farthings. And we hereby pray and require you out of his Maties. Treasure that is or shall be in your hands to pay unto Mr Charles Melville, Agent to the said Regimt., one fourth of the said Sum of £134 8s. 5¾d. in money to be by him paid over to the said Serjts, Corporalls, and Drumers being Twenty in number according to the proportions due to them respectively by the Stated Accots. above mentioned, and to issue Debrs. for the remaining three fourths of the said arrears which you are to place to Accot. of the cleerings due to the Regimt. aforesaid upon the Establishment of this Kingdome.

> And for so doing this together with the Receipt of the said Mr Melville shall be to you and the Commrs. of your Accots. a sufficient Warrant.[2]

On the 28th of September, 1698, the Receivers and Paymasters General receive fresh authority:

> These are to pray and require you out of his Majesties' Treasure that is or shall be in your hands to advance and Pay unto Coll. Henry Conyngham the sume of three hundred forty five pounds, twelve shillings for providing Hay for the six winter months for the Sergts. Corplls. and private men of the Regiment of Dragoones under his command at four shillings each man p. month which you are to stop in the Treaẽry.[3] and deduct out of the Subce. of the said Regiment for the six winter months at seaven pounds four shillings p. month from each Troope. And for so doing this together with the Receipt of said Coll. Conyngham or his Agent shall be your sufficient Warrant.[4]

[1] *Mart. Aff.*, 1 E, 3.4, p. 4.   [2] *Mart. Aff.*, 1698, 1 E, 3.4, p. 71.
[3] Treasury.   [4] *Mart. Aff.*, 1698, 1 E, 3.4, p. 83.

Each of the regiments of dragoons had thirty-three officers and thirty sergeants training only two hundred and sixteen men. It is easy to understand the current jest that our army was an army of officers.

On the 26th of May and the 10th of August, 1698, the amount of powder received consideration. On the former date this instruction was sent out to the regiments concerned :

Wee hereby pray and require you to cause to be delivered out of his Maties' Stores of Warr under your care to the Coll. or Officer in chief of the severall and respective Regiments of Horse Dragoons and Foot within mentioned of his Maties. Forces in this Kingdom the quantity of Powder within exprest for each Troop and Company in the said severall Regts. being the usual allowance of Watch Ammunition to the Regimts. aforesaid for six months comencing the Twenty fifth day of March last, and ending the 29th of Septr. next ensuing. And forsoe doing this together with the receipt of the several Colls. or Commanding Officers or any persons authorized by them the same shall be your sufficient Warrant and discharge.

Given the 26th Day of May, 1698.

Major Genll. Levesons
and Brigadier Langstons } Regiment of Horse.

Six Troops in each Regiment and a quarter of a Barrell for each Troop.

Coll. Rosses
Coll. Robert Echlins   } Regiments of Dragoones.
Coll. Henry Conyngham

Eight Troops in each Regiment, halfe a Barrell of Powder for each Troop.[1]

On the 10th of August, 1698, Conyngham received a special order, instructing him "to have out of the Stores three Barrells of Pistoll Powder and to receive from him in lieu thereof three Barrells of Musquet Powder formerly issued to him out of the Stores for the use of his Regimt. of Dragoons."[2]

On the 24th of May, 1698, Conyngham granted licence to Captain Henry Wood to be absent from his command for two months from this date, and on July he did the same for Quartermaster Del Isle.

[1] *Mart. Aff.*, 1 E, 3.4, p. 89.   [2] *Mart. Aff.*, 1 E, 3.4, p. 64.

In 1698 there were four movements of troops. On the 25th of January one troop marched from Newtown Limavady to Artikelly, Dungiven, and Muff.[1] On the 29th of March one troop marched from Cavan to Belturbet; one to Sligo; one to Letterkenny, Ramelton, and Rathmullan; one to Newtown Limavady, Muff, and Artikelly, and Dungiven; one to Armagh, Caledon, and Glasslough; one to Ardee, Dundalk, and Castletown Bellew; one to Monaghan; one to Clonish; and one to Newry and Loughbrickland. On the 14th of April the several troops marched to the quarters following:—One to Cavan and Killeshandra; one to Belturbet; one to Enniskillen and Lowtherstown; one to Strabane; one to Letterkenny and Rathmullan; one to Newtown Limavady and Muff; one to Coleraine; and one to Navan and Kells. On the 11th of June Captain Robert Stewart marched part of his troop from Lowtherstown to Enniskillen, where his whole troop was quartered. On the 27th of June the following is the distribution of the troops:—One at Cavan and Killeshandra; one at Belturbet; one at Enniskillen; one at Strabane; one at Letterkenny and Rathmullan; one at Newtown Limavady and Muff; one at Coleraine; and one at Navan and Kells.

Men were far more cosmopolitan in the Middle Ages than they are to-day. It was common for an undergraduate to spend a year at Oxford or Cambridge, then travel to Paris for the sake of some celebrated teacher there, and then to Bologna or Prague. Erasmus, the great humanist of the sixteenth century, was technically a Dutchman, yet he belonged to the whole of literary Europe. Nor is this feeling foreign to the army. The Duke of Berwick, an Englishman, was to command the army of the French in Spain. Schomberg had served under Frederick Henry, Prince of Orange; had served with the Swedish army in Germany under Bernhard of Weimar; under Rantzau in Franche-Comté; under the Prince de Tarente in Holland; was captain of the Scots Guards in the French army with the rank of maréchal-de-camp; raised an infantry regiment in Germany and was lieutenant general; captured and became governor of Bourbourg; was maréchal-de-

---

[1] *Mart. Aff.*, 1 E, 3.1, p. 83.

camp in the Portuguese service; came to England and entered the service as commander under Prince Rupert; commanded the army between the Sambre and the Meuse and received the rank of Duc; became Marshal and commanded the army on the Meuse; on the Revocation of the Edict of Nantes entered the service of the Elector of Brandenburg; and finally accompanied William III to England. Such a varied set of commands would be quite out of the question in our time, and no doubt was exceptional even for the seventeenth century. We do well, however, to remember that the spirit of nationalism, save in the British Isles, is largely a creation of the nineteenth century. The cosmopolitanism of the forces present on the winning side at the Battle of the Boyne would have occasioned but little surprise in any country in Europe except our own. It occasioned some feeling with us shortly after 1691, and men noted with regret the leaning of the King to his Dutch troops. The feeling passed from regret to anger, as men continued to witness the favour shown to men who, after all, were the countrymen of the sovereign. Did the Dutch not hold the most lucrative posts in the royal household? Did Dutchmen not occupy the finest manors of the Crown? Did Dutchmen not command the army? In 1698 the common cry was: No standing army; no grants of Crown property; and no Dutchmen. The influence of the agitation passed to Ireland in 1698, and accordingly we have the following document with its pithy marginal note:

"Major Genl. Leveson, Brigd. Langston, Coll. Rosse, Coll. Echlin, and Coll. Conyngham, to discharge out of their Regt. all forrainers." The terms of the actual document are:

Having received his Majties. comands forthwith to give Order for the disbanding of all such Officers and Soldiers now in the several Regts. of the Army in this Kingdome as are not his Majesties' natural borne Subjects; Wee do in Order to the execution of his Majesties' Pleasure therein hereby authorize, direct, and require you forthwith to discharge all Officers and Private Soldiers in the Regt. under your Command that are not his Majties. Naturall borne Subjects, being foraigne natives, and in doing thereof to observe the directions following.

1st, You (or such Officer as you shall appoint and for whom you will be answerable) are to repaire without delay to the several Troopes of the Regt. of Horse under your Command and there see those Officers and Soldiers who are not natural borne Subjects of his Majtie. disbanded and declare them discharged of the present Service by his Majties. Order.

2ndly, You or such Officer aforesaid are to settle the accounts between the Officers and such men as shall be disband on this occasion and see that they shall be satisfied all their just ptentions from their Officers and to let them know they shall be paid what is due to them from the King to the day of their discharge, of which you are to give them a certificate under your hand.

3ly, The Accts. of all Non Comd. Officers that come within these Rules are to be stated and adjusted and given to them and his Majtie. of his Royall bounty being gratiously pleased to allow to each non Commd. Officer and Private man ten days Subce. from the time of his Discharge. You are to advance the Sume to him and returne a Certificate thereof to the Muster Master Genll. or his Deputy at Dublin, with the names of the Officers and Soldiers you shall discharge in pursuance hereof and the day of their discharge, and thereupon the Recr.[1] Genll. will give you credit for the money so advanced.

4thly, The Armes delivered out of the Stores to the Non Commsd. Officers and Private men are to be returned into the next Store and Receipts taken for the same of which you are to send us an Acct. and if any Officer have a pretence to such Armes, upon application to us they shall have right done them.

5thly, You are to permitt each Non Commd. Officer and Private Soldier to carry away his Cloakes, Cloathes, Sword and other necessarys and accoutrements, and you are to give them Passes, and therein to signifie that they are not to continue together above six in number after they are disbanded upon.

The Dutch Guards were driven by popular clamour out of England, and the foreigners in the army out of Ireland. Past services are proverbially soon forgotten, and yet no one who remembers the splendid services of the Dutch can read this page in our annals with unmixed satisfaction. One rude spectator, who witnessed the passing of the Dutch, was heard to remark that Hans

[1] Receiver.

made a much better figure, now that he had been living on the fat of the land, than when he first came. "A pretty figure you would have made," retorted a Dutch soldier, "if we had not come." The retort, we are glad to think, was generally applauded. It is pleasant to read that on the 2nd of June, 1699, Lieutenant Noah Cadroy, on taking out his naturalisation, was restored to his commission in the Eighth.[1]   On the 22nd of February Conyngham had granted twenty-eight pounds to his French officers in order to enable them to become naturalised.[2]

On the 20th of November, 1699, we meet with an order "for discharging Sergt. Ash of Capt. Davis's Troop . . . for his mutinous behaviour and to declare him for ever incapable to serve his Majtie. in any post whatsoever."[3]   There are no details throwing light on his conduct.

In 1700 we learn that there were two troops at Sligo, one at Carrick, Jamestown, and Charlestown, and one at Ballinrobe, whence a sergeant and ten men were to set out for the redoubt at Ballaghy.

Throughout this year the question of arrears bulked once more prominently. On the 8th of January, 1700, an order was issued to four regiments. Its terms are:

> Wee hereby direct and require you to produce sevll. Warrts. and present them to our Signature for paying to the two Regiments of foot commanded by Brigd. Hanmer and Coll. Gust. Hamilton and the Regiments of Dragoones command. by Coll. Echlin and Coll. Conyngham the full pay due to them according to the late establishment from the first day of Jan. $169\frac{1}{2}$ to the 31st of Dec. 1697 both includ. deducting thereout all such Sumes as shall have been paid to each of the said Regimts. upon Acct. of the Subce. or arrears and make the said Warrant payble. to the respective Agents of the said Regimts.[4]

On the 27th of February, $1\frac{699}{700}$, the agent of the 8th received an order for the payment of £1496 10s. o$\frac{1}{4}$d. to the officers and £54 1s. 8d. to the non commissioned officers.[5]

---

[1] 1 E, 3.5, p. 5.   [2] 1 E, 3.5, p. 5.   [3] 1 E, 3.6, p. 36.
[4] 1 E, 3.6, p. 77.   [5] 1 E, 3.6, p. 56.

On the then New Year's Day, the 25th of March, 1700, another general order appeared. According to it,

> Wee hereby direct and require you to prepare a Warrant and present the same to our Signature for paymt. to the agent of Brigad. Langstons Regimt. of Horse the allowance due to the severall officers thereof according to the establishment in lieu of their servants from the first day of January last to the 31st of Mch. inst. both included. . . .

The like order of the severall regiments following.
    Coll. Harveys.
    Coll. Rosses.
    Coll. Echlins.
    Coll. Coninghams.
    Earl of Orkneys Royall Regts. . . .[1]

Warrants enough were issued, but did they secure payment? There is little reason to think that they did.

One way out of the difficulty of securing proper payment was to lessen expense by disbandment, and accordingly on the 18th of May Colonel Echlin was told to "cause two of the Regiments of Dragoones under your Command to be disbanded so soone as conveniently may be after rect. hereof in the doing whereof you are to observe the following directions—Vizt. The like Order to Coll. Conyngham for disbanding four Troopes of the Regiment of Dragoons under his Command with the alteraċon that the best men and horses are to be preserved."[2] The rest of the Eighth was dismounted. In the British Army, unlike most armies, mounted and dismounted men felt they belonged to one great body. Such a gentleman as Bayard refused with disdain to fight alongside infantry. Our traditions were entirely unlike the French, yet entirely in keeping with our national characteristics.

On the 24th of June, 1700, the order of the 8th of January is amplified. Now we read :

> Whereas Wee have directed the paymaster Genll. to pay the cleering or arrears of pay due unto the regimt. of Dragoones commanded by Coll. Robt. Echlin, the regimt. of Dragoones commanded by Coll.

[1] 1 E, 3.6, p. 65.   [2] 1 E, 3.6, pp. 80–1.

Henry Coningham, the regimt. of foote commanded by Sr. John Hanmer, and the regimt. of foot commanded by Coll. Gust. Hamilton in full of all that is due to the said Regimts. from the 1st day of January, 169½, to the 31st of December, 1697, according to the Establishmt. And whereas divers Comd. and Noncomd. Officers that served in the aforesaid regiments to whome arrears of cleerings are due are either removed out of this Kingdome or dead whose respective arrears or cleerings. Wee have caused to be stopt in the Treaſy. untill such time as the sd. officers shall appeare either by themselves, their Heires, Exrs., Admrs., or assignes and produce good proofe of their being duly intituled to the sd. arrears or cleerings and to the end that the accounts and Warrants for cleerings of the sd. regimts. may be closed Wee are pleased to issue this our proclamaꞇon. to publish and make known unto all persons that are concerned yt.[1] they do before the 31st of Mch. next, 1701, apply themselves unto the paymr. Genll. or his deputy (for the time being) at the Treaſy. Office in Dublin, and there make out by due proofes the arrrs. due to them in order to their satisfaꞇon., it being intended the said Warrts. shall be closed from and after the 31st day of March 1701 aforesaid.

Proclamations like the foregoing appear and reappear with the utmost persistency. The only appearance that really mattered to officers and men alike was the appearance of pounds, shillings and pence sterling, and there is unfortunately only too much reason to apprehend that such appearances were much rarer than the warrants that continued to pour forth. It is a relief to turn from the perusal of such documents to the announcement that Capt. George Breholt, Commander of his Majesty's yacht, the *Loesdyke*, received on the 11th of July, 1700, an order " for sayling wth. Coll. Coningham, his Lady, and servts. to Bristoll."[2]

The dangers due to the designs of Louis XIV on the throne of Spain threatened to give a defeat to William III in the lifelong duel between the two monarchs. The authorities regretted the disbandment of the four troops in 1700, and two troops were at once to be raised in 1701. In this year there was certainly one troop stationed at Kinsale. On the 13th of August an order for

---

[1] That.   [2] 1 E, 3.6, p. 100.

money was granted for the regiment to be remounted.   On the 8th of November, 1701, we read :

> Whereas his Majty. had thought fitt to direct the Regimt. of Dragoons comãnded by Coll. Henry Conyngham to be forthwith Remounted, and two new Troopes to be raised and added to the said Regimt. and for their subsistence has made an additional Provision upon the present Establishment commencing the first day of August last, and whereas Major John Pepper, Commanding in Chief the said Regimt., has engaged to Remount the said Regimt. and raise and add Two new Troopes to the same by the first day of January next.   We are pleased the better to enable the said Major to perform the said Service that the allowance contained in the said Establishment from the first of August last past to the 31st of Dec. next over and above what is usually paid to the Regimt. as being unmounted shall be forthwith issued and paid to the Agent of the said Regimt. to be disposed of to the severall Capts. thereof for remounting their respective Troopes as the said Major shall direct, which said additionall allowance being eightpence a day to each Sergt., fourpence to each Corporall, sixpence a day to each Drummer, and fourpence halfpenny to each private Dragoone, doth for four Troopes within the time above mentioned amount to the sume of four hundred and sixty nine pounds four shillings.[1]

There were six troops in an English regiment, but there were to be eight in the Eighth.

The old dread of the Roman Catholic had by no means disappeared.   None was to be allowed to serve in any regiment in Ireland, so runs an order of December, 1701.   Rewards were offered for their discovery, and threats of breaking and suspension were held over the heads of the Captain of the troop and the Colonel of the regiment if they knowingly allowed them to serve. Such soldiers were to be discharged with infamy and subsequently were to be prosecuted by law.

On the 16th of July, 1702, detachments of Conyngham's Dragoons were ordered to join headquarters at Limerick, there to await orders.   While the regiment was there, on the 17th of November, 1702, Captain Robert Stewart and Cornet William

---

[1] *Book of Military Events (Miscellaneous,* 1701–03).

Nesbitt were placed on half pay. When the four troops had been disbanded in 1700 and the remainder dismounted, their saddles, slings, and the like, had been retained with strict orders for their preservation. Naturally some of the men disposed of them. Equally naturally Brigadier Conyngham suffered loss. He therefore petitioned on the 10th of December, 1702, for six months' off-reckonings, amounting to £714 10s. 8d., in order to replace the loss, and his petition was granted.

On the 7th of July, 1703, the regiment was at Nenagh.[1] We find that for some time past the question of precedence had been vexing the soul of Brigadier Conyngham. In the infantry the officers took precedence according to the seniority of the regiments to which they belonged. In the Horse they took precedence, as is the case now, by date of commission. On the 3rd of August, 1703, Brigadier Conyngham addressed the Duke of Ormonde, the Lord Lieutenant:

May it please your Grace

I humbly beg leave this way to remind your Grace of the memoriall I lately gave your Grace, to be layd before her Matie. and can not doubt, but when the justice of my pretentions have the advantage of coming before the Queen with your Grace's recommendation the misfortune I now lie under will soon be remov'd by makeing my Commission of Brigadr. of equall date with those her Matie. first granted, tho the great worth of those her Matie. did earlyest promote to that station gives them a just title to that mark of her Maties. favour, yet I hope I may be allow'd to say, which I do with all submission, that it is a very great mortification to me to be now commanded by those I had the precedence of for ten years past. I beg leave to add that I am very ready to serve her Matie. abroad in any station she shall be pleas'd to imploy me in, but I must say that I shou'd goe with much more satisfaction were her Matie. pleas'd to grant my present request, or add such further marke of her favour as may leave the world no roome to think I have fail'd either in my duty or affection to her Maties. interest. This would lay a lasting obligation on me to grasp at every opertunity that might best express the duty and gratitude I owe both as a subject and servant.[2]

[1] *S.P., Ir.,* Bundle 363.   [2] *S.P., Ir.,* Bundle 363.

It was usual in those days for an officer to sit in the House of Commons, and accordingly Brigadier Conyngham was a member of parliament. He proposed that the Government might be allowed to borrow £50,000 or £60,000 for which the hereditary revenue might stand as security. This proposal he made in order that funds might be at once forthcoming. On the other hand, the serious consequences of running into debt were duly explained, and the House soon dropped it.[1] On the 27th of December, 1703, Conyngham was still so put out by his lack of proper precedence that he thought of selling out. The news of French designs came to his ears, and he seemed off his plan of selling, "especially now that plots are on foot and there might be an opportunity to show his zeal."[2] Conyngham petitioned the Queen:

Most humbly representeth

That the said Brigadr. lately sent the Secretary of State a Memorial to be laid before yor. Majtie. setting forth the many discouragements the said Brigadr. lyes under by having had several younger Colls. put over him, who are now either elder Brigadrs. or Majr. Genlls.

That the said Brigadr. some time since received from Lt. Genl. Erle the coppy of a Letter directed to him from Mr Secrety. Hedges declaring it to be yor. Majties. pleasure that Mr O'Farell shoud have the comãnd and conduct of the Troops now designed for Portugal ; It is given as a reason in ye. said letter, that ye. said Brigadr. did not make known his pretensions till the Troops were imbarkt and ready to sayle ; The said Brigadr. most humbly begs leave to assure yor. Majtie. that that matter has been misrepresented, for ye. said Brigadr. the very day he first received an account that it was yor. Majties. pleasure his Regimt. shoud serve in Portugal, put the Question to Lt. Genl. Erle whether Majr. Genl. Offarel was to serve by Comission from yor. Majtie. or from ye. King of Portugal, to wch. he answered that it was not to be doubted but yt. Majr. Genl. Offarrell had yor Majties. Comission, for that he had writ to him he was on ye. English establishmt., and ye. said Brigadr. had still acquiesct. under so positive an assurance, had not a new occasion of doubt occurd. to him after Lt. Genl. Erle left Cork.

[1] *S.P.*, *Ir.*, Bundle 363.
[2] *Hist. MSS. Com. Reports, the Ormonde MSS.*, VIII, p. 52.

F

The said Brigadr. most humbly offers to yor. Majties. consideration if ever any man who had the honour to serve yor. Majtie. as a Genl. Officer or indeed in any Station, was layd under so unfortunate a distinction, wch. may be interpreted as if he had don somthing infamous in his post, or at least were judgd incapable of doing his duty.

The said Brigadr. begs leave to assure yor. Majtie. that it is a true zeal for yor. service and the success of ye. present war that are his only inducements to serve ; and that tho' he can never want inclination under the most unfortunate circumstances to pay obedience to yor. Majties. pleasure, yet he is sensible he cannot go with this convoy to Portugal wthout. runing the hazard of suffering at least in his reputation.

The said Brigadr. therfore most humbly begs leave to go to London, in order to acquaint yor. Majtie. more fully of the great difficultys he now lyes under, hoping yor. Majtie. will be graciously pleasd in yor great justice so to order matters that he may be able to serve on honourable terms.[1]

The authorities treated this petition with the attention it deserved. The Duke of Ormonde, the Lord Lieutenant, wrote to Lieutenant-General Erle on the 10th of August, 1704 : ". . . . As to Brigadier Conyngham's pretension, the Lords Justices will take care to do him right. He will be allowed for his accoutrements, and everything else that is justly due to him ; but he must consider he has troops with accoutrements in lieu of those which went off (to Portugal). . ."[2] As the Duke of Ormonde was then in London, the Lords Justices remained the supreme authorities in Dublin. Early in 1704 we find that a general statement on the pretensions of General Officers of Ireland was issued to the Major Generals. On Conyngham's case there is this note :

. . . Brigr. Conyngham. That his Com̃ission as Colonell of Dragoons bears date on Febry. 170$\frac{2}{3}$, and at the time of the Queens accession to the Crown he was second Col. of Horse or Dragoons in her Maties. Service.

[1] S.P., Ir., Bundle 364.
[2] Hist. MSS. Com. Reports, the Ormonde MSS., VIII, p. 107.

That upon the first promotion of General Officers wch. her Majtie. made, there were 5 or 6 younger Colonells of Horse and Dragoons, and Severall younger Colonells of Foot made Brigadiers ; And when her Matie. was pleased to advance him to that Post, his Comission was not made to bear equall Date with those of the younger Colonells, so that he remains under the discouragement of being at present commanded by a great many Gentlemen whom he had the honour to command for Ten years before, wch. he humbly hopes will be redrest upon the first promotion of Genll. Officers wch. her Majtie. shall make.[1]

We now return to the other events of 1703. A declaration had been sent out, directing officers not to absent themselves without licence, and those absent without licence were directed to return immediately. In spite of this declaration, Brigadier Conyngham received a sharp order on the 9th of September, 1703, to this effect :

Whereas Capt. Arthur Davis, Lieut. Thomas Knox, Cornet Andrew Nesbitt, Cornet Alexr. McGowan, Quar. Masr. George Knox, Quar. Gideon Wardlaw, and Quar. Masr. Andrew King, all of Brigadr. Conyngham's Regiment of Dragoons have (notwithstanding Our Expresse Ordrs. requiring all officers to repair to their commands) absented themselves from their respective Troopes without leave from us Wee think fitt that the sd. several officers be suspended from their comands and duty till further Order. And Wee hereby direct and require you to suspend the said severall officers for such disobedience.[2]

Nor is this at all an unusual state of affairs, in spite of the generous leave granted, in the early years of the eighteenth century. On the 9th of September it was decided that "the said officers be suspended from their Comands and Pay till further Order And doe hereby direct and require you to respit the Pay of the sd. Officers."[3]

The ever-green question of deductions emerged again on the 25th of October, 1703, when the Duke of Ormonde issued a proclamation :

Whereas a Deduction of two pounds fourteen shillings and two pence p. month was formerly by directions of this Government made from each Regiment of Foote in this Kingdome and stopt in the Treasury for providing medicines for one year for such Regiments

[1] *S.P., Ir.,* Bundle 365.   [2] *Mart. Aff.,* 1 E, 3.8, p. 8.   [3] *Mart. Aff.,* 1 E, 3.8, p. 19.

Wee now think fitt that that Method be discontinued and that in lieu thereof the like stopage be made by the Agent of your Regiments to comence from the first day of October last and to be continued monthly till further order and the same when deducted to be paid from time to time to the chirurgeon of the said Regiment to be by him expounded in furnishing and providing the proper medicines. And Wee hereby direct and require you to cause the Agent of your Regiment to make the said Stoppages and to pay the Sume in manner aforesd. accordingly. For doing whereof this shall be a Warrant given ye. 25 Octr. 1703.

EDWARD SOUTHWELL.

To Brigadr. Thomas Fairfax at
the office in Cheife with the
Regiment of Foote under his
Comand.

The like Order dated and sygned as above for the severall Sumes to be stopt as affixed to the name of the Regimts.

Brigadr. Tidecombe	2	14	2	Coll. Gorges	2	14	2
Coll. Nicholas Sankey	2	14	2	Major Gen. Langton	2	14	2
Coll. Farrington	2	14	2	Lord Windsor	1	13	4
Coll. Stringer	2	14	2	Brigd. Echlin	1	13	4
Sr. Richard Temple	2	14	2	Coll. Conyngham	1	13	4
Lord Mohun	2	14	2	Coll. Cadogans 3 Troops		16	8
Coll. John Gibson	2	14	2	Coll. Rosses 2 Troops		13	4
Coll. Pearce	2	14	2[1]				

The soldiers required medicine for their maladies, and the country no less required it. The pages of Story[2] bear convincing testimony to the annoyance inflicted by the rapparees upon the prosperity of the people. He narrates how, when they feared detection, they would sink down in the long grass, how they would dismount the locks of their pieces and stow them away in some dry spot, or about their clothes, how they would then stop the muzzles of their pieces with corks, and the touch-holes with small quills, and then throw them away confidently into a pond or other equally secure place; "you may see a hundred of them without arms who look like the poorest, humblest slaves in the world, and

[1] 1 E, 3.8, p. 24.
[2] Cf. his fascinating *A True and Impartial History of the . . . Wars of Ireland.*

you may search till you are weary before you find one gun; and yet when they have a mind to do mischief they can be all ready in an hour's warning." A proclamation was issued for committing the priest of the parish where the rapparees were last "out upon their keeping," also their relations, and other harbourers and abettors. This somewhat drastic measure was to continue until all the Tories or rapparees had been captured and killed. The militia was specially charged with the duty of arresting the offenders, and commissions of Oyer and Terminer were issued for their immediate trial.

Small detachments of men could not quiet the disturbed tracts; in County Cork, for example, three zealous magistrates complained that the mountains were so extensive, the fastnesses so strong, and the whole countryside—gentry, commonalty, and clergy—so much their abettors that the militia completely failed to reduce them. "But after all, as there ever have been, so we fear there always will be Tories in several parts of this Kingdom. It is not to be wondered at that, after a war wherein many have been totally undone, and others fear being dragged into prison and languishing there, for debt or causes of action arisen during the war, many have gotten a loose way of living and cannot betake themselves to a laborious, honest calling; some perhaps receive private encouragement from abroad or concealed enemies at home still to alarm the Government, and the country being so ill planted, there are more of this sort of rogue now than at other times."[1] Among the hardiest annuals in Parliament were the statutes against Tories, rapparees and robbers, furnishing melancholy evidence of the unguarded state of the kingdom. As the Eighth were stationed at Limerick it occasions no surprise when we find that the Duke of Ormonde requests Cornet Andrew Knox on the 29th of November, 1703, to help the militia. His instructions run:

Haveing received certain Acct. of Severall Robberys lately comitted near Newcastle in the Country of Lymerick and that Rapparees are now out in that Country in great numbers These are therefore to direct you so many men as you will think fitt, to goe in search of the said

[1] *S.P., Ir.*, Bundle 356, No. 65.

Rapparees and in concert with the Gentlemen of the Country to use your best Endeavours to apprehend and bring them to justice And Wee hereby require all officers of Foot and Dragoons to be aiding and assisting you herein, as they will answer to the contrary.

As the War of the Spanish Succession loomed increasingly on the horizon we note that on the 23rd of March, 1704, Lieutenant Bentley entertained fourteen recruits, and on the 29th of the same month Captain Stewart received eighty pounds for the subsistence of recruits.

One of the most interesting documents for 1704 gives the routes for the marches of the Eighth:

1 Troop from Athlone	
To Fairbane	19th June
Ballybay	20
Mountmellick	21
Rest	22
Ballynakill	23
Camp	24

1 Troop from Nenagh	
To Thurles	22
Freshford	23
Camp	24

1 Troop from Charleville	
To Kilworth	20
Clonmell	21
Rest	22
Kells	23
Camp	24.[1]

1 Troop from Cappoquin	
To Clonmell	21st June
Rest	22
Kells	23
Camp	24

1 Troop from Mallow	
To Kilworth	19
Clogheen	20
Rest	21
Clonmell	22
Callan	23
Camp	24

As we watch the character of the orders and instructions for the period from 1693 to 1704 we come to understand how the actions of a regiment were then controlled. No doubt some of these orders and instructions are apt to seem to the casual reader merely

[1] *Marching Order*, 1703-05.

tiresome material—perhaps to be skipped. Yet it is only by their perusal we can come to possess a grasp of what manner of men Conyngham's Dragoons really were. They had achieved great deeds at Derry and Enniskillen, at the Boyne and Aughrim, and at Limerick, before their actual formation in 1693. These deeds lay in the background of all their work from 1693 to 1704, and we can feel equally confident that the work from 1693 to 1704 enabled them to take their share in the War of the Spanish Succession.

We now enter upon our survey of the working of the regiment from 1693 to 1704. Commissions were purchased as a matter of course. In 1695 Colonel Hastings of the Thirteenth Foot had taken evidently more than the usual amount of money for commissions in his regiment. In the Mutiny Act of this year a clause was inserted compelling officers to take the following oath before their commissions could be registered in the Commissary-General's Office: "I, *A. B.*, do hereby declare that I have neither directly nor indirectly, by myself or any one for me with my knowledge, given or promised to give any sum of money, present, gift, or reward, to any person whatsoever for obtaining my Commission to be (Cornet) in the Regiment of (Horse) commanded by (so-and-so), other than the usual fee to the Secretary of State or the Secretary of the Commander-in-Chief of the Army countersigning such Commission." The oath was regularly taken by the newly-joined subaltern, and just as regularly violated. Generally speaking, the commission of a Lieutenant-Colonel cost about £3440, that of a Captain ranged from £1720 to about £6000, that of a Lieutenant ranged from £600 to £1075, that of a Cornet about £2100, and that of a Quarter-Master about £1000. Of course these are simply examples of the prices current towards the end of the seventeenth century, and they inevitably fluctuated with the state of the market. Nor is the sale of commissions in any wise peculiar to the British Army; it was every whit as common in the French army. If we take the value of money at the level of 1913, in order to ascertain the value of money in 1693 we must multiply it by $2\frac{3}{4}$. A hundred pounds then bought as much as £275 in 1913.

The exchange of an officer from one corps to another was freely permitted, but such exchange required the royal sanction, even for an exchange from one company or troop to another of the same regiment.[1]

Disbanded or reduced officers were placed upon half pay until they could be absorbed. It was simply a retaining fee: it was not a permanent reward or pension. It was originally calculated as an exact half of the full pay, and in the reign of William III the half of the servant's allowance was also included.[2] The rates of subsistence in Ireland in 1697 were:

	Horse.		Dragoons.		Foot.	
Colonel, as such ..	5	0	5	0	5	0
Lt.-Col. do.	3	0	3	0	2	6
Major	6	8	6	8	1	8
Captain	7	0	5	0	4	0
Lieut.	5	0	3	0	2	0
Cornet	4	6	2	6		
Adjutant	2	6	2	6	2	0
Surgeon	3	0	3	0	3	3 and Assistant
Qr.-Master	3	0	2	0		
Chaplain	3	4	3	4	3	4
Sergeant			1	6	0	9
Corporal	1	6	1	3	0	6
Trumpet	1	6				
Drummer	1	6	1	6	0	6
Private	1	0	0	$9\frac{1}{2}$	0	4[3]

In 1701 the rates of subsistence in the Eighth were:

	Per diem.		Per annum.		
Colonel, as such	12	0	219	0	0
Lt.-Col. do.	7	0	127	15	0
Major do.	5	0	91	5	0
Chaplain	6	8	121	13	4
Adjutant	4	0	73	0	0
Surgeon	4	0	73	0	0
Gunsmith	2	8	48	13	4

[1] *Orders*, Dublin, June 24 and 26, 1697.   [2] *Royal Warrant*, March 16, 169$\frac{7}{8}$.

[3] *Orders*, Dublin, August 3, 1697; *Proclamation*, Dublin, July 26, 1697. *Cf.* pp. 844–5, for the last, in Walton's admirable *History of the British Standing Army*.

ONE TROOP.

	Per diem.	Per annum.
Captain	10 0	182 10 0
Lieutenant	5 0	91 5 0
Cornet	4 0	73 0 0
Quarter Master	3 0	54 15 0
Two Sergeants, each 2 6 ..	5 0	91 5 0
Three Corporals, each 2 0 ..	6 0	109 10 0
Two Drummers, each 1 6 ..	3 0	54 15 0
Sixty Soldiers, each 1 2 ..	3 10 0	1277 10 0

There are eight troops altogether.

The colonelcy of a regiment is now honorary, given usually to a distinguished general. Normally the colonel was the real commanding officer of what was called his regiment, but what was in a large measure his private property. He was always present with it, whether at home or in the field. He had his troop in the regiment, for which he drew pay as captain as well as his pay as colonel.[1] The Paymaster-General sent the money due to the regiment to the colonel, and with the latter its distribution entirely rested. Once the money was issued, it is amazing to learn that there was no audit of the regimental accounts. The muster of the regiment is the assembling of the soldiers in order to ascertain if all nominally on its roll are really present. Such a muster was supposed to avoid fraud through the colonel claiming pay for men who simply existed on paper, and it afforded an opportunity for the regular inspection of men, horses, arms, and accoutrements by the Commissary. For a time musters were taken monthly, but by an order of 1697 it was laid down that they were to be held at least four times a year.[2]

The frauds at musters had become so grave, that in 1690 orders were issued that certificates of absence from sickness were to be signed in the commissary's presence by the major or adjutant, by the surgeon, and by the two senior captains not belonging to the company to which the soldiers in question were attached. For

[1] *Warrant, Ir.*, May 2, 1698 ; *Account*, Dublin, April 30, 1698.
[2] *Regulations for Musters*, Dublin, July 29, 1697. *Cf.* Appendix No. XLVII in Walton, p. 804.

soldiers on furlough there were to be similar stringent certificates. The rolls were to be finally closed on the spot, and the parchment copy was to be transmitted by the very next post to the Commissary-General, who passed it on to the Paymaster-General.[1] In order to distribute the pay and keep the accounts, the colonel employed a civilian clerk, who received no salary, but paid the colonel for his appointment. In time this clerk became the agent, who practically occupied the position of a modern regimental paymaster. Some of these agents looked after two, three or even seven regiments.[2] Indeed the banking firm of our time, Messrs. Cox & Co., for instance, traces its origin to these agents.

The Commissary exercised some check over the appearance of fictitious names in the musters: the agent exercised none, and as a matter of fact often he created such names. Indeed there were loopholes of which even the conscientious colonel need not hesitate to take advantage. Was not his servant a soldier?[3] Could he not claim pay for him? Inevitably the number of servants increased, and in 1698 there were six or seven of them in each troop.[4] In 1695 it was reckoned that there were 5747 men authorised to pass among the musters. Nor was the question of servants the only ambiguous one. If a man died or was discharged after a muster, was not the captain entitled to the money thus due? If the captain did this, why should not the colonel do the like in his company? If the captain kept vacancies in the ranks unfilled and also kept the pay for such vacancies, why should not the colonel keep vacancies in the officers unfilled and also keep the pay for such vacancies? The captain could—and indeed did—argue that sometimes he had to pay a crimp one or two pounds for recruits, and he was surely entitled to receive a return for what he had expended. When in 1704 Lieutenant Bentley entertained fourteen recruits, he must have felt that all the expense ought not to come out of his pocket. With a view to stamping out the creation of fictitious

[1] *Regulations for Musters*, Dublin, July 29, 1697.
[2] *Proceedings of House of Commons*, January 25, 169$\frac{4}{5}$.
[3] *Regulations for Musters*, Dublin, July 29, 1697.
[4] An Order, Dublin, January 11, 169$\frac{7}{8}$, reduced troops of Horse and Dragoons to "46 soldiers per troop, the servants included."

names, the muster-roll indicated precisely the age, place of birth, date of enlistment, and even the complexion of each soldier.[1] Yet if the colonel was allowed six servants—this was his legitimate allowance; the lieutenant-colonel, major, or captain, three; and the subaltern two, it certainly, in spite of the muster-roll, left room for, to say the least, stray loopholes.

The pay of the soldier was divided, like Gaul, into three parts. First of all, there was his subsistence-money at the regulated rate of one and two pence out of one and sixpence for a Dragoon. There were, secondly, the gross off-reckonings, which were the difference between the total pay and subsistence. Lastly, there were the net off-reckonings, which were the balance of the gross-reckonings after all lawful deductions. The net off-reckonings formed the clothing fund of the regiment, and the colonel exercised sole control over it.

The Sovereign granted the licence or leave of absence except to General Officers or Members of Parliament who might absent themselves at discretion. In the absence of the Lord Lieutenant, the Lord Justices granted leave to officers. No matter how much the question of precedence vexed the soul of Brigadier Conyngham, the question of leave did not. Was he not an M.P., entitled to as much leave as he pleased? Not more than one-third of the number of officers could be given a licence of leave. The limit of leave was supposed to be two months in the year, but this was as much a supposition as the accuracy of the muster-roll. For it is not unusual to meet with leave for six months. Leave for a year was not unknown, though in this case the officer usually went abroad in order to pursue the improvement of his education. Two officers were always to remain with each troop.

The lieutenant-colonel was simply the deputy or lieutenant of the all-important colonel. He was then the senior captain of the regiment, retaining a troop and taking rank above the captains.[2]

The title of major is simply a contraction of sergeant-major, and in his duties he combined the functions of the major and the

---

[1] *Regulations for Musters*, Dublin, July 29, 1697. *Cf.* Walton, p. 804.

[2] *Warrant, Ir.*, May 2, 1698; *Account*, Dublin, April 30, 1698.

sergeant-major of our day, adding to them much of the work now assigned to the adjutant. In fact, he was pretty well a maid-of-all-work. He formed the medium of communication between the colonel and the regiment; he received and distributed into their proper channel all orders, detailed parties and guards, and visited or inspected the latter; he drilled and exercised the regiment, corrected errors or disorder on parade or on the march, and saw that the men had their quarters or their tents in due order. At first the major had no troop, but on the 27th of June, 1698, a warrant allowed to the majors that have troops three shillings a day for subsistence, in addition to their subsistence as captain.[1]

The colonel, the lieutenant-colonel, and the major constituted the regimental "Field-Officers," who did not take a place in the ranks, but ranged over the whole space of operations, as they were officers of the field. These three Field-Officers, with the adjutant, the quarter-master, and the surgeon, formed the regimental staff. All the other officers, the captain, the lieutenant, and the cornet, were troop officers.

The senior lieutenant acted as captain of the colonel's troop, being designated the captain-lieutenant. As such, he took precedence as the youngest captain. The two next senior lieutenants acted in similar capacity for the companies of the lieutenant-colonel and the major respectively. The cornet carried the colours of the troop. The guidon was simply the standard colour rounded and slit at the end, and the designation of the standards of dragoons as guidons persisted to the nineteenth century.

The colonel appointed the chaplain, the surgeon, and the quarter-master, as well as the agent. The quarter-master, ranked between the commissioned and the non-commissioned grades. His rank then, however, was higher than it is to-day, for we often meet with officers on half-pay or even full pay seeking it. A regiment of horse or dragoons had a quarter-master to every troop. It was the duty of the quarter-master to arrange for the distribution of quarters and billets, the receipt and the distribution of regimental supplied and stores of all kinds.

[1] *Warrant*, Dublin, June 27, 1698. Yet see Fortescue, I, pp. 318–23.

Trumpets were peculiar to horse regiments, hautboys[1] to dragoons and infantry, and fifes to foot regiments, while drums[2] were common to all of them. As a sign of how much the regiment belonged to the colonel, it was quite usual to meet with his crest, not the royal arms, painted on the side of the drums. All cavalry regiments had one kettle-drummer. The ordinary sounds of drum and trumpet were the "Gathering," or "Assembly," or "General" (*i.e.* the fall-in); the "Troop" (*i.e.* from the battalion); the "March"; the "Preparative" (*i.e.* prepare to engage); the "Battle" or "Charge"; the "Retreat"; the "Tap-to" or Tattoo (*i.e.* evening watch-setting); and the "Revally" or Reveille (*i.e.* the morning relief of the watch). All these were beats of the drum, and the sounds of the trumpet were the "Auguet" (corresponding to the Tap-to), the "Boutez-selle" (*i.e.* put on your saddles), whence our corruption of "Boot-and-saddle"; the "Mont-a-caballo" (*i.e.* bridle and mount); the "A-la-stendardo" (corresponding to the troop); the "Tucquet" or March; and the "Carga" or Charge.[3]

The pay of the private soldier in 1697 was $9\frac{1}{2}$d. a day, and out of this he had to provide for his own subsistence and that of his horse. In theory he had:

Gross Pay	Viz.				Deductions.		Net off-reckonings, being gross off-reckonings less the deductions.
	Subsistence.		Gross off-reckonings.		12d. per £.	One day's pay per Kilmainham	
Per diem.	Per annum.	Per diem.	Per annum.	Per diem.	Per annum.	Per annum.	Per annum.	Per diem.	Per annum.
s. d.	£ s. d.	s. d.	£ s. d.	s. d.	£ s. d.	£ s. d.	s. d.	d.	£. s. d.
1 6	27 7 6	1 2	21 5 10	0 4	6 1 8	1 7 4½	1 6	3.05	4 12 9½

As the net off-reckonings provided for his clothing, we learn from the proclamation of the 26th of July, 1697, that every year he was supposed to receive one pair of breeches, one hat; every

---

[1] "Hautboys" had other uses. The names of fictitious men in the musters are generally to be found in their ranks. Such names among them as John Doe, Richard Roe, and Peter Squib repeatedly occur.

[2] We meet with kettle-drums in 1542. *Cf.* Fortescue, I, p. 124.

[3] Here I use the convenient summary in Walton, pp. 466–7.

two years one coat of better cloth than usually, and one cap ; and every three years one cloak, one housing, one saddlery and harness, with sword, bayonet, belt, cartouch-box and slings.

The captain of each troop of horse was ordered on the 13th of August, 1697, to stop four shillings per month from each trooper for the six grass months, that is, from the 1st of May to the 31st of October, and during the other six months there was to be no such stoppage.   The intention of this regulation was excellent, for the money so stopped was to be laid out in buying horses in the room of such as died or became unserviceable.   Captains, unlike colonels, were to account for this stoppage on the 1st of May annually, and the surplus was to be divided among the troopers, except those remounted within the year out of the fund.   Troopers remounted out of the fund were to pay eight shillings instead of four shillings in the ensuing year.   Here too the intention was excellent, for, according to this order,

> By this method the horses being in common to the whole troop, such trooper as shall be discharged upon his own desire, or shall be broke by a sentence of a Court Marshal, or by the order of the Chief Governor or Governors or the General shall have no pretence or challenge to his horse, neither is he to have any money for him, but the horse is to remain in the troop for H.M.'s service and to mount the trooper that shall be listed in his room.   For which reason no Captain shall stop or make any deductions for the horse from the new enlisted trooper, neither shall any Captain discharge any man, without first acquainting his Colonel, and giving the reasons thereof.
>
> And if it should happen that any of the troops should be disbanded the several horses of such troops are hereby declared to belong to the troopers that shall ride them, and not to the Captain, and each trooper shall carry off the horse on which he served.

The order of the 13th of August was supplemented on the 2nd of September, 1697, when the stoppage of four shillings and eight shillings respectively was reduced to three shillings and sixpence and seven shillings a month.   The captains were to refund to the non-commissioned officers and men according to length of service on the ground that "there has been more stopped from some than either the value of their horses or the Contingent charges and expenses amounts to." The order proceeds to state that "whereas it appears that there has been a stop from each dragoon" in Conyngham's regiment of "one pound four shillings in order to provide them pistols, which arms His Majesty having not thought should be given them. Each Dragoon hath received a good broad sword value twelve shillings, and the Colonel designing to employ the remaining twelve shillings so stopt towards the better arming that regiment with fuzees. . . . 1st May next by which time that money is to be expended for the use aforesaid. . . . No dragoon who shall hereafter be discharged at his own request, or be broke by sentence of Court Marshal or order of Government or General shall have any challenge or pretence to his arms; but if any troop shall be disbanded each Dragoon shall carry off his sword, and receive the twelve shillings stop towards buying his fuzee."

In billets the soldier was to pay fair prices, which must not exceed his subsistence money. He paid for his provisions and forage, and the billet found quarters, light and fuel. Nor was the landlord compelled to furnish soldiers with more than "lodging and candle, and to let them have the necessary use of one fire with those of the family": he was not even forced to supply salt, pepper or vinegar.

The age of the recruit was from seventeen to forty. The power of the colonel is apparent in the regulation that no captain could enlist soldiers till they were first examined by the colonel, "nor," adds the proclamation of the 26th of July, 1697, "shall any soldier be disbanded but by consent or order of the Colonel or Officer Chief commanding" the regiment. Men had to obtain permission to marry, and married men were not in favour. At the great reduction of 1697, on the termination of the Nine Years' War, the married men were discharged whether they desired it or not, while the unmarried ones were forced to remain. In 1698 the Eighth was composed of single men. It was generally considered desirable to recruit the regiments from the counties where they were originally raised or to which their colonels belonged.

True as this is generally, it is especially so of the Eighth, who were mainly composed of men of Derry and Enniskillen. Nor must we overlook the circumstance that a recruit belonged more to the troop than to the regiment at large.

The outstanding year for disbandment during this period from 1693 to 1704 was undoubtedly 1697. Disbanded infantry were allowed to carry away with them their clothes, belts, and knap-sacks; and cavalry their horses and saddlery as well. As their clothes and accoutrements were provided out of the off-reckonings of the soldiers themselves, it was but fair that they should take them home with them. They received three shillings for the swords they were not permitted to take. Troopers and dragoons were allowed to remove their horses under the limitations indicated in the regulations of the 13th of August and the 2nd of September, 1697. The soldier also received ten days' subsistence, not ten days' pay. When a regiment was reduced, not disbanded, the "youngest troop" was to be first selected for reduction.

On the 11th of January, 1698, the troops of Horse and Dragoons were reduced to forty-six soldiers a troop, the servants included.[1] The horses, it was then decreed, were to be the property of the men if paid for out of the levy-money, and the soldier had a year's service; otherwise, the horses are to be sold, and the money retained for the present. Troopers with horses were to receive seven days' full pay, and those without fourteen days' pay. On the 20th of March, 1699, it was ordered that each troop of light horse should have two corporals, one trumpeter, and thirty-six private soldiers in addition to officers. Each troop of dragoons was to have one sergeant, two corporals, one drummer, one hautboy, and thirty-six men in addition to officers.

The seventeenth century took for granted that there was little need to learn drill. The prevalent view was that it could best be picked up in front of the enemy. Fortunately for us, our chief enemy then, the French, entertained pretty similar notions. When mounted, dragoons were drawn up in three ranks and were exercised

---

[1] *Warrant* to Denny Muschampe, Esqr., Muster-Master-General; with reference to the *Royal Letters* of January 1, 1698, and of December 31, 1697.

as horse; and when dismounted, they formed and exercised as the foot did. The words of command to mounted dragoons were:

Dragoons have a care (take heed).
Sling your muskets.
Make ready your links.
Clear your right foot of your stirrup.
Dismount and stand at your horses' heads. (The six outside men remained mounted to take charge of the horses.)
Link your horses to the left.
March clear of your horses, and shoulder as you march.
Halt.

The battalion was then formed up in the same way as a foot regiment.

Have a care of the exercise.
Officers to the right-about.
Take your posts in rear of the battalion (*i.e.* for exercise).
March.
Dragoons have a care (the men pull off their right-hand gloves and stow them under their waist-belts).
Lay your right hand on your musket.
Poise your musket.
Rest your musket.
Cock and guard.
Present ; fire.
Recover your arms with the cock half-bent (*i.e.* half-cock).
Rest upon your musket.
Handle your daggers (*i.e.* the bayonets).
Draw forth your bayonets (or daggers).
Fix them in the muzzle of your muskets.
Poise your muskets.
Charge to the front.
To the right (left, right-about, left-about), charge.
Recover your arms.
Rest upon your muskets.
Handle your bayonets.
Withdraw your bayonets.
Place (*i.e.* return) your bayonets.

Poise your muskets.
Rest your muskets.
Clean the pan (with the ball of the thumb).
Open your cartridge-box.
Handle your primer.
Sink and prime.
Return your prime.
Shut your pan (with your forefinger).
Blow off your loose corns (recovering arms at the same time).
Cast about to charge.
Handle your cartridge.
Take out your cartridge (and shut the box).
Open it with your teeth.
Charge with powder and ball.
Draw forth your scourers (*i.e.* ram-rods).
Shorten them to an inch (against your right breasts).
Put them into the muzzle of your muskets.
Ram down powder and ball.
Withdraw your scourers.
Shorten them to an inch (as before).
Place (*i.e.* return) your scourers.
Poise your muskets.
Shoulder your muskets.
Poise your muskets.
Rest your muskets.
Lay down your arms.
Quit your arms.
To the right-about.
March clear of your arms and break.

The men being dispersed, the drum beat and the men, drawing swords, ran to their arms "with a Huzza."

Return your swords.
Handle your arms.
Rest your arms.
Poise your muskets.
Sling your muskets.
To the right-about.

March to your horses.

Unlink your horses.

Shorten your bridles.

Put your left foot in the stirrup.

Mount.

Fasten your links.

Unsling and advance your muskets (on the right thigh).

Join your left hands to your muskets.

Cock and guard.

Rest your muskets on your bridle-hands.

Present ; fire.

Recover your arms with the cook half-bent.

Billeting led to such trouble with the civilian population that we are surprised to find the army forty-two years in existence before there were permanent barracks. In 1697 the erection of such barracks in Ireland was first sanctioned, and then, as its many advantages presented themselves, it was continued. Inns were the only quarters sanctioned by the Mutiny Act. As there were very few of them in Ireland, there was an urgent necessity for the construction of barracks. The very next year several eight-day camps were formed at different places in Ireland.

After 1697 a deduction for medicines at the rate of twenty pounds a year was made.[1] In spite of the fact that the subsistence money of the soldier was supposed to be untouchable, yet we find by the orders, issued at Dublin on the 10th of July, 1699, and the 20th of October, 1699, that the deduction for medicines came "out of the monthly subsistence of the regiments to which the same was delivered."

In 1698 the contractor for bread was not bound to supply more than a pound to each man daily.[2] It is scarcely credible that throughout the wars in Ireland and Flanders the full value of provisions issued to the regiments was charged.[3] It is even more incredible that troops paid not merely for the arms they carried but also for the powder and ball they shot against the enemy.

[1] *Orders*, Dublin, October 20, 1698, and July 10, 1699.

[2] *Order*, Dublin, July 7, 1698.   [3] *Harl. MSS.*, 7018, and *Harl. MSS.*, 7194.

Occasionally the trooper, in true feudal fashion, brought his horse with him when he enlisted, and no doubt his ownership induced him to take care of his charger. Whether he did this or not, the horse became the property of the trooper, paid for out of his own money, and his to carry him home on his discharge. If a cavalry soldier lost his horse, he *ipso facto* lost his qualification to serve unless he was able to buy another animal. Not seldom he was quite unable to do so, with the outcome that it was felt to be increasingly necessary for the horse to become the property of the regiment. For the purchase of remounts in 1697 the captain of each troop was allowed to stop from his men four shillings a month during the six "grass" or summer months.[1] In order to purchase remounts in the 6th Dragoons in 1698 the subsistence of one troop was reduced to five pence a day for six months, and the saving was expended on horses.[2] The following year there was an unwonted liberality to the soldiers respecting horses bought by the Government. For a warrant appeared directing that "Where any Non-Commissioned Officer or Trooper hath served a whole year, the Horse which H.M. has paid for by the Levy-money is to be given to him, His Majesty being graciously pleased to give his whole right in such horse to said Non-Commissioned Officer and Trooper." On the other hand, if the soldier had not served a whole year, the horse was to be sold and the amount credited to the Government.[3] It was customary for horses to have "cropped ears," "shorn manes," and "bob-tails" or "cut-tails."[4] The trooper's subsistence money was "for himself and his horse,"[5] yet occasionally for strategic and other reasons the Commissariat had to supply forage, and its value was subsequently deducted from the subsistence of the regiment. For instance, during the war against James II, hay was largely supplied by contract. The rations proposed for troops encamped were for the horse 16 pounds of old hay, 1 peck of oats, and 1 truss of straw a week, and the same for dragoons less $\frac{1}{2}$-peck of oats.[6]

---

[1] *Rules*, Dublin, August 3 and September 2, 1697.
[2] *Order*, Dublin, October 22, 1698.   [3] *Warrant*, Dublin, March 11, 169⅞.
[4] The advertisements in the *London Gazette* prove this.
[5] *Proclamation*, Dublin, July 26, 1697.   [6] *Add. MSS.*, 28947 (Brit. Mus.).

The question of deductions is a never-ending one, and yet we feel some sympathy for those made on behalf of Kilmainham Hospital, the first stone of which was laid by the Duke of Ormonde on the 29th of April, 1680, and the second by the Earl of Longford, as Master-General of Ordnance. For it was to be a home for the soldier maimed in war, or who after at least seven years' service had become aged, infirm, or unserviceable. The deduction of sixpence in the pound out of *all* pay on the military establishment was the rate. The diet laid down at Kilmainham Hospital was:

Sunday Monday Tuesday Thursday	} Breakfast, 1 pint water-gruel. Dinner, 1 lb. beef or mutton. Supper, 1 quart broth.
Wednesday	} $\frac{1}{2}$ lb. cheese ; or 3 pints of pease-porridge, and butter; 1 quart water-gruel.
Friday	Fish and butter ; 1 quart gruel.
Daily	1 lb. bread, and three pints of beer.

The men were allowed twopence a week " for tobacco."[1]

While the inner man was thus fortified, the outer was looked after in a fashion truly marvellous. As the trooper had to feed his own horse, so he had to clothe himself out of the net off-reckonings of his pay, which he handed over to the all-powerful colonel. For each dragoon this amounted to £4 12s. $9\frac{1}{2}$d. in 1697. Even if we multiply this sum by $2\frac{3}{4}$, the multiplier for the value of money then, the total is not considerable for clothing for a year. Sir Albert Conyngham felt this in 1691 when he stood desperately in want of saddles, "and the stores are not provided with them that we might have them for payment; I wish the stores could furnish both Horse and Dragoons with so necessary accoutrements." This wish was shared by his son.

The following list gives the prices of the various articles of clothing and equipment up to the year 1700:

	Horse.	Dragoons.	Foot.
Shirts, Sergeant's			6/-
„ Private's			3/- to 3/6
Coat, Sergeant's		and breeches 50/- to 70/-	and breeches 45/- to 72/-

<hr>

[1] *Royal Hospital Registry-Books*, April 7, 1693.

	Horse.	Dragoons.	Foot.
Coat, Corporal's	60/- to 90/-	and breeches	and breeches 32/-
„ Private's	50/- to 65/-	26/- to 42/-	and breeches 20/- to 38/-
Hats, Sergeant's		10/- to 15/-	10/- to 15/-
„ Private's	11/- to 15/-	4/4 to 8/6	4/- to 7/-
Waistcoat	16/- to 25/-		
Gloves	5/6 to 7/6		
Boots and shoes	21/- to 26/-	10/- to 12/-	4/- to 4/6
Knapsack			3/6
Cravat, Sergeant's		1/8 to 2/6	2/-
„ Private's		1/- to 1/6	9d.
Sashes for Pikemen			2/6
Caps, Grenadier Sergeant's			14/- to 15/-
„ „ Private's			8/- to 9/6
Cap, Dragoon Sergeant's		6/- to 10/-	
„ „ Private's		3/- to 5/-	
Stockings, Sergeant's		3/6 to 6/-	4/- to 6/-
„ Private's		1/4 to 2/-	1/8 to 2/-
Cloak, or Surtout	28/- to 45/-	26/- to 40/-	7/6 to 18/-
Housings, Sergeant's		12/- to 18/-	
Holster Caps, Private's	18/- to 25/-	7/6 to 12/-	
Drum carriages			10/-
Drummer's suit		35/- to 50/-	
Hautboy's suit		50/- to 70/-	
Corporal's suit		35/- to 50/-	
Coat, Drummer's			and breeches 31/- to 60/-
Badge			3/6

The Harleian manuscript 7018 gives particulars of the clothing for a regiment of dragoons about the year 1696, and it forms instructive reading:

				Former prices.			Prices now proposed.		
				£	s.	d.	£	s.	d.
411	Coats and breeches		..	2	2	0	1	6	0
483	Cloaks	..	..	..	2	0	0	1	6	0
467	Hats	..	..	..	0	8	6	0	4	4

		Former prices. £ s. d.	Prices now proposed. £ s. d.
467	Caps	0 5 0	0 3 0
467	Neckcloths	0 1 6	0 1 0
483	Pr. boots	0 12 0	0 10 0
467	Waist belts	0 4 6	0 2 4
467	Swords	0 7 6	0 4 6
483	Leather bags	0 4 0	0 2 6
467	Hoose and caps, embroidered	0 12 0	0 7 6
411	Daggers	0 2 6	0 1 6
411	Cartouch boxes	0 2 6	0 1 6
467	Pr. stockings	0 2 0	0 1 4
16	Sergeants' coats and breeches	3 10 0	2 10 0 .
16	Hats	0 15 0	0 10 0
16	Caps	0 10 0	0 6 0
16	Cravats	0 2 6	0 1 8
16	Swords	0 10 0	0 7 0
16	Belts	0 6 0	0 3 0
16	Pr. stockings	0 6 0	0 3 6
16	Hoose and caps	0 18 0	0 12 0
24	Corporals' suits	2 10 0	1 15 0
16	Drummers' suits	2 10 0	1 15 0
16	Hautboys' suits	3 10 0	2 10 0

The same manuscript provides other particulars of the prices of some of the arms and accoutrements:

	Sergeants.	Privates.	Drummers.
Swords, Horse		7/6 to 10/-	
,, Dragoons[1]	7/- to 10/-	4/6 to 7/6 and 12/-	
,, Foot	10/-	5/-	4/6
Hanger		6/6	
Collar of bandaleers		5/6	
Fusil		12/-	
Pistol		12/-	
Cartridge-box		1/8 to 2/6	
Plug-bayonet		1/6 to 2/6	

[1] *Order*, Dublin, September 2, 1697.

	Sergeants	Privates	Drummers.
Sword-bayonet		4/6	
Grenade-pouch		2/6 to 6/-	
Match-box		1/-	
Sword-belt, shoulder		6/- to 10/-	
„ waist	3/- to 6/-	2/4 to 4/6	4/6
Carbine-belt		4/- to 7/-	

The twelve shillings was the price charged to the men of the Eighth Dragoons in 1697 for "a good broad sword," and twelve shillings for "a fuzee."[1] Dragoons wore a sort of cap as well as hat, and were the only troops, save the Horse Grenadiers, to whom both were issued.[2] As a rule, the face was clean shaven, with the exception of the grenadiers, who were sometimes allowed to grow the hair on the face. In 1695 it had become common to club the wig or the hair behind in order to keep it out of the way, thus giving rise to the pig-tail.[3] The cravats of the officers were rich and voluminous, those of the men plain and less voluminous. The coat, which used to be collarless, grew gradually longer and fuller in the skirts. About 1696 it was looped back on to a button placed on the sides in such a way that the two corners of each skirt met on the button. As a rule dragoons wore waistcoats, and yet it is singular to notice that in the Harleian manuscript 7018 there is no mention of them. Coats were lined and faced on the cuffs with the regimental colour, whence the term "facings." The coats of drummers were of the colour of the regimental facings with red facings. At a later period hautboys were subject to a similar rule, but then they wore coats of the same colour as the men.

The cavalry, whether Horse or Dragoons, always had loose cloaks with small capes to them,[4] and these were of scarlet or red cloth often faced with the regimental colour. These cloaks were carried *en croupe*, rolled up and attached to the saddle by straps. Dragoons wore cloth breeches. The Horse wore jacked-boots and the Foot shoes, while the Dragoons wore a sort of short boot, termed by

[1] *Order*, Dublin, September 2, 1697.
[2] *Harl. MSS.*, 7018.
[3] In the military prints of 1695 and 1696 there are many clubbed wigs.
[4] *Harl. MSS.*, 7018.

the French " bottines."   All officers, from the General to the
Sergeant, whether of Horse, Dragoons, or Foot, wore the sash.
With commissioned officers its fringes were of gold or silver.

The arms of a trooper were at first a sword, a pair of pistols
fourteen inches long in the barrel, a cuirass, or rather a back and
breast, and a pott or iron skull cap.   Carbines were added before
1696.   Sword-belts, carbine-belts, and cartridge-boxes completed
the accoutrements of troopers.   In 1695 dragoons still carried
"leather bags" or grenade-pouches, bayonets, and cartouch-boxes.
When they ceased to have pistols we do not know.   In 1697,
however, we note that the Eighth were refused leave to provide
themselves with them.[1]   It is curious to meet with the antiquated
fusil among the equipment of the Eighth so late as 1697.   Was it,
as Walton suggests,[2] that this regiment was regarded at the time it
was raised as one likely to be disbanded during peace rather than as a
permanent part of the regular army ?   Was it, accordingly, equipped
in haste with whatever spare arms there might be at hand ?   Be
that as it may, it is clear that dragoons laid aside the grenade-
pouch between 1695 and 1697.[3]

Swords, of course, formed part of the armament of dragoons,
and the sword of the Eighth in 1697 was styled "a good broad
sword."[4]   Nor is it without significance that in 1691 the Inniskilling Dragoons demanded "good broad cutting swords with
three barred hilts."   The term cross-belts is applied to the sword
and carbine belts crossing each other on the chest.   In the days to
come the Eighth were to make a name for themselves in action, and
accordingly it was given the privilege of wearing cross-belts as
a mark of honour.

[1] *Order*, Dublin, September 2, 1697.

[2] *History of the British Standing Army*, pp. 423–4.

[3] It is not mentioned in the *Proclamation*, Dublin, July 26, 1697.

[4] *Order*, Dublin, September 2, 1697.   *Cf.* the reference to sabretaches of the regiment in
The Cavalry Journal, VI, p. 212.

APPENDIX

COMMISSIONS CHIEFLY EXTRACTED FROM THE HOME OFFICE MILITARY ENTRY BOOKS, VOLS. 2, 3, AND 4, AND FROM THE WAR OFFICE COMMISSION BOOKS, 1693 AND 1704.

HENRY CONYNGHAM Esqr. to be Lieut. Col. in Col. Echlin's Regt. of Dragoons and to command a troop in the same. Kensington, 31 Dec. 1691.

WILLIAM NESBITT to be Cornet of Capt. PEPPER's troop in Col. Henry Conyngham's Regt. of Dragoons. July 27, 1693.

ROBERT KILLIGREW Esqr. to be Major of our Royal Regt. of Dragoons commanded by Col. Edw. Matthews. February 15, 1694.
    [Lt. Col. same Regt. April 23, 1697.]

WILLIAM CONWAY to be Cornet to Col. CONYNGHAM's own troop. May 7, 1694.

ANDREW NESBITT to be Cornet to Capt. STEWART in Col. Henry Conyngham's Regt. of Dragoons. 1694.

ANDREW LINDSAY to be Lieut. to Capt. John Davis in Col. Conyngham's Regt. 1694.

PETER TELFER to be Chirurgeon. May 7, 1694.

Additional Officers, 1694 :
    Captain   JOHN DAVIS.
    Lieutenants ANDREW LINDSAY.
                WILLIAM MORTIMER.   October 27, 1694 (to Capt. Davis).
    Cornet   ANDREW NESBITT.

THOMAS CRESPIGNIE Esqr. to be Captain Lieut. to Col. CONYNGHAM. Feb. 7, 1695.

WILLIAM PRESTON to be Capt. of that troop late Major POLLOCK's in the same Regt. Same date.

MATTHEW STONE to be Lieut. to Major HUME's in Col. Conyngham's Regt. Same date.

ARCHIBALD PRIMROSE to be Cornet to Capt. DOUGLAS in ditto Regt. Same date.

JOHN PEPPER Esqr. to be Major and to be Capt. of a troop in Col. Henry Conyngham's Regt. of Dragoons. Welbeck, November 1, 1695.

THOMAS KNOX to be Capt. of the troop whereof Lieut. CHARLES CALDWELL was late Capt. November 1, 1695.

TOBIAS MULLOY to be Capt.-Lieut. of Col. Conyngham's troop. November 1, 1695.

HENRY NIX Gent. to be Cornet of Capt. John Davis' troop.   October 8, 1696.

Capt. ROBERT STEWART to be Captain of that troop whereof Capt. THOMAS KNOX was Capt. in Col. Henry Conyngham's Regt. of Dragoons. Kensington, March 22, 169$\frac{6}{7}$.

JAMES UNIACKE to be Lieut. to Capt. STEWART.   Same Regt., same date.

WARREN BAXTER to be Cornet to Capt. STEWART.   Same Regt., same date.

ALEXANDER MCGOWAN to be Cornet.   July 1, 1697.

ANDREW KNOX to be Cornet, July 20, 1697.

In 1697 the following with others were with the Regt., Lt. Col. ARTHUR DILLON, Captains ROBERT STEWART, HENRY WOOD and ALEXANDER STEWART.   Captain THOMAS KNOX had then left.

PATRICK WHITE to be Chaplain.   December 4, 1698.

JOHN MCLANE to be Chaplain.   December 8, 1699.

FLEETWOOD WATKINS Gent. to be Cornet.   January 2, 1700.

CLOTWOTHY GOWAN to be Chaplain.   December 19, 1700.

Brit. Mus. Add. MSS. 15897, f. 122.

A list of the half-pay Officers which is supposed not to be provided for at this time.

28 March, 1702.

COL. CONYNGHAM'S.

	Per diem.			Per annum.		
	£	s.	d.	£	s.	d.
Capt Henry Wood	0	4	0	73	0	0
Robt. Stewart		4		73		
Lieut. Noah Cadroy		2	6	45	12	6
„ James Uniacke		2	6	45	12	6
Corntt. Wm. Nesbitt		2		36	10	
„ Fleetwood Watkins						
Qr. Mr. Hugh Nesbitt		1	6			
Q. Mr. Wm Parr		1	6			

fol. 114.   List of Commissioned Officers in Her M. Army in Ireland.

COL. CONYNGHAM'S REGT. OF DRAGOONS.

Captains.	Lieutenants.	Cornets.
Hen. Conyngham, Col.	Toby Mulloy	Andw. Nesbitt
Arth. Dillon, Lt. Col.	Hugh Morgan	Andw. Knox
John Pepper, Maj.	Alexr. Sanderson	Coningby Brown
Henry Wood	Thos. Knox	Hen. Nix
Arthur Davis	John Pacy	Alex. McGowan
Wm. Stewart	Wm. Mortimer	Warren Baxter

Qr.-Masters.	Staff Officers.
Geo. Knox	Clotworthy Gowan, Chaplain
John Rice	John Stewart, Chyrurgeon
Richd. Gash	
Andw. King	
Gid. Wardlow	
Cha. King	

Chapter II

The Intrigues of Louis XIV

If the challenge cup of Europe from 1870 to 1914 has been the possession of Alsace Lorraine, then the challenge cup from 1701 to 1714 had been Spain. For the rôles of Louis XIV and William II, in not a few respects, were identical. The French King spent a longer period in maturing his plans than the German Kaiser, and for that reason they came closer to success. Many of his thoughts of fifty years centred around the determination that a Bourbon should occupy the throne of the dying Charles II.

A genealogical key is required to grasp the intricacy of the problem of the Spanish Succession :

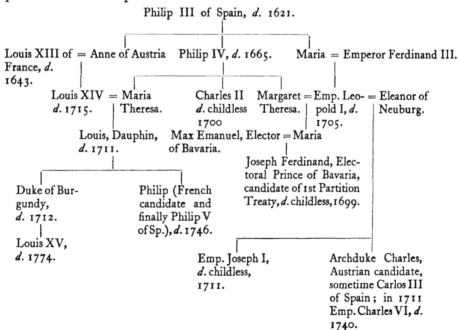

Philip III of Spain, *d.* 1621.

Louis XIII of = Anne of Austria   Philip IV, *d.* 1665.   Maria = Emperor Ferdinand III.
France, *d.*
1643.

Louis XIV = Maria   Charles II   Margaret = Emp. Leo- = Eleanor of
d. 1715.   Theresa.   *d.* childless   Theresa.   pold I, *d.*   Neuburg.
                          1700   1705.

Louis, Dauphin,   Max Emanuel, Elector = Maria
d. 1711.   of Bavaria.

                                         Joseph Ferdinand, Elec-
Duke of Bur-   Philip (French   toral Prince of Bavaria,
gundy,   candidate and   candidate of 1st Partition
d. 1712.   finally Philip V   Treaty, *d.* childless, 1699.
                   of Sp.), *d.* 1746.

Louis XV,
d. 1774.
                   Emp. Joseph I,   Archduke Charles,
                   d. childless,   Austrian candidate,
                   1711.   sometime Carlos III
                                        of Spain; in 1711
                                        Emp. Charles VI, *d.*
                                        1740.

Ever since the death of Philip IV of Spain in 1665, Europe had lived under the shadow beneath which we lived from 1890 to 1914. Who was to succeed the childless Charles II, the last male representative of the Habsburgs in Spain? The House of Bourbon, the House of Habsburg, and the Bavarian House of Wittelbach all provided claimants. Obviously the succession ought to go to the sisters of Charles II. Of them, the elder, Maria Theresa, had married Louis XIV, and their eldest son, the Dauphin, was clearly the rightful heir. By the Treaty of the Pyrenees, Maria Theresa, in consideration of a dower of 500,000 crowns, had expressly renounced all claims for herself or her descendants upon the throne of Spain. Philip IV had not paid her dowry. Was not her renunciation accordingly of none effect? The younger daughter of Philip IV, Margaret Theresa, had married the Emperor Leopold I. The only issue of that marriage was a daughter, Maria, who married Max Emanuel, Elector of Bavaria. They had a son, Joseph Ferdinand, generally known as the Electoral Prince, who was therefore the representative of the rights of Maria Antonia by descent. But she, like her sister, had expressly renounced her claims on the Spanish inheritance.

If the children of Philip IV had their claims barred, recourse must be had to the other children of his father, Philip III. Here, again, the question lay between two sisters. The elder daughter of Philip III was Anne of Austria, the wife of Louis XIII and the mother of Louis XIV. On her marriage, Anne had renounced her claims on the crown of Spain. The younger daughter, Maria, had married the Emperor Ferdinand III, and was the mother of Leopold I, who was the representative of her rights. She, unlike her sister and her nieces, had made no renunciation. Though he had legality on his side, Leopold I was far too sensible to imagine that Europe would permit him to revive the empire of Charles V, and he passed on his rights to his second son, the Archduke Charles. Louis XIV was also far too sensible to imagine that Europe would allow a Bourbon to rule over both France and Spain, and he and the Dauphin passed on their rights to the second son of the Dauphin, Philip, Duke of Anjou.

Louis XIV and William III, by the first Partition Treaty of 1698, agreed that Spain, the Indies, and the Netherlands should go to the Electoral Prince of Bavaria. Unfortunately in 1699 he died of smallpox, and this scheme failed. By the second Partition Treaty of 1699 the rivals agreed that the Archduke Charles received Spain, the Indies, and the Netherlands, while the Dauphin received the Milanese. At Madrid, however, the intrigues of the French King persisted, with the result that Charles II signed the will, giving the whole inheritance of the crown of Spain to Philip, Duke of Anjou, the second son of the Dauphin, and in the event of his death to his younger brother, the Duc de Berri. If Philip refused to accept the inheritance, the right to it was to pass wholly to the Archduke Charles. Louis XIV accepted the will, and accepted with it as one of its legacies the downfall of the Bourbon monarchy. If he could say, "Il n'y a plus de Pyrénées," a Frenchman in 1789 could also say, "Il n'y a plus de Bourbons." There was a scrap of paper in August, 1914, and there was also a scrap of paper in October, 1700, when by accepting the will, Louis XIV proved that he regarded honesty, private honour, and public faith as words devoid of meaning in international affairs. It rested with William III to build up the Grand Alliance in 1701. Then England, the Emperor, the Dutch, the King of Prussia, and the Grand Duke of Hesse joined themselves together with the object of destroying the tyranny of Louis XIV and breaking up the Franco-Spanish monarchy, by giving Italy to the Emperor and the Indies to the maritime powers. The machine of opposition to France was put together on workmanlike principles, yet the master workman did not live to see it in operation. For William III passed away in 1702.

The gravity of the situation had long been realised by John Churchill, Duke of Marlborough, who now steps on the scene as the greatest general our race has ever produced. Nor must we overlook the circumstance that since the Battle of Rocroi in 1643, the French army was universally regarded as the foremost army in Europe. Throughout the long reign of Louis XIV, French soldiers had come to regard themselves as invincible, and it is not the least of Marlborough's merits that he taught our army to believe in itself as second to none. The immediate effect of the declaration of the war against France was the augmentation of our regiments.

On the 1st of March, 1704, Captain Mulloy received an order to raise a troop. On the 5th of July a warrant was issued for completing and then embarking the Eighth for Portugal.[1] On the 27th of July, 1704, we learn from a letter of J. Dawson to Lieutenant-General Erle that

> Her Matie. having ordered the Regt. of Dragoons commanded by Brigadr. Henry Cunningham to be transported to Portugal for her Service there, and the transport Ships appointed for that Service not yett being ready to receive them on board, we hereby pray and require you to give the necessary orders to the severall troops of the said Regt. to quarter their Horses in the stables of the barracks of Clonmell, Charleville, Mallow, Cappoquin and the officers and private men on the inhabitants of those towns wh. you are to cause to be done in such manner as you shall think most convenient till you shall receive notice of the arrival of the Transport Ships at Cork, Kinsale, and then to cause them to march on Shipboard pursuant to former directions and for so doing this shall be your Warrt.[2]

The Eighth Dragoons had won their spurs in Ireland at the sieges of Derry and Enniskillen, at the Battles of the Boyne and Aughrim, and at the siege of Limerick, and in all these exploits they had been really fighting the plans of Louis XIV for the domination of Europe. It is accordingly thoroughly in keeping with their traditions that their first foreign service should be to aid in repelling the designs of the French monarch in Spain. Brigadier Conyngham had taken his share in these exploits, and was determined once more to do what he could. Now with reason the question of his precedence broke out again. In Ireland he had felt it, and in Portugal he realised that he must feel it even more acutely. We are not surprised to read the letter of the 19th of October, 1704, from C. Hedges to Erle:

> I send your Lordship's Letter of 28th past concerning the difference arisen between Mr Offarell designed to be a Major Genll. in Portugall and Brigr. Cunningham, about the Command of ye. Troops ordered to be sent from Ireland to Portugall, with a copy of ye. said Brigrs. Letter to you and your answer to him upon that Subject, which having laid

[1] *W.O.*, 25/3149.   [2] 1 E, 3.8, p. 89.

before the Queen, I am commanded by her Majty. to signify to you that in regard M. Offarell had the care and command of the Troops committed to him, and did many things relating to that expedition before Brigr. Cunningham's Regimt. was designed to be sent thither and since, and that the latter did not make known his pretensions 'till the troops were embarqued and ready to sail, it is her Majty's pleasure, that the said Troops doe remain under the comand and conduct of the said Mr Offarell 'till they arrive in Portugall, and then the Earl of Gallway, her Majty's Genll. there, will give such orders concerning them, as he shall think necessary, which declaration of her Majty's pleasure I desire you will please to signify, as well to Mr Ofarell as to Brigr. Cunningham, that the Queen's Service may not suffer by any contest between them.[1]

The Duke of Ormonde could have informed Hedges differently, for in 1703 Conyngham had been in communication with the Lord Lieutenant on this very question of precedence. On the 22nd of October, 1704, Conyngham wrote from Cork to Secretary Hedges:

Lieutt. Genll. Erle sent me the copy of a letter from you to him declaring that it is her Majesties pleasure that Mr Offerrell is to command this expedition to Portugall. I am very unfortunate that I should be thought so undeserving as to have him preferr'd before me in so unusuall a manner as laies me under so very great difficulties how to behave my selfe, that I most humbly beg her Majesties leave to take another way to Portugall than with this convoy, and I intreat the favour of you that by next post you will be pleased to lett me know her Majesties pleasure.[2]

On the 31st of October, 1704, a warrant was issued by J. Dawson: "These are to direct and require you to prepare a Warrant and present the same to our signature for paying the Agent of Brigadier Cunningham's Regt. of Dragoons the full pay due to them according to the establishment from the 18th of October just to the 31 following both included the day of their embarcation out of which is deducted. . . ." Here the warrant abruptly breaks off.

The 31st of October was the very day the regiment embarked for Portugal, whose King Pedro favoured the claims of the Archduke

[1] *S.P., Ir.*, Bundle 364.   [2] *S.P., Ir.*, Bundle 364.

Charles, the Austrian candidate for the throne of Spain. The newly-captured fortress of Gibraltar claimed three battalions for garrison. Portugal demanded ten thousand men, and Flanders from twenty to twenty-five thousand. The strength of a battalion in the Peninsula varied from 750 to 850, and the regiments of dragoons varied from a normal strength of 400 to 450, rising in occasional instances to 600. The campaigning season lasted from the 1st of April to the 1st of October, and the recruiting season covered the remaining six months.

During November, 1704, three thousand troops arrived at Lisbon from England, and these included Conyngham's Dragoons under Lieutenant-Colonel John Pepper, who afterwards became their colonel, a battalion of the Guards, made up from the 1st and 2nd Regiments under Colonel Richard Russell, and Donegal's Foot, just returned from the West Indies. For want of horses the Royal and Conyngham's Dragoons remained at St. Ubes and Lisbon. Nor were horses the only lack, as we see by the letter of Henry St. John of the 18th of December, 1704:

> These are to Authorize You by beat of Drum or otherwise to raise and receive so many Volontiers as shall be wanting to Recruit and fill up the respective Troops of Our Royal Regiment of Dragoons under your Command for Our Service. And for the more Speedy Recruiting Our said Regiment to receive into your Custody any such Able Body'd Men as shall be rais'd and Levy'd to Serve as Soldiers by any of Our Justices of the Peace, or other Magistrates or otherwise listed in pursuance of severall Acts made this last Session of Parliament for raising Recruits for Our Land Forces And for discharging such Insolvent Debtors as should serve or procure a Person to Serve in Our Army. Wherein all Magistrates, Justices of the Peace, Constables and other Our Officers whom it may Concern are hereby required to be Assisting to you in Providing Quarters, Impressing Carriages and otherwise as there shall be Occasion.[1]

Such was the letter Lord Raby, Colonel of the Royal Regiment of Dragoons received, and a like letter was addressed the same day to Brigadier Conyngham.

[1] *W.O.*, 26/12.

How terrible a voyage in those days might be is evident from a memorial of Conyngham to Lord Galway dated certainly after the 18th of December, 1704:

Thatt the 31st of October and 1st of November last the Regimt. of Dragoons under his Command with their horses, were Imbarked on Eleven Transport Ships att Corke, all in good order and compleate according to the Establishment of Ireland as appears by the Account and Certificate on the other side.

Thatt 141 of the said horses dy'd for want of roome, all the said Transports except two being only from 83 to 145 Tunns—whereas they ought to have been from 300 to 400 Tunns, as is usuall for such long voyages which wou'd have prevented this loss.

That there was 36 men detached out of the said Regiment to compleat Majr. Generall Harvey's Regiment of horse to the Inglish Establishment where they were order for Portugall who carry'd with them all their clothes and accouterments, and a Troop was allso taken from the said Regiment, to bee added to Ld. John Hayes Regiment of Dragoons who tooke likewise with them all their clothes and mounting for which as Yett there has been no satisfaction made.

Thatt Whereas itt is Her Majties' pleasure the said Regimt. of Dragoons shou'd bee now fill'd up to the numbers of those on the English Establishment, there will bee wanting 22 private men and one Drum to each Troop which for the six amounts to 132 private men and six drums, he therefore humbly desires that the Officers who goe over to receave them may have leave to choose good men, and hopes they will bee deliver'd with their cloths and intire accouterments as he deliver'd his men or otherwise that he bee reimbursed for these that were soe taken from his Regiment with the detachment and Troop before mentioned.

That there is 114 horses now wanting for the non Commissiod. officers and dragoons that came from Ireland besides 27 of the Commissioned officers horses who allsoe dy'd in the voyage and itt is to be feared that 8 or 10 may yett dye of their wounds—and 138 horses more will bee necessary to mount the men to bee added to his said Regiment soe that in the whole 287 horses will be wanting, and he humbly conceaves the most speedy and Efectuall way to have the said

Regiment monted and made fitt for Service will bee that the detachment of 138 men doe bring with them their horses and that 122 horses may bee bought in England and sent over att the same time to remount the men now on foote here.

The said Brigadeer humbly beggs leave to represent further that most of the Officers who lost the 27 horses above mentioned are not in a condition to remount themselves, which he humbly prays Your Excellency wou'd bee pleased to lay before Her Majie. that by Her Royall bounty they may bee in a condition to serve.[1]

Put shortly, this means that out of 70 chargers 27 perished, and out of 216 troop horses no less than 141 perished. Such a loss was due to want of room and to the animals being beaten to pieces. Nor was this state of affairs in any wise unique. Till Marlborough took the matter into his own hands with his characteristic thoroughness, there was the same carelessness in both hiring and fitting transports. It is easy to understand how eager Conyngham was that his officers should be recipients of the royal bounty, for the levy-money was merely at the rate of twelve pounds a horse.[2]

We glean not a little about the state of the regiment from a letter of Henry St. John of the 16th of February, 1705:

Major General Harvey designing to present another memorial to my Lord Treasurer concerning the additional men to Brigadier Cunningham's Regiment of Dragoons, I thought it might be proper to transmit to you the inclos'd account. This Regiment came on ye. Portugal Establishment ye 25th of October last and is by Parliament provided for from that time att ye. rate of 1 Serjeant, 1 Corporal, 1 Drummer, 1 Hautbois, and 24 private men in each troop more than their numbers on the Irish Establishment, of which they still consist ; so that to ye. last of this month there is a sum sav'd which I suppose is applicable to ye. charge of raising them to ye. numbers of ye. Establishment they are now upon. You will see how much has been already allow'd them, and what remains of these Savings. The Officers still continue here, tho' ye. Service requir'd that they shou'd have been some time ago in Ireland, in order to raise their men.[3]

[1] *S.P., Dom., Military*, Bundle 3.
[2] *Miscellaneous Orders (Guards and Garrisons)*, May 17, 1707.
[3] *Treasury*, 1/93, No. 50.

Usually the enclosed account or the annexed list is lost: this is the exception. Here it is:

Saved upon the Establishmt. of Brigadr. Cunningham's Regimt. from 25th of October 1704 to 28th of February following.

					One day's pay. £ s. d.	127 days' pay. £ s. d.
6	Sergeants	each	2 6	..	15	95 5
6	Corporalls	each	2 -	..	12	76 4
6	Drummers	each	2 -	..	12	76 4
6	Hautbois	each	2 -	..	12	76 4
144	Dragoons	each	1 6	..	10 16	1371 12
168					13 7	1695 9

For Saddles and Accoutremts. for 144

Dragoons at £3 each   432

The Price of 144 Horses at £5 each ..   720

                                               1152

                                               543 9 [1]

In Ireland the Duke of Ormonde was urging officers to bestir themselves with the task of recruiting. On the 20th of February, 1705, he ordered Captain Stewart thus:

Her Matie. having signifyed unto Us her royall Will and pleasure for allowing Recruits to be raised in this kingdome for compleating Brigr. Conyngham's Regt. of Dragoons now in Portugall to the English establishment, these are therefore to authorize and impower you by beat of Drum or otherwise to raise and inlist as many volunteers as shall come and enter themselves in her Maties. service in the sd. Regt. and as often as any such Volunteers shall be so entertained you are to cause them to be carryed before the next Justice of the Peace who is to certifye to the Musr. Masr. Genll. the day of their inlisting and appearance before him and wee also hereby require the Musr. Masr. Genll. to muster all those Volunteers who shall come and appear before him as Soldiers inlisted to serve in the sd. Regt. and to make a roll of all such as shall be so mustered and certified by the Justices of the

[1] *Treasury*, 1/93, No. 50.

Peace whereupon directions will be given for their Subsistce. till they can be transported to Portugall, and we hereby direct and require all officers, civil and military, Magistrates, Constables, and others, whom it may concern to be aiding and assisting you herein in providing such Recruits with Quarters, and otherwise as there shall be occasion.[1]

Captain Stewart exerted himself to some purpose, for we find that on the 26th of February he received fifty pounds for providing subsistence for recruits and on the 15th of March he received another fifty pounds. A letter written by Edward Southwell on the 26th of February, 1705, at Dublin, tells us somewhat more about Stewart's activities: "Capt. Stewart who is come over for Col. Conynghams Recruits has received all his Dispatches from my Lord Lieut. and 50l. in hand to begin wth. and that he may have no delay, his Grace has directed the Dragoon Officers here to raise him Men in their respective Quarters, wch. I hope will facilitate that work. Capt. Stewart says he has left Cornet Knox behind him in London to take care of the Cloathing, etc."[2]

On the 10th of April the recruits set out for their destination. From Cork Stewart wrote: "According to your Commands I give you the Trouble of this to acquaint you that I have shipt here on board the Transports for Portugall seventy five men for Brigadr. Cunningham's Regimt. and doe dayly expect from the North 29 Men more, which in probability may come in good time, the Winds being like to continue Contrary. And whilst I have any time here, I will doe my Endeavour to raise more Men."[3]

From Cork the scene now changes to the Peninsula, where we encounter the Earl of Peterborough, the commander-in-chief, one of the most curious characters in the annals of history. An enigma he was to his contemporaries, and an enigma he has remained ever since. A friend declared that his eminent talents were dashed with something restless and capricious in his nature. All air and fire, he is described as turning life into a wild romance; as one of the phenomena produced by nature once in the revolution of centuries to show to ordinary men what she can do in a fit of prodigality. Had he, as Lord Stanhope declares, a talent for partisan warfare

[1] 1 E, 58.   [2] *S.P., Ir.*, Bundle 365.   [3] *S.P., Ir.*, Bundle 365.

which has seldom been equalled and hardly ever exceeded? He is, in the judgment of Sir Walter Scott, one of the most heroic characters, according to ancient ideas of heroism, which occur in English history. On the other hand, for all the enterprises attributed to Peterborough, Colonel Parnell, in his accurate history of *The War of the Succession in Spain*, simply substitutes the name of Prince George of Hesse Darmstadt. As well as this, Colonel Parnell puts different personages in Peterborough's place, and practically obliterates him. Now in so doing this author has been deeply influenced by his discovery that *The Military Memoirs of Captain Carleton* are thoroughly untrustworthy.[1] His reasons for this important conclusion are cogent to the last degree. As these memoirs exalt Peterborough to an unduly high place, it is no matter of surprise that Colonel Parnell debases him to a low one. Unfortunately, Mr. Richard Cannon, in his *Historical Record of the Eighth, or, The King's Royal Irish Regiment of Hussars*, accepts these memoirs as trustworthy, with the result that his whole account of the part taken by the Eighth in the War of the Spanish Succession must be received with great caution.

Like all discoverers, Colonel Parnell has gone too far. No doubt Peterborough has been the subject of undue appreciation, yet that is no reason why he should now be the subject of equally undue depreciation. In spite of *The Military Memoirs of Captain Carleton*, the figure of Peterborough remains pretty much where it was, though its pedestal undoubtedly has been lowered.[2] Jonathan Swift sketched him not untruly in his inimitable lines:

> Mordanto fills the trump of fame,
> The Christian world his deeds proclaim,
> And prints are crowded with his name.
>
> In journeys he outrides the post,
> Sits up till midnight with his host,
> Talks politics, and gives the toast.

---

[1] *Cf.* his *War of Succession in Spain*, pp. 316–26.

[2] *Cf.* T. Miller Maguire's article on Peterborough in *The United Service Magazine*, Vol. 33 (N.S.), p. 184.

Knows every prince in Europe's face,
Flies like a squib from place to place,
And travels not, but runs a race.

From Paris gazette à-la-main,
This day arriv'd, without his train,
Mordanto in a week in Spain.

A messenger comes all a-reek
Mordanto at Madrid to seek ;
He left the town above a week.

Next day the post-boy winds his horn,
And rides through Dover in the morn :
Mordanto's landed at Leghorn.

Mordanto gallops on alone,
The roads are with his followers strewn,
This breaks a girth, and that a bone ;

His body active as his mind,
Returning sound in limb and wind,
Except some leather lost behind.

A skeleton in outward figure,
His meagre corps, though full of vigour,
Would halt behind him, were it bigger.

So wonderful his expedition,
When you have not the least suspicion,
He's with you like an apparition.

Shines in all climates like a star ;
In senates bold, and fierce in war ;
A land commander, and a tar :

Heroic actions early bred in,
Ne'er to be match'd in modern reading,
But by his namesake, Charles of Sweden.[1]

¹ Swift, *Poems*, I, pp. 48–9 (Bell's ed.).

The career of Conyngham we can understand, but it is difficult to understand the career of Peterborough. He seems indeed to be a crusader of the thirteenth century who has strayed into the eighteenth. Conyngham had at last obtained the rank he had won for his services. He was second in command as Major-General to Peterborough, and the working commander of the English troops. Under him were Brigadier-Generals the Earl of Donegal, Viscount Charlemont, Richard Gorges, James Stanhope, and Viscount Shannon. Major-General Scratenbach and Brigadier-General St. Amant commanded the Dutch contingent. The army comprised three English, three Irish, and four Dutch regiments, numbering six thousand men in all. Naturally the character of Peterborough affected the whole enterprise. He possessed desirable qualities, but among his undesirable ones we must place the circumstance that he was a good hater and an accomplished reviler. Conyngham he termed an "eternal screech-owl." Nor did Charles III and Prince Lichtenstein fare a whit better. They were always the "Vienna gang."[1] A Pauline qualification for a bishop is that he should be able to suffer fools gladly. It ought also to be a qualification for a general, who ought to be able to suffer fools, especially of the political variety, gladly. Of this qualification, Peterborough had not a trace. Nor can a commander do without the invaluable quality of patience. To the lasting loss of the expedition, its commander had not a trace of this quality. William Pitt selected patience as the first requisite of the statesman: it is also the first requisite of the commander; "patience," as Marlborough, the contemporary of Peterborough, himself once wrote to Godolphin, "which can overcome all things."[2]

In the seventeenth century Blake and Monk had served as generals as well as admirals, and it is not altogether surprising to find that Peterborough enjoyed the post of joint Admiral with Sir Cloudesley Shovell.[3] On the 24th of June, 1705, Peterborough wrote to Secretary Hedges:

> We are safely arrived, having had a most prosperous voyage and the Dutch not long in port before us, . . .

[1] S. Martin Leake, *The Life of Sir John Leake*, I, p. lxxxvi.
[2] Mahon, *History of England*, III, p. 368.   [3] *S.P., Foreign, Spain*, Bundle 6.

All the ministers and Generalls are sent for and I believe they would have made (gr)eat efforts Towards Taking Cales.   I wish the first orders had stood and I had been left att Liberty.   I believe they would have made me up fourteen thousand foot and Two thousand Horse, as the case standes, to repaire their own scandalous campaigne.

They are all against the attempts in Catalonia espatially Shotenbergh the Dutch envoy. . . .

Sometime or other I must writt you a letter of complaints for in truth some services are executed very scandalously, there is nothing so infamous as all that relates to the marines, and the Queen has been out of measure abused in the horses bought in Ireland, it is ill husbandry to Transport a horse att Twenty five pounds expence which is worth forty shillings and that indeed is the case.

The shipp that came to-night from Villa Franche bring no news. I wonder Sr. Cloudesly has no letters from the Person you know of, but they have been very long in their passage, they touched att Gibraltar and the Prince of Hesse is ill hurt with the kick of a horse.   We expect Ld. Galloway and all the great men in Town, as soon as they arrive I shall trouble you with particulars all matters here being in the Hyest confusion.[1]

Peterborough's views about the prices of Irish horses are not to be trusted implicitly, for we learn from the State Papers that on, say, the 27th of February, 1705, "good squat dragoon horses" could be bought in Ireland for five pounds apiece.[2]   In May, 1705, a batch of men and 420 horses arrived from Ireland.   Of the latter Harvey's Regiment of Horse received 120 and Conyngham's 300. Did Peterborough share Marlborough's prejudice in favour of English horses as superior to all others?   The cheapness of the Irish horse proved of no pecuniary advantage to the officers.   They were expected to pay for the transport of their horses at a fixed rate, and though at length, in reply to their complaints, free transport was granted for twenty-six horses to a battalion, yet this privilege was again withdrawn as soon as it was discovered that Irish animals were to be purchased at a low price.[3]   Nor must we

[1] *S.P., Foreign, Spain*, Vol. 75.
[2] *S.P., Dom.*, February 27 and August 10, 1705.
[3] *Secretary's Common Letter Book*, February 27 and August 10, 1705.

overlook the expense of obtaining recruits. No doubt the officers received levy-money for this purpose. This, however, was insufficient, and, besides this, no allowance was made for recruits lost through desertion, sickness, and the like, over which the officers could exercise no control. Officers in the Peninsula complained in the bitterest terms that because of the heavy mortality in the transports their recruits, by the time they reached them, had cost them eight or nine pounds a head.[1]

One of the outstanding differences between the War of the Spanish Succession and the Peninsular War is that popular sentiment was as decidedly against us in the former as it was on our side in the latter. One of the exceptions was the Catalans, who favoured the Austrian candidate, the Archduke Charles. Accordingly an army and a fleet under Admiral Leake and Admiral-General Lord Peterborough were sent to their assistance. The army consisted of six British and four Dutch battalions, comprising about 6500 men. On the 20th of June, 1705, they arrived at Lisbon, when it was in due time determined that the fleet should proceed to Barcelona, the capital of Catalonia. Galway lent his two regiments of dragoons, the Royals and the Eighth. Here we may say that the former were under Colonel Robert Killigrew, who subsequently served as a brigadier-general and subsequently commanded the Eighth. There is, therefore, difficulty in disentangling the actions of the Royal Dragoons and the Eighth Dragoons. Peterborough pursued his way to Gibraltar, where he picked up the eight battalions of the garrison, leaving two of his own in their place, and proceeded to his destination, which ultimately proved to be Barcelona.

A Council of War had been held at Lisbon on the 28th of June, O.S., and among others present was Major-General Conyngham. "Finding," we read, "that the number of Horses offered by the Portuguese is far less than Ld. Gallway considers sufficient, and finding that he could get nothing in writing from the Portuguese as to their concurring in some design in Catalonia or against Cadiz, and even if he could, they could not be depended upon to comply within reasonable time. It is therefore the unanimous resolution

---

[1] *Cal. Treas. Papers*, November 18, 1710; January 6, 1711.

of the Council to waste no more time but proceed with their instructions.   Ld. Gallway having ordered two Regts. of Dragoons to proceed with the Fleet, the season of the year requiring everyone to go on immediate service."[1]

At Gibraltar a plan of operations was settled, and on the 5th of August, 1705, the confederate fleet of English and Dutch sailed towards the north-west.   It anchored for a time in Altea Bay in Valencia.   A manifesto was here circulated in which the Spaniards were told that the allies came to deliver the Spanish nation from the insupportable yoke of foreigners, that is, Frenchmen, and that they were escorting the true King, Charles III.   The fortified town of Denia surrendered, and Juan Basset y Ramos was appointed its governor.   Charles III was duly proclaimed King of Spain and the Indies.   On the 22nd of August Sir Cloudesley Shovell arrived off the coast, and anchored three miles east of Barcelona.

According to the rumours printed in the *London Gazette*, Barcelona was ill-fortified and ill-garrisoned.   The presence of Peterborough was to be simply a variation of Caesar's despatch. Peterborough was to come, to see, and of course to conquer.   No doubt the standard of fortification attained by a Vauban or a Cohorn had not been reached.   Like every other town in Spain or in Ireland supposed to be fortified, Barcelona was defended by a stout wall flanked at intervals by a few bastions and many small towers, preceded by a ditch of moderate depth, with a covered way and a low glacis.   On the south-western side, at a distance of eleven hundred yards, stood a hill seven hundred feet higher than the fortress, crowned by the small fort of Montjuich.   This weak fort had a line of bastioned advance works, commenced but left incomplete.   Artillery might create a breach.   Should there then be an assault?

On the 22nd of August a Council of General Officers was held at Major-General Scratenbach's quarters.   There were present Peterborough, Scratenbach, Brigadier St. Amant, Brigadier Richard Gorges, Viscount Shannon, Colonel Hans Hamilton, the Quartermaster General, Major-General Conyngham, the Earl of Donegal,

[1] *S.P., Foreign, Spain*, Vol. 75.

Viscount Charlemont, Brigadier James Stanhope, and Lieutenant-Colonel Wills, Adjutant-General. According to the minutes, "Having well weighed and debated the King of Spain's Letters dated of this day, and upon a second consideration (as His Majesty desired) of his Speech on board the *Brittannia*, and well examined all our Circumstances and those of the Garrison.

"It is proposed to this Council of war to give their Votes whether Real and Vigorous Attack on this place by creating a battery of Fifty pieces of Cannon against the Courtain, in order to the bringing on the speediest assault possible on the breach shall be undertaken, or can be made with hopes of Success? Which pass'd in ye Negative."[1]   All so voted except Peterborough. His reasons were :

Because I am sensible that the Queen My Mistress, besides the engagement of treaties and the motives of Public Interests has a most particular and tender Friendship for the King of Spain, therefore I think it expedient to pay him the utmost respect in complying as far as possible with his desires in any attempt wherein there is ye. least hopes of Success, after having as in duty bound with all sincerity and plainess represented to him the difficulties and hazards to wch. he exposes his interest, and the Troops of ye. Queen and her Allyes.

Because that His Majesty persisting with so much firmness in his Opinion about Barcelona upon a belief the town would surrender if a Breach was made.   This may create some dispute in the World, what might have been the Event, which nothing but experience can demonstrate, whatever reasons some may have to judge the contrary, and it may be thought by some our duty to have tryed the Experiment, tho at the utmost hazard.

Lastly because no other reason but plain disobedience to her Majesty's orders have hinder'd me from complying with any Commands that came from his Catholick Majesty.   But the Queen has repeatedly commanded me in all my Instructions to be guided in Councills of war by a Majority, even in express words, in those cases where the Kings of Spain and Portugall, or their Ministers should offer anything in writing to me, wch. orders I communicated to his Catholick Majesty, as all my Other Instructions and I had often Opportunity of repeating

[1] *S.P., Foreign, Spain*, Vol. 75.

them before the Ministers of the King of Spain, the King of Portugall and the English and Dutch Embassadour and Envoy, being thus fetter'd by such positive Orders, wch. I must comply with, this hath again made me Offer the Kings Proposalls about Barcelona, and use may utmost efforts to gain ye. Assent of a Councill of War, declaring then as I doe now, that I would most willingly engage in any attempt which could have been Agreed to in a Councill of War, having received him his Majesty aboard the Fleet, with a Resolution to serve and obey him in all things in my power.

The proposal was made on the 26th of August, 1705, to attack the town for eighteen days. Peterborough, Stanhope and St. Amant voted for this proposal. Hamilton, Charlemont, Shannon, Gorges, Wills, Scratenbach, and Conyngham voted against it. Conyngham stated : "I am of opinion that the Siege of Barcelona ought not to be undertaken for the reasons I have allready signed to, and that the Armys remaining here Eighteen daies may make a good retreat impracticable, or at least so farr wast the Army and time, as to render all other Attempts impossible, but am ready to Obey all such Orders as I shall receive from my Superior Officers."[1]

At the meeting on the 26th it was realised that the garrison of the town was large and under a governor, Francisco Velasco, unpopular, it is true, but vigilant to a degree. Colonel Petit, our Chief engineer, had simply proposed to erect a large battery at five hundred yards from the walls, to make a breach, and then to storm it, and all this would have to be undertaken when exposed to heavy fire.

Conyngham was present at the Council of War held on the 26th of August at Peterborough's quarters. The General Officers present agreed that

Since the King of Spain is resolved to lay the whole successe of his affairs upon making an Attempt on Barcelona for Eighteen daies (expressed in his Letter to us) notwithstanding all our unanswerable arguments to the contrary at three several Councils of War and tho we have reason to fear the Result will too much justifie our Opinions,

[1] *S.P., Foreign, Spain*, Vol. 75.

yet in regard that our General the Earl of Peterborow has complyed with the Kings desires, and that we are extreamly pressed to do the same by the King and his Ministers, who still continue to give positive assurances of their Intelligence from the Place, being resolved that no blame be imputed to us, We are willing to comply with the Kings desire for the above-mentioned attempt (tho' at the same time we must expresse our concern that this undertaking will debarr us of all future Services for this Campaign) provided we are sustained by the Fleet and Miquelets[1] in the workes and Trenches as we have reason to expect to give a possibility of making a Breach and Sustaining the Trenches.

It is evident to this Council of Warr by the demands from the Engineers and the Opinions of all the General Officers that this Attempt cannot be made with less than five thousand Men on Duty every day to work and Guard the Trenches.   That of this Number our Army not exceeding seaven Thousand Men including the Eleven hundred Marines besides the Dragoones and Guards, cannot furnish above two thousand five hundred.

That this service absolutely requires two thousand five hundred Men daily out of the Fleet and Miquelets, and we desire (the Admirals having promised their utmost assistance) to let us know whether they can furnish fifteen hundred p. day, and whereas they have promised to assist this undertaking with Fifty two Battering Guns it is understood that all things thereunto belonging must be furnished with the Guns and Men.[2]

On the 28th of August, 1705, all the General Officers met at Major-General Conyngham's quarters in the camp before Barcelona. The question of the experimental attack for eighteen days was again debated. The outcome is that

we are confident his Majtie. (of Spain) will allow we gave even a most unreasonable Mark of our respect, having consented to expose the Troops under our care to visible ruin without any prospect of successe, and against all the Rules of Warr. . . .

We were obliged to Land the Forces without the least Advice, and that made an Argument for an Attempt against a Town with a Garrison near as strong as our Selves, without any Correspondence in it Suitable to what we have been told, which Siege must require more than two

---

[1] These are Catalan peasants with arms.   [2] *S.P., Foreign, Spain*, Vol. 75.

third parts of our Men on Duty every day by the demand of our Engineers.

And having notice from Admiral Wassenaer of the positive time of the departure of the Dutch Ships, some dayes before which the Dutch General assures us, he will embark his Troops, and the Engineers not undertaking to make a Battery even in that time, since the Fleet besides the Marines which in all our Computations of the strength of the Army we had reckoned upon to compose a part of it, are not able to furnish towards carrying on our Workes above nine hundred Men, of which onely three hundred can work each day, instead of fifteen hundred for daily Service as we had desired ; so that the whole Assistance that the Fleet can give, being added to the Number of Effective Foot we have now fit for Service, including the Battalion of Guards will make in all but Eight Thousand five hundred and fifteen Men. . . .

And since Eight Deputies from the Catalans did declare to the Earl of Peterborow and her Majties. Envoy that they could not promise any number of Men to work at our Trenches and Batteries, or in any place where they should be exposed to Fire, which they said could not be expected from undisciplined country people. . . .

It is the unanimous opinion of this Council of War that the proposed attempt on Barcelona for eighteen daies cannot be made, but that the Troops be immediately Embarqued for the probable service and the support of the Duke of Savoy.[1]

Behind Charles III was Prince George, who stoutly contended that the attempt on Barcelona ought to be made. He stated that he had sure intelligence of the good disposition of the citizens and the disaffected state of part of the garrison ; and he added that, if only the walls were breached, Velasco would be glad to capitulate with honour. Another debate ensued. On the one side stood the Prince, Sir Cloudesley Shovell, the admirals, and all the Germans, and on the other side Peterborough, and all his generals. Summing up the objections urged by the General Officers, Charles finally declared that even if the English general should leave him, he himself would never consent to desert the Catalans. With such pressure Peterborough was forced to agree that the English and the Dutch forces should join in making an attempt on Barcelona.

[1] *S.P., Foreign, Spain,* Vol. 75.

Within a weak fortress Velasco had a garrison of 800 horse and 3200 foot, composed of Spaniards and Neapolitans who were by no means loyal to the Bourbon cause. The Catalan citizens of the town were of course warmly attached to Charles III. On the allied side there were 6600 British soldiers, 2500 Dutch, and 570 Catalans, or 9670 men in all. Beside this army there was a fleet of sixty-sail of the line, led by the enterprising Sir Cloudesley Shovell, carrying 24,000 sailors with 3500 heavy guns. The Miquelets numbered some 3000, and were daily increasing. The battery manned by seamen, and eight field guns on the hills, fired, but the fire was barely sufficient to reply to the fire of the enemy. In this fruitless fashion the prescribed eighteen days were all but spent. Of course more Councils of war were called both ashore and afloat, and it was decided that further attempts were useless. Soldiers and sailors, especially the latter, manifested their disgust at leaving the place without serious fighting. The Catalans, dreading the vengeance of Velasco, agreed not only to work in the trenches, but even to storm the town themselves, if only the allies would first make a breach!

There was much ill feeling between Prince George and Lord Peterborough, and for a time they were not on speaking terms. In September, however, Peterborough and his General Officers were induced to entertain a design for another stroke at the city. Peterborough had not, in spite of his views at Councils of War, thrown himself very heartily into the support of the siege. Still, was it not possible to assault Montjuich? True, it enjoyed a strong natural position. Yet for that very reason the officers of the garrison, deeming it impregnable, had not sent more than 200 men to it. Of course the possession of the Fort of Montjuich by no means carried with it the possession of Barcelona, though, psychologically, such a success must exercise a serious effect on the garrison of the city. In his diary Colonel St. Pierre holds that he hazarded the suggestion of the attack upon the Fort. Yet we know that no delusion is more common among the most honest subordinates in the army than that they are the authors, the real authors, of decisive movements which their chief has simply the credit of carrying out. Peterborough determined to capture the fort by escalade. Four hundred grenadiers, supported by 600 musketeers, were the men detailed for this piece of work, and the reserves were 300 dragoons and 1000 foot under Stanhope. It was their task to watch the San Antonio gate of Barcelona and to prevent any sortie from it. The whole attempt was undertaken with the utmost secrecy, for Peterborough used to say of himself, "When I desire a thing extremely, I rather conceal than own my intention."

The assault began badly. Instead of reaching the Fort of Montjuich before dawn the troops arrived in broad daylight. Prince George approached the inner fort imprudently, falling mortally wounded, and two hundred of his men were taken prisoners. A panic seized the men in the outworks. Falling into the horriblest rage, according to Richards, that ever man was seen in, with bravery and resolution Peterborough led the troops back again to the posts which they had quitted. He persisted in the attack, and on the fourth day the Fort fell. Success, however, was dearly bought by the loss of Prince George, who was only thirty-six. Devoted to the cause of Charles III, his death was a piece of supreme good fortune for Louis XIV and of supreme bad fortune for the Allies. Never till now, wrote Paul Methuen, had the English been aware of the extreme devotion borne by the Catalans towards one who had been their former viceroy.

The attitude of Peterborough towards the siege completely altered.[1] He now set himself seriously to the capture of the city. He dropped—for a time, at least—sneers at the "Vienna gang," and Conyngham was no longer an eternal screech-owl. Formidable batteries were erected, and regular approaches planned. Fifty-eight guns and mortars were soon in action. Peterborough and Charles III exposed themselves with reckless regard of danger. The foe within was almost as serious to Velasco as the foe without. For he realised how readily the smouldering hostility of the

[1] *Cf.* a curious article in *Colburn's United Service Magazine*, Part III, 1869, p. 361.

Catalan citizens might break out. They attacked the Bourbon troops, and the carelessness or the complicity of the sentries had allowed the Miquelets to steal inside. All was over, and Velasco was forced to apply to Charles for protection. On the 9th of October Barcelona was in the hands of the Allies. With its capture, combined with the subsequent reduction of Tarragona by the fleet, Charles III had won Catalonia.

On the 28th of October, 1705, Peterborough wrote to Messrs. Arundell & Bates, English merchants at Genoa:

> The news of our success In Catalonia I doubt nott are as agreable to Every English man, as they are surprising to the Ennemye, to take a Capital Whose Garrison Consisted of above five thousand foot and eight hundred horse, when our Army was but seven thousand Foot and four hundred Dragoons the Enemy resisting to the last Extremity, and att same time Gironna taken by surprise and Tarragona (souldiers and Officers Prisoners of Warr) this is a beginning which Heaven has favourd almost with Miracles, since wee begun with taken Mangui[1] with sword In hand, which Castle is much stronger then the place, they had five hundred men to defend itt, and wee but eight to attack itt, I thought itt of such Importance that the Prince of Hesse and myself attacked it with the Grenadiers wheere wee had the Misfortune to lose that Gallant Generall, since Lerida, Tortosa, all the strong Castles, Towns and Villages have submitted to King Charles the third Except Rosas just upon the Frontiers of France. Now, Gentlemen, I must Inform you that the embarcation of the King of Spain was nott thought of at home nor provided for, butt this expedition I have supported att my own expense. . . .

> You will likewise do me the favour to negotiate with the Dutch Consul or Merchants the Dutch bills I send than which nothing is more sacred, they are starving and so are wee all with those considerable members of Horse and Foot which have deserted the Ennemy and Come Into our Service which amount to three thousand. Judge whether these must bee entertained or forced back to the ennemy. I have already lain out Forty thousand pounds of my own and have no more.[2]

---

[1] Montjuich.   [2] *Treasury*, 1/96, fo. 176.

The point of view of the general is valuable: the point of view of the commanding officer is no less valuable. On the 6th of October Robert Killigrew wrote a singularly ill-spelt letter from Barcelona:

I was favord with Yours of July the 25, and by ye. Pakett, I had a Letter from Mr. La Never, how tels me that Sr. Charles Hedges ashourd the Lord Galloway, that att his request the Queen had made a Bregader, but with out pay, that is nothing, it is a post still gand (*sic*), and I should have it by the verre firs opportunity it sent to me heare. I am not a Littill pleased att my Good fortun, tho nothing shall make me for gett, your frendships[1] att all times to me, I am againe under some deficoulty, for in a former Letter to me, you ware pleased to say you know no ressen why Mr. Pulford should not sell, and he has bin so informed, by Mr Ellison. Now writt to me the same as from yr. Lordship, now Mr Pulford insist on your Leve ; I most confes I wos to blame, when I recommended him to be Lieut. Capt. Green complained of him. I shall take him att his word, and offer it to Mr Barrett, and the rest of the Qr. Mr. wich I think is the fairest way.

As to Mr Pairce I shall make him accordin to your commands, the First Leut. that fall.

I am sorre sombody has misrepresented young Mr Kitson to Your Lordsp. I Ges this come, he has bin advised not to Keep so much companne, to avoyed drinken, he is a verre sober Zaiett youth, and dos mind his Bisnes, or wonts he seen, and if I may be but a Levid (allowed) a moderate Jeug, I think he is as hopfull a young man, and as likely to make an offisser, as anne wee have had seen I came to the Regement, wich his capt. will geve him the same carrextor, it is vere strang, that some men cant recomen them selves, by by defamin of other, its a bas princepell. for I have often Inquired in to his behavir, as he wos by Your Lordsp. so strongly recomended to me, and my kin (?) and so have an eye over him, wich make me writt what I know, and have seen and obsarved of him.

As to what you dissier consarning your nephewe, it is my oppinnion that his bein a Leut. or a cortt, matter nothing, is not the Regement yours, for by that time he will be fitt to sarve, you may att anne time give him a Troop, I ned not tell Your Lordsp., that a Leut. is the Life

---

[1] This letter does not tell us to whom it was written. Obviously it was to the Colonel.

of a troop, the post of cornett is only for young Gentelmen to begin the world, and to Larne thare douty, and now in time of sarvies it will not loke well, pardon me, if I dissagre with you, but I sobmett to your Better Gogement, but if you will have it so, it shall be don, and the same for Mr Manvill, Your Lordsp. may make him a Leut. att once when ever your Lordp. shall think fitt to have him To is douty, to advance him, and that att some time, but I most on, this is not a proper time.

Sarjant Jones is left seke att Lisbon, and by nomenes fitt, for Sargant Caper, wine is chep and he is not to be advised, he is a good sadler, and of sarvice in your Troop, or I had Broke him long agoe. That smith you writt of, had been ded a bofe this twelfe month, you ware deserved in the man, he wos not that man you toke him for, he is dead, so I will say no more of him.

As to my Liken or disliken the recrouts, Mr Jasen may afarm what he please, I have only this to say, I returned severrell, wich ware either lame, or to old, or Blind, and I sent them for England, and thare wos amongest them severell Boyes brought over, wich I made to be taken for Dromes, or sarvants. In souch a nomber thare most with out all dispouts, some good men, some Bad, not all so excelent as ma be he would have you beleve, it is his way, it Hortes not me ; and seen it please him, lett them be all souperexcellen with all my Harte.

I shall be sheure to take care to obsarve your commandes, as to Capt. Jasen.[1]

The triumph of Charles III had been dimmed by the tragic death of Prince George, yet he could not help feeling that his anticipations of the capture of Barcelona had been entirely justified. He entered its gates joyfully on the 23rd of October, and was proclaimed amidst the plaudits of the Catalans King of Spain. He had written to Queen Anne the preceding day that the Earl of Peterborough in particular had evinced throughout the expedition constancy, bravery, conduct, zeal, and application. He expressed his admiration of the troops for their abstention from the common practice of pillage, and for their good faith in appeasing the disorders with a discipline and generosity without example.

[1] *Add. MSS.*, 31134, fo. 144.

Peterborough was neither trustful nor exultant. He besought Godolphin for supplies. "We perish," he wrote on the 12th of October, "for want of money. I have in a manner supported all here with my little stock. I sold, mortgaged, and took up a year's advance upon my estate, got all my pay advanced, took all the money up at Lisbon upon my account that I could anywise get. I have left my wife and children nothing to live upon." The fact that he was forced in November to lay an embargo, for the sake of the safety of Barcelona, which was destitute of powder, upon half the stock some ships in port were conveying to North Italy, testifies his need. That same month Messrs. Arundell & Bates, English merchants at Genoa, informed Godolphin that, from a sense of patriotism, they had advanced to Peterborough after the capture of Barcelona the sum of twenty thousand pounds. Peterborough's letter of the 2nd of November to Secretary Hedges speaks for itself:

It was impossible for me to think of the happy progresse of her Majtys. arms in this Country, and not resolve to stay with the Troops, tho' the circumstances in which we are give very melancholy considerations, the people of the Country have no money, and I stay here with a King and a Court without a Farthing, with the Dutch and Marines for whom there never was any provision, and nothing left to subsist the Troops, all the money I could gett being spent in the siege, and for the Kings support. . . .

We are att a full stop for want of money, a summe proportionable to such a design would in two months secure Valentia and Arragon, or carry us to Madrid.[1]

On the 18th of November Peterborough announced that "Our Troops are now marching towards Valentia and some Towards Arragon, if the Enemy continue on the Frontiers we may chance to make them such an other visitt as att Fraga where fower Hundred of (ours) beat Two Thousand out of the Town, and took three Hundred foot and a Hundred horse Prisoners."[2]

One outcome of the capture of Barcelona was the occupation of the various fortresses of Catalonia. The richest and largest

---

[1] *S.P., Foreign, Spain,* Vol. 75.   [2] *S.P., Foreign, Spain,* Vol. 75.

province of Spain was now on the side of Charles III and in his
possession. Valencia, with its capital, followed the example set
by the Catalans. Conyngham, on this occasion, was advanced
to the local rank of Lieutenant-General in Spain. His dragoons,
the English marines, two battalions of Dutch, two of Neapolitans
and Ahumada's newly-raised regiment of Catalans, consisting of
3700 men, moved in December to the strong town of Lerida,
beautifully situated on the slope of a hill on the right bank of the
Segre. This force was commanded by Conyngham, under whom
were Colonel Wills and the Dutch Colonel Palms. With the
Miquelets, its business was to guard the Arragon frontier, since the
Bourbon soldiers must advance from that direction. By its bridge
across the Ebro Tortosa formed the key to Arragon and Valencia.
To garrison Tortosa Brigadier-General Killigrew had under him
the Royal Dragoons, with Barrymore's, Donegal's and Mountjoy's
foot, mustering in all 1400 men. King Charles had represented
that the army of his opponent, the Spanish General de Las Torres,
was but two thousand strong, and had added that thousands of
peasants were up in arms against it. Peterborough, with only
thirteen hundred men, made the disagreeable discovery that the
Spaniards numbered no less than four thousand foot and three
thousand horse, while the thousands of Miquelets existed only in
the imagination of the King.

The force of General de Las Torres was too strong for Peterborough, and on his arrival at Traguera in January, 1706, he
resorted to stratagems. The enemy captured a spy, and on him
was found a letter from Peterborough to Colonel Jones, who had a
few dragoons and a thousand irregular infantry. "I am at
Traguera," so it ran in effect, "with six thousand men and artillery.
You may wonder how I collected them: but for transport and
secrecy nothing equals the sea. Now, be ready to pursue Las
Torres over the plain. It is his only line of retreat, for I have
occupied all the passes over the hills. You will see us on the hill-
tops between nine and ten. Prove yourself a true dragoon, and
have your miquelets ready for their favourite plunder and chase."
Las Torres was completely taken aback by this communication.

On threats of death the spy offered to betray another messenger of Peterborough's, who was hidden in the hills. The Spaniards captured this spy, and found a copy of the same letter upon him. Both were cross-examined. One of them declared that he knew nothing of the strength of Peterborough's force, while the other declared that he knew everything, and that all the letter contained was accurate. Confirmation of this was furnished by the appearance of the red-coats at different points on the hill-tops. At this moment Las Torres was additionally startled by the accidental explosion of one of his own mines before San Mateo. The sudden appearance of the red-coats combined with the equally sudden explosion proved too much for him, and he beat a retreat forthwith. On the spot Jones and his men sallied forth, and the retreat turned to a rout. Peterborough with his thirteen hundred men thereupon took possession of San Mateo with the whole of the Spanish camp and material of war. Of course the two spies had been in the pay of Peterborough. He had taken the precaution to hold their families as sureties for their good faith, and he had cut off Las Torres from all veracious intelligence.

On the second day of the retreat, as Las Torres was beginning to grasp the nature of the trick played upon him, a friendly spy came to inform him that an English force was marching parallel to his left flank, endeavouring to cut off his retreat by seizing the passes into the plain of Valencia. Las Torres, acting on the principle "once bitten twice shy", could not believe the spy, who offered, if two or three officers accompanied him, to prove that he was right. Disguised as peasants, two officers accompanied the spy in search of confirmation of the truth of his story. A picquet of ten dragoons took them prisoners. The resourceful spy gave the picquet wine, and the dragoons succumbed to their national failing. Seizing three of the dragoons' horses, the two officers and the spy galloped back to Las Torres, who, on seeing the housings of the horses, could no longer deny credence to the story told to him. At once he broke up his camp, and hurried away in the direction where he was least wanted by Peterborough. Las Torres wanted to secure the precious passes into Valencia. The spy was in Peterborough's pay, and, saving the ten dragoons, there was not an Irish or English soldier within twenty miles of Las Torres.

The minutes of a Council of War, consisting of General and Field Officers, including Killigrew, held at the town of Albocazer on the 12th of January, 1706, says nothing of these stratagems, but simply records that

> the enemy employed 3 of their best Regts. of Horse besides 200 Horse of the D. of Anjou's Guards, amounting to above 2000 Horse and 16 Hundred Foot.

> The Forces with which the siege of St. Mattheo' was raised consisted of 1000 Foot, and less than 200 Dragns., the enemy being surprised. Upon their retreat "the Forces march'd after them a long and tedious March over ye. Mountains to Albocazar," where the Troops of the D. of Anjou were encreased to 1200 men on the frontiers of Arragon besides 6000 between him and Valentia.

> The 900 Foot that remained "being fatigued and almost barefoot with continued marches over ye. Rocks and Mountains," his Lordship called a Council of War at which it was decided not to advance further, but to attempt Peniscola marching towards Veneros—not so far from Tortosa, and employ the troops to the relief of Catalonia.[1]

The plan of Louis XIV for the recovery of Catalonia was sufficiently extensive. A French Marshal, the Comte de Tessé, was proceeding with the rival King Philip through Arragon towards Tortosa ; a second force of four or five thousand men under Comte Tserclaes de Tilly was menacing Lerida ; and the Duc de Noailles was marching upon Barcelona from Roussillon with eight thousand men. The optimistic Charles III and his advisers were now reduced to the depths of pessimism. Peterborough made his preparations, hampered by his lack of men and of money. At Tamarite, not far from Balbastro, Conyngham had posted an outlying detachment of horse. As he felt certain that they would be attacked, he sent Colonel Wills with 600 marines to their support. On the 23rd of January, 1706, he followed with his own dragoons and a battalion of Dutch foot under Colonel Palms.

[1] *Add. MSS.*, 28058, f. 9.

The next day with 39 horse and 400 foot, Wills advanced to San Estevan de Litera, and on the 25th stoutly assailed the French vanguard, driving them back on their main body. At night Conyngham and the rest of the troops joined Wills. Lieutenant-General D'Asfeld, with nine squadrons and nine battalions, numbering 4500 men, set out to attack Conyngham, who had only 1200 men, of whom 800 were English and the rest Dutch. There were no Spaniards on either side. At 8 a.m. sharp fighting began. Brigadier-General Polastron drove back two companies of marines with his overwhelming force till Major Burston of Wills's brought up the supports, charging and repelling the French. Fierce fighting ensued, and Conyngham, in spite of his inferiority of numbers, held his ground. At length he was wounded and carried off the field, Wills assuming command. After a desperate struggle of seven hours, at three D'Asfeld withdrew his men to Fons. Wills remained two hours longer on the field, and then retired to Balaguer. The French lost 400 killed or wounded. Our loss was 150 men, besides several officers, among whom were Palms and Burston, who were both severely wounded. On the third day after the fight Conyngham died at Balaguer, leaving behind him as his legacy to the regiment he raised the memory of a life devoted to King and Country. At the Battles of the Boyne and of Aughrim he had taken his part in the defeat of the schemes of Louis XIV. Not a few remember these battles simply as among the many contests fought in Ireland, but to Conyngham they were far more than that. To him they were part of the eternal struggle mankind has to wage against tyranny. "The price of liberty is eternal vigilance," so wrote John Stuart Mill. That price Henry Conyngham was content to pay. Some of it he paid on the soil of Ireland and the rest of it on the soil of the Peninsula. To him all the time, as to his master William III, the figure of Louis XIV was never absent from his thoughts. He must be defeated, be the struggle long or short.

Did Peterborough regret the fashion in which he had vilified his second in command? There is not a sign he did. We hardly like to record the fact that after the fight at Tamarite, Peterborough, on being called to account for heavy deficiencies in money, promptly suggested that Conyngham's estate should bear the charge.

APPENDIX

1707–14.

MAJOR-GEN. R. KILLIGREW'S REGIMENT OF DRAGOONS.

James Johnson to be Qr.-Mr. to Major-Gen. Killigrew's Troop	Valencia,	Mar. 9,	1707
Brig.-Gen. Pepper to be Col. *vice* Robt. Killigrew	Xativa,	Apr. 15,	1707
Andrew Nesbitt to be Capt. of Major-Gen. Killigrew's Troop	,,	,,	,,
James Norris to be Lieut. to Capt. Adam Bellamy	,,	,,	,,
Francis Godfrey to be Cornet to Major John Upton	,,	,,	,,
Andrew Knox to be Capt.-Lieut.	,,	,,	,,
Richard Stedman to be Lieut. to Capt. Wm. Mathews	,,	,,	,,
William Berkeley to be Cornet to Brigadier Pepper's Troop	,,	,,	,,
John Dedier to be Surgeon	Las Borges,	Nov. 1,	1707
Stephen du Casse to be Lieut. to Lt.-Col. Stewart	Camp at Vals, June 13, 1708[1]		
Thomas Erle to be Major	Barcelona,	Dec. 24,	,,
Andrew Knox to be Capt. *vice* Major John Lastangues	,,	Jan. 20,	1709
Major Lastangues was a Capt. in the Regt. in 1708.			
John Stanhope to be Capt.-Lieut.	,,	,,	,,
Major John Upton to be Lieut.-Col.	St. James's,	Apr. 12,	,,
John Upton was a Major in the Regt. in 1707 and remained so till April 12, 1709, when he was promoted.			
Thomas Pitt to be Capt. of Lt.-Col. Stewart's late Troop	,,	,,	,,

[1] The above ten commissions were signed by Lord Galway.

Thomas Gleinham to be Capt. *vice* Wm. Mathews		June 6,	1709
William Wolseley to be Cornet to Capt. Andrew Nesbitt	London,	Feb. 15,	1710
Sir Richard Vernon to be Lieut.-Col. ..	,,	Feb. 23,	,,
Thomas Erle to be Capt. of Andrew Nesbitt's late Troop	Saragossa,	Aug. 9,	,,
Robert Stevenson to be Cornet to Capt. Wm. Cosby	Madrid,	Oct. 24,	,,
James Pelham to be Capt. *vice* Wm. Cosby	St. James's,	Mar. 7,	1711
William Cleland to be Capt. *vice* Gleinham	,,	Jan. 23,	1712
John Knox to be Lieut. to Capt. ——— *vice* Jas. Norris	Dublin,	Sept. 17,	1713
James Norris to be Capt.-Lieut. *vice* John Stanhope	,,	,,	,,
John Pitt to be Capt. *vice* Peter Lamaison	,,	Mar. 1,	1714[1]

[1] Dalton, VI, pp. 40–1.

Richard St George Esqr Major General in
his Majesty KING GEORGE the IId Forces

LIEUT.-GENERAL RICHARD ST. GEORGE.

CHAPTER III

The Resistance to Louis XIV's Domination

ON the 26th of January, 1706, Robert Killigrew was appointed to the vacant command of the Eighth. A highly capable officer, he rose to the command of the Royal Dragoons. He served under William III in Ireland and Flanders and during the campaigns of 1702 and 1703 in the Netherlands under the Duke of Marlborough; and in 1704 and the early part of 1705 under the Earl of Galway. Accompanying the Earl of Peterborough to Catalonia, he served at the siege of Barcelona and also took part in the brilliant enterprise in Valencia. The Dragoons were no longer Conyngham's; they were to be for little more than a year Killigrew's. Other commanding officers to come from Marlborough's army were Phineas Bowles, Richard Munden, Sir Robert Rich, Charles Cathcart, Sir Adolphus Oughton, Clement Neville, and Richard St. George. The Marlborough tradition was to understand the soldier. Our greatest commander, as Sir John Fortescue justly observes, took care to feed the soldier well, to pay him regularly, to give him plenty of work, and to keep him under the strictest discipline; and with all this he cherished a genial feeling for the men, which showed itself not only in strict injunctions to watch over their comfort, but in acts of personal kindness kindly bestowed.[1] His soldiers, like Wellington's, were for the most part the scum of the nation. Yet they not only marched and fought with a steadiness beyond all praise, but actually became reformed characters, and left the army, sober, self-respecting men. It is not the least part of the good fortune of the traditions of the Eighth that among its commanding officers have been eight men who grafted on to the Ulster tradition the Marlborough tradition of discipline and of good firing. The new and improved musket,[2] which carried

[1] Fortescue, I, p. 590.
[2] *H.O.M.E.B.*, October 14, 1704; *Commons' Journals*, March 19, 1707.

125

bullets sixteen to the pound, as compared with the French weapon, which carried bullets of twenty-four to the pound, combined with the superiority of discipline, rendered the fire of the British incomparably more deadly than that of the French. Busy as the Duke of Marlborough was, he found time to put the whole army through its platoon-exercise by signal of flag and drum before his own eye. Tactically too our side possessed the advantage, for we fired by platoons according to the system devised by Gustavus Adolphus, whereas the French fired by ranks. If there was no musketry school at Hythe in those days, there was a commander who keenly appreciated the advantages of deadly fire. What the army of Marlborough learnt, in turn the Eighth learnt, and for this teaching they owe much to such commanding officers as the eight imbued with the Marlborough tradition.

The garrison of Lerida was composed of the Eighth Dragoons, the 30th and 34th Foot, with two Dutch and two Neapolitan battalions. Summoning it to his assistance, Peterborough, with a reinforcement of Spaniards, resumed the pursuit of Las Torres. At Alcalá de Chisvert he had a brush with the vanguard of Las Torres, sending it flying twenty leagues backward. Galloping with an insignificant escort he reached Nules, where the Spanish commander had left arms sufficient to equip a thousand of the townsmen. Riding up to the gate with his handful of dragoons, Peterborough offered the town six minutes for capitulation. The inhabitants opened fire. In a rage Peterborough ordered them to send out a priest or a magistrate instantly, on pain of having their walls battered down and of being themselves put to the sword. Priests, familiar with Peterborough's ways, appeared. "I give you six minutes;" so the General informed them, "open your gates or I will not spare a soul of you." This game of bluff was not called, and the gates were opened. In rode Peterborough at the head of his tattered dragoons, demanding immediate provision of rations and forage for several thousand men. The news soon reached Las Torres, who for the third time found that an imaginary enemy had beaten him. In life the fictions of history are quite as important as its facts, and Peterborough found—for a time, at least—that imaginary troops served his purpose just as well as real ones.

Nules fell in January, 1706, and on the 30th of this month John Hepburn told Secretary Hedges that "My Lord Peterborows prudence and Conduct is admir'd and lov'd by all men especially by the Spaniards, we have had a severe conflict with the Enemie at Lerida, where the Enemie was soundly bate tho double our number. We lost in that action Lovtennant Grãll Cunningham, and severall other officers."[1]   From Valencia on the 22nd of February, 1706, Peterborough wrote:

I wish the news of her Majesties Troops entering into Valentia were of as much consequence to the affaires of Spain, as I think it is honarable for her Matys. Arms.   I hope we have done our duty every where, but if not soon relieved (having to this hower wanted all necessaries) you will soon find a fatall conclusion of this hitherto happy Enterprise, for to have received All this while neither reinforcement of men, nor the supply of a Farthing from England is very hard, not so much as a letter this fower month from any part of the world, I have made the uttmost efforts a man could make but longer there is no resisting above Twenty thousand men.   I have carryed a handfull of men pretty far into Spain, and uninterrupted by German ministers.   I could have carried them to Madrid with the least assistance, I am in the proper place to receive succours, and if we must perish here for want of them, I hope my manner of getting hither will show the world, I should have made a good use of the Troops if I had had a competent force, it is surprising they doe nothing of (off) the side of Portugall the Ennemy having no Troops on that Frontier.   I have given so large an account to Ld. Godolphin that the repetition to your self is unnecessary.   I hope you have had an Easy Session, and that ye. divertion we have made here however we suffer makes the game more easy in other places.[2]

The question of unity of command is invariably a difficult one with Allied armies.   Prince Eugene put the point when he informed Marlborough, "I do not think Alexander the Great would have conquered the world at so early an age if he had had to contend with the Dutch deputies."   For Dutch deputies in the

---

[1] *S.P., Foreign, Spain*, Vol. 229.   [2] *S.P., Foreign, Spain*, Vol. 76.

case of the Peninsula campaign we can substitute Portuguese. There was an allied army in Catalonia under Peterborough and there was an allied army in Portugal under Galway. In the Peninsula, and even in England, they were treated, for administrative purposes, as two distinct and separate establishments. Nor did the fault lie with either Peterborough or Galway. The Portuguese were afraid to move any distance from their frontier, and hence Galway was hampered. Charles III ever watched the passes through which the French might advance on Catalonia, and hence Peterborough was hampered, at least so far as he ever allowed anyone, King or General, to hamper him.

Recovering from his astonishment at the three stratagems practised on him by Peterborough, Las Torres crossed the northern frontier of Valencia, capturing Montroi and Morella, and advancing to San Mateo, defended by Colonel Jones. Jones secretly sent messengers to Killigrew, requesting relief. As Las Torres was vigorously attacking San Mateo, news reached Jones that a relieving column was on its way from Tortosa. This column of Killigrew's consisted of 470 horse, 1100 foot, and 500 Valencian Miquelets, with artillery. By a fresh and scarcely creditable stratagem, Peterborough marched into Valencia without firing a shot. After the relief of San Mateo, he and Killigrew proceeded with a portion of their horse to Castillon. Las Torres executed a forced night march to secure precious passes.

On the 10th of March, 1706, Admiral-General Lord Peterborough issued the following proclamation to the Admiral:

> Whereas it is of ye. highest Importance for ye service that ye. Men, Mony, Ammunition and Artillery on board of ye. Fleet[1] be landed in this Kingdome of Valencia where I am in person at ye. head of a good body of Troops and in very favourable Circumstances if joyned by a fresh Body of Men to March towards Madrid. You are hereby required and directed to come with ye. ships under your command at a distance off this place[2] sending ye. light frigate and ye. Smaller Imbarcations nearer to ye. shore with ye. Men and other things to be disimbarqued, having Barks and boats ready to make all imaginable

---

[1] The Fleet was close to Barcelona.   [2] Valencia.

Dispatch, but if it be dangerous in this place you must make for Denia or Altea and make your landing there sending me an Express of your Arrival at either of ye. said places, that I may repair thither with a body of Horse to joine them.   And whereas there is at present a French Squadron of Twenty sayle in Barcelona Road, ye. great ships may proceed thither, ye. opportunity being very favourable to Destroy ye. said Squadron if you can surprise and bear down upon them in ye. Night.[1]

The next day Brigadier Stanhope told Mr. Secretary Hedges that "we are informed by captain Cavendish, who left Denia but twelve days agoe, that My Ld. (Peterborough) continued at Valencia in a prosperous condition.   We have had the misfortune of loosing two Major-Generals in the Countrey, the one Mr. Cunnyngham, killed in an action near Lerida where he commanded, and gott a considerable advantage over 3000 of the Ennemies with 1200 of our men, the other Mr Schratenbach who commanded the Dutch forces there and was a very deserving man."[2]

Conyngham had spent himself in the effort to prevent the French swooping down on Barcelona.   Its capture had irritated and alarmed Philip and his grandfather, Louis XIV.   The French King determined to recover it, and at the beginning of April, 1706, Marshal de Tessé appeared before it with twenty-five thousand men.   Its governor was Count Uhlfeldt, and he had a garrison of 3600 regulars, including a dismounted detachment of Killigrew's dragoons.   Wills had sent the last from Lerida to join Prince Henry, who, knowing Uhlfeldt's wish for English troops, had embarked the dragoons at Mataro.   The French pursued their siege works steadily, and on the 4th of April the Capuchin convent of Montjuich was captured.   On the 13th General de la Para, the chief French engineer, cannonaded the Fort of Montjuich, which since the former siege Colonel Petit had powerfully strengthened.   On the 21st Killigrew, with 600 English and Spanish dragoons, arrived from Valencia.   Peterborough overtook Killigrew, and on his arrival the commander infused fresh courage into the besieged.   In the meantime a Council of War of Flag Officers and Captains had been held on board H.M.S. *Ranelagh*

[1] *Add. MSS.*, 28058, fo. 13.   [2] *S.P., Foreign, Spain*, Vol. 76.

at Gibraltar on the 6th of April. There "it was unanimously resolved and agreed to proceed to Altea, and if they got certain intelligence there that the enemy had no more than 27 sail before Barcelona, to proceed there and give them battle, but otherwise to proceed as determined by another Council of War."[1]   The relieving squadron under Admiral Leake set sail, and with their arrival the siege was raised.   On the first day of the French retreat there was a total eclipse of the sun lasting two hours.   As Louis XIV was Le Roi Soleil, the allied army naturally concluded that the sun of France was destined to undergo a complete eclipse.   During the siege and retreat the French lost 6000 men, and they left behind them 129 guns and mortars, 5000 barrels of gunpowder, much ammunition, 8000 trenching implements, 16,000 sacks of meal, 6000 bags of oats, much rye and wheat, 10,000 pairs of shoes, and other valuable stores.   In London men then set the relief of Barcelona alongside the glorious victory of Ramillies, and both triumphs furnished the reason for ordering a day of general thanksgiving.[2]

On the 30th of April, 1706, Captain F. Butler wrote to his relative, the Duke of Ormonde :

I hope your Grace received mine from Lisbon, whence we sailed for the Mediterranean with six men-of-war and our Irish forces on the 9th of April, and on the 22nd joined Sir John Leake abreast Altea, as Sir George Bynge had done a little before.   We then made a line of battle of fifty good ships and so stood with all the possible speed (we) could make to the relief of Barcelona and anchored in the road of it the 27th, but to our great surprise we found that Fort Mountjoy[3] had been taken and demolished fifteen days before, in which action my Lord Donegal was killed.   The enemy had so good intelligence of our fleets being near them that they got away the night before and had we not been so very much becalmed they had been secure enough from ever having made so lucky an escape.   The town lay under very great extremity and the King was got into a boat to preserve his person, the enemy

[1] *S.P., Foreign, Portugal*, Vol. 19.

[2] *S.P., Foreign, Spain* (1700–13), pp. 132, 133, 134.   *Cf.* Marlborough's letter, June 17.

[3] This form would recall Derry to an Irishman like Butler.

having brought their works quite up to the foot of the bastion, and so securely too that they could not be seen in their trenches and keep a continual fire from six several places.   Abundance of bombs flies into the town, which they had certainly carried in two days had we not come so timely to their assistance, for their people being few were worn off by extra duty and killed by the enemy, but now we think we are ten thousand strong, besides inhabitants within the walls, and every night brings about some effect or other, and there comes into us ten, fifteen or twenty deserters every night, and they say that the Duke of Anjou looks very sorrowful upon it, and though he is computed to have about fifteen thousand men, yet in all likelihood he has besieged himself, not being able to look round him anywhere but he has in view a sad presage of ruin, for there is not above four days' provisions in his camp, and he is surrounded on the side of the country with about forty thousand Miquelets, who are resolved to revenge the cruelty the French has treated them with in their coming hither.   The only deliverance they expect is taking the town and by battering the walls to enter, which if they attempt they will meet with a very warm reception, for our people has raised inward works and are ready to cut them in pieces if they dare venture it, and all things look very promising with success of their getting any point of us as matters stand to-day, and this is the account our present case affords, all which must have an end in a very short time.[1]

Butler's letter of the 1st of May is not a whit behind his first one in giving us the point of view of an Irishman.

Since my sending up the enclosed of yesterday's date it is with inexpressible joy that I am to add the following account.   This morning at three o'clock the enemy went off in a most confused manner, leaving behind them 27 mortars, 140 brass cannon, 40,000 cannon balls, 5000 barrels of powder, with shells of all sorts to a great number, pickaxes and spades near 10,000, with a great store of habiliments of war, meal in sacks for 12,000 men for eight months and great quantities of provisions and answerable thereto, three large hospitals of sick and wounded said to be about 5000, and the enemy is pursued by most of the Miquelets of the country, from whence we expect a miserable account of such an army as is gone off in mutiny and disorder, and all this is done without their offering battle or one attack to the town, though governed by

---

[1] *Hist. MSS. Com. Reports, Ormonde MSS.*, VIII, p. 233.

Duke Anjou, Marshal de Tessé and their mighty general Noales.[1] At the time of my writing this we believe the enemy takes the nearest way into Provence, but attacked all the way and must suffer. Count de Tessé writ to my Lord Peterborough in these words, that the glory of the day was his, that the French fleet was gone and the English gained the victory, but prayed his Lordship to use humanity and kindness to preserve the sick and wounded, on which my Lord ordered a guard for their security, but before their coming thither it is said the Miquelets had destroyed some of them. Abundance of things is to be said of our glorious victory which I cannot comprise here, but expect the whole monarchy is and will be in a short time devoted to King Charles. We are all in a good condition and hope this will not be the last stroke we shall give them this summer.

This account I took at the King's palace as the very same he had himself at that time, and if you will please to receive it at second hand from me it will be the greatest obligation to him who is . . .[2]

At bottom the rivalry between France and the Holy Roman Empire turned round the command of the Mediterranean, and the raising of the siege of Barcelona proved a step towards the consolidation of the power of Charles III. During the eighteenth century the aim of France was to transform the Mediterranean into a French sea. This meant during the War of the Spanish Succession that the English should keep a fleet in the Mediterranean, and it also meant the possession of Majorca or some other Spanish port where the fleet could winter. A spacious inlet like Port Mahon was, from this point of view, eminently desirable. Nor can we ignore the fact, weighing much in Peterborough's eyes, that the inhabitants of Majorca were fervent haters of France and Castile, and accordingly were prepared to support Charles III, if not for liking of him, at any rate for dislike of his adversary. For our generalissimo realised acutely that if Charles III defeated Spanish armies they were not thereby conquering Spain—if there was no control of the sea. With such thoughts in his mind Admiral-General Peterborough, always sensible of the importance of cavalry in Spain, had purchased some hundreds of serviceable horses at

---

[1] Noailles.   [2] *Hist. MSS. Com. Reports, Ormonde MSS.*, VIII, p. 234.

ten pounds a head.   On the 8th of June, 1706, he wrote to General Wyndham : "I am seeking mules for them (*i.e.* Alnutt and South-well) and providing horses for Killigrew ; as soon as he can march, I will send him towards Requena ; when three troops are horsed they shall march."   On the 23rd of June, O.S., Wyndham wrote to his superior officer : "As for the marching of the troops forward, I am as much for it as your Lordship can be, but the two Irish regiments have no mules, so that they can carry neither tents or baggage along with them, for all the mules they brought hither were sent back again."[1]

In a letter of the 13th of June, 1706, Peterborough hinted to Charles III some of the considerations in his mind :

> I see very well the importance of Aragon.   It would be a very good one if we had the necessary troops and money ; . . . Besides, I must tell your Majesty that our men, especially the new comers, are most of them sick and in hospitals, that they will not be able to bear the marches through the burning mountains which they must pass to Aragon, it is impossible for the infantry, and your Majesty has not reflected upon the condition of the horse, which has marched from Valencia to Catalonia and from Barcelona back to Valencia ; the regiment of Conyngham has not above 40 horses that can move. . . .
>
> As for the disposal of your royal person, I can only say that Valencia and Saragossa are rivals, and that I believe both desire your presence passionately, . . .
>
> But Sir, for God's sake seek the way to Madrid by all means possible, and do me the honour to believe me, when I tell your Majesty, that the Allies cannot support this war, and that your Majesty will see extraordinary orders, if we do not push the present opportunity. . . .[2]

The hints to the King of Spain are openly avowed in Peter-borough's letter of the 18th of June, 1706, to the Count de Noyelles, his general :

> I gave him (*i.e.* Charles III) a hint, which I hope you will improve, if his Catholic Majesty should come to you, which was, that he might perhaps oblige both nations and not ruin our affairs, if he made no

---

[1] *Printed Calendar of MSS. of the House of Lords*, Vol. VII, New Series, No. 2426, p. 498.

[2] *Printed Calendar of MSS. of the House of Lords*, Vol. VII, New Series, No. 2426, p. 472.

stay in Aragon, but came with the horse directly towards Requena, which we must possess before we can carry the King into Castile. . . .

The King might direct them (*i.e.* the Portuguese) to send some of their horse and dragoons towards Valencia.   You know the wretched condition of mine, and that 1000 are diverted which were allotted me by the council of war ; the least assistance of this kind from them, who had no fatigue, would make it safe for the King to go for Madrid immediately, and not stay till I can put my foot in condition, and marching so with the horse is an excuse for want of a splendid equipage, which they amuse themselves with preparing, instead of securing a Crown.[1]

With Madrid and the advance through Valencia in his schemes, Peterborough sent his movable column of 1500 men, under General Wyndham, consisting of three regiments of foot and one of dragoons, to besiege the small fortress of Requena, thirty miles off, on the road to Madrid.   Wyndham, as he advanced, took Cuenca ; Gorges marched against Alicante ; Alnutt invaded Murcia ; while the commander-in-chief kept Killigrew with five regiments at Valencia.   Alnutt had his own foot and a detachment of Killigrew's Dragoons, and Killigrew had his own Dragoons and the Royal Dragoons.   On the 17th of July Peterborough informed General Wyndham :

So fatally averse to his own interest his advisers have made the King, that not only he is not to be persuaded to come by Valencia to Madrid, he not only sends his troops directly out of the way, but uses his utmost endeavours to make me incapable of serving him, and the mortal sin that I can commit is to go towards Madrid.   Towards which end, he has sent solemn orders that a solemn council of war should be held, in order to consider the speedy seizing the islands of Majorca and Minorca, and this represented as a service of the highest importance, and any troops to be sent from hence towards Madrid as unnecessary ; and all the insinuations given that, if I enter into any such resolutions, it is only an impatience I have to go to Madrid before the King, either for vanity or diversion.   This is a very agreeable circumstance, and a grateful acknowledgment of all my fatigues and services.   However,

---

[1] *Printed Calendar of MSS. of the House of Lords*, Vol. VII, No. 2426, p. 474.

Sir, I shall do what I can to save him, to the best of my power, and to prevent all ill consequences of such mistaken measures. I have taken the utmost precautions and with the advices of a council of war and the viceroy, have resolved to march towards Madrid.[1]

Troops are composed of flesh and blood, and the men felt the hardships of the continual marching. On the 22nd of July, O.S., Wyndham told Peterborough that "I arrived here (at Campiglio) this day with the three battalions, your Lordship's troops and Killigrew's dragoons, who are all so very much fatigued, that I must be necessitated to halt here tomorrow for their refreshment. . . . The weather is so excessive hot, that our foot drop down dead on their march . . . the three battalions do not make above 300 men."

On the capture of Alicante by Gorges, he, with Killigrew's Dragoons and a strong column of English foot, marched to Origuela and occupied it. Then he entered Murcia with the intention of surprising its capital. When within eight miles of Murcia, Gorges discovered that a division of Berwick's army was advancing to cut him off from Alicante. On his retirement he left a force under Colonel Bowles with no artillery at Elche, the Illici of the Romans. This force consisted of 300 English foot, 150 of Killigrew's Dragoons, and 900 armed peasants. On the 21st of October Geoffreville, with 5000 French and Spaniards, appeared before Elche. Alnutt's men had left Carthagena and joined Gorges's main body. With no hope of succour Bowles held out for two days, making brisk use of his musketry. It was all, however, of no avail, and on the 23rd he and his troops became prisoners. Peterborough had been discouraged by the turn events had taken, and had bethought himself of an old plan of setting out for Genoa, for a descent upon a Mediterranean port exercised a lively attraction over his nature, ever eager to seize any opportunity.

We have spent space over the eventful year of 1706, the year of Ramillies, and yet as we survey its accomplishments we endorse Sir John Fortescue's verdict, "memorable for two of the most brilliant, even if in some respects disappointing, campaigns ever

---

[1] *Printed Calendar of MSS. of the House of Lords*, Vol. VII, No. 2426.

fought simultaneously by two British generals."[1]   This year marks the turning of the tide against Charles III.   He was painfully learning that to proclaim himself a king was not equivalent to the detachment of the Spanish people from the crown of their choice. As in the days of Wellington, the nation rose in guerilla bands, but against the allies, not for them.   Madrid had been occupied, and it had to be abandoned, and on the approach of winter Leake was forced to retire from Lisbon.   Shovell did not reach the Tagus till January, 1707, when he at once hurried on and landed seven thousand men for Peterborough.   Marlborough thought that nothing could save Spain but an offensive movement against France from the side of Italy, and this lay at the back of Peterborough's mind when he set out for Genoa.   He was overruled, and relieved of his command.   Galway, who succeeded Peterborough, decided first to destroy Berwick's magazines in Murcia, and then to march northward up the valley of the Guadalquivir into Arragon.   When he turned the head of the Tagus, his plan then was to descend along its basin to Madrid.

On the 7th of March, 1707, we are fortunate to possess the reports of Joseph Fredenham and Arthur Moore, Comptrollers of Army Account, who submit one on the clothing of Killigrew's Dragoons to the Duke of Marlborough:

In Obedience to your Graces Commands signifyed to Us by Lre. from Mr. St. John upon a Memorial presented to your Grace by Lieut. Colonel Pepper of Brigadr. Killigrews Regiment of Dragoons Complaining of the badness of the Cloathing provided here for the said Regimt. and that no provisions is made of Saddles, Cloaks and Swords, which are Entirely wanting, altho' the OffReckonings of the Regimt. are upon the best footing And thereupon directing Us to examine into the matter of this Complaint, and whether the said Cloathing is in quantity and Quality answerable to the State of the Offreckonings of the said Regiment the nature of the Service they are employ'd in, and what is fitting for the Souldiers, and Report the same to your Grace.

We humbly acquaint your Grace, That having conferred wth. Lt. Coll. Pepper, and with Mr Wilk's the Agent and Capt. Man the former

[1] Fortescue, I, p. 486.

Agent and others, And having Caused the contract and other papers relating to the Cloathing complained of to be laid before Us, as also the Paterns seald only by Brigadr. Killigrews Brother who was authorized to provide the said Cloathing, and having View'd most of the particulars of the Cloathing it self, We find that the said Cloathing was provided by Contract dated to Novr. 1706 for the sum of £3483 17s. od. payable out of the OffReckonings of the said Regiment to Commence from the 24th of December 1706.   That though many particulars of the said Cloathing might have been excepted against as to their quality, yet the Lieut. Collo. not insisting thereon by reason they were actually provided, but desiring they might be made up to their full Complement, in regard the Regiment being lately taken prisoners wented all manner of Cloaths and Accoutrements.

We have Considered the State of the Offreckonings of the sd. Regiment and find the last Assignmt. made by Major Generall Cunningham for £1500 expired the 27th July last.

We also find an Assignmt. made by Brigadr. Killigrew to his Brother for £710 15s. od. dated 19 Septemr. last mentioned to be for severall necessary Clathings and Accoutrements provided by ye. said Brigadr. payable out of ye. OffReckonings after the Assignments made by the late Majr. Genll. Cunningham who had the Regiment before, But there being no particulars mentioned of what is so alledged to have been provided, And the Act of Parliament directing the Paymasters not to Comply wth. any Assignment but for Cloaths deliver'd.   We conceive the said £710 15s. od. ought not to be charged on the OffReckonings till it shall appear to have been for Cloaths deliver'd.   And the rather for that both Lieut. Collo. Pepper and Captain Man the late Agent say, That no Cloths or Accoutrements has been provided for that Regiment since the above mentioned Assignmt. from Majr. Genll. Cunningham nor is any Satisfaction as yet given Us what Clothes or Accourtrments were provided for the Regimt. for those OffReckonings.

We have hereunto Annexed a Schedule of a full Cloathing and Accoutremts. for the Regimt. which wee are humbly of Opinion ought to be provided and sent away and that the Offreckonings from the 27th July last to the 24d. of Decemr. and from thence for Two years will be sufficient to pay for the said Cloathing And if it shall hereafter Apeare that Brigadr. Killigrew hath provided any of the said Cloathing and

Accoutrements That he be paid for the same out of the future Off-Reckonings, But that a like quantity of such Cloathing and Accoutrements be Reserved and kept in store for the future Cloathing of the Regiment.[1]

Most of these documents have lost their schedules, but this schedule is still in the Record Office, London.   It is a schedule of clothing and accoutrements wanting to make up the full complement for the regiment in Spain on the 3rd of March, 1707, over and above what is included in the contract of the 6th of November, 1706.

Provided.	Wanting.	Full No.	12 SERGEANTS.
12		12	Coats of Crimson Cloth in grain, Sleeves and Flaps laced with gold lace
12		12	Waistcoats) the same colour as the Lining of
12		12	Pair of Breeches) the Coats
	12	12	Cloaks
12		12	Hats laced with gold lace
12		12	Pair of Gloves
12		12	Pair of Boots and Spurs and Spur Leathers
12		12	Sets of Belts, Carbine belts or broad Cross belts for Muskets, and Waist-belts large and strong, to carry basket hilted Swords, with Cartridge Box belts laced.
	12	12	Cartouch Boxes or Pouches
12		12	Housings and Holster Straps Embroidered
12		12	Pair of Holsters with Straps
12		12	Buckets with Straps
12		12	Horse Furniture, as Headstalls, Reins, Breast plates and Cruppers, Bits, Bosses and Collars and Cloak Straps
	12	12	Saddles with Straps, Girths, Stirrup leather and Irons
	12	12	Spit Socket Bayonets to serve over a large full bored Musket, and the longest size Bayonet
			Pair of White Worsted Stockings to roll
	24	24	Shirts and as many Cravats
	12	12	Baskets Hilted highland Scotch broad Swords.

[1] *Audit Office*, 17/28, p. 150.   See the reference to the clothing of the regiment in 1707 in *The Society of Army Historical Research Journal*, Vol. I, p. 262.

Provided.	Wanting.	Full No.	
			18 CORPORALS.
18		18	Coats, Flaps and Sleeves with a Narrow gold Orrace
18		18	Waistcoats and Breeches
	18	18	Cloaks
18		18	Hats laced with Gold Orrace
18		18	Pair of Gloves
18		18	Pair of Boots, Spur and Spur Leathers
18		18	Sets of Belts as before
	18	18	Cartouch Boxes or Pouches
18		18	Housings and Holster Caps embroidered
			Pair of holsters with straps and as many buckets with straps
18		18	Horse furniture as before
	18	18	Saddles with Straps, Girths, Stirrup leathers and Irons
	18	18	Spit Socket Bayonets as before
18	18	36	Pair of Stockings
	36	36	Shirts and 36 Cravats
	18	18	Basket Hilted Swords as before.
			12 DRUMS.
12		12	Coats laced
12		12	Waistcoats and Breeches
12		12	Hats laced with gold Orrace
12		12	Pair of Gloves
12		12	Pair of Boots and Spurs and Spur Leathers
12		12	Drum Slings or Carriage and Waist belts laced
	12	12	Horse furniture as before
	12	12	Saddles with Straps, Girths, Stirrup leathers and Irons
	12	12	Swords
12	12	24	Pair of Stockings
	24	24	Shirts and 24 Cravats.
			4 HAUTBOYS.
4		4	Coats for Liveries laced as the Sergeants
4		4	Waistcoats and breeches
4		4	Hats

4 Hautboys—*continued.*

Provided.	Wanting.	Full No.	
4		4	Pair of Gloves
4		4	Pair of Boots, Spurs and Spur Leathers
4		4	Waistbelts suitable to the Coats laced as the Sergeants
	4	4	Horse furniture as before
	4	4	Saddles with straps, Girths, Stirrup leathers and Irons
	4	4	Swords
4	4	8	Pair of Stockings
	8	8	Shirts
	8	8	Cravats.

306 PRIVATE DRAGOONS.

Provided.	Wanting.	Full No.	
306		306	Coats, Waistcoats and breeches
100	206	306	Cloaks
306		306	Hats laced
306		306	Pair of Gloves
306		306	Pair of Boots, with Spurs and Spur leathers
100	206	306	Sets of belts, Carbine belts, or broad Crossbelts for Muskets and Waist belts, large and strong to carry Basket Hilted Swords, with Cartridge Box belts laced
100	206	306	Cartouch Boxes or Pouches
306		306	Slings for Pouches
306		306	Housings and Holster Caps
216	90	306	Holsters with Straps
306		306	Buckets and Straps
306		306	Horse Furniture as Headstalls, Reins, Breastplates and Cruppers, Bits, Bosses, Collars, and Cloak Straps
50	256	306	Saddles with Shirts and Furniture with Straps with Girths, Stirrup leathers and Irons
100	206	306	Spit Socket Bayonets, to serve over a large full bored Musket and the longest sized Bayonet

Provided.	Wanting.	Full No.	
			306 Private Dragoons—*continued*
100	206	306	Basket Hilted Highland Scotch broad Swords
306	306	612	Pair of Stockings
	612	612	Shirts
	612	612	Cravats

For a Second Mounting.

4		4	Hautboys' Suits
348		348	Hats for large Sergeants, Corporals, Drums and private men
348		348	Pair of Gloves for Ditto
348		348	Collars for Horses
	348	348	Shirts for large Sergeants, Corporals, Drums, and private men
	348	348	Cravats for ditto
	348	348	Stockings.[1]

Napoleon and Wellington declared that whatever they might know about warfare, they both knew at least how to boot, spur and feed their men. We may take booting and spurring in the larger sense, and we may accordingly contend that when Marlborough asked for precise information of the state of the clothing of the Eighth, he was also asking for men drilled and disciplined. Nor is any detail of uniform without value in the early days of the history of a regiment. The *esprit de corps* of the dragoons came from their common memories of dangers sustained at Enniskillen and Derry, the Battles of the Boyne and Aughrim, and the Siege of Limerick. It was but right that men with such a roll of battle honours already should be fitly clothed. Their total strength in 1707 was 443 officers and men.

On the 10th of April, 1707, Galway crossed the Murcian frontier, and laid siege to Villena. In the meantime Berwick gathered his army, marching towards Almanza. Before gaining possession of Madrid, it was clear that an action must be fought by Galway,

---

[1] *Audit Office*, 17/28, p. 152.

with his 15,500 men, with Berwick and his 25,400. It is curious to note that a Frenchman commanded the English army and an Englishman commanded the French army. Galway had more than one half of poor Portuguese levies, while not quite one third were English. Berwick had nearly one half of French and the remainder Spanish. There were only 51 of Killigrew's Dragoons present, for no less than 150 of them had been captured at Elche. The rest of the regiment was sick, absent on duty with different posts, and the like. Brigadier-Generals Killigrew and Carpenter led brigades of dragoons. The cavalry present at the Battle of Almanza were :

	Squad.
Harvey's Horse	2
Killigrew's Dragoons	1
Col. E. Pearce's ,, ...	2
Col. Green's ,, ...	2
Carpenter's ,, ...	1
Essex's ,, ...	1
French Regiment	1

Another list differs from this by adding Peterborough's Dragoons with two squadrons and omitting Colonel Green's with two squadrons.[1] There were, according to the divergent lists, ten squadrons of cavalry at the battle. In Catalonia and other parts of Spain there were :

	Batt.	Squad.
Royal Dragoons		2
Royal Regiment of Fusiliers ..	1	
Hotham	1	
Sibourg	1	
Blosset	1	
Elliot	1	
Watkins	1	
	6	2

[1] *S.P., Foreign, Spain*, Vol. 230, Part I.

THE FOOT AT THE BATTLE.

					Batt.
Guards	..	..	..	..	1
Portmore	..	..	..	..	1
Southwell	..	..	..	..	1
Stewart	..	..	..	..	1
Hill ..	..	..	..	..	1
Blood ..	..	..	..	..	1
Mountjoy	..	..	..	..	1
Alnutt ..	..	..	..	..	1
Gorges ..	..	..	..	..	1
Mordaunt	..	..	..	..	1
Wade ..	..	..	..	..	1
Bowles ..	..	..	..	..	1
Macartney	..	..	..	..	1
Breton ..	..	..	..	..	1
Mark Kerr	..	..	..	..	1
Nassau..	..	..	..	..	1
					16

If we reckon ten squadrons at 80 men each, we have 800; and if we reckon sixteen battalions at 300 men each we have 4800, with a grand total of English troops of 5600. Besides, 50 men of each of these regiments were on party duty or at the blockade of Montesa. This does not of course include the sick in the various hospitals. True, the whole twelve squadrons according to the establishment would make 150 men in each, but computed at 80 effective men in each, we have 960 horse. Equally true, the whole 22 battalions according to the establishment would make 550 men in each, but computed only at 350 men in each, we have 7700 foot.[1]

When Galway heard of Berwick's advance, he determined to fight. His Portuguese claimed the post of honour on the right

[1] *S.P., Foreign, Spain*, Vol. 230, Part I.

wing, and Galway conceded this claim. Weak in cavalry, he committed the mistake, after the manner of Gustavus Adolphus, of interpolating battalions of foot among his horse. Berwick drew up his army in the usual two lines on a plain to the south of Almanza. At three o'clock in the afternoon of the 25th of April, 1707, Galway opened the attack by leading an advance of the horse on his left wing. The brigade, to which the small squadron of the Eighth was attached, was posted on the left of the line. Sheer weight of numbers overpowered the cavalry, and they were driven back. Our losses were heavy, and four of the cavalry regiments left their commanding officers on the field. Wounded in the first charge, Killigrew continued to fight with all his wonted gallantry, and was killed in the second charge. The British and the Dutch fought with determination, but the Portuguese showed their sense of the honour conferred upon them by galloping off the field. The English foot on the left centre attacked, and drove back the hostile infantry. Berwick then brought up his French, and the infantry fought desperately, but the weight of numbers was too much for them. Galway received two sabre cuts near his right eye, and was forced to retire from the field. In spite of this disaster, Tyrawley, with the horse under Carpenter, Killigrew and Winterfeldt, supported by Wade's foot and Hill's foot, offered a stout resistance to the attacks of Popoli and D'Asfeld. At the end of two hours the allies were thoroughly routed. They lost about four thousand killed and wounded and three thousand prisoners. The fallen English officers comprised one brigadier-general, five colonels, seven lieutenant-colonels, two majors, thirty captains, and forty-three subalterns, or eighty-eight in all. Those taken prisoners were 286, of whom no less than ninety-two were wounded. As a plain matter of fact, the moment the Portuguese galloped off the field, the Battle of Almanza resolved itself into a contest between eight thousand British, Dutch and German against thrice their number of French and Spaniards, in an open plain. Such a contest could not be long in doubt, and there is no disgrace, save for the Portuguese, in our complete defeat. All was lost—save honour. Dormer, Lawrence, and Green, commanding respectively Essex's,

Carpenter's and Peterborough's dragoons, laid down their lives. The order of battle shows the disposition of the forces:

Left
1st line.

Wade's Brigade.

Horse.

Left Wing Only.
Macartney's Brigade.

Two Dutch Brigades.

Right.

Royal Dragoons.
Carpenter's Dragoons
Essex's Dragoons.
Guiscard's Dragoons.

Southwell's Foot.
Wade's Foot.
Killigrew's Dragoons
Peterborough's Dragoons.
Blood's Foot.
Mountjoy's Foot.

Two Regiments of Dutch Horse.
Harvey's Horse.
Four Dutch Regiments of Horse.

Queen's English Guards.
Gorges's Foot.
Macartney's Foot.
Mordaunt's Foot.

2nd Line.

Hill's Brigade.

Breton's Brigade.

Four Squadrons Portuguese Dragoons.

Stewart's Foot.
Alnutt's Foot.
Three Portuguese Squadrons.
Mark Kerr's Foot.

Four Portuguese Squadrons.

Portmore's Foot.
Breton's.
Nassau's,
Bowles's. [1]

Of the 51 men of the Eighth present at Almanza, 31 were killed or taken prisoners, and 20 escaped to Alcira. Among the killed were Brigadier-General Killigrew and Lieutenant Baxter. There is a monument to Killigrew in Westminster Abbey, the Valhalla of the British race. There is also a monument to him left in the traditions of the Eighth. Our regiment had only been fourteen years in existence, and its record is that its first two commanding officers were killed in the battlefield. Carpet knights its officers had never been, for their baptism was baptism by fire. Some of

[1] *Postboy*, June 5–7, 1707.

our dragoons escaped out of captivity, some joined from command, some from sick leave, and accordingly we find eighty-one private dragoons brought into the field, encamping for some time on the banks of the Ebro. Letters of the time have much to say about the Battle of Almanza. On the 17th of April, O.S., Captain Cleland informed the Earl of Mar that "Our foot generallie did well as did part of our cavalrie, the Portugueze, lyke cowards, or as some say they believe without reason lyke traitors, leaveing us the honor to begin and end the action which for the tyme was, as old and experienced people say, one of the hottest ever known."[1] Writing from Tortosa on the 6th of May, O.S., Major Henry Killigrew, with inherited bad spelling, said : "I suppose before this Comes to yr. hands you will hev had the unhappy news of my unkele Roberts death. I shall not Repeat to you the particulars of his behaviour in the action, for that will onely renew yr. sorrow. Lett it suffice that no man there, gave up his Life with greater bravery than he did for the Service of his Country."[2]

The lieutenant-colonel of the Eighth, John Pepper, was appointed colonel of the corps on the 15th of April, 1707. His career had been an honourable one, and we attach but little credence to the letter written on the 13th of May, 1707, by Henry St. John to Robert Harley : "When I heard to-day at the Cockpit that Pepper was the man pitched upon to go express to the King of Spain I imagined you did not know how scandalously he procured this year a commission of brigadier by imposing a false date of his colonel's commission on the Duke of Marlborough. The thing deserved cashiering, and he seems to have a mark of favour conferred upon him."[3] He justified this mark of favour, for in 1710 he attained the rank of major-general, distinguishing himself at the Battle of Almenara and at Saragossa. In the retreat from Madrid he was taken prisoner at Brihuega. After the Peace of Utrecht his regiment was disbanded in Ireland, but George I restored it in 1715. We find Pepper on the 1st of June, 1715,

[1] *Hist. MSS. Com. Reports, MSS. of the Earl of Mar and Kellie. Cf.* the *London Gazette,* May 1–5.
[2] *Add. MSS.,* 20032, f. 37.   [3] *Hist. MSS. Com. Reports, MSS. of the Marquis of Bath.*

Adjutant-General of the forces in Ireland.[1]   In 1715, after the fashion of those times, Pepper sold his commission.[2]   Then he became a member of parliament, holding the posts of Governor of Kinsale and ranger of Epping Forest and of Enfield Chase.[3]   His war services at length told on his constitution, and he withdrew to Montpellier for the benefit of the air, dying there on the 22nd of December, 1725.

In his appointment as commanding officer, Pepper manifested care and consideration in the restoration of the Eighth to its old condition of efficiency.   The men of the regiment taken prisoners at Elche were exchanged.   Recruits and horses arrived from Ireland, while drafts of men and horses were received from Carpenter's (third) and Essex's (fourth) dragoons.   In Spain, in spite of the high prices, horses were bought, and the efforts of the commanding officer, backed by Lieutenant-Colonel Stewart and Major Boyd, restored the Eighth to its former state.   Still, improvement took time, and the muster rolls of November, 1707, attest this in furnishing a return of the British troops in Catalonia :

HORSE.

Harvey's,	now 2nd Dragoon Guards		148	men

CAVALRY.

Royal,	now 1st Royal Dragoons	..	..	320	,,
Carpenter's,	,, 3rd Light ,,	..	..	95	,,
Essex's,	,, 4th ,, ,,	..	..	120	,,
Pepper's,	,, 8th Hussars	..	..	81	,,
Pearce's,	since disbanded	..	..	192	,,
Guiscard's,	,, ,,	..	..	287	,,
Nassau's,	,, ,,	..	..	223	,,
	Total Cavalry	..	..	1466	,,

[1] *S.P., Dom., Entry Book,* 177.

[2] On March 21, 1711, it was laid down that unless an officer had twenty years' service or had been disabled, he could not sell his commission.   The minimum age for officers was then fixed at sixteen.

[3] In 1743 the Earl of Stair remarked on the soldier-member of parliament : "I thought it hard to refuse them leave when they said that their preferment depended on the interest of their friends at court.   They had no notion that it depended on their exertions here" on the battlefield.   The biting sarcasm was amply merited.

Foot.

Portmore's,	now 2nd Queen's Royal	..	..		410	men
Southwell's,	„ 6th Foot ..	..	..	..	411	„
Stewart's,	„ 9th „	..	..	..	386	„
Hill's,	„ 11th „	..	..	..	437	„
Blood's,	„ 17th „	..	..	..	266	„
Blosset's Catalans, Spanish in English pay				..	915	„
Galway's „	„ „	„ „		..	993	„
Saragossa Regiment „	„ „	„		..	424	„
	Total Infantry	..	..		4242	„

Dissatisfied with the course of affairs, Galway pressed upon the home authorities his retirement. He realised how hopeless it was to convert the Spaniards into enthusiastic supporters of Charles III, and he also realised the excellence of Berwick and the men serving under him. No doubt Louis XIV never realised the importance of the sea, yet he always realised the importance of land and of land operations. In reply to such a letter as that of the 11th of December, 1707, in which Galway urged his retirement, the Earl of Sunderland on the 18th of December has much to say about the unsatisfactory nature of the way in which Peterborough had commanded his forces.[1] Inevitably Galway thought such a letter entirely irrelevant.

Colonel Pepper still laboured at his task with the result that when the Eighth took the field in 1708 the Count de Noyelles, the commander-in-chief in Catalonia, cordially commended its condition. A few men of the regiment were left dismounted at Barcelona. During the summer of 1708 the regiment remained encamped at Montblanco and Constantino, occupied in patrolling the mountains and valleys of Catalonia and in taking outpost duty. The question of sea-power still engaged the attention of the allies. The occupation of a Spanish port became increasingly indispensable. Was not Port Mahon, in Minorca, the finest harbour in the whole Mediterranean? Majorca had already tendered its allegiance to Leake, and now an attempt was made on Minorca. Toulon was

---

[1] *S.P., Foreign, Spain*, 77.

the port whence the French could sally forth.   Savoy, in spite of Peterborough, could afford no help with Toulon.   "It remains," concluded Leake, "that you should dispose yourselves to be masters of Port Mahon."[1]

The English force commanded by Stanhope comprised 1000 horse, 800 foot, and a train under Carpenter, Wills and Richards respectively.   With these men he hoped to relieve the fortress of Tortosa, which in May Orleans was about to besiege.   The English troops were Harvey's Horse, the Royal, Pepper's, Nassau's (lately Peterborough's), a few of Guiscard's Dragoons, with Southwell's and Wade's Foot.   The fortress of Tortosa was vigorously assailed, and it surrendered.   The forces set free were accordingly able to turn their attention to Minorca.   Stanhope fitted out an expedition against Minorca, and the dismounted Eighth Dragoons left at Barcelona took part in it.   Leake effected a landing, and before the end of September, 1708, the whole island submitted to Stanhope.   Louis XIV took alarm.   France, stunned by the blows she had received through the genius of Marlborough, was making desperate overtures for peace, even to offering Marlborough four million of livres to secure it on terms that would not absolutely paralyse her in the Mediterranean.   The capture of Minorca was therefore a cause of additional anxiety to the French King.

In 1709 the regiment returned to Catalonia, pitching its tents near the Segre.   In August it forded that stream, taking the fortresses of Balaguer and Ager.   Placing garrisons in these fortresses, it repassed the river, settling down into winter quarters. In a letter of the 8th of July, 1709, we learn that Lieutenant-Colonel Upton received licence of absence for six months in order to enable him to recover his sight, and that Captain Gleinham was already ordered to the seat of war.[2]

In 1710 there were 61 squadrons of Horse and 56 battalions of Foot.   There were 10 squadrons of English Horse and Dragoons,

---

[1] *Life of Leake*, June 22, 1708.

[2] *S.P.*, *Military*, Bundle 3.   On the general situation in 1709, *cf. Colburn's United Service Magazine*, 1866, Part III, p. 517.

including two of Pepper's.   All told, there were 589 officers and
soldiers in our regiment, and their charges for the year were
estimated at £15,868 7s. 6d.   The total cost of 14,311 men was
reckoned at £232,653 12s. 1d. The cost of the Allies, the British, the
Italians, the Germans, and the Portuguese, was £927,778 0s. 11½d.
The number of Italians was 12,900 and of Portuguese 3879.
In June, 1710, the regiment was at the camp at Balaguer, where
Charles III joined the army.   His rival, Philip, Duke of Anjou,
grandson of Louis XIV, also joined his French and Spanish army.
On the 13th of June the French attacked the allies, when General
Stanhope led Harvey's Horse and Pepper's Dragoons against the
right of the enemy, and succeeded in throwing it into confusion.
Craggs wrote to the Earl of Sunderland on the 13th of June:

> This day being ye. 13th inst. their whole army march'd up towards
> us at abt. 7 a clock in ye. morning, and seemed resolved to attack us
> upon our left where Mr Stanhope commanded the English, but after
> having come close enough to observe our disposition, they darst not
> venture, but retired wth. ye. loss of severall horse and foot soldiers
> from our cannon.   If the Enemy had attack'd us, I believe he would
> have been able to send your Lordp. an accot. of an entire victory obtained
> by the Queen's troops and commanded by himself.   He is so weary
> yt. he cannot write himself, he has been on horseback these 48 hours ;
> but he bids me acquaint yr. Lp. yt. ye. Army will march within these
> two hours to cut off ye. Enemys returne to Lerida and their provision(s)
> at Fraga.   And in two or three days he will be detach'd to goe to
> Valencia wth. 2 regimts. only from Tarragona, and he will be joined
> by sea by Sr. Jn. Norris wth. ye. German troops. . . .[1]

In a letter of the 16th of June Craggs amplifies the details in his
letter of the 13th:

> By ye. first intelligence we had of them they were marching wth.
> ye. utmost diligence to repass ye. Segra and prevent us from taking
> their camp, for wch. reason Mr Stanhope who comãnded ye. Cavalry
> and was got to Noguera by 4 in ye. afternoon percieving some squadrons
> of ye. Enemys horse on t'other side ye. Segra, and fering they might
> pass it before he could receive ye. Marescls. orders resolved to ford ye.

[1] *S.P., Foreign, Spain,* 77.

Noguera wch. he did tho' ye. stream was very rapid, and pass'd with ye. left wing at Corvines taking possession of ye. Enemys camp there and a good deal of forage wch. he found there, And Count Atalya pass'd wth. ye. left wing at Albeces.   We had but 4 men and horses carried away with ye. stream. . . . Mr Stanhope had laid all ye. night of ye. 14th to ye. 15th upon ye. ground at ye. head of ye. Cavalry believing the Enemy who had forced their march might attack him wth. their horse in wch. they are much superior, before our foot could get over.[1]

On the 15th of June the army encamped at Portella.   The dragoons had occasional encounters with the enemy, and on the 19th they brought in seventeen Spanish troopers and their horses. The next day a captain, lieutenant, cornet, and twenty men of the enemy were also taken.   Staremberg, the commander of the Allies, was an experienced officer, bearing a high reputation.   In July he had 4900 horse and 24,500 foot with a good train.   Of these troops the Germans numbered 14,000 ; the English, 4200 ; the Spanish, 3500 ; the Dutch, 1400 ; and the Portuguese in English pay, 1400.   Under Stanhope Lieutenant-General Carpenter commanded the English horse, consisting of five regiments ; Lieutenant-General Wills the foot, consisting of eight battalions ; and Brigadier-General Richards the train.   Major-General Pepper and Brigadier-Generals the Earl of Rochford and Count Francis of Nassau led the brigades of cavalry, while Major-General Wade and Brigadier-General Gore led those of the infantry.   The English troops were Harvey's Horse, the Royal, Pepper's (with whom were incorporated the remains of Guiscard's and Rochford's Dragoons), the Scots Guards, Harrison's (late Southwell's), Wade's, Bowles's, Dormer's, Munden's, Dalzell's, and Gore's regiments of foot. With his increased forces Staremberg took the offensive, carrying the war into Arragon.   As he crossed the Segre, he ordered Stanhope to seize the pass of Alfaraz before the Spaniards could reach it. Advancing with the utmost speed, Stanhope with a force of twelve squadrons of dragoons under Carpenter and twenty companies of grenadiers, supported by six guns and a pontoon train under Eck, reached Noguera on the 27th, throwing several bridges across it,

[1] *S.P., Foreign, Spain,* 77.

and posting his horse advantageously on the Almenara heights above the right bank.   As Philip was thus unable to seize the pass of Alfaraz his army under the Duc de Sarno fronted the ground occupied by Stanhope.   Twenty-six squadrons of Allied cavalry faced forty-two of the enemy.   Stanhope and Carpenter dashed at the Bourbon horse, and brilliantly discomfited them.   Pepper's Dragoons began the attack with the utmost vehemence, bearing down their opponents in their grim determination.   All the available evidence points this out as the occasion when the regiment overthrew a corps of Spanish cavalry with extraordinary completeness.   The dragoons equipped themselves with the Spanish cross belts of the fallen foe, and these cross belts were, in the days to come, worn by them as a mark of the honourable distinction they won at the Battle of Almenara.[1]

On the 31st of July, 1710, Stanhope sent home a long despatch, furnishing details on the Battle of Almenara.   In the course of it he remarks that

Our next thought (at a council of war) was to Cross the Segre at Balaguer, and push to gett over the Noghera ; to which purpose I was detached with 8 Squadrons of Dragoons, and 1000 Grenadiers, with which I marched at midnight, and took post at Alfaraz on the Arragon side of the Noghera at 6 in the morning of the 27th . . . about noon our left wing of horse passed the river, which I formed on a plain about Cannon shot from the river, between which plain and the river was a deep Valley.   By this time the Ennemies horse came up a pace, and formed before me about 15 Squadrons Which I was going to attack when the Marechal (Staremberg) came up and prevented, seeming still determined not to hazard any thing ; both armies continued marching to gett up, and about 6 all our Infantry had passed the river, and crossed the Valley I mentioned, and gott upon the high ground behind our horse.   The Marechal was pressed several times to attack the Ennemies horse which was before us, their foot marching at a great distance behind them in the Valley, where they could be of no use, about 6 the Ennemies having gott up all their horse, marched several Squadrons down a little hill which was between us ; upon which we all

---

[1] Severne holds the view that the occasion of the winning of the cross belts was the Battle of Almenara, and he was pretty sure to know.   See *S.P., Ireland*, 449, f. 74b.

cryed out shame, and I did earnestly press the King we might have leave to dislodge them, which was at last complied with, but not 'till sunsett. I therefore marched to them with the left wing, which consisted of 22 Squadrons, which were formed into two lines, and a Corps de Reserve of 4 Squadrons, the ground we were drawn up in not allowing us to make a greater front.   So soon as we begun to move the Ennemies Squadrons which had come down the rising I mentioned, retired to their line, consisting but of 10 Squadrons, we found the Ennemie drawn up in two lines, the first of 22 Squadrons, and the second of 20, with two batallions of foot betwixt their lines, and a Brigade of foot on their right, I was therefore forced so soon as I came in presence, to make a halt to gett up some Squadrons from the second line ; the Ground where the Ennemies were being so much wider than that which I had marched from ; besides that getting up the hill had put our line in some disorder, the Ennemies were so good as to give us the time we wanted, we brought up 6 Squadrons and putt our line in good order, which consisted thus of 16 in all, Six English, 4 Dutch, and 6 Palatines[1]; Mr Carpenter and I were on the left, Mr Frankenburg the Palatine General, and Major Genl. Pepper on the right.   So soon as ever we were thus formed, we attacked them, and by the blessing of God broke their two lines, which consisted of 42 Squadrons ; on the right were the Gardes Du Corps, and other choice Regiments which did not doe ill.   I can not sufficiently commend the behaviour of all the troops that were engaged, which never halted till we had driven their horse of (off) the plain, beyond their Infantry which was in the Valley, and if we had had two hours day light more, your Ldp. may be assured that not one foot Soldier of their Army could have escaped ; the night gave them the opportunity to escape to Lerida, which they did in such confusion that they threw away their tents, lost good part of their baggage, and some of their cannon, and have continued ever since encamped within and about the Glacis of Lerida. . . .[2]

In the pursuit Pepper's Dragoons drove off the Spanish squadrons opposed to them, cutting down their opponents in the heat of their ardour. Among the fallen were Brigadier-Generals the Earl of Rochford, who had joined with his regiment only the day before on his return from Italy, and Count Nassau, Colonel Travers,

---

[1] Natives of the Palatinate.   [2] *S.P., Foreign, Spain,* 77.

Captain La Porte, Cornets Carson and Webb, one quarter-master, and seventy-three men.   Among the wounded were Lieutenant-Generals Stanhope and Carpenter, Lieutenant-Colonels Bland and Montgomery, Captains Ravenel, Willis, Moor, and Naizon, Lieutenants Mills, Patterson, Jobber, Heron, and Wood, Cornets Wildgoose and Du Cane, Quarter-master Smith, and one hundred and thirteen men.[1]   In spite of these losses, Charles III ordered the guns of Barcelona to be fired in honour of this triumph, though he postponed the singing of the *Te Deum*.   On the evening of the 17th of August Colonel Crofts arrived in Whitehall with the despatches of General Stanhope, giving fresh details of the victory. Among them is this notice : "The Majors-General Franquenberg and Pepper began the attack with such Resolution and Bravery that the whole Cavalry of the Enemy was routed, even before the Assailants could be joined by our Right Wing."[2]

Philip called in his detachments and proceeded towards Saragossa. The Allies eagerly followed, and on the 19th of August at five o'clock in the evening arrived at the banks of the Ebro.   Carpenter crossed the river with the cavalry, including Pepper's Dragoons. Stanhope and Carpenter advanced with their horse to reconnoitre ; and on their report Staremberg determined to attack the enemy. His army amounted to 23,500, and the Bourbon army did not exceed 20,000, and these were entirely Spanish.   With much forethought Bay, the Bourbon commander, drew up his troops on a plain in front of Saragossa, with his left on the Ebro, and his right on the brow of a hill.   In similar manner Staremberg arrayed his men, with a reserve in the rear of his second line.   On the morning of the 29th of August, 1710, Pepper's Dragoons took post near the left of the line.   The Battle of Saragossa opened with the usual artillery duel, which lasted six hours.   The Spanish cavalry were superior in number and in excellent condition.   Placing himself at the head of the brigade of cavalry, of which the Eighth formed part, Stanhope charged the Spanish horsemen on the right. Crossing a deep ravine, the opposing squadrons fought amazingly

---

[1] *S.P., Foreign, Spain*, 77 ; *Hist. MSS. Com. Reports, the Marquess Townshend MSS.*
[2] *London Gazette*, No. 4732, cf. Aug. 17–19.

well. Six squadrons of Portuguese dragoons fled without striking a blow. Now was the time for the Spanish cavalry, which gained some advantage. Stanhope and Carpenter were forced to recoil to their second line. Here they rallied. The Spanish general, Mahoni, continued his progress against the Austrian squadrons on the extreme left. In the centre the Germans drove back the Spanish foot, and on the right the Spanish horse were rolled back. In the meantime Stanhope brought up fresh squadrons, and re-arranged his old ones. Mahoni, like Prince Rupert, had pushed home his attack too far, and had much to do to regain his own line. The rout of the Spanish foot involved their horse on the left, and the outcome was that the Bourbon army was compelled to retire in disorder along the Ebro. On our side the killed and wounded amounted to 2000, and on the Bourbon side to 3000 killed or wounded and 4000 taken prisoners. Saragossa surrendered, and, to the dismay of Louis XIV, Philip fled in confusion. He sent off his Queen, his infant son, and the Court to Valladolid, where he temporarily established the Bourbon government.

With celerity the French monarch repaired his defeat, at once forming an army of the garrisons on the frontier and sending it southward under the command of Vendôme. Before either the Portuguese or Stanhope could reach Almaraz, Vendôme gained it, destroying the bridge. He advanced down the Tagus to the historic ground of Talavera. In consequence of this rapidity, Stanhope had to evacuate Toledo and Staremberg Madrid. Popular hostility to Charles III declared itself with increasing plainness, and our spies were foiled in their efforts to obtain news of the movements of Vendôme. The Allies also found themselves in grave want of money and want of bread. In spite of the battle of Saragossa, we learn by a letter of the 4th of October, 1710, that "not one officer in the D. of Anjou's service has left him."[1]

For the sake of forage and supplies the Germans, Spaniards, Dutch, and Portuguese of the Allied army marched close to one

[1] *S.P., Foreign, Spain,* 77.

another, and on the 6th of December, 1710, were cantoned in Cifuentes and the neighbouring villages; for the weather was too wet for encamping. Stanhope with the bulk of the English division formed the rear-guard, and he diverged to the left, taking up his quarters within a small town named Brihuega. He had noted a large body of horse following him during his march. He reported this circumstance to Staremberg, but neither he nor Staremberg believed for a moment that it was Vendôme's cavalry. Nevertheless, it was. Nor was this the only surprise, for Vendôme's infantry also appeared. It had covered one hundred and seventy miles in seven days, a march of incredible speed, which, in Stanhope's words, was his undoing. The truth is that part of the surprise was due to the fact that the peasants foiled the efforts of Stanhope's spies to extract information. By five o'clock in the evening nine thousand men had surrounded Brihuega. All Stanhope had within its walls were 2536 officers and men. The cavalry, under Lieutenant-General Carpenter and Major-General Pepper consisted of Harvey's Horse, and the Royal, Pepper's and Stanhope's (late Nassau's) Dragoons, numbering in all 640 troopers. The foot, under Lieutenant-General Wills and Brigadier-General Gore, consisted of the Scots Guards, Harrison's, Wade's, Bowles's, Dormer's, Munden's, Dalzell's, and Gore's regiments, mustering 1896 men.

The town of Brihuega possessed a high wall of Moorish construction, without artillery and without a banquette for musketeers. Hills commanded it within range of artillery and even of musketry. True, it contained a small castle, capable of offering some resistance. In the hope that he might be able to hold out till Staremberg came to his relief, Stanhope refused to listen to the summons to surrender. During the night a field train of twelve guns joined Vendôme, and in the morning speedily made two breaches in the old walls. He began to mine, thus forming a third breach. When this mine was fired the enemy effected an entrance almost before they were perceived. Stanhope repelled the assaulting columns several times. The deadly English fire drove the French back. They withdrew in order to wait for reinforcements.   The 2500 men resisted with all their might and main, horse and dragoons fighting dismounted alongside the foot. In their desperation they set fire to the houses captured by the enemy, and after four hours fighting against superior numbers and superior equipment they still held the best part of the town of Brihuega.   Never during the War of the Spanish Succession was there fiercer fighting.   Ammunition began to fail, and Staremberg did not appear.   Accordingly at 6 o'clock Stanhope surrendered. Our casualties were 300 killed and 300 wounded, and the French roll was thrice as great.   They had 900 killed and 1800 wounded, with 1936 of our men as prisoners.   These included Stanhope, Carpenter, Wills, Pepper, Gore, and 231 officers of lower rank. The names of the officers who, when taken prisoners, were in command of regiments were Colonel Dormer, Lieutenant Colonels Otway of Harvey's, Montagu of the Royals, Hawker of Stanhope's, Ramsay of Harrison's, Howard of Wade's, Strickland of Bowles's, Nevill of Munden's, and Pearson of Dalzell's, with Major Pinfold of Gore's and Major Erle of Pepper's.   For the second time during this war the Eighth had been captured *en masse*.   None could doubt its bravery, but could any doubt its misfortune?   Recalling old Derry days, when the Eighth found ammunition running short, they employed bricks and stones.   The tragedy is that the resistance of them and of the garrison almost won, for the van of Staremberg's army reached the neighbouring hills half an hour after Stanhope had ordered the chamade to be beaten.

The military correspondence for the rest of December is filled with details of the fall of Brihuega.   One paper strikingly summarises the list of prisoners :

3	Lieutenant Generals	10	Majors
1	Major General	60	Captains
1	Brigadier	76	Lieutenants
1	Colonel	64	Ensigns
15	Lieutenant-Colonels	3	Adjutants or Quarter-Masters[1]

[1] *S.P., Foreign, Spain,* 77.

The list of the Eighth is:

Major Genl. Pepper
Major Erle

Captains
- Bellamy
- Knox
- Pitt
- Gleinham

Capt. Lieut. Stanhope

Lieutenants
- Stedman
- Norris
- Du Casse
- D'Hourse

Lieuts.
- Skinton
- Alexander
- Zobell

Cornets
- Godfrey
- Berkeley
- Harwood
- Lavergne
- Wolseley.[1]

On Christmas Day, 1710, Pepper gave the Duke of Ormonde his version of the fall of Brihuega:

I did myself the honour to write to your Grace from Madrid, wherein I gave you an account of the success of this campaign to that time, since which we have lost eight battalion of foot and four regiments of horse, being taken at Brihuega by the Duke of Vendome, who invested us with thirty-four battalions of foot and eight thousand horse with thirty-three pieces of artillery, we being separate from the rest of the army on our march towards our winter quarters. The enemy having made four several attacks at once, which continued three hours and having spent all our ammunition, we defended the breaches half an hour sword in hand, then finding it impracticable to defend it any longer, a chamade was beat, but not till the enemy had above two thousand of their troops in town and a great part of the town all in fire, where was a great number of the enemy as well as our own men destroyed. We were made prisoners of war. General Stanhope commanded ; there were General Carpenter, Wills, myself and Brigadier Gore, who are all come hither (to Valladolid) and have been extremely well treated. The 9th instant at ten at night Mr Stanhope signed the capitulations, but not with my consent, nor had I any hand in this unfortunate affair otherwise than the defence of the town, which was defended to the last, nor General Wills, and it was against both of our opinions in coming to that place, and had dispositions been made as they ought we should not have been, I may say, surprised. As I am not answerable for the

[1] *S.P., Foreign, Spain*, 78.

troops coming to Brihuega, nor for our being surprised, but to the contrary did all within my power to prevent both, so I must beg your Lordship to have an honourable opinion of me till you be informed of the truth of this unfortunate affair.   Marshal Honunburgh marched with all diligence imaginable to our relief, but came too late, we having marched out of Brihuega the 10th instant about eleven o'clock.   The Marshal came up with the Duke of Vendome's army about twelve towards our relief, who engaged the enemy very vigorously.   The battle held till ten at night, and how it is decided I am altogether a stranger to, being prisoner.   Of the horse there are taken at Brihuega Raby's, Harvey's, my own and Stanhope's ; of the foot the Guards, Harrison's, Wade's, Dormer's, Bowles's, Gore's, Munden's and Dalzell's.   I have here enclosed your Grace a copy of the capitulations. I long to be in England that I may have the opportunity once more to see your Grace to own with all gratitude the many favours that you have shown upon all occasions to (me). . . .[1]

Colonel Clement Scott, Paymaster, declared the accounts of the Eighth who were captured. Pepper's pay from the 23rd of December, 1710, to the 31st of March following, less deductions of poundage and hospital, was £232 1s. 7d. The subsistence of his regiment from the 23rd of December, 1710, to the 23rd of December, 1712, amounted to £9795 19s. 8d. The pay of several sick men and others who did not arrive at Bayonne by the 23rd of December, 1712, from this date to the 1st of March following, when they embarked for England from the Port of Passage in Spain was £76 5s. 4d.[2]

From Barcelona the Duke of Argyll wrote to Lord Dartmouth on the 18th of January, 1711 :

This will be Deliver'd Your Lordsp. by Majr. Genll. Pepper who being Exchang'd just as I arrived in this Country, Came and Offered himself To serve here this Campaign, Which I could not Refuse Upon the Acct. that We had so few Genll. Officers to Do the Duty, but he not being upon this Establishmt. Cannot be paid here, Which is the Reason of my now Desiring Your Lordsp. to lay his Case before Her

[1] *Hist. MSS. Com. Rep., Ormonde MSS.*, VIII, p. 234.
[2] *Audit Office, Declared Accounts*, Bundle 324.

Majty. That as he has been Att an Extrary. Expense he may be paid
in England, I could not In Justice to him but Recommend him to
Your Lordsp.[1]

On the 18th of April, 1711, Pepper himself wrote from Barcelona
to Lord Dartmouth :

Being taken Prisoner att Brihuega and now Exchanged for Count de
Boucour, am come hither in order to act in my post. Wee have now
only one Regiment of the British Horse here Mounted, with the Complement of men on foot to make up 2 other Regiments, 350 of which
were sent from England, and the Rest Deserters from our English
Cavalry taken att Brihuega, and there are daily more comeing in to us,
we have Officers for one Regiment here, and expect others so I do not
doubt, but that if her Majty. be pleased to Raise two of the Regiments
here, that were taken att Brihuega, it may be Accomplished with a great
deal of facility, in case orders be sent for the Immediat buying of horses
in Italy, which are to be had att a Reasonable Price, and should her
Majty. think fitt to send Dismounted Cavalry here, it will be proper to
send Officers from hence, and from England as soon as possible, to
buy such numbers of Horses as will be wanting, and if her Majty.
should think Proper to Raise my Regiment here, I have orderd my
Agent to send my Cloathing Immediately hither (which is all Ready),
and to wait on your Lordhsp. for orders therein.

The Court here has Agreed to a Generall Exchange, leaving the
Whole to Generall Stanhope on their side, and the Duke of Anjow
has left it likewise to a Lt. Generall of theirs. In my way hither I
overtook severall of their Troops on their March towards our Frontier,
not being above 11 Leagues from hence but most of them since are
retired over the Segra, which are in a most miserable Condition, and
especially their foot, which is never to be made up here, unless Forces
be sent them from France, they have great numbers of horse but in
bad order, and in case the Troops designed for this place come in time
with Money to pay Off our Debts, and withall to Enable us to take the
Field, I hope we shall be able to March to any part of Spaine we please,
and that with Ease, unless the Enemy does Expect Troops from thence ;
I do not doubt but we shall be able to make up the Misfortune of our

[1] *S.P., Foreign, Spain*, Vol. 230, Part I.

last Campaigne in this, we daily expect our Forces from Italy here, and Likewise those from Brittain. I shall be glad to Receive your Lordships Commands which shall be observed with the Greatest Chearfulness by (me).[1]

In a list of officers absent from their commands we find that all of the Eighth were present in Spain when Pepper was leaving Barcelona except himself and Sir Richard Vernon. Pepper had exchanged out of Lieutenant-General Echlin's regiment into the Eighth with Colonel Upton. On taking up his duty he found that his troop was charged with a debt of £815 19s. 4d. He obtained leave from General Stanhope to return to his original regiment in order to remove this incumbrance on his troop.[2] In 1712 it was suggested that the horses belonging to the Dragoons should be bought by the King of Portugal for his service, and the value deducted from the subsidy payable by our Government to him.

The War of the Spanish Succession lingered on till 1713. Practically the Eighth were finished with it when Brihuega fell. The first chapter in the foreign service of our regiment is before us, and seemingly it ends in failure. For Philip V remains King of Spain, not Charles III. In appearance Louis XIV had won in the south if not in the north. The glorious record of Marlborough owns such names as Blenheim, Ramilies, Malplaquet, and Oudenarde, four victories that settled the question of the invincibility of the French soldier. He remained a great soldier, yet a soldier whom the British could conquer. In the south there is on the bead-roll of the soldiers of the War of the Spanish Succession such names as the capture of Barcelona, the Battle of Almenara, and the Battle of Saragossa. On the reverse side there are, no doubt, the Battle of Almanza and the fall of Brihuega. Yet, in spite of the boast of the French King, the Pyrenees remained, for Philip V turned, like Charles V, into a thorough Spaniard. The French navy had been the greatest navy afloat, yet since the Battle of La Hogue ours had disputed its supremacy. The capture of Gibraltar and Minorca testified to the worth of the weapon of sea

[1] *S.P., Foreign, Spain*, 78.   [2] *S.P., Dom., Military*, Bundle 4.

M

power.   Nor can the beginnings of our commercial greatness be overlooked, supported as it was to be in the days to come by the trade of the Thirteen Colonies, Canada, and India.   The thoughts of youth are supposed to be long, long thoughts.   Whether this is true of youth or not, it is emphatically true of nations.   The War of the Spanish Succession was no more than the second round in the contest with France.   There had been the Nine Years' War from 1688 to 1697.   There were to be the War of the Austrian Succession from 1740 to 1748, the Seven Years' War from 1756 to 1763, and the contest with France from 1793 to 1815.   In all these wars England was to be found on the one side and France on the other. For throughout the whole of the eighteenth century these rivals were contending for a prize of incalculable worth, and that prize was no less than the colonial headship of the world.

To illustrate the
WAR OF THE
SPANISH SUCCESSION

Greenwich 0° Meridian

Spanish Leagues
10   5   0   5   10   20   30   40

English Miles
10   0   10   50   100   150

FRANCE

BISCAY

NAVARRE

ASTURIAS

OLD CASTILE

NEW CASTILE

ESTREMADURA

PORTUGAL

ANDALUSIA

MURCIA

ARAGON

CATALONIA

VALENCIA

MADRID

LISBON

MINORCA

MAJORCA

IVICA

MEDITERRANEAN SEA

ATLANTIC OCEAN

MOROCCO

Corunna
C.Finisterre
Santiago
Pontevedra
Vigo
Lugo
Oviedo
Leon
Benevente
Zamora
Braga
Oporto
Braganza
Salamanca
Valladolid
Palencia
Burgos
Vitoria
Pampelona
Tudela
Saragossa
Calatayud
Daroca
Caspe
Lerida
Balaguer
Agramunt
Manresa
Gerona
Barcelona
Mataro
Villa Franca
Reus
Tarragona
Tortosa
Peniscola
Benicarlo
Castellon
Valencia
Nules
Almenara
Morella
Albocazer
Alcala de Chisvert
Requena
Alcira
Denia
Altea Bay
Villena
Alicante
Elche
Origuela
Murcia
Cartagena
Almanza
Montessa
Almeria
Granada
Malaga
Cordova
Constantina
Seville
Cadiz
Gibraltar
Straits of Gibraltar
C.St Vincent
Evora
Elvas
Badajos
Campo Mayor
Placencia
Almaraz
Talavera
Toledo
Ciudad Rodrigo
Madrid
Colmenar
Brihuega
Cifuentes
Fraga
Fonz
Balaguer
Tudela

R.Ebro
R.Douro
R.Tagus
R.Guadiana
R.Guadalquivir
R.Minho
R.Douro

CHAPTER IV

Service at Home

A CAMPAIGN brings honour and glory: it also brings sorrow and death. The latter aspect appears in the pensions paid quarterly to Elizabeth Baxter, whose husband had fallen with Killigrew, and Anne Nesbitt. The husbands of each had served as cornets, and the widows received twenty pounds a year.[1] Still, if we multiply it by $2\frac{3}{4}$ in order to ascertain its value in 1913, the amount was fifty-five pounds, by no means a meagre allowance in the year 1712.

With the end of the War of the Spanish Succession the question of the release of the captives emerges. On the 25th of July, 1712, a warrant was issued:

> Our Will and Pleasure is that the Severall Regimts. following (Vizt.) Our Regimt. of Horse Comanded by Lt. Genll. Harvey, Our Royall Regt. of Dragoons Comanded by the Earle of Stratforde, Our Regt. of Dragoons Comanded by Majr. Genll. Pepper and our Severall Regiments of Foot Comanded by Colonel Harrison, Brigr. Wade, Brigadier Dormer and Brigadier Bowles which were taken prisoners in Spain, and are Suddenly to be Released, as also our Regt. of Foot whereof Collo. Windress is Colonel now in Brittain, Shall be put upon that (*i.e.* the Irish) Establishmt. to replace the like number of Regimts. wanting thereupon as aforesaid. . . .[2]

Pepper manifested deep anxiety for the raising of his regiment in Spain, and had ordered his agent to send him the clothing for

---

[1] I E, 3.1, pp. 110, 119.   [2] *W.O.*, 8/1, p. 18.

it at once in order to save all delay.   He had sent a memorial to his friend, the Duke of Ormonde, in 1713.   In it he pointed out:

That the said Regimt. had the misfortune to be taken Prisoners at Brehuga and Severall of the Officers obtain'd Her Maties. leave to be absent from their Posts, others came over upon their Parole, and Recēd. full Subsistce. according to the English Establishmt. from 23d. Decembr. 1711 to the 22d. Augt. following During which time they were ordered upon the Irish Establishment.

That the Rest of the Officers who Remain'd Prisoners were likewise Subsisted with the Serjeants, Corporals, and privt. Men, according to the afore-menc̄oned Establishmt. untill they were released which was in December 1712.

That notwithstanding by an Accot. from the Pay Office this Regt. is now charged with the money Arising from ye. Difference of ye. English Establishmt. to that of the Irish for one year, by which means the Officers Cleerings are taken up, and they brot. vastly in Debt, by the Overpaymt. of their Men besides the Adjutants Subsistce. the Irish Establishment allowing no such Officer.

He therefore humbly Prays Your Grace will be pleased to take it into consideration, that the Officers and Men may be Allowed their Subsistce. on the English Establishmt. to December 1712, otherwise it will be a great hardship upon the Officers and Men to be allowed less than others who served in the same Station during that time.[1]

Nor was the Eighth the only regiment to find itself in this predicament.   For Colonel Bland's Regiment, Brigadier Pearce's Regiment of Dragoons, Lord Mountjoy's and Lieutenant-General Gorges's Regiments of Foot also stood in it.   The difficulty arose from the fact that there were differences between the Irish and the English Establishments in the number of officers and men and also in the number of troops.   Thus the Irish Establishment allowed eight troops, the English only six.   Hence two troops and several officers of the Eighth were, according to the English Establishment, struck off as supernumeraries.   These two troops were Captain Gleinham's and Captain Cosby's.   Accordingly,

[1] *Audit Office*, 17/31, p. 60.

Ormonde granted this reasonable petition, and Pepper enjoyed the relief he sought.[1] The following table shows what it involved :

Officers' Names.	Pay per diem.			To which time paid abroad or here.	No. of days demanded for.	Total sum demanded for each Officer.		
	£	s.	d.			£	s.	d.
Major-Gen. Pepper as Col. and Capt.	1	6	6	Dec. 22, 1711	244	323	6	0
Sir Rich. Vernon, Lt.-Col. and Capt.		18	6	,,	244	225	14	0
Major Erle		16	6	Feb. 23, 17$\frac{11}{12}$	181	149	6	6
Capt. Knox		11	6	,,	181	104	1	6
„ Bellamy		11	6	,,	181	104	1	6
„ Pitt		11	6	,,	181	104	1	6
„ Pelham		11	6	Dec. 22, 1711	244	140	6	0
„ Cleland		11	6	,,	244	140	6	0
Lt. Norris		6	10	,,	244	83	7	4
Cornt. Knox		5	10	,,	244	71	3	4
„ Wolseley		5	10	June 23, 1712	60	17	10	0
„ Stevenson		5	10	Dec. 22, 1711	244	71	3	4
„ Carpenter		5	10	,,	244	71	3	4
Qr.-Mr. Willington		4	2	,,	244	50	16	8
„ Pepper		4	2	,,	244	50	16	8
„ Johnson		4	2	Feb. 23, 17$\frac{11}{12}$	181	37	14	2
Dr. Finglas, Chaplain		5	0	Dec. 22, 1711	244	61	0	0
Mr. Dedier, Surgeon		4	6	,,	244	54	18	0
„ Held, Gunsmith		3	0	,,	244	36	12	0
„ Henry Rd., Mate		1	0	,,	244	12	4	0
Geo. Conner, Corpll. ...		1	0	,,	244	12	4	0
4 Privt. Dragoons, each 8d. ...		2	8	,,	244	32	10	8
						1954	6	6[2]

The dragoons had sold their horses in Spain, and had returned dismounted. They proceeded to Ireland, and during the month of April,[3] 1713, they received *inter alia* twenty-two horses from the late Regiment of Dragoons commanded by the Earl of Wharton, and for these they had to pay twelve pounds apiece.

[1] *Audit Office*, 17/31, p. 61.   *Cf.* a popular sketch of the history of British cavalry in *Colburn's United Service Magazine*, 1867, Part I, p. 168.

[2] *A.O.*, 17/31.   [3] April 25, 1 E, 3.12, p. 142.

On the 23rd of April, 1713, a general order settled the rank and precedency of the forces.   The place of the Dragoons was to be:

Royal Regt. of Drags. Commanded by the Earl of Strafford
The Royl. Regt. of North Britain Command. by the Earl of Stair
Our Own Regt. of Drags. Command. by Lt. General Carpenter
Late Sir. Richd. Temple's Regt.
The Royl. Regt. of Ireland Cõmand. by Genl. Ross
Lieut. Genl. Echlyn's Regimt.
Colonel Kerr's
Majr. Genl. Pepper's
Earl of Hyndford's
Brigadr. Lepell's
Colonel Morris's
Lt. Genl. Stanhope's
Majr. Genl. Pearce's
Col. La Bouchetier's
Col. Foissac
Brigadr. Withers's
Col. Desbordes's
Col. Magny's
Col. Gually's
Col. Sarlande's
Marqs. D'Assa's
The Regt. late E. of Wharton's.[1]

On the 18th of April, 1713, Mr. Kane of Dublin received £2628 16s. 2d. for the clothing of the Regiment; and this was the off-reckonings for two years, commencing from the 28th of September following.[2]   On the 27th of June a warrant was issued for the sum of three hundred and sixty pounds for the forage for the coming winter.[3]

The two supernumerary troops, according to the English Establishment, had been struck off. Their officers, however, had been

[1] *W.O.*, 26/14, *Miscellany Books, Warrants, etc.*
[2] I E, 3.12, p. 143.   [3] I E, 3.12, p. 155.

given half pay from the 23rd of December, 1711, and accordingly on the 10th of July, 1713, we meet with this order:

	P. diem.			P. diem.		
	£	s.	d.	£	s.	d.
Capt. Cleland	0	4	0			
„ Pelham	0	4	0			
Lt. Christ. Zobell	0	2	6			
„ Stephen Du Casse	0	2	6			
Cornet Willm. Wolseley	0	2	0			
„ Robt. Stevenson	0	2	0			
Quarter Master Henry Willington	0	1	6			
„ „ Jon. McClane ..	0	1	6			
				1	0	0
Capt. Wm. Mathews				0	4	0
				1	4	0[1]

On the 30th of September the principal officers of ordnance were directed to deliver out of the stores 198 muskets, 204 cases of pistols, and six drums.[2] On the 6th of October, 1713, the usual quantity of watch ammunition was issued. For the ensuing half year, from the 29th of September last to the 25th of March, each of the six troops received half a barrel of powder for this purpose.[3]

The first case we meet of trouble arising within the Regiment is the case of Captain English, whose name, curiously enough, does not occur in the lists of officers. A meeting of General Officers was held on the 22nd of July, 1713, when Lieutenant-Generals Withers (President) and Carpenter, Major-Generals Baines, Whetham, Primrose, Davenport, Braddock, Evans, and the Earl of Stair were present. The proceedings run:

Majr. Genl. Pepper having complained to the Board against Capt. Wm. English, late Adjutant and Quarter Master, in the Regt. of Dragoons under his Command, for Aspersing him, the said Major General, in relation to Mony Alledged to be due to him for Mule-Maintenance while in that Regt. The said Matter was this Day heard. Whereupon it Appeared, That the said English in Order to Obtain

[1] *W.O.*, 8/1, f. 25.   [2] 1 E, 3.12, p. 173.   [3] 1 E, 3.12, p. 182.

Payment had made Affidavit before a Master in Chancery, That not any of the said Mule-Mony had been paid unto Him, when at the same time he had Reced. part, if not the whole thereof, as by his Receipt was found. It further appeared that on the said Officers producing the said Affidavit to the Agent of the Regt. in Order to payment as aforesaid, he did the same with very insolent Expressions towards the Major General, which he scrupled not to own to the Board without the least extenuation.

Upon due Consideration of all which, It is Ordered

That Capt. English, for his making Oath so very contrary to Truth, and for his Insolent Behaviour towards his Superior Officer, Be suspended, as he is hereby suspended, from his Half-Pay during Her Majts. Pleasure ; And be in Arrest for so long time as His Grace the Duke of Ormond, General of the Forces, shall think fitt.   And it is likewise Agreed humbly to move Her Majty. that She will be pleased not to take off the said Suspension but thro' the Application of the said Major General, who is without Delay to make up the Acct. of Mule-Mony Demanded by the said Officer, and, if anything shall be found due unto him to pay the same.[1]

On the 27th of August Captain English presented a memorial to a meeting of the General Officers, praying the Board to take off the suspension. He produced some witnesses to extenuate his offence. He asked the pardon of Pepper, who thereupon supported his request to the Board to take off the suspension, and accordingly it was so done.[1]

On the 12th of March, 1714, the question of the extra two troops of Captains Gleinham and Cosby cropped up once more. Colonel Thomas Pitt, on behalf of himself and other officers of the Eighth, petitioned the Duke of Shrewsbury, when Lord Lieutenant of Ireland, to be relieved of a charge of £1251 18s. 5d., being the subsistence of two troops according to the Irish establishment. This of course was the payment made to eight troops from the 23rd of December, 1711, to the 7th of January, 1712, and when the Duke of Shrewsbury referred this petition to the Lords Justices they recommended payment.[3]

---

[1] *W.O.*, 71/2, p. 187.   [2] *W.O.*, 71/2, p. 198.   [3] *Treasury Papers*, Vol. 192, No. 44.

The Peace of Utrecht had been signed. At the conclusion of the Nine Years' War the Eighth had been disbanded, and now it was to suffer the same fate when the War of the Spanish Succession had been formally concluded. Ormonde may have been a friend of Pepper, but he could not like the tone of the Regiment. For it was staunchly Protestant and equally staunchly anti-Jacobite. Ulster memories, consciously and subconsciously, prejudiced officers and men alike against any son of James II, even so splendid a son as the Old Pretender. The intrigues of Louis XIV still persisted. Nor did Anne remain unmoved by the ties of blood, for she offered the crown to her step-brother, James, if he would consent to become a member of the Church of England. To his eternal honour he refused. Bolingbroke, already plotting the succession of the Old Pretender to the throne, was bent on remodelling the army. This meant his determination to get rid of every regiment that favoured the succession of the House of Hanover. On the conclusion of the war, the regular practice was the disbandment of regiments. The rule, however, was that the first to undergo this process were the youngest regiments. In flagrant violation of the rule, the Seventh and Eighth Dragoons, the Sixth, the Fourteenth, the Twenty-Second, the Twenty-eighth, the Twenty-ninth, the Thirtieth, the Thirty-second, the Thirty-third, and the Thirty-fourth were all dissolved.[1] The warrant for the immediate disbandment of Pepper's Dragoons was issued on the 9th of March, 1714.[2] The officers then were:

Captains.	Lieutenants.
Jno. Pepper, Col.	Jon. Stanhope, Capt. Lt.
Thos. Erle, Lt. Col.	John Alexander
Adam Bellamy, Majr.	James Norris
Sir Richd. Vernon	John Skinton
Andrew Knox	Henry D'Hourse
John Pitt	Richard Stedman

[1] *Commons Journals*, April 18, 1713; *Secretary's Common Letter Book*, July 29, 1712; July 23, 1715; *H.O.M.E.B.*, July 26, 1715; *Miscellaneous Orders* (*Guards and Garrisons*), October 25, 1715.

[2] *W.O.*, 25/3152, *Register of Warrants, Ireland.*

Cornets.	Quarter Masters.
Willm. Berkeley	Francis Sempill
Richard Harwood	James Johnson
John Knox	John McManus
Francis Godfrey	Richard Croft
Samll. Blount	Robert Benson
Willm. Wolseley	John Gordon

Staff Officers.

Nichs. Finglas, Chapl.

Jon. Dedier, Chyrurn.[1]

Though Major Bellamy was suffering by this disbandment, yet he was eager that the arrears of the troops of Captains Gleinham and Cosby should be paid to them.[2] On the 18th of May, 1714, he petitioned the Duke of Shrewsbury on behalf of these troops and on behalf of the rest of the officers who had not received their proper subsistence, since the charges of the two supernumerary troops fell on the other six. Naturally Bellamy desired that the six troops should be freed from the necessity of having their subsistence lessened by the amount necessary to provide for the troops of Captains Gleinham and Cosby. The promise made to Pepper, though granted by the Duke of Ormonde, does not seem to have reached the stage of performance. Bellamy pressed for its performance, though we are left in doubt of his ultimate success. On the 25th of May, 1714, a list was compiled of the officers in the regiments of dragoons commanded by Major-General Pepper and Colonel Kerr, and the regiments of foot commanded by Colonel Churchill, Lord Mountjoy, Major-General Wade, and Brigadier-General Corbett, who on disbandment were to receive half-pay, but this list is not forthcoming.[3]

The suddenness of the death of Queen Anne shattered the schemes of Bolingbroke, and George I tranquilly ascended the throne. His accession was the indirect means of restoring the Eighth Hussars, for the Jacobite Rebellion of 1715 startled people to find

---

[1] *W.O.*, 8/1, *Out-Letters, Ireland.*   [2] *A.O.*, 17/31 ; also in *T.*, 192/44.

[3] *Treasury*, 1/176, f. 16.

how unprovided they were for the duty of repelling invasion. It is pleasing to note that the care of the widow was not forgotten, for we learn that Mrs. Mary Maxwell received from the 25th of December, 1713, to the 24th of June, 1714, thirty pounds.[1] The first of the new regiments of dragoons was Pepper's. On the 22nd of July, 1715, the commissions for its formal restoration were issued. The *London Gazette* of the 25th of July contained this joyful news. Many of the former officers, non-commissioned officers, and men who had served in Spain gladly joined their old corps. Here is the list of officers:

Field Officers and Captains.
John Pepper, Col. and Capt.
Thos. Erle, Lt. Col. and Capt.
Adam Bellamy, Major and Capt.
James Pelham
Edward Wills
John Pitt

Lieutenants.
Thos. Echlin, Capt. Lieut.
Richard Harwood
Vincent Peyton
John Skinton
William Kerr
Christopher Zobell

Cornets.
James Johnson
Samll. Blount
Robt. Stevenson
John Withers
Guy Vissouse
George Pepper

Staff Officers.
Roger Royston, Chaplain
Richard Harwood, Adjutant
John Dedier, Surgeon.[2]

On the 30th of July, 1715, Pepper received a letter, imploring him to use all possible dispatch in providing clothing for his regiment.[3] He was asked to send his patterns for the same for inspection by the Board of General Officers appointed for this purpose at ten on the morning of the 2nd, 4th or 6th of August. On the 20th of August the Board of Ordnance returned 153 swords given up on disbandment. For each sword he was to pay three shillings, the amount paid for them when they were returned to the Board of Ordnance.[4] The Eighth was distinguished by buff

[1] I E, 3.13, p. 245.   [2] *S.P., Dom., Entry Book*, 177.
[3] *W.O.*, 7/24.   [4] I E, 3.13, p. 162.

sword-belts suspended across the right shoulder. This was in accordance with the other regiments of horse, whereas the other regiments of dragoons had buff sword-belts fastened round the waist. There is a tradition of long standing that this distinction was given to the Eighth because of its signal victory at the Battle of Almenara over a corps of Spanish cavalry, which it annihilated. The victors equipped themselves with Spanish belts, and were afterwards permitted to wear them as a mark of honour. Nor is the dress of the Regiment, as detailed on the 3rd of March, 1707, without significance.

Now there were six, not eight, troops, and they were stationed in the south of England. On the 25th of August, 1715, appeared the following royal warrant, restoring to Pepper's Dragoons its former rank in the army:

GEORGE R.

Whereas We have thought fit to raise the Regiment of Dragoons commanded by our trusty and well-beloved Major-General John Pepper, which was broke on the 16th day of April, 1714.

Our Will and Pleasure is, that the said Regiment shall have, hold, and enjoy its former Rank, as if the same had not been broke, notwithstanding any former Order, Direction, or Instruction to the contrary, and of this Our Pleasure all the General Officers and Colonels of Our Army, and all other persons whom it may concern, are to take notice, and govern themselves accordingly.

Given at Our Court at St. James's this 25th day of August 1715, in the second year of Our Reign.

By His Majesty's Command,

(Signed)   WM. PULTENEY.[1]

The general order of the 23rd of April, 1713, had not been waste paper, for the precedency then given to the Eighth was now confirmed. At their quarters at Aylesbury the Regiment encountered a trace of the "Fifteen." Matthew Arnold has pronounced that the University of Oxford is the home of lost causes,

[1] *W.O.*, 26/14.

and forsaken beliefs, and unpopular names, and impossible loyalties. Actuated by a similar belief, Colonel Owen, who had recently been dismissed the army, and a number of other Jacobites, proceeded to Oxford. The treatment meted out by James II to this University might be thought sufficient reason to prevent any of its members joining the ranks of his son. Colonel Owen and those associated with him, however, found supporters both in Oxford and in its University. Memories of the attachment manifested by the University to Charles I began to revive.

Major-General Pepper was ordered to take the six troops of his Regiment with him and seize the Jacobites. On the evening of the 5th of October the six troops were assembled within sixteen miles of Oxford. The memory of the commander could carry him far back into the past. He could recall that the men of his Regiment had foiled, on a grand scale, the designs of Louis XIV in Ireland and in Spain. Now it was their turn, on a small scale, to foil the same designs by arresting sympathisers with the Old Pretender. In civilian clothes an officer visited Oxford, ascertaining the precise places where the Jacobites lodged. In the early morning of the 6th the Regiment seized the avenues of the old-world town. An officer summoned the astonished Mayor and the Vice-Chancellor of the University to meet Major-General Pepper. Supported by these officials, who extended their ready help, a number of suspected people were seized, though Owen unfortunately escaped. In his haste Pepper refused to stop in the quarters provided for the Regiment by the Mayor. Marching to Abingdon on the 6th of October, he sent the prisoners on to London. On the 7th of December three of them, Captain William Kerr, John Dorrel and John Gordon, were executed at Tyburn.

George Clarke, son of Sir William Clarke, who was Secretary at War, adds in his autobiography to our knowledge of this episode. He tells us:

> Not long after Brigadier Pepper came to Oxford with some troops and orders to seize several persons named in a list, and the Vice-Chancellor, Dr. Gardiner, was required to assist him in searching for them and such others as the Brigadier should acquaint him. I think

he met with but one of the persons in his list, Capt. Halsay, whom he carried away with him about the noon of the day he came in. He behaved himself very civilly the little time he was here, and never let his men go from their arms all the while they were in town, to prevent any disorders that might have happened. By something the Brigadier said to me, I had good grounds to believe that he was advised by some persons here to have taken me up, but he said he would be hanged first or to that effect. After he marched away, in some short time, there were soldiers[1] quartered in Oxford, who were very rude and made everybody uneasy, but at last those who had not done anything to deserve it, and from whom there was no colour of danger, and so removed them.[2]

The Eighth spent their winter quarters in 1715 at Warwick and Banbury. On the 7th of March, 1716, a petition was presented for the payment of £2318 16s. 4d. for clothing, and it sought to obtain a proportion of the off-reckonings for this purpose. There is reason to think that this petition was granted. On the 11th of July, 1716, the question of the number of servants allowed to the officers was raised.[3] The precedents of William III's reign were set forth. Then the Colonel had six, the Field Officers and Captains had three each, the Lieutenants, Cornets and Quarter-masters had each one. With the exception of the Lieutenants, Cornets and Quarter-masters, all the officers lost a servant apiece on the conclusion of the war in 1697, and this arrangement received fresh confirmation. On the 16th of May, 1717, five regiments of Dragoons, including Pepper's and eight regiments of Foot, which were in Great Britain, were transferred to the Irish Establishment.[4] This order was evidently meant to be carried out, for we meet with it in no less than three forms.[5] On the 11th of July Pepper received the licence for payment made to him for his work as Adjutant-General.

---

[1] These belonged to General Handasyde's regiment of foot (now the Twenty-second).
[2] *Hist. MSS. Com. Rep., Popham MSS.*
[3] *W.O., 7/122.*
[4] *W.O., 8/1, f. 76.*
[5] *W.O., 8/1, f. 76; 1 E, 3.15, p. 81; 1 E, 3.15, p. 281.*

In 1717 it was perceived that the danger of a Jacobite rebellion had passed away, and accordingly we meet again with a slight reduction in the army. On the 12th of August three regiments of Horse, Major-General Davenport's, Brigadier Waring's and Major-General Sibourg's, and four regiments of Dragoons, Major-General Pepper's, Col. Newton's, Brigadier Dormer's, and Major-General Wynne's, were told:

His Majesty having signified unto us His Royal Will and Pleasure that Five Private Men be reduced out of the several Troops of the Regiment of Horse under your Command on or before the 24th day of August instant by which Reducement (the Officers' servants being to be thrown into their Personal Pay and the Widows Men put into a separate Article) each Troop is to consist of Twenty Five Effective Private Men ; These are to direct and require you forthwith to cause the several Troops of the said Regiment to be reduced to the number before mentioned accordingly. In the doing whereof you are to observe the following directions. Vizt.

1st That the Arms delivered out of His Majesty's Stores of Ordnance to the Troopers to be disbanded be returned into His Majties. Stores wth. in this Kingdom.

2nd That the Accounts between the Troopers and their Officers be made up to the day of their Discharge and that they be fully paid and satisfied their Arrears or other just Pretension, whereof the said Officers are to produce Acquittances or Discharges from them respectively.

3rd That each Trooper be permitted to carry away with him his Cloak, Cloaths, Accoutremts., Belt and Knapsack, and be paid Three shillings for his Sword which is to be returned into the Stores of His Majties. Ordnance, And as for the Horses of the Troopers they are to be disposed of according to the Regulations following. Vizt.

1st That where any Trooper who shall be discharged in Pursuance hereof hath served a whole year, the Horse which His Majesty paid for by the Levy Money is to be given to him, His Majty. being graciously pleas'd to grant His whole right in such Horse to the said Trooper.

2nd That where any such Trooper hath not serv'd His Majesty one whole year such Horse is to be sold and an Account kept in Order to the Disposal of the Money in such manner as His Majesty shall direct.

3rd That where it shall appear that any officer has furnish'd a Horse to a Trooper, the officer is to be satisfied for such part of the Value of the said Horse upon sale, for which he has not been already paid by Deductions or otherwise from the Trooper.

4th That where any Difference shall arise between the Trooper and his Officers, the same shall be determined by you cy[1] to Right shall appertain.

And you are further to take care that each Trooper to be disbanded who in pursuance to this Regulation shall keep his Horse to be paid seven days full Pay, and those who shall not keep their Horses Twenty days Full Pay, which His Majesty is pleased to allow them of His Royal Bounty to carry them to their respective Habitations, written Papers are to be given allowing them convenient time to repair thither.

And to the end the Troopers so to be disbanded may be the more sensible of the care taken of them upon their Dismifsion, the Instructions given you in pursuance hereof, are to be read at the Head of each Troop in order to a more exact Complyance therewith.

Lastly you are to take care that His Majties. Pleasure hereby sygnified be duly executed as soon as possible and return an Account thereof to us with all convenient speed.[2]

Every line of such an order testifies in the plainest terms that the soldier contributed to his equipment, and that when he was disbanded this equipment of right belonged to him. On the 18th of November, 1717, a warrant was issued for the Vice-Treasurer of his deputy to pay Elias Cripps of Dublin for the clothing he had supplied to the Eighth of the value of £2218 14s. 2½d., "Gross Poundage, Hospital, and Pells included by equal monthly Gale."[3] This was the net off-reckonings for two years from the 30th of

---

[1] I cannot interpret this word.   [2] 1 E, 1.52, p. 100.   [3] 1 E, 3.15, p. 202.

July, 1717, and had not the private soldier contributed to these off-reckonings?

On the 27th of September, 1717, the usual allowance of half a barrel of powder for watch ammunition to each troop was issued.[1] On the 29th of October the Agent of the Regiment was to receive ten pounds three shillings for the provision of earthenware trenchers, and the like,[2] for one year. This was at the rate of one and two pence for each non-commissioned officer and private. On the 10th of June, 1718, the Treasury was to pay the Agent six hundred pounds for forage for the winter, "and the same is to be Deducted out of the Subsistence that shall grow due and payable to the same Regiment at One hundred Pounds per. month commencing the first day of November next, untill the whole Sum so advanced as aforesaid be fully Stopped."[3] On the 23rd of August, 1718, the Muster Master General was asked to prepare a warrant, giving the Agent the full pay due to the Regiment, commencing on the 1st of October, 1717, and ending on the 31st of December following, both inclusive.[4]

For almost twelve years Major-General John Pepper had commanded the Eighth, and on the 23rd of March, 1719, he received permission to sell his commission, and Major-General Bowles, from the 12th Dragoons, succeeded him in the colonelcy. Bowles had distinguished himself under William III, and had served with the Duke of Marlborough. In July, 1705, he received command of a regiment of foot, which served under Stanhope in Spain. His connection with the Eighth was an old one, for he had been at Elche with Killigrew, he had been at the Battle of Almanza, he had been at the Battle of Almenara, and he had been at the fall of Brihuega. Like other regiments, his was disbanded in 1714. The Jacobite Rebellion gave him a fresh start, and in 1715 he raised, equipped, and disciplined a corps of dragoons, now the 12th Royal Lancers.

On the 25th of March, 1719, Brigadier Bowles received the following letter from George Treby of Whitehall: "Severall Inkeepers of ye. Town of Barnstaple having sent up a Complaint

[1] I E, 3.15, p. 143.   [2] I E, 3.15, p. 174.   [3] I E, 3.15, p. 301.   [4] I E, 3.15, p. 345.

to be delivered into ye. House of Commons agt. two Troops of yr. Regiment setting forth that ye. sd. Troops embarked for Ireland without paying Their Quarters, I have taken care to stop ye. same for ye. present and should be glad to talk to you about it here to morrow morning."[1]

In the spring of 1719 the Regiment proceeded to Ireland, where it was stationed for the next quarter of a century. This was a specially peaceful time in Ireland, and accordingly there is not much to chronicle save the ordinary routine. On the 20th of August we meet with the regular order, directing the Muster Master General to give the Agent full pay for three months, commencing the 1st of January last to the 31st of March following, both inclusive, "out of which you are to deduct all such Sums of Money as have been issued to the said Regiment either upon Account of Subsistence, Arrears or otherwise, within that time. As also all such sums as have been stopped upon account of any cheques imposed on the said Regiment within the time mentioned and yet unremoved. And we hereby further require you to deduct out of the said Full pay so much as the charge of the Damage or Injury done to the Bedding Utensills, etc., of any of the Barracks by any of the Troops of the said Regiment during the time of their being quarter'd therein doth amount unto."[2]

In 1721, nine years after the fall of Brihuega, Pepper presents a petition, informing George I of the services he had rendered:

Most humbly Sheweth

That Yr. Petr[3] having laid before ye. Parliament his claim for £5000 (wch. Sum ye. late Lord Stanhope, when he was Plenipotentiary and Genl. in Spain, had promis'd yr. Petr. as a reward for ye. great Hazards he underwent. and ye. expences He was at in order to the Relief of Barcelona, wch. appears, as well by ye. Letter of ye. present Emperour to ye. late Queen, as by the certificate of ye. late Lord Stanhope to have been ye. means of saving ye. then King and Kingdom of Spain) the House of Commons did unanimously agree in their Opinion of ye. Justice of yr. Petrs. claim, and voted a Clause should be brought in to empower ye. Commissrs. of Accots. to certify for ye. same.

[1] *W.O.*, 4/22, p. 67.   [2] I E, 3.16, p. 33.   [3] Your Petitioner.

That Mr Walpole and ye. late Mr. Secretary Craggs thinking it for yr. Majesty's Service in Parliament prevail'd on yr. Petr. to drop ye. sd. Clause, they giving yr. Petr. assurance that He should receive his Satisfaction for ye. sd. Sum from yr. Majesty.

Yr. Petr. humbly begs leave further to Represent to Yr. Majty., that it is upwards of two years since He quitted ye. Governmt. of Kinsale upon the Earl Cadogan's delivering him Yr. Majty.'s Message, that it would be pleasing to Yr. Majty. that yr. Petr. should do so, rather than a Person no way attach'd to Yr. Majty.'s Interest should come into his Seat in Parliament, as was then most probable : And that Yr. Petr. should receive from Yr. Majty. an Equivalent for that Government.

That Yr. Petr. having ye. honour to be told that his Serving in Parliamt. would be agreeable to Yr. Majty., notwithstanding his great expences on ye. former Election, did attempt being chosen into this present House of Commons, and by his own Strength without other assistance was return'd, against ye. Opposition made by Sr. Harry Goring and others, in both wch. Elections Yr. Petr. expended upwards of £5000 pounds.

That a Zeal for Yr. Majty.'s Service has made Yr. Petr. on every occasion to forego ye. Private Regards he should otherwise have had for himself and his Family : Nor would he notwithstanding his late Indisposition have been prevail'd upon to quit Yr. Majty.'s Service in ye. Army had he not Yr. Royal Promise that if he should recover his health, he should be honour'd again with the command of a Regiment.

Yr. Petr. therefore being now restor'd to his health, humbly prays that Yr. Majty. out of Yr. Royal Justice and Goodness will be Graciously pleas'd to give such directions with regard to ye. premisses as may enable Yr. Petr. to purchase a Regimt. ; or by Pension on ye English or Irish Establishment to grant such Equivalent as Yr. Royal Wisdom shall seem meet.[1]

On the 12th of December this indefatigable petitioner again approached George I :

Sire

A mon retour du Bourg, ou je suis Choisis membre de Parlement, et ou autre secours que le credit, que j'ay acquis je me suis asseuré une nouvelle Elextion.

[1] *S.P., Military,* Bundle 5.

J'ay apris que Le Bureau de garde magasin de la Tour Etoit vacant par le mort du Chevalier Thomas Wheat (et quoi que cet Employ ne soit pas equivalant, au Gouvernement de Kinsale que j'ay quite pour le Service de vôtre Majesté.

Si Votre Majeste, Sire, veut bien m'honorer de cet Employ, Je recevray avoie toute la reconnoissance possible cette Faveur, comme une marque de sa bonté Royalle Etant avoie un tres profond respect.

Sire

De Votre Majesté
Le tres humble, tres obeissant Et
tres fidele Serviteur et Sujet.[1]

On the 10th of November, 1724, Pepper wrote another petition, setting forth that information has been laid against him suggesting His Majesty had not power to grant him the offices of "Head Ranger, Stwd., Head Bailiff and Woodward" of the Manor and Chase of Enfield in the Duchy of Lancaster.[2]

We shall not meet John Pepper again in these pages, and we feel just a shade sorry to note him placing such a high value on his services.   He had attained the exalted rank in those days of Major-General, and on his retirement he had become Adjutant-General. He had been Governor of Kinsale, and ranger of Epping Forest and of Enfield Chase, and now sought to become Constable of the Tower.   We know of no service he rendered at Barcelona that would entitle him to claim no less a sum than £13,750 in the currency of 1913.   It is well to set a high value on your services, but did not the retired Major-General set an unduly high one?

The remaining period of the command of Major-General Bowles is uneventful.   On the 31st of August, 1722, we meet with the regular warrant to the Vice-Treasurer to give Samuel Braithwait of Dublin £2218 18s. 2½d. for the clothing of the regiment.[3] This formed the net off-reckonings for two years.   On the 19th of November, 1722, Phineas Bowles died in harness.

George I conferred the colonelcy on Major-General Richard Munden of the 13th Dragoons.   Like Bowles, he had served with William III and the Duke of Marlborough.   He was with the

---

[1] *S.P., Military*, Bundle 5.   [2] *Add. MSS.*, 36135, f. 90.   [3] 1 E, 3.16, p. 471.

First Guards at Schellenberg in 1704. There he behaved with the utmost bravery, his hat riddled with bullets, yet cheering his men on. He led the forlorn hope at Schellenberg, bringing back with him but twenty out of eighty men. Like the Duke of Marlborough, he was a devoted Protestant, manifesting as much zeal for religion as for his profession. He became colonel in 1706, receiving the colonelcy of a newly-raised regiment of foot in 1709, and this corps served in Spain. It was present at the combat of Caya in 1709, at the Battle of Almenara, and at the fall of Brihuega. In 1710 it was disbanded, and in the following year Munden was promoted Brigadier-General. In 1714 he succeeded Lord Lansdowne as Governor of Pendennis Castle.[1] In 1715 he raised a corps of dragoons, now the 13th Hussars. In June, 1722, we find him Outranger of Windsor Forest, caring for the growth of the woods in his charge.[2] With the deepest regret he this month attended the funeral of his old chief, the Duke of Marlborough. On the 19th of November, 1722, he was appointed commanding officer of the Eighth.

On the 31st of January, 1723, there is the orthodox warrant for the clothing of the Regiment by Elias Cripps of Dublin,[3] and on the 20th of May the no less orthodox warrant for its full pay.[4]

On the 24th of March, 1724, the Muster Master General received orders to prepare his warrant for clearing or paying the arrears of the Regiment.[5] On the 13th of June the Treasury was to pay the Agent £360 for forage for next winter, and the stoppage thereof was to be at the rate of sixty pounds a month until the whole sum advanced is paid.[6] On the 8th of August a warrant was prepared for paying the executors of Phineas Bowles the allowance due to him as Quarter-Master-General from the 1st of January, 1721, to the 4th of August following.[7] On the 8th of September, 1724, Munden was asked to give Richard Borough the allowance due to him as Town Major of Dublin "pursuant to His Majesty's Establishment for Payments of Military Affair."[8]

[1] *S.P., Military*, 5. [2] *Treasury Papers*, 1/239, f. 71. [3] 1 E, 3.17, p. 85.
[4] 1 E, 3.16, p. 471. [5] 1 E, 3.17, p. 104. [6] 1 E, 3.18, p. 9.
[7] 1 E, 3.18, p. 59. [8] 1 E, 3.18, p. 82.

The matter of officers' servants and of filling up the vacancies due to death and other causes is dealt with in an order sent from Dublin Castle on the 30th of November, 1724. "The Forces here," it runs, "according to all accounts, are in as good condition and kept in as strict order as an Army can be, and tho' the Number of Non-Effectives in several Regiments is very great, . . . yet by the Orders His Majesty commanded me to transmit, the whole Affaire is now come to His knowledge, . . . the Officers will, for their own honour as well as His Majesty's Service, take care to fill up those Non-Effectives before the 25 of March next, at which time I have let them know His Majesty expected the Army should be complete, . . . since the Order for reducing two Irish out of each Foot annually and for listing none but British Born subjects, between Seventeen and Eighteen hundred Recruits have been brought over from Great Britain, in such numbers as might complete the several Regiments once every Year."[1]

Major-General Richard Munden died on the 20th of September, 1725, and was succeeded by Major-General Sir Robert Rich, Baronet, from the 13th Dragoons. He was the second son of Sir Robert Rich, of Roos Hall, Suffolk, a descendant from the elder branch of the powerful family of Rich, Earls of Warwick and Holland. He began his military career with a commission as ensign in the Grenadier Guards in 1700. Before he was twenty he was twice wounded, first at Schellenberg in 1704, and afterwards at Blenheim on the 13th of August of the same year. In 1708 he was made captain of a company of Grenadier Guards, with the rank of lieutenant-colonel, and received his commission as colonel in 1709. On the death of his elder brother, Sir Charles, he succeeded in 1706 to the title and estates. In 1708 he fought a duel in Suffolk with Sir Edmund Bacon, Bart., whom he ran through the body. The effects were "wrongly supposed to be mortell," but Sir Edmund survived to 1755. Rich served in the 18th Foot until that regiment was broke in 1714. In the summer of 1715 he raised a regiment of dragoons which took its share in the suppression of the Jacobite Rebellion, but in 1718 it was disbanded.

[1] *S.P., Ir., Entry Books*, 8.

On the 19th of November, 1722, he obtained the colonelcy of the 13th Light Dragoons, on the 23rd of September, 1725, that of the Eighth, and on the 1st of January, 1731, that of the 6th Dragoon Guards. This was his last command, and he held it to his death in 1768. His service in the army amounted to over sixty-seven years. He entered Parliament in 1715, and retired in 1741. As a member of the House of Commons he extended steady support to Sir Robert Walpole. In 1718 he was appointed a groom of the bedchamber to the Prince of Wales, on whose accession to the throne he became a groom of the bedchamber to the King. He also became Brigadier-General in 1727, Major-General in 1735, Lieutenant-General in 1739, General in 1747, and Field-Marshal in 1757. In 1740 he received the coveted life appointment of governor of the Royal Hospital at Chelsea at the salary of five hundred a year.

In 1742 he embarked with his regiment of dragoons for Flanders to join the Earl of Stair's army, fighting at Dettingen in 1743. In 1745 his was one of the regiments to march through London on their way to Kent and Sussex to oppose any landing of the French which might have aided the "Forty-Five." He was one of the three lieutenant-generals placed upon the staff of the army formed under the chief command of Field-Marshal the Earl of Stair to oppose an apprehended invasion from France in 1744. Indirectly he had to do with one of the exploits of the Eighth in 1756, when he presided at the court-martial upon Lieutenant-General Thomas Fowke, Governor of Gibraltar, for disobedience of orders in connection with the loss of Minorca.

In 1725 we meet with the following :

> Whereas His Majesty hath thought very fit and necessary for the support and maintenance of the Service and to preserve and keep up good order and Discipline among the Troops, that a strict Review should be made of all His Majesty's Forces, and it being for His Majesty's Service that a true and faithful Account of their present strength and condition, with their Behaviour in their Quarters, should be Reported to Us, and be ready to be transmitted to His Majesty as soon as possible : We do hereby pray and require you to make an exact Review of such

of His Majesty's Forces Quartered in and near the Province of Connaught in this Kingdom, as are mentioned in the annexed List,[1] and to observe the following Instructions in the said Review.

1—That you do repair to the several Quarters of each Regiment, Troop and Company to be reviewed by you, and to cause the said Troops to pass in Review before you, and to take an Account of their numbers, with the goodness of their Men and Horses and also of the condition of their Cloathing, specifying in your Returns what Day the new Cloathing of each Regiment for the present year was received by the Men, and giving particular directions to the officers that the soldiers do from the time of receiving such New Cloathing contrive to wear the same ; you are also to take an account of their Arms and Accoutrements, distinguishing those Regiments which have received their New Arms made according to the last pattern pursuant to His late Majesty's orders, and to inform yourself if they are provided with Tents and all other Camp necessaries fit and ready to March and take the Field upon any Occasion, and to be particular in your Inspection of the officers Horses and whether they are such in every respect as may answer the ends His Majesty proposes from them, should they have any occasion to enter upon any immediate Action or Expedition.

That you take an exact account of the number of officers present with each Regiment, Troop and Company, and who are absent, with the reason of their absence, and the respective times they have been from Quarters, specifying whether in or out of the Kingdom.

That you take an exact account of the British Recruits which have been raised since the last General Review now remaining in their respective Companies, mentioning when and where they were Listed ; that you can take an account of the soldiers Dead, Deserted or Discharg'd since the said Review, and if you have any reason to believe or suspect that there are any Papists in the said Troops or Companies you are to discharge them.

That you cause each Regiment, Troop, and Company to be exercised before you, and carefully observe the manner of their performance, and take notice of any defects or negligence of the officers in the discharge of this part of their duty, and strictly command and enjoin them to use their utmost diligence and endeavour to teach and perfect their Men in

[1] There is no such list.

the knowledge and use of their Arms, that they may upon Action be ready and expert in all the parts of discipline which the Service requires ; And that you see the same exercise be used throughout the Forces, according to the orders that have been given thereupon.

That you do in the fitting and proper manner see that the officers do justly account with and pay the Non-commissioned officers and Private Men all their just demands, and that they do not make any illegal or undue Stoppage from them ; That you take effectual care that the method of paring the Dragoons be pursued according to the Governments order of the 6th of May 1725, And in case of any complaints upon these heads, that you do enquire into the Truth of the Fact and upon due Examination thereof, if the said complaint is found reasonable, that you order justice to be done, and upon the refusal of any officer to report the same to Us for our further direction.

The scheme of quarters for 1725 and 1726 was the same. According to it there was to be one troop at Roscommon, Castlebar, and Headford, and one-and-a-half at Portumna and Loughrea, thus making up the six.[1] At Sligo on the 21st of October, 1725, the Eighth were inspected by an officer whose name is not given, but who was probably Lord Tyrawley.   Here is the list of officers :

Field Officers and Captains.	Where.
Sir. Robt. Rich	Quarters
Lt. Col. Samll. Whitshed	Dublin
Major De Grangues	Quarters
Capt. Willm. Bland	,,
Capt. Cuff. Ellison	Gt. Britain, by licence
Capt. Sheff. Austin	,,

Lieutenants.	Where.
Capt. Lt. Thos. Echlin	Quarters
Christ. Zobell	Dublin
Thoms. Erle	G. Britain, by licence
Cha. Bowles	Quarters
Jas. Johnson	,,
Rich. Harwood	,,

[1] *Add. MSS.*, 23636, *Tyrawley Papers.*

Cornets.	Where.
Rich. Skinton	Quarters
Willm. Berkeley	,,
John Withers	,,
Fair. Jenkins	,,
Fra. Baillie	,,
Whitt. Mackean	,,

Quarter Masters.	Where.	Sergeants.	Corporals.	Drums.	Private Dragoons.	Horses.
— Byrne	Quarters	1	2	1	20	24
Willm. Skinton	,,	1	2	1	20	24
Fort. Low	,,	1	2	1	20	24
Jams. Graham	,,	1	2	1	20	24
Willm. Martin	,,	1	2	1	20	24
Dell. Miller	,,	1	2	1	20	24

Staff Officers.	Where.
Chapl. Wm. Cross	Dublin
Surgn. John Hogge	Quarters.

According to the report of the inspecting officer: "The Horses are very little Ridden, or Bitted, and the Men ride very ill, and doe their Exercise on Horseback very indifferently, but are pretty well on foot.

"The majors Troop is a good Troop of Men, but 25 Men must be chang'd out of the other five Troops, and 55 Horses out of the Six Troops to make it a Tollerable Regiment."[1]

Among the Tyrawley Papers there is an abstract of the report of the General Officers in the year 1726, and it appears from these papers that Lord Tyrawley was the inspecting officer. He was an extremely popular officer who had been present at the siege of Barcelona in 1703 and the Battle of Almanza in 1706. He afterwards served under Marlborough, and was severely wounded during the Battle of Malplaquet. That is, he knew the worth of the Eighth of old, and he also knew the Marlborough tradition. He declared that the barracks were in very bad order, and this reacted on the condition of the men. His report is: "Bad Arms,

[1] *S.P., Military*, 6.

a great many horses wanting, but said to be on the road, Clothing not delivered. Col: Whitshed at his House."[1]

So far as we can judge Sir Robert Rich had taken trouble with the clothing, though no doubt with a change in command there was a change in contractor, giving rise to delay. On the 27th of August, 1726, Rich had concluded a contract with Joseph Kane of Dublin for clothing and accoutrements. The first mounting was to be on the 28th of April, 1726, and the second mounting on the 28th of April, 1727, and Rich had assigned to him the off-reckonings of the Regiment for the period commencing the 25th of March, 1726, and ending the 24th of March, 1727, inclusive. The amount of the contract was £2154 6s. 5d.

The Tyrawley Papers furnish us with the estimate of the subsistence of a trooper, a dragoon, and a foot soldier with the constant and necessary deductions with which each is charged in 1727. We give the plight of the dragoon:

	s.	d.	£	s.	d.
A Dragoon for the winter 6 months at 11½d. a day for 28 days			1	6	10
Subsistence at 3s. a week for 28 days ..	12	0			
Forage at 4½d. a day for Do. ..	10	6			
Surgeon a week 1½d.					
Clerk Do. is a month	2	0			
Farrier Do.					
Riding Master at ¼d. a day is a month ..		7			
Stable-Man at 2d. a week is a month ..		8			
Sheets		1			
Remaining to be accounted for	1	0			
			1	6	10
A Dragoon for the Summer 6 Months					
Subsistence at 3s. a week for 28 days ..	12	0			
Grass at 1s. 2d. a week is	4	8			
Surgeon, Clerk, Farrier, and Riding Master	2	7			
Sheets		1			
Stock-Purse[2] at 1½d. a day	3	6			
Remaining to be accounted for	4	0			
			1	6	10

[1] *Add. MSS.*, 23636, *Tyrawley Papers.*   [2] This was the recruiting fund of the regiment.

The order for clearing or payment of arrears came on the 25th of February, 1727.[1]   During the next year the following regulations for clothing were issued.   For a dragoon it was to be:

A new Cloth Coat well lined with serge.

A new waistcoat.

A pair of new breeches.

A new laced hat.

A pair of new large buff coloured gloves with stiff tops.

A pair of new boots as they shall be wanting.

Saddles to be left to the judgment of the general officer who may be appointed to review them.

Housings, caps, new horse furniture, bits, stirrup irons, and cloaks faced with the livery of the regiment, entirely new, as they shall be wanting.

New buff or buff coloured accoutrements.

A shoulder belt with a pouch, a waist belt sufficient to carry the sword, with a place to receive the bayonet, and sling for the arms such as the general officers appointed to inspect the clothing shall approve of as they shall be wanting.

The second mounting is to consist of new laced hats, gloves, and horse collars.[2]

The order for the payment of forage for the next winter was issued to Sir Robert Rich on the 19th of June, 1728, and the amount was three hundred and sixty pounds to be repaid on the usual conditions.[3]   By an order of the 2nd of February, 1729, the clothing, accoutrements, and horses of the Regiment were all to conform to the standards laid down.   Particular directions are given for the dragoon:

A strong well bodyed Horse, at fifteen hands and not exceeding, Men not under five foot Ten inches, in Stockings, is a Sufficient Size for the Horse and Dragoons ; and that they may be chosen Men with good countenances, good limbs, and broad shoulders—

And that the size of the Men for the Foot Guards be Five Foot nine Inches ; and Marching Regiments Five Foot Eight Inches with shoes such as are given in the Cloathing.[4]

[1] I E, 3.19, p. 118.   [2] I E, 3.20, p. 110.   [3] I E, 3.20, p. 110.   [4] I E, 3.21, p. 78.

Sir Robert Rich provided, as we find by a letter of the 28th of April, 1729, horse furniture, to use the phraseology of the eighteenth century, and suitable accoutrements to be imported from England for the use of his Regiment.[1] Naturally he objected to paying duty on them, and accordingly the Commissioners of Revenue were ordered to admit them free from all duty. Nor was this privilege confined to Sir Robert Rich as a commanding officer. He was, like Charles Cathcart, also a groom of the bedchamber, for which he received his quarterly annuity of one hundred and twenty-five pounds.[2] As a Member of Parliament, he, like Charles Cathcart[1] in the days to come, was exempted from the duty of paying four shillings in the pound.[3] On the 17th of August, 1730, orders were issued for the special care of the Barracks, the bedding, utensils, and firing, and a monthly return was to be made. In the case of billeting, the officers are earnestly asked to reconcile any differences between the troops and the inhabitants, maintaining at all costs "good order and exact discipline."[4]

Sir Robert Rich's period of office ceased, and on the 1st of January, 1731, the Honourable Charles Cathcart, son of Alan, seventh Lord Cathcart, succeeded him as commanding officer. Rich had joined the service in his fifteenth year, whereas Cathcart was in his eighteenth. In 1704 he commanded a company in Colonel Macartney's regiment (since disbanded), serving against the French on the frontiers of Holland. As the fifth commanding officer to serve with the great Duke, he continued the Marlborough tradition with the Eighth. Like Rich, he fought at Ramillies, and, like Rich, he served with the Earl of Stair, acting in 1707 as brigade-major with the Earl. Indeed he took part in most of the actions we associate with Marlborough. In 1709 he was appointed major of the Greys, soon attaining the rank of its lieutenant-colonel. Like Rich, on the accession of George I, he was appointed one of the grooms of His Majesty's bedchamber. Like Bowles, Munden and Rich, he took part in the quelling of the Rebellion of 1715. His share, however, was more active than theirs, for on joining the

---

[1] T., 14/11, p. 331. [2] *Treasury Papers, Calendar*, 1729–30.
[3] *Treasury Papers, Calendar*, 1731–34. [4] I E, 3.22, p. 12.

Duke of Argyle in 1715 he, with a party of dragoons, encountered on the 23rd of October, 1715, a body of Jacobites, consisting of one hundred horse and two hundred foot. Meeting these at five o'clock on the morning of the 24th, he attacked and defeated them, taking seventeen prisoners. With the dragoons he fell upon the Jacobite flank at the Battle of Sheriffmuir. In 1717 he received the colonelcy of the Ninth Foot; in 1721 of the Thirty-first Regiment; and on the 1st of January, 1731, of the Eighth. In the following year he succeeded to the title of Lord Cathcart. In 1733 he became colonel of the Seventh Horse, now Sixth Dragoon Guards; in 1735 he attained the rank of brigadier-general, and in 1739 that of major-general. In 1735 George II appointed him lord of the bedchamber. He was one of the Scots representative peers. In Ireland he held the posts of Governor of Duncannon Fort, and, as was befitting a former commanding officer of the Eighth, of Londonderry. On the outbreak of the War of Austrian Succession Cathcart was selected to command the expedition against the Spanish possessions in South America. He was appointed commander-in-chief, but dying on the passage on the 20th of December, 1740, he was buried on the beach of Prince Rupert's Bay, Dominica, where a monument was erected to his memory.

The first activity of Charles Cathcart we encounter is his receiving 138 swords from Scotland by a warrant of the date of the 18th of May, 1731.[1] The next year his six troops were quartered in Dublin, and were reviewed there by Lieutenant-General Pearce.[2] The care of the widows still continued, for we find an order dated the 29th of April, 1732, going back to the command of Sir Robert Rich, giving £257 15s. 1¾d. out of the Stock Purse, or recruiting fund of the Regiment, to the widows.[3] The Muster Master General prepared a warrant paying to the agent the additional allowance of threepence a day to the non-commissioned officers and men for doing duty in Dublin.[4] The usual warrants for off-reckonings, forage, watch ammunition, and the like, of course continue to be issued, but there is nothing noteworthy in them.

[1] *Treasury Papers, Calendar*, 1731–34.   [2] I E, 3.22, p. 301.
[3] I E, 3.22, p. 278.   [4] I E, 3.24, p. 49.

On the 7th of July, 1735, the order for the annual review was sent out. By the time it took place there was a new commanding officer, for Sir Adolphus Oughton, Baronet, was appointed on the 7th of August, 1733.

Sir Adolphus Oughton belonged to Tachbrook, Warwickshire. He was appointed a captain and lieutenant-colonel in the First Footguards in 1706, was aide-de-camp to Marlborough, during his retirement on the continent in 1712,[1] and in 1718 was regimental lieutenant-colonel of the Coldstream Guards. When the Prince of Wales (afterwards George II) was made a K.G., Oughton acted as his proxy, for which he was created a baronet in 1718. He was long member of parliament for Coventry. In 1735 he was promoted to the rank of brigadier-general. Leaving no issue by his marriage, he died in 1736, when the Tachbrook baronetcy became extinct. By his will he left the sum of fifteen hundred pounds to be invested for the benefit of "my natural son James Adolphus Dickenson" Oughton on his attaining the age of twenty-one. On the 29th of October, 1741, the son was appointed lieutenant in St. George's (lately Oughton's) Dragoons.

Major-General Naper made a tour of inspection and reviewed Oughton's Dragoons in 1735 at Philipstown. One troop was stationed at Granard, Mullingar, and Navan, and three at Philipstown.[2]

Lord Cathcart, though he has severed his connection with the Eighth, we meet again, for on the 29th of July, 1735, he petitioned for an allowance similar to that grant to others who had occupied, as he had, the position of Receiver General of all Land, Rents, and Casualties, and Paymaster of all Salaries, Pensions, and Allowances paid in Scotland.[3] We feel, however, a more lively interest in the petition he presented to the Queen in 1735:

Sheweth

That Your Petitioner served in Flanders from the Beginning of the Year 1704 'till the End of the War, in the Stations of Captain of Foot, Captain of Dragoons, Major of Brigade, Major and Lieut. Colonel of Dragoons.

[1] *Marlborough Despatches*, V, pp. 579–80. [2] 1 E, 3.25, p. 248.
[3] *Treasury Papers*, 1735–38.

That his services were approven of by the Duke of Marlborough, and by the other Generals by whom he had the honour to be commanded.

That he commanded the Grey Dragoons during the unnatural Rebellion in Scotland, when he had the good fortune to strike the first Stroke against the Rebels with Success at Dumferling, and when his Conduct at Dumblain received the Approbation of His late and Present Majesty.

That he had an old Regiment of Foot given him, the beginning of the year 1717.

That he had the honour to be Groom of His Majesty's Bedchamber soon after His coming into England ; in which Station he had an Opportunity to Shew his Zeal for the King, by adhering to His Person and Interest at a time when he had large Offers made him by the late King's Servants, and when all his Relations were on that side of the Question.

That during the Eighteen years he continued in the Bedchamber, his greatest Study and Endeavour was to do his Duty in the manner he thought the most agreeable to His Majesty.

That by his Father's death, which happened in the end of the Year 1732, his Services in the Bedchamber Ceased.

May it therefore please Your Majesty to intercede with the King that Your Petitioner may succeed to Major Genl. Russel lately Deceased in the Government of Berwick upon Tweed, as a mark of His Majesty's favour in Consideration of the Petitioner's long and faithful Services in the Army and in the Bedchamber.[1]

From an order to the Muster Master General on the 3rd of April, 1736, it is quite clear that the six troops were engaged for almost the whole of December of the preceding year on duty in Dublin, and were accordingly to receive an additional allowance.[2] On the 20th of June, 1737, the lieutenant of Major Ellison's troop received a grant towards the hire of lodgings at Carrickfergus from the 23rd of June, 1736, to the 20th of June, 1737. During this time the barracks were being prepared, and he was allowed

---

[1] S.P., Dom., Military, 9.   [2] 1 E, 3.24, p. 49.

three-and-six a week for fifty-one weeks, according to the rule of the barracks. The sum was thus apportioned:

	£	s.	d.
The Barracks		8	16	6
Quarter Master		8	16	6
Net		47	8	4
Secretary			13	6
Poundage		1	4	$0\frac{3}{4}$
Pells			4	$11\frac{1}{2}$
Gross		49	9	$6\frac{1}{4}$[1]

Like Phineas Bowles, Sir Adolphus Oughton died in harness on the 4th of September, 1736, and for the first time in the annals of the Eighth the colonelcy remained vacant for some time till George II filled it up by the appointment of Major-General Clement Neville, from the 14th Dragoons, on the 27th of June, 1737.

Neville entered the army at the Revolution, and William III signed his first commission in 1688. He served with distinction in the wars of King William and Queen Anne, receiving the rank of colonel at the close of the campaign of 1711. On the 9th of April, 1720, he became colonel of the 14th Dragoons, and on the 27th of June, 1737, colonel of the Eighth. In 1739 he was promoted major-general, and the next year received the colonelcy of the Sixth Horse, now the Fifth Dragoon Guards. In 1743 he became lieutenant-general, serving several years on the staff in Ireland.

The year Clement Neville was appointed to the Eighth he became Brigadier upon the Establishment on the 22nd of September,[2] and on the 27th of the same month he became Brigadier of the Forces *vice* Lieutenant-General Robert Naper.[3] Towards the end of 1739 there are hints of war with Spain, and indeed the War of the Austrian Succession was to break out the very next year. As with every outbreak of war, there was at once a call for more soldiers.[4] Accordingly there were orders for nine additional men in all

---

[1] 1 E, 3.25, p. 52.   [2] *S.P., Ir., Entry Books*, 11.
[3] *W.O.*, 8/3, p. 41.   [4] 1 E, 3.26, pp. 178, 182, 311.

regiments of horse and dragoons. Levy money, clothing, arms and accoutrements for each additional dragoon required £37 2s. 8d.[1] according to the order of the 2nd of April, 1740. The pay of the non-effective men was to be discontinued, and all vacancies due to deaths were to be forthwith filled up.

The main feature of the policy of Sir Robert Walpole had been the preservation of peace, and naturally the declaration of war against Spain found the army in a signally unprepared condition. Realising all that Marlborough had accomplished for the service, he muttered, "They may ring their bells now ; they will be wringing their hands before long." Recruits flocked to the colours. A bounty was offered, and the Irish came to England to enlist only to be informed that as Roman Catholics they could not be admitted.[2]

In 1740 the colonelcy of the Sixth Horse was given to Major-General Clement Neville, and on the 6th of May, 1740, Richard St. George took his place with the Eighth. An ensign of foot in 1689, he served under William III and the Duke of Marlborough. He was promoted to the lieutenant-colonelcy of the Seventh Horse, now the Sixth Dragoon Guards, and in 1737 to the colonelcy of the Twentieth Foot, and in 1740 to the colonelcy of the Eighth. He attained the rank of brigadier-general in 1743, of major-general in 1744, and of lieutenant-general in 1747. The persistency of the Marlborough tradition is remarkable, for no less than eight commanding officers served with the great Duke. Robert Killigrew, Phineas Bowles, Richard Munden, Sir Robert Rich, Charles Cathcart, Sir Adolphus Oughton, Clement Neville, and Richard St. George are the names on this list, and we are not even sure that John Pepper is not entitled to a place on it. If this were so, all the commanding officers except the founder of the Regiment had served with John Churchill.

Orders came to St. George on the 12th and the 20th of May, 1740. By the first all officers, except general officers, were directed to repair immediately to their posts, there to attend to their duty, and not to absent themselves from their commands on any pretext

[1] *T.*, 14/12, *Out-Letters, Ireland.*
[2] *Secretary's Common Letter Book*, June 19, October 9, 1739.

whatever.[1] By the second Colonel St. George was directed to
repair forthwith to Kilkenny to take upon him the command of
the forces there and at Waterford and Duncannon Fort.[2] On the
25th of March, 1741, there was to be a further augmentation of
nine men to each troop. Next year,[3] on the 21st of December,
we find the route for officers and men with forty recruit horses
from Northampton to Chester or Holyhead :

Daventry	
Coventry	To rest not more than two nights in a place during
Coleshill	this march
Lichfield	
Stone	
Nantwich	
Chester	To remain in either of those places till they can embark
Parkgate	for Ireland ; or if it should be more convenient for
	the young horses then to march from Chester
Holywell	
Radland	
Conway	
Bangor	
Holyhead	There to remain till they can embark for Ireland.[4]

Eighteen men had been added to each troop in 1740 and 1741,
and on the 11th of October, 1742, there was to be another adjutant
with one sergeant, one corporal, one drummer, and twenty private
men to each troop. At the beginning of 1743 a draft of men
and horses proceeded to Flanders.

The Lord Lieutenant received peremptory orders on the 26th of
January, 1744, to augment and recruit the several regiments of
horse and dragoons, serving in Flanders, with all expedition, by
drafts to be made from the regiments of horse and dragoons in
England and Ireland.[5] No time was to be lost in providing the

[1] 1 E, 3.26, p. 195.   [2] 1 E, 3.27, p. 258.

[3] Cf. a quarto volume of drawings entitled *A Representation of the Clothing of the King's
Household, and of all the Forces in the Establishment of England and Ireland for the Year* 1742.

[4] *W.O.*, 5/35, *Marching Orders. Cf. Colburn's United Service Magazine*, 1875, Part I,
p. 432.

[5] *S.P., Ir., Entry Books*, 11.

necessary transports to carry this body of troops to Flanders by Ostend, Bristol or Chester. On the 30th of January, 1744, the Duke of Devonshire commanded these reinforcements to embark at Dublin and disembark at Chester under Lieutenant-Colonel Pole. Minutes were enclosed for the proper drafting of the regiments of horse and dragoons. These stated:

It is His Majesty's Pleasure that Ten Men and Horses p. Troop be drafted from each of the Regiments of Horse in Ireland.

That Fourteen Men and Horses p. Troop be drafted from each of the Regiments of Dragoons in Ireland. . . .

Fifteen Men out of each Troop of Dragoons to be Reserved and the Drafts to be made from the Remainder and to be sent Compleately Accoutred as the Horse. . . .

One Captain, Two Subalterns, a Qur. Mar. and 2 Serjeants to march with the Drafts from each Regt. of Dragoons to the Place of Em-Barkation, and one Commission'd Officer, and Qur. Mar. be Ordered to Accompany them to Ostend.

The Horse and Dragoon Officers to deliver the Drafts there to the Officers appointed to Receive them.

No man to be Drafted as a Volunteer or otherwise who is lame, bursten, or disqualified for His Majesty's Service, Nor any Horses which are disqualified for the Service, not above the Age of Nine Years last Grass.

These Orders to be Read at the head of each Troop at the time of drafting.

The said Drafts are to be upon the British Establishment from the 25th of last December inclusive.

That the expense of this Embarkation is to be born by Great Britain.

That His Grace the Duke of Devonshire will appoint one General Officer, to have the Care of this Embarkation.

That one Field Officer do attend the Draughting of each Troop to see that these His Majesty's Orders be punctually executed.

That the Officers who deliver the Men do take a Receipt for the Drafts from the Persons appointed to Receive Them at Ostend.

It is His Majesty's Pleasure that this Embarkation be made as soon as possible And that His Grace will Order This Embarkation to be made at such Place, as he shall think proper.

That the Genl. Officers appointed to have the Care of this Embarkation be Ordered to Reject such Men and Horses as he shall find not conformable to His Majesty's Instructions, and that others be furnished in their Room.

The Subsistance from the 25th of December last inclusive to the time of the delivery of the Drafts at Ostend to be repaid by the Agents or Paymasters of the respective Regiments into which they shall be incorporated And that the Days of their delivery at Ostend be certified to the Lord Lieut. of Ireland or his Secretary in Order that the said Subsistance be reserved in Bank as a Fund towards replacing and re-mounting a like Number Men in the respective Regiments from which they were drafted.

That His Grace will Order one Field Horse or Dragoon Officer to Command the whole and see them delivered at Ostend.

His Majesty leaves it to His Grace whether this Embarkation may be made at one or more Embarkations.

That His Grace will give directions to Contract for Transports for this Service.

That it be left to the Government of Ireland to Transport the Drafts of Horse and Dragoons either directly to Ostend or to Bristol or Chester as they may think most for his Majesty's Service.

That in Case the Drafts should debark in any part of England that Notice should be sent thereof to the Secretary at War in order to send Routs for them.

That the Officers and Non Commissioned Officers do return to their respective Regiments after the delivery of the Drafts at Ostend.[1]

We give these minutes at length because they are typical. They illustrate a system that had deplorable effects not merely upon the Regiment, but upon the whole British Army. The soldier lost the feeling that he belonged to his old regiment, and he scarcely

[1] *S.P., Ir., Entry Book*, 11.

felt that he belonged to his new one. Regimental *esprit de corps* is the very lifeblood of our army, and it suffered a severe shock by the method of drafting. Serious as the primary evils of drafting always are, the secondary ones are by no means to be ignored. For the transfer of every man from one regiment to another entailed also a transfer of cash, and an adjustment of the Stock Purses between regiment and regiment. It also meant the re-placement of the transferred men who were well aware that they might be drafted, and so the ills of the system revolved in a vicious circle. An order of the 30th of November, 1744, insists on the replacement of men taken from the Eighth[1]: it has nothing to say about the harm inflicted upon regimental tradition. No doubt this feeling can be carried too far, too far perhaps when a man felt that his loyalty was claimed more by his troop than by his regiment. We see the worst side of this in the answer of the Swiss who was asked whether he cared more for his own canton than for Switzerland, "My shirt is nearer to me than my waistcoat." Of course this spirit is regrettable. Still, we prefer devotion even to a company rather than devotion to nothing at all. The soldiers of St. George's Dragoons realised that it was an honour to be admitted to it. All recruits had to bring recommendations from the rector of the parish, and a justice of the peace. Nor was it easy to obtain these recommendations. The system of drafting tended to a complete breach with the county or the provincial feeling. The men of the Eighth came largely from Ulster, animated by the Ulster feeling. In the order of the 31st of January, 1745, such a provincial feeling is rudely shattered, for Major-General St. George is told he is authorised "by Beat of Drum or otherwise to Raise so many Volunteers in any County or part of Our Kingdom of Great Britain as are or shall be wanting to Recruit and fill up the respective Troops."[2]

Order after order poured forth as the needs of the War of the Austrian Succession demanded more men. The cry was, Men at any cost, even at the cost of every tradition the army ought to hold

[1] 1 E, 3.28, p. 44.   [2] *W.O.*, 26/20.

dear. The mechanical side of drafting was carefully looked after, but the officials who dictated the orders overlooked the fact that the letter kills while the spirit, and the spirit alone, gives life. Walpole had inflicted grave harm on the British army, and, thanks to his supreme carelessness about the means of defence, the authorities his system bred continued to inflict every whit as grave harm. Take such an order to the Lord Lieutenant, the Duke of Devonshire, as that of the 1st of March, 1745:

> His Majesty having given Directions, That the Men, intended to replace Those, which were draughted from the several Regiments of Horse and Dragoons in Ireland, should be raised and disciplined, but paid only as Men dismounted till further Order ; I am now to signify to your Excy., That Horses, Arms, and Accoutrements be forthwith provided, out of the present Savings on account of those Draughts, for as many of the Men so to be raised, as may be, and that such Men do appear compleatly mounted at the Muster, to be taken of His Majtys. Regiments of Horse and Dragoons, in that Kingdom.[1]

Take the warrant of the 27th of April, 1745, insisting upon deduction for the subsistence of two men in each troop from the captains in case they do not keep it complete according to establishment.[2] A second order on the 27th of April urges that no new charge be added to the Regiment without authorisation by the High Treasurer or the Commissioners of Treasury.[3] Orders of this type are of course required, yet it ought to have struck some of the authorities that drafting was seriously injuring the *esprit de corps* of regiment after regiment. Nicholas Murray Butler astonished a New York audience by stating in 1917 that he was a peace-at-any-price man. He developed his thought by adding, "The present price is war, and I am prepared to pay it." The spirit at headquarters in 1745 appeared to be, Win the war at all costs. The price was drafting, even at the cost of destroying the proper pride the soldier feels in his own regiment. Officials, inspired by this spirit, owned little regard for the intangible. What they owned was a mania for the tangible of the following

---

[1] *S.P., Ir., Entry Book*, 11.   [2] *W.O.*, 24/238.   [3] *W.O.*, 24/238, *Establishments*.

type: in this their soul delighted. A regiment of dragoons consisted of:

Field and Staff Officers.	s.	d.	Per diem. £ s. d.			For 365 days. £ s. d.		
Colonel as Colonel	15	o						
In lieu of his servants ..	4	6						
			19	6		355	17	6
Lieut. Colonel as Lieut. Col.			9	o		164	5	o
Major as Major			5	o		91	5	o
Chaplain			6	8		121	13	4
Adjutant			5	o		91	5	o
Surgeon			6	o		109	10	o
			2	11	2	933	15	10

There were six troops of 59 men in each commanded by Major-General St. George.

One Troop.	s.	d.	Per diem. £ s. d.			For 365 days. £ s. d.		
Captain 8s. and 3 Horses 3s ..	11	o						
In lieu of his servants ..	4	6						
			15	6		282	17	6
Lieutenant 4s and 2 Horses 2s ..	6	o						
In lieu of his servants ..	3	o						
			9	o		164	5	o
Cornet 3s and 2 Horses 2s. ..	5	o						
In lieu of his servants ..	3	o						
			8	o		146	o	o
Quarter Master for himself and Horses	4	o						
In lieu of his servant.. ..	1	6						
			5	6		100	7	6
Two Serjeants each 2 9 ..			5	6		100	7	6
Three Corporals „ 2 3 ..			6	9		123	3	9
Two Drummers „ 2 3 ..			4	6		82	2	6
Hautbois			2	o		36	10	o
59 effective Dragoons each 1 9 ..			5	3	3	1884	6	3
Carried forward			8	o	o	2920	o	o

One Troop.	Per diem.			For 365 days.		
	£	s.	d.	£	s.	d.
Brought forward	8	0	0	2920	0	0
Allowance to Widows		2	0	36	10	0
Allowance to the Colonel for clothing lost by deserters, etc.		2	6	45	12	0
Allowance to the Captain for recruiting		2	4	42	11	8
Allowance to the Agent		1	2	21	5	10
	8	8	0	3066	0	0
The pay of the five troops more to complete the Regiment of the like numbers and rates as the troop above mentioned.	42	0	0	15330	0	0
	52	19	2	19329	15	0[1]

St. George had maintained the healthy Marlburian traditions carried on by his seven predecessors who had served with the Duke. The process of drafting hurt one of his subordinates so much that even in time of war he felt that he could not retain his command. Accordingly, on the 14th of June, 1745, we read:

To the Right Honble. Sr. Willm. Yonge, Barrt.

His Majesty's Secretary at Warr.

Memorial of Sr. Sheffield Austin, Barrt., Lieutenant Colonel to the Regiment of Dragoons Commanded by Major General Richard St. George.

Most Humbly Sheweth

That he has served upwards of Twenty nine years and has always Attended his Duty hitherto, but his Familys Affaires have been left by his Predecessor in such a state as require his presence and constant Attention.

That Major John Arabine, the Eldest Captain, Thomas Erle, Captain Lieutenant Whitney Mackean, the Eldest Lieutenant Robert Saunderson, the Eldest Cornet George Bingham, and the Eldest Quarter Master Thomas Major and the Gentlemen of the Regiment in regard to their promotion have agreed to make his Retirement easy Allowing him full pay during Life.

That this pay is to be made up by these Gentlemen and their respective Successors serving on their present pay, after they are promoted,

[1] *W.O.*, 24/238, *Establishments.*

that is the Lieutenant Colonel or Majors pay, Major or Captains pay, the Captain or youngest Capt. for the time being on Lieutenants pay, the Lieutenant or youngest Lieutenant for the time being on Cornets pay, the Cornet or youngest Cornet for the time being on Quarter Masters pay, and the Quarter Master or youngest Quarter Master for the time being to serve without pay during the Memorialists Life.

That they have Major General St. George's Consent and Recommendation in favour of the Above Mention'd Officers.

The Memorialist therefore Most Humbly prays that Major John Arabine may be made Lieutenant Colonel in his room, the eldest Captain Thomas Erle may be made Major, Capt. Lieutenant Robert Saunderson may be made Captain Lieutenant and that Quarter Master Thomas Major may be made Cornet, and that His Majesty would be Graciously pleased to Grant the Warrant as is usual in such Cases, that the Memorialist may have his pay during Life and for the Pension of Lieutenant Colonels Widow to his wife should she survive him.[1]

No doubt such a form of promotion was fairly frequent during the eighteenth century, yet we cannot help connecting it with the system of drafting. The petition was granted, and on the 9th of July the Agent of the Regiment was directed to pay Sir Sheffield Austin twenty-four and six a day.

Since 1719 the Regiment had been stationed in Ireland, and in July, 1744, this long spell in one country came to an end. For the next twelve months it spent its time at Coventry, Warwick and Stratford-upon-Avon. For a regiment with the sporting traditions of the Eighth, it is not unsuitable to give the marching orders of the 3rd of August, 1745: "It is the Lords Justices Directions that you Cause the Two Troops belonging to Major-General St. George's Regiment of Dragoons under your Command at Warwick to March from thence three days before the Horse Races begin there to Stratford upon Avon where they are to remain untill the said Horse Races are over, and then to return to Warwick and Continue there untill further Order."[2] We shrewdly suspect that the officers in the two troops suddenly realised that urgent family affairs required their presence—at Warwick.

[1] S.P., Dom., Military, 16.   [2] W.O., 5/36, Marching Orders.

CHAPTER V

The "Forty-Five" and After

VON SCHLEIFFEN developed a splendid scheme for the invasion of France when war with that country was to be declared. In August, 1914, the disciple, Von Moltke, attempted to improve the scheme of his master, Von Schleiffen, and the result was the supreme disaster of the first battle of the Marne. Germany then lost the war, though it took four years to demonstrate this fact, just as Napoleon was beaten in 1806, though it took nine years to demonstrate this fact. The truth is that it is never easy even for one able man to meddle with the plans of another. Of course when the man is less than able, it is simply courting disaster. Louis XIV devoted himself heart and head to the question of the succession to the throne of Spain, and, despite the formidable opposition of William III and Marlborough, he achieved his end—outwardly, at all events. We now know that Louis XV was a far more capable man than historians used to imagine.[1] Still, he gave to Venus the devotion that Mars claimed, and the outcome was the disasters that mar his reign. Louis XIV had given support, staunch support, to James II in Ireland. His untimely death had ruined the prospects of the "Fifteen," and that gallant gentleman, the Old Pretender, met with the failure he scarcely deserved. Louis XV never ceased to give fair promises never destined to performance. So the Old Pretender found, and so the Young Pretender, Bonnie Prince Charlie, was destined to find in the "Forty-Five."

Sir Walter Scott refused to write the biography of Mary Queen of Scots on the ground that his heart went one way and his head another. A similar predicament lies before the biographer of

---

[1] *Cf. Louis XV et les Jacobites*, 1743-1744, by Captain Colin, and *cf. The Army Quarterly*, Vol. 4, p. 288 ; *The United Service Magazine*, Vol. 15 (N.S.), p. 107.

Prince Charles Edward, for his heart goes one way and his head another. To this moment emotions are aroused when the band plays, "Will ye no come back again?" The pity, however, is that it is not possible for anyone who cares to set down the truth to represent Charles as "a very perfect gentle knight." Indeed we are quite unable to find in him the shining figure that bewitched our fancy in our childhood. His figure is beheld in a lustre not its own : in the splendour of love and loyalty that gave themselves ungrudgingly for him and for his cause, that cherished his memory, and was content to endure exile and death for his sake.

In 1715 and in 1719 the aims of the Jacobites had been encouraged, but they had been effectively discouraged by the policy of peace pursued by Sir Robert Walpole. The War of the Austrian Succession offered them a fresh opportunity for the realisation of their deferred hopes. They appealed to Cardinal Fleury for French support, and in 1743 an expedition was equipped. In 1744 Prince Charles left Rome in order to assume command of it. The expedition sailed from Dunkirk, but returned in a shattered condition. Louis XV henceforth evinced but little real intention of renewing the enterprise, though Charles continued to cherish and to express confident hopes of his further co-operation. Without such assistance the Jacobites refused to contemplate war, and in 1744 John Murray of Broughton visited Charles on their behalf. As the prospect of French support became fainter and yet fainter, and as hope deferred made the heart of the young man sick, he at length determined to raise Scotland, "if he brought only a single Footman" with him. At the back of his mind he felt convinced that a successful effort on his own part would enlist the co-operation of Louis XV. The Prince's arrival with an insignificant armament aroused surprise and consternation, and at the outset he received but slight encouragement. When Lords Ogilvy, Pitsligo, Kilmarnock, Balmerino, Nithsdale, Kenmure, and others joined his standard, France at length bestowed outward countenance. At Holyrood Charles received the Marquis d'Eguilles with much ceremony as the titular French Ambassador. We are all familiar with the early successes of the Jacobite rising of 1745, the victory of Prestonpans, the capture of Carlisle, and the arrival at Derby on Black Friday, the 4th of December. As Carlisle had resisted, so London would resist even more strongly. The Scots dared not besiege the metropolis with Cumberland's and Wade's unbeaten armies operating in the field. Even had the Prince obtained and kept possession of it, he would inevitably in his turn have been besieged. Neither from France nor from Scotland was there any prospect of adequate reinforcements, and he and his army would have been obliged to face the necessity either to surrender or to cut their way out in a desperate rush towards Scotland. His assent to the retreat from Derby was therefore wisely, if reluctantly, given. .

In the meantime, what steps were the English taking? About the end of September, 1745, George II ordered a strong body of troops to march to Scotland under the command of Field-Marshal Wade.[1] They were appointed to assemble at Doncaster. The Field-Marshal arrived there on the 9th of October, and remained till the 21st; he then proceeded to Newcastle, where he arrived on the 29th. St. George's Dragoons arrived at Doncaster on the 8th of December. When Wade heard of the homeward flight of the highlanders from Derby, he at once despatched Major-General Oglethorpe, with St. George's Dragoons, commanded by Lieutenant-Colonel Arabin, and a detachment of Montague's and Wade's Horse (now the Second and Third Dragoon Guards) to cut off the retreat of the Jacobites.

Wade's army consisted of his own and Montague's Regiment of Horse, St. George's Dragoons, and the Yorkshire Hunters, just raised by Major-General Oglethorpe. The Foot consisted of Howard's, Barrell's, Wolfe's, Pulteney's, Blakeney's, Cholmondeley's, Munro's, Fleming's, and Battereau's Regiments, the 2nd Battalion of the Royal Scots, and Dutch troops. In all they amounted to about 8000 British and 6000 Dutch, with twenty field pieces. They suffered much from sickness at Newcastle. On hearing that the Jacobites were again attacking Carlisle, Wade set out from

---

[1] On cavalry in the '45 see the article by W. Little in *The Cavalry Journal*, Vol. 13, p. 81, and Lieut.-Col. Thompson's article in the same, Vol. 15, p. 3.

Newcastle on the 16th of November, and marched as far as Hexham, fifteen miles west of Newcastle, where he arrived at midnight on the 17th. As the fields were covered with snow, and as the roads were almost impassable, the march proved most fatiguing. On receiving intelligence of the surrender of Carlisle, Wade set out for Newcastle, where he arrived on the 22nd, having lost many of his men by sickness.

The Duke of Cumberland was pursuing the retreating enemy, and Field-Marshal Wade also advanced to cut him off, and reached Wakefield on the 10th of December. Finding, however, that Prince Charles had evaded him by a very forced march, Wade returned to Newcastle, sending his Horse, Dragoons, and the Yorkshire Hunters under the command of Major-General Oglethorpe on the 11th to join Cumberland's army. They reached Preston on the 13th of December, having performed a march of one hundred miles over roads choked with ice and snow and accompanied by most inclement weather in less than three days. The Jacobites quitted Preston on the 13th, a few hours before the arrival of St. George's Dragoons. There they joined a detachment of cavalry from the forces of the Duke of Cumberland. They pursued the Jacobites, fighting a skirmish in the village of Clifton with the rearguard of the enemy. In this skirmish three hundred dragoons are said to have defeated a thousand men, though the Jacobite reports affirm exactly the opposite. St. George's Dragoons arrived at Hesket, eight miles from Carlisle, on the 19th, where they lay till the next day. This station they occupied as an advance post to the army, which halted on the 29th at Penrith. As the Duke of Cumberland thought that the foe would make a stand at Carlisle, he halted there in order to allow his whole force to come up.

When the Duke ascertained that the Jacobites had not stayed at Carlisle, he marched on again on the 21st at four in the morning. At noon he arrived at Carlisle, and invested it. St. George's Dragoons with three hundred men of Bligh's Regiment (now the Twentieth Foot) were posted on the Scots side of the city, with orders to prevent anyone passing the bridge on the Eden. The

Duke was obliged to send to Whitehaven for a train of battering cannon, which arrived on the 28th, and on the 30th of December the garrison capitulated.

On the 15th of January, 1746, the Duke of Newcastle informed Lieutenant-General Hawley that "His R. Highness the Duke of Cumberland will send orders that Lord Mark Kerr's Regiment of Dragoons should go to Kelso, and Jedburgh (as you desire) and the Remainder of St. George's Dragoons to Dunse." On the 24th of January the Duke of Newcastle is clear that St. George's Regiment is to be ordered to Edinburgh to join Hawley there, "in whatever condition it is."[1] It arrived in Edinburgh in the early part of February, 1746. A body of Hessian troops arrived in Scotland, and were stationed in the vicinity of Edinburgh. St. George's Dragoons marched westward, and were cantoned at Earn Bridge, and, with a detachment of Ligonier's and Hamilton's Dragoons stationed at Bannockburn, were left under the command of the Earl of Crawford and the Prince of Hesse, while the Duke of Cumberland, then only twenty-three, followed the Jacobites. His plan was to hold Perth and Dunkeld as the gates to the Highlands.

On the 24th and 25th of February, 1746, the Duke of Cumberland wrote to the Duke of Newcastle. In the first letter he says: "St. George's Dragoons will be cantoned at Earn Bridge and the two Remains of Naizon's and Hamilton's, will be cantoned at Bannock-burn, near Stirling. With this Cavalry, which I put under your Command, the Prince will have a corps sufficient to destroy the Rebells, should they either attempt to avoid me, by rashly going South; or dare to attack our Posts, at Blair Castle, Castle-Menzie, etc., of which you shall have a List." In the second letter he says: "His Majesty will see by the enclosed Copys of my Letters to Prince Frederick and Lord Craufford, the disposition that is made for the Hessians, who with St. George's Dragoons, and the two remnants of Naizon's and Hamilton's will form a second Army at the foot of the Hills, near as numerous as that which is now here (at Montrose)."[2]

---

[1] *S.P., Scot.*, Series II, 27.   [2] *S.P., Scot.*, Series II, Bundle 28.

Early in March Prince Charles finally learnt that Louis XV proposed to send no French expedition. As our men hunted in the Peninsular War when not much was happening at the front, so Prince Charles fished for salmon in the River Beauly. All his life he had been a sportsman. "At six and a half," wrote the Duke of Lerida, "he could split a rolling ball ten times in succession with his crossbow." He hunted on the Duke of Hamilton's estate, and was said to have been every day at the chase. The fates were closing in about him.

On the 14th of March, 1746, Major-General St. George was once more empowered to raise volunteers in any county or in any part where he could enlist them.[1] On the 21st of the month the Duke of Cumberland wrote to Lord Crawford: "I have this moment received yours of the 20. by which I see that Blair Castle is actually invested by the Rebells and that there is no thoughts at Perth of relieving it; which much Surprises me. But, still more the Reasons you seem to mention viz. that I had ordered the Troops should not engage themselves too far in the Hills, even after a Victory. But I take this case to be entirely different; as they have but two Marches up to Blair. Wherefore I think it absolutely necessary for His Majesty's Service, that the Castle of Blair be immediately relieved; and that for that Purpose Prince Frederick should immediately, on the Receipt of these Letters, march his whole Hessian Corps, now at Perth, and St. George's Dragoons, forward to Dunkeld the first Day, and the next, on to Blair. I am very sure that on the Hessians moving, the Rebells will quit their Attempt. Or, should they not, that the Prince will purchase a Victory at a very cheap Rate."[2] Crawford, upon receipt of this letter, not unnaturally asked to be relieved of his command.

To Prince Frederick at Perth the Duke of Cumberland wrote on the 21st of March: "Mon cher Frere, Par la lettre du Comte de Craufurd du 20e: que j'ai receue ce Soir, il me paroit que les Rebelles ont Dessein d'assieger le Chateau de Blair. Ainsi, je vous prie de faire marcher immediatement a la Reception de cette

[1] *W.O.*, 26/20, p. 355.   [2] *S.P.*, *Scot.*, Series II, 29.

Lettre, tout votre Corps Hessois, qui est actuellement à Perth, et Le Regiment de Dragons Anglois de St. George qui est a portée, droit à Blair, pour chasser les Rebelles de ce voisinage. Je m'assure qu'ils n'oseront jamais hazarder une affaire serieuse contre vos Troupes aguerries et que s'ils osent le faire, votre Corps sera en etat et aura la Gloire de donner un coup decisif à ces Rebelles audacieux."

Light is thrown on the movements of the Eighth by a letter of the Duke of Atholl to Lord Justice Clerk written from Dunkeld on the 29th of March:

The Prince of Hesse arrived here with all the Hessian Troops that was in Perth and a few Dragoons, they were all ferryed over here that night except one Regiment that is encamped at Invar . . . and St. George's Regt. of Dragoons that came here the 27th. are in a field behind the Garden.   These Troops with the Cannon and a great deal of Baggage were easier ferryed over than can be well imagined but most of their largest Carriages with the one Regt. were left on the other side and the Prince of Hesse or some of His Generals Insist to have a bridge of boats made which I believe is impracticable.   However I have ordered up all the boats upon Islay from Coupar of Angus to Kincleaven and from Kincleaven to this place (the boats upon Tay above this being brought before) and all these boats arrived here last night.   They are all very well provided of Forrage hitherto and Straw, etc., but it is not to be imagined that it can last long in this part of the world.   They have got all that I had of that sort but in two days more they can not be provided unless it is brought from Fife. . . .

Partys of the Hussars with some Dragoons keep constantly patroling as far up as they can safely and there has been several shott exchanged at different times between them at first not above six miles from this. Last night our advanced party of 15 Hussars and as many Dragoons came up with a party of the Rebels half way betwixt (*sic*) and Blair at a place called Haugh of Dalshian with whom they had a Skirmish, the Dragoons say they killed four of them and they brought a Rannoch boy here prisoner who tho' very young carryed arms and owns himself he was at the Battle of Falkirk. . . .

This morning at six there was an alarm by an Hussar come from the advanced post that a body of two or three thousand of the Rebels were

P

within four or five miles of this Upon which the Hessian Troops with their Cannon and the Dragoons Together with the Regiment that was encamped on the other side of the water were drawn up upon a rising ground just above this Town but just now half an hour after eight a Servant of mine is returned . . . and could perceive no body of Men."[1]

Prince Frederick received another letter from the Duke of Cumberland written on the 30th of March: "Mon cher Frere. J'ai receu votre Lettre du 27e: de Dunkeld, et je me flate qu'avant que ma Reponse puisse vous joindre, vous aurez deja fait lever le Siege de Blair. J'aprouve fort que les deux Battalions Hessois, et la Cavalerie qui est avec eux avance a Tay-bridge."[2]

Lord Crawford told Sir Everard Fawkener on the last day of March:

Yours of the 28. came to my Hand last Night, just as General Brandt arrived with the two Battalions from Crief, and the Remains of the two Regiments of Dragoons Naizon's and Hamilton's, who have Orders this Day to pass the Tay and join St. George's with which Corps and 200 Grenadiers, I am to march this evening towards the advanced Posts of the Rebells on this side of the Pass, thereby to entice a greater Corps to sustain me, so as to accomplish what H.R.H. the Duke inclines should be done. . . .

I dread the worst for Blair, if our whole Corps moves not forward by to morrow. . . .

P.S.   It is at present given out the Rebells have had a Reinforcement join'd them, about Blair ; but it wants confirmation.[3]

Lord Crawford advanced on Monday, the last day of March, with St. George's Dragoons to relieve the garrison of Blair Castle, and five hundred Hessians under Prince Frederick followed him. The next day they arrived at Pitlochry, when the Jacobites there prepared to offer battle, and then withdrew before there was an opportunity to attack them.   The Duke of Atholl gives his version of this in his letter to Lord Justice Clerk on the 2nd of April:

Monday about three o'Clock in the Afternoon the Erle of Crawfurd marched with 400 Hessians, St. George's Regt. of Dragoons and some

---

[1] *S.P., Scot.*, Series II, 30.   [2] *S.P., Scot.*, Series II, 29.   [3] *S.P., Scot.*, Series II, 30.

Hussars to Dowlie near five miles from this (Dunkeld), and there Encamped,

Tues . . . the Earl of Crawfurd with most of the Dragoons and Hussars marched towards Pittlochry, when he came within a mile of it, the Rebells to the Number . . . of about 500 were plainly seen drawing up upon the side of a rising ground near to Pittlochry, and immediately after marched . . . to the pass of Killychranky, upon which the Earl of Crawfurd advanced with some of the Dragoons and Hussars, and in less than a quarter of an hour was on the ground the Rebells left, and went forward to within a little mile of the pass of Killychranky, when many of the Rebells were seen going up to the Tops of the Different hills betwixt that and the pass. I waited on the Earl of Crawfurd all the way, and had brought severall who could be depended upon as Guides, that if the Earl of Crawfurd had had a sufficient Number of Troops he could have marched them safely without going through the pass of Killychranky, and might have been at Blair by three oClock that day but as he had no foot with and too few Dragoons, Mulluarne (sic) half way betwixt Blair and Dunkeld, in hopes of having Foot sufficient to march with next day. . . .

But betwixt Six and Seven this morning the Dragoons, Hussars and Foot all returned to their Camp here. It seems the Earl of Crawfurd had got a Letter from the Prince of Hesse at Ten oClock last night, wherein he wrote it was the Opinion of his Generalls that this Expedition could not be supported, and therefore that he had ordered his troops back again to this place.

12 oClock Wednesday.

Just as I had finished the above, and was regrating much that the Garrison at Blair, was without prospect of relief, a messenger came with Accounts that the Rebells had abandoned Atholl before day light this morning ; And that he judged they were as far as Dallnacardoch eight miles beyond Blair early this morning, that he believes the Garrison were at full liberty. . . . Upon this I understand that the Earl of Crawfurd is to march towards Blair Immediately with the Dragoons, and I suppose the Hessians, or at least a sufficient number of them will also march.[1]

[1] *S.P., Scot.,* Series II, 30.

As the dragoons approached the pass of Killiecrankie the Jacobites made off towards Badenoch. St. George's men followed close on their track, and arrived at Blair Castle at five o'clock on the morning of the 3rd of April. The siege was raised, the enemy decamped, and the Regiment were cantoned in and about Hunting-town. Prince Charles had attempted to break through the cordon protected by Blair Castle and Fort William, and he had attempted in vain. He could not break through the barrier of Loch Lochy and Loch Ness. In a word, the Duke of Cumberland was closing him in. Prince Frederick was too timid to defend Blair Castle as it ought to have been defended. The Duke of Cumberland spoke out to him with the utmost frankness in his letter of the 4th of April:

Mon cher Frere. Hier au Soir je receu votre Lettre du 31e. de Mars, datee de Dunkeld. J'ai ete surpris d'y voir que vous y fussier encore, après les deux Lettres par lesquelles je vous avois prié de marcher incessamment pour faire lever le Siege de Blair. Je ne vois pas comment vous pouvez regarder le Marche de Dunkeld à Blair comme risquant les quatre milles Hommes qui sont sous votre Ordres : et la meme Raison que vous alleguez seroit valable pour que l'on n'osat jamais entreprendre de faire lever de Siege. Quelle Honte seroit-ce ! pour un Corps aussi considerable que celui de vos Troupes, si vous laissier prendre 300 Hommes dans le Chateau de Blair, par une Poignée de Miserables, à une Marche de vous. Ce seroit bien mortifiant qu'un tel Affront arrivât a vos Troupes pour la premiere fois, etant sous vos Ordres. . . .

Je suis assure que vous ne penser pas a repondre à la Lettre qu'un Rebelle au Roi votre Beau Pere, vous écrit, et dans laquelle meme il ne donne à Sa Majeste que le Titre d'Electeur. J'admire l'insolence de ces Rebelles qui osent proposer un Cartel, aiant aux memes la Corde au Cou.

Comme tout votre Corps est a l'heure qu'il est joint ensemble, j'espere qu'il ne se trouvera plus à present de Difficultez pour faire lever le Siege, si au moins le pauvre Chevalier Agnew[1] a pu soutenir aussi long tems."[2]

[1] Sir Andrew Agnew.   [2] *S.P., Scot.*, Series II, 30.

The spirit that inspired this stern letter to Prince Frederick is the same as that in which he addressed his men on the field of Culloden, "Now I don't suppose that there are any men here who are disinclined to fight, but if there be, I beg them in God's name to go, for I would rather face the Highlanders with a thousand resolute men at my back than with ten thousand half-hearted." The cheers provoked by this speech put heart even into Prince Frederick. At Earn the Eighth were stationed, and there they remained during the Battle of Culloden. St. George's Dragoons were afterwards stationed at Glamis, Arbroath, Coupar of Angus, Dumfries, Broughton, and other places, where they apprehended the defeated Jacobites. Lieutenant-Colonel John Arabin wrote to Lord Justice Clerk on the 21st of June, 1746 :

I am directed to send your Lordship a list of such Rebells as Surrendered to me or to the Officers of General St. George's Dragoons before his Royal Highness's late order and an account also of the prisons in which they are confined which I now have the honour to do and shall hope for Your Lordships directions what further is to be done.

Mr. Campbell Shiriff depute took yesterday the declarations of several witnesses concerning the murder of one John Catenoch and suppose he will forward to Your Lordship the whole proceedings. Catenoch was servant to Mr Ogilvie a Captain among the Rebels and was taken about three weeks ago by some of my men, but finding he had only attended his master as a servant and had never born arms I offered him his liberty on condition that he would bring me Intelligence as I could not get any from any of the Inhabitants of this Neighbourhood And that I heard several Rebel Officers were often near this place (Glamis). The fellow proved faithfull and met my Sergeant once or twice according to appointment (for he told me his life would be in danger if he was seen coming to me too often). On my receiving his R.H.'s late order I sent to him He signed the Obligation of which I gave him a Certificate as I did to others thinking he might appear with safety and be of more service. But it did not protect him from the hands of a set of villains. Your Lordship will best judge by reading the declarations of the Barbarity of this murder and hope the Criminals will accordingly be brought to speedy Justice. I shall wait Your

Lordships Commands what is now to be done. But in the mean time I shall keep the Criminals as well as the witnesses (who are but poor people and might possibly be spirited away) in close confinement. I am afraid but few or none of the Inhabitants of Renney but what knew of the design of putting this man to death.[1]

Arabin received the thanks of the Government for his apprehension of the criminals and for finding the proper evidence against them.

In August, 1746, we find the Regiment at grass quarters at Dumfries. There is a return of it given on the 1st of September, 1746:

MAJOR GEN. ST. GEORGE'S (No COLONEL PRESENT).

1	Lieut. Col.	12 Sergeants
1	Major	12 Drums and Hautboys
3	Captains	226 fit for duty
4	Lieuts.	2 sick present
5	Cornets	5 sick in hospitals
1	Adjutant	2 left behind with horses
1	Surgeon	75 on command
6	Quarter Masters	310 total effective
372	horses fit for duty	
38	men wanting to complete	

ABSENT OFFICERS.

Capt. Baillie on his return from England where he was buying horses.

Lieut. St. George
Cornet St. George } In Ireland Aides de Camp to the General

Dean Cross Chaplain in Ireland.[2]

The alternative presented to the victor after a civil war is, Cruelty or Clemency. After the Williamite Wars in Ireland and the Jacobite Risings in Scotland, the cruel policy was tried. English gaols were filled with Jacobite prisoners, and many were condemned to the scaffold. The vengeance exacted expressed the sense of danger experienced by the Government. Within the bounds of Britain Celticism had been an independent and threatening force. The time had at last come, so the Government

[1] *S.P., Scot.*, Series II, 32. [2] *S.P., Scot.*, Series II, 33.

deemed, to reckon with it. In the Lowlands the policy of Anglicising had been tried with success, and now the same policy was to be applied to the Highlands. Let Sir Walter Scott testify to the results :

There is no European nation, which, within the course of half a century, or little more, has undergone so complete a change as this kingdom of Scotland. The effects of the insurrection of 1745—the destruction of the patriarchal power of the Highland chiefs—the abolition of the heritable jurisdictions of the Lowland nobility and barons—the total eradication of the Jacobite party, which, averse to intermingle with the English, or adopt their customs, long continued to pride themselves upon maintaining ancient Scottish manners and customs, commenced this innovation. The gradual influx of wealth, and extension of commerce, have since united to render the present people of Scotland a class of beings as different from their grandfathers, as the existing English are from those of Queen Elizabeth's time. . . . But the change, though steadily and rapidly Progressive, has, nevertheless, been gradual ; and, like those who drift down the stream of a deep and smooth river, we are not aware of the progress we have made until we fix our eye on the now-distant point from which we have drifted. Such of the present generation as can recollect the last twenty or twenty-five years of the eighteenth century, will be fully sensible of the truth of this statement ; especially if their acquaintance and connexions lay among those who, in my younger time, were facetiously called "folks of the old leaven," who still cherished a lingering, though hopeless attachment, to the house of Stuart. This race has now almost entirely vanished from the land, and with it, doubtless, much absurd political prejudice ; but also, many living examples of singular and disinterested attachment to the principles of loyalty which they received from their fathers, and of old Scottish faith, hospitality, worth, and honour.[1]

The reconciling force of literature is amazing. Take an instance. Sir Walter Scott writes :

> Breathes there a man with soul so dead,
> Who never to himself hath said,
> This is my own, my native land ?

---

[1] *Waverley,* chap. XIII.

These lines describe the love of the Highlander for Scotland, but Scott's own patriotism is as much British as Scots. The Irish never had a man of genius of this embracing order. Scott, too, described his native land so that the English love it as much as Scots. It is a tribute to him that the English no more think of Bannockburn as a defeat than Scots think of Culloden as a defeat by a hated foe. Alas! the Irish so still regard on one side Benburb and on the other the Boyne.

There was peace in Scotland in 1746, and there was peace in Europe in 1748. In April, 1748, there were 21 officers, 30 non-commissioned officers, 328 privates, and 371 effective horses. There were 26 men and 19 horses wanting to complete the allowances. There were 44 men and 37 horses wanting to complete the establishment.[1]

In May three troops were at St. Andrew's, Dundee, and Montrose respectively, and three troops at Aberdeen. On the signing of the Peace of Aix-le-Chapelle in 1748 George II approved on the 31st of October a plan of putting the army in Ireland on a peace establishment, consisting of four regiments of horse of six troops each and twenty-one privates per troop, five regiments of dragoons of the same number and one other of nine troops, and twenty-six battalions of infantry of ten companies each and thirty privates per company. The following month this was altered to twenty-seven battalions of twenty-nine men per company. The total number contemplated was 11,850.

On the return of peace in 1697 and in 1713 we have the inevitable reduction of the army, and in 1748 we are face to face with the same process. Accordingly, on the 3rd of November, 1748, the decree of doom went forth:

Whereas His Majesty hath thought fit to Order the six Troops of each of the Regiments of Dragoons respectively Commanded by Lt. Genl. St. George and Colonel Naizon to be forthwith reduced, so that each of the said Troops is to consist of one Captain, 1 Lieutenant, One Cornet, One Quarter Master, One Serjeant, 2 Corporals, One Hautbois, One Drum, and Twenty One effective private men, and no more. . . .

[1] *S.P., Dom., Military,* 19.

Non Commission Officers and private Men hereby to be reduced, be permitted to carry away with him his Cloak and Cloaths which he now wears and that their Horses be dispos'd of according to the Regulation following. . . .

That the Captains of each Troop of Dragoons have been at a very extraordinary Expence in Completing their Troops fit for Service. We do further Direct that the Horses of the Reduced Men, at the Time of such Reduction, shall be absolutely given to the respective Captains of each Troop, except the Horses of such Dragoons only, as shall have served One full Year or upwards to whom the Captains shall leave their respective Horses or Three Pounds in lieu of each Horse, either of which shall be in the Captain's Option ; And that where any Difference shall arise between the Dragoon and his Officer, the same be Determin'd by you[1] or such as You shall appoint. . . .

That the said Dragoons, who in pursuance of the aforesaid Regulations, are to have their Horses, be paid Nine Days Full Pay ; And those who shall not have their Horses Eighteen Days full Pay. . . .
to give them Passes, in Case they shall desire the same to the Places of their former Residence . . . and giving them likewise a Strict Charge not to presume to Travell with Arms, nor more than three in Company together, upon Pain of the Severest Punishment. . . .

And to the end the said Non Commission Officers and private Dragoons may be sensible of the Care His Majesty hath taken of them upon their Reduction ; You are to cause these Our Directions, to be read at the Head of each Troop.[2]

Arms were to be returned to the Ordnance.

In 1749 the Agent was John Bayly, and the officers with the quarters of the Regiment were :

Officers' Names.		Quarters.
Col. L. Gen.	Richard St. George	Colooney
Capt. Lieut.	James Graham	
Corn.	Thomas Major	
Q.M.	Nath. Proctor	

[1] Lieutenant-General Humphry Bland.
[2] *W.O.*, 16/21, *Entry Book of Warrants and Precedents.*

Officers' Names.		Quarters.
L. Col.	Christ. Clarges	Longford
Lieut.	George Bingham	
Corn.	John Arabin	
Q.M.	Thomas Hunt	
Major	Tho. Erle	Longford
Lieut.	Arthur Johnston	
Corn.	James Fleming	
Q.M.	John Hunt	
Capt.	Francis Baillie	Granard
Lieut.	John Agnew	
Corn.	Christ. Conyers	
Q.M.	Nath. Cook	
Capt.	Whitney Mackean	Sligo
Lieut.	Richard St. George	
Corn.	Thomas Hall	
Q.M.	St. George Hatfield	
Capt.	Tho. Hamilton	Granard
Lieut.	Faustin Low	
Corn.	William Nugent	
Q.M.	Rob. Young	
Chapl.	George Hely	
Surg.	George Ross.[1]	

In 1750 there are three troops at Charleville, Mallow and Cappoquin respectively, one partly at Mallow and Cappoquin, and two at Tullough. The following year there are two troops at Loughrea and Headford respectively, and three at Portumna. In 1752 there are three troops at Tallow, Nenagh and Charleville respectively, and two at Doneraile.[1]

In the royal warrant of the 1st of July, 1751, the regiment was numbered the Eighth Dragoons; and its uniform, guidons, and the like, were commanded to be as follows:

Coats—scarlet; double-breasted; without lapells; lined with yellow; slit sleeves, turned up with yellow; the button-holes worked with

[1] Newspaper Room, British Museum.

narrow white lace ; the buttons of white metal, set on three and three ; a long slash pocket in each skirt ; and a white worsted aiguillette on the right shoulder.

Waistcoats $\left.\begin{array}{l}\\\end{array}\right\}$ yellow.
Breeches

Hats—three-cornered cocked hats, bound with silver lace, and ornamented with a white metal loop and a black cockade.

Boots—of jacked leather, reaching above the knee.

Cloaks—of scarlet cloth with a yellow collar, and lined with yellow shalloon ; the buttons set on three and three upon white frogs, or loops, with a yellow stripe down the centre.

Horse Furniture—of yellow cloth ; the holster caps and housings having a border of broad white lace, with a yellow stripe down the centre ; $_D^{VIII}$ embroidered on a red ground within a wreath of roses and thistles on each corner of the housings ; and on the holster caps the King's cypher and crown with $_D^{VIII}$ underneath.

Officers—distinguished by silver lace ; their coats bound with silver embroidery, the button-holes worked with silver ; and a crimson silk sash worn over the left shoulder.

Quarter Masters—to wear a crimson sash round the waist.

Serjeants—to have narrow silver lace on the cuffs, pockets, and shoulder-straps ; silver aiguillettes ; and yellow and white worsted sashes tied round the waist.

Drummers and Hautboys—clothed in yellow coats, faced and lapelled with red, and ornamented with white lace with a yellow stripe down the centre ; their waistcoats and breeches of red cloth.

Corporals—narrow silver lace on the cuffs and shoulder-straps ; and a white silk aiguilette.

Guidons—The first, or king's guidon, to be of crimson silk, embroidered and fringed with gold and silver ; in the centre the rose and thistle conjoined, and crown over them, with the motto, Dieu et mon Droit, underneath ; the white horse in a compartment in the first and fourth corners, and VIII.D., in gold characters on a blue ground, in the second and third corners. The second and third guidons to be of yellow silk ; in the centre the rank of the regiment in silver Roman characters, on a crimson ground, within a wreath of roses and thistles on the same stalk; the white horse on a red ground in the first and fourth compartments ; and the rose and thistle conjoined upon a red ground in the second and third compartments.   The distinction of the third guidon to be a figure 3, beneath the wreath.[1]

All of us remember the potato famine of 1846.   What was new in that famine was the care taken of the starving : the famine was not new, for such a condition was chronic in Ireland during the eighteenth century.   Terrible were such years as 1727, 1728, 1729, and 1730.   "In twenty years," declared W. E. H. Lecky, "there were at least three or four of absolute famine, and that of 1740 and 1741, which followed the great frost at the end of 1739, though it hardly left a trace in history, and hardly excited any attention in England, was one of the most fearful upon record."[2] Bishop Berkeley, a sane saint if ever there was one, told his friend Prior in 1741 : "The distresses of the sick and poor are endless. The havoc of mankind in the counties of Cork, Limerick, and some adjacent places hath been incredible.   The nation probably will not recover this loss in a century.   The other day I heard one from the county of Limerick say that whole villages were entirely dispeopled.   About two months since I heard Sir Richard Cox say that five hundred were dead in one parish, though in a county I believe not very populous."[3] During the "fifties" of the eighteenth century the potato crop failed again.   Inevitably with such distress in the country the price of provisions increased, and accordingly we have the following issued on the 12th of March, 1752 :

Right Trusty and Right entirely beloved Cousin and Councillor We greet you well.   Whereas We have taken into Our Royal Consideration your Letter to the Commissioners of Our Treasury of the 25th day of February 1752 which they have laid before Us Representing the distressed Condition of the Dragoons on the Establishment of that Our Kingdom occasioned by the dearness of Provisions and Forage and proposing that from the 1st day of January last inclusive there be an Increase of One Shilling a day to the pay of each Lieutenant, Cornet,

[1] *Cf. The Journal of the Society of Army Historical Research*, Vol. 3, pp. 248–9.   In this article the Rev. P. Sumner records changes in the regimental uniform from 1768 to 1792.
    [2] *History of Ireland*, I, pp. 186–7.   [3] Fraser, *Life of Berkeley*, p. 265.

and Quartermaster and two pence a day to each Serjeant, Corporal, Drummer and Private man by reason of which addition their pay and Subsistance will be as follows.   That is to say

	Full pay p. diem.		Subsistence p. diem.		
	s.	d.	s.	d.	
For each Lieutenant of Dragoons	7	2	5	9	
For each Cornet	6	2	4	10	Parts.
For each Quartermaster	4	0	3	8	96
For each Serjeant	2	8	1	9	10
For each Corporal	1	10	1	3	87½
For each Drummer	1	8	1	2	36
For each Private Man	1	6	1	1	50

(Marginal notes: *Addl. pay of one shilling a day.* for the first group "which makes their"; *Addl. pay of 2d. a day without deduction.* for the second group "which makes their")

We are graciously pleased to condescend and agree thereto.   Our Will and Pleasure therefore is And we do hereby Direct and Command that you give the necessary Orders and Directions for placing on the Establishment of that Our Kingdom from the said 1st day of January last inclusive the several Allowances of pay and Subsistance above mentioned and to direct that the several sums aforesaid be paid to them and every one of them in like manner as other pay or Subsistance on the said Establishment is paid or payable All which said several Additional Allowances as aforesaid will amount to £13 19s. 6d. a day or £5100 17s. 6d. a year And Whereas you have represented that it will be usefull and necessary that an Adjutant be appointed to each Regiment of Horse and Dragoons on that Establishment and that an Allowance of Four shillings a day for each amounting to Forty shillings a day or £730 a year will be necessary to be inserted on the Establishment for this Service to which We being graciously pleased to consent and agree.   Our further Pleasure is that you cause to be inserted on the said Establishment the said Allowance of Four shillings a day for each Adjutant or Forty shillings a day or Seven hundred and thirty pounds a year for the whole the same to commence from the said 1st of January 1752 payable in like manner as other payments on the said Establishment are made of which three shillings a day is to be paid to each of the said Adjutants for Subsistance.   And for so doing this shall be as well to you as to all other Our Officers and Ministers who shall or may be concerned herein a sufficient Warrant.[1]

[1] *Treasury*, 14/13, *Ireland*.

That officers had suffered through the rise in prices is evident
from the Court Martial held at Dublin Castle on the 6th of December, 1752, when Cornet William Nugent was charged with keeping
four pounds for four years, part of the pay of a dragoon, for
challenging his captain, and with conduct unbecoming a gentleman.
He was found guilty on the first charge.   The Court, however,
took into account the fact that he had paid the dragoon his four
pounds, that he had been arrested three weeks, and that his colonel,
General St. George, had interposed on his behalf.   Accordingly,
he was acquitted of the first article of his accusation.   With regard
to the second, it was proved that Nugent challenged Captain
Hamilton.   Were there mitigating circumstances?   The members
of the Court were of opinion that

> he was guilty of a Breach of the 2nd Article of the 7th Section of the
> Articles of War ; But that Cornet Nugent, by the information given
> him, that Capn. Hamilton had cruelly aspersed his Character, and
> from the further Information given the Court, by the several officers of
> the Regiment, of his good Character in General, and being a Man not
> given to quarrelling, but in every respect a diligent officer in the
> discharge of his Duty, the Court humbly recommended him to us
> for mercy.

And that in regard to the third Article, It appearing to the Court
from the Circumstances of the Challenge given by Cornet Nugent to
Captain Hamilton, that the Captain might reasonably imagine by the
Cornet's hasty retreat, that he intended to load his Pistol again, and
that by the Nature and Situation of the Wound, Captain Hamilton
had received, he might not have heard the Cornet beg his Life, in the
manner he mentions, no Evidence Appearing in proof, the Court could
judge only from circumstances, were therefore of opinion that neither
the Captain or Cornet have acted in the quarrel unbecoming gentlemen.

Upon consideration of the aforesaid Proceedings We are of opinion
that the said Cornet Nugent is guilty of a Breach of the 2nd Article of
the Seventh Section of the Articles of War, But upon some favourable
Circumstances we are pleased hereby to pardon the said Cornet Nugent
for having committed the said offence, and do hereby discharge him
from all Pain or Punishment on account thereof, Whereof the Commander

in Chief of His Majesty's Forces under the Government of this Kingdom is to take notice, and to give the proper orders that the said Cornet Nugent be discharged from his Confinement.[1]

This order was not issued till the 24th of March, 1753.

Lieutenant-General St. George died at Dublin on the 12th of January, 1755, and the officers and men alike regretted the loss of one so much respected. He was succeeded on the 22nd of January, 1755, by Colonel the Hon. John Waldegrave, from the Ninth Foot. He obtained a commission in the First Foot Guards in 1737; in July, 1743, he was appointed captain-lieutenant in the Third Foot Guards; in the September following he obtained the command of a company, and in 1748 he was promoted to a commission of major in the same corps. He received the colonelcy of the Ninth Foot on the 26th of June, 1751; that of the Eighth in 1755; and that of the Second Irish horse in 1758. As major-general he proceeded to Germany to take part in the Seven Years' War. He commanded a brigade in the attack on St. Malo in 1758.[2] The next year he made his mark in the Battle of Minden; and Walpole ascribes the victory chiefly to a manœuvre conducted by him. In September, 1759, he was removed to the Second Dragoon Guards, and conducted himself with credit during the rest of the Seven Years' War. Nor was he unmindful of the welfare of the soldiers who served under him. In 1763 he succeeded to the title of Earl Waldegrave. In the early years of the reign of George III he acted mainly with the opposition, but was in 1765 made master of the horse to Queen Charlotte. He was promoted to the rank of general. When in 1770 Lord Barrington declared in parliament that no officer in England was fit to be commander-in-chief, he, according to Walpole, "took up the affront warmly without doors." In 1773 he obtained the colonelcy of the Second Foot Guards, and in 1781 he was named lord-lieutenant of Essex. He died of apoplexy in his carriage near Reading on the 15th of October, 1784.

In June, 1755, there were 16 officers, 19 non-commissioned officers, and 122 privates in the 8th Dragoons. One private

[1] E, 3.30, pp. 153–4.   [2] *Grenville Correspondence*, I, p. 238.

was sick and seven were on furlough. There were 6 drummers and trumpeters and 8 privates wanting to complete the establishment. There were 140 horses fit for duty, and 16 horses were wanting to complete the establishment.[1]   In July, 1755, the regiment was at Sligo.   On the 15th of April, 1756, 400 firelocks and bayonets were issued out of the stores in England for the use of the additional eight men per troop ordered to be made to the regiments of dragoons in Ireland.   The list of officers on the 15th of May, 1756, is:

Colonel.	Regl. Rank.	Army Rank.
John Waldegrave	22nd Jan., '55	25th Feb., '48
Lieut.-Col.		
John Severne	20th Feb., '50	
Major.		
John Pomeroy	4th Sept., '54	
Captains.		
Thomas Hamilton	31st Aug., '47	8th May, '46
James Mansergh	4th Sept., '54	
Clement Wolseley	16th Feb., '56	
Capt.-Lieut.		
James Graham	15th Feb., '48	
Lieutenants.		
John Agnew	31st Aug., '44	
George Bingham	22nd June, '45	
Arthur Johnson	19th March, '47	
Christopher Conyers	7th April, '50	
James Fleming	27th April, '56	
Cornets.		
Edward FitzGerald	16th Aug., '49	
Lewis Moore	20th June, '53	
Nathaniel Cook	20th March, '54	
Francis Brooke	10th Dec., '55	
Henry Irwin	27th April, '56	
Richard Jones	27th April, '56	

[1] *S.P., Ir.*, 417.

Chaplain.	Regl. Rank.
George Hely	May, '46

Surgeon.	
Thomas Wetherill	24th Jan., '52

Adjutant.	
St. George Hatfield	3rd June, '52

Quartermasters.

John Hunt (became Capt.-Lieut. and Paymaster)
Thomas Hunt
St. George Hatfield (became Adjutant, died in 1807)
John Franklin
Richd. St. George Conyers (became Lieut., and was alive in 1809)
Robert Young.

In October, 1758, John Waldegrave was removed to the Second Irish Horse, now the Fifth Dragoon Guards, and the new commanding officer was, on the 23rd of October, 1758, Major-General the Hon. Joseph Yorke, from the Ninth Foot. The third son of Philip, first Earl of Hardwicke, Yorke entered the army at an early age, serving as aide-de-camp to the Duke of Cumberland at the Battle of Fontenoy. He was appointed captain and lieutenant-colonel in the Second Foot Guards on the 27th of May, 1745. Becoming aide-de-camp to George II, in 1755 he was appointed colonel of the Ninth Foot. In 1758 he was transferred to the Eighth; in 1760 to the Fifth Dragoons; and in 1787 to the Eleventh Dragoons. In 1788 he was created Lord Dover, Baron of Dover-court in the county of Kent; and in the following year he was appointed colonel of the First Life Guards.

On the 15th of May, 1759, we meet with the first separate mention of one who has the long connection of over thirty-seven years with the Eighth and the exceedingly long connection of over seventy-one years with the Army, John Severne. He was allowed a pension of two hundred and fifty a year for his office as Barrack Master General, a post about to be discontinued. On the removal of Yorke to the Fifth Royal Irish Dragoons in November, 1760, George III promoted, on the 27th of November, 1760, the

Q

lieutenant-colonel of the Eighth, Colonel John Severne, to the colonelcy of the regiment. Few men can ever have known the regiment so well as the new commanding officer, and few can ever have served it so devotedly. He was cornet in 1715, captain in 1735, major in 1740, lieutenant-colonel in 1740, and colonel in 1760. He attained the rank of major-general in 1761, of lieutenant-general in 1770, and of general in 1782. The new lieutenant-colonel on the 29th of November, 1760, was William Lushington.

The precedents of 1697, 1713 and 1748 were followed on the conclusion of the Seven Years' War in 1763, and reduction was once more the order of the day. On the 30th of March, 1763, Lord Egremont informed the Lord Lieutenant, the Earl of Halifax: "The King now being come to a resolution forthwith to disband a part of his forces in Ireland, and to send some other Regiments thither; also to make such a reduction of his corps remaining on the establishment of that kingdom, that his army thereon may not exceed the number of 12,000 men, Commissioned and Non-Commissioned officers and Drummers including, I have received His Majesty's commands to signify to your Excellency his pleasure . . .

"And that in the Regiments and battalions hereinafter respectively mentioned there be reduced as follows, Viz. . . . In each of the 8th, 9th, 12th, 13th, and 14th Regiments of Dragoons 54 private men."[1] Severne's Dragoons were to consist of one Colonel, one Lieutenant-Colonel, one Major, three Captains, six Lieutenants, including the Captain Lieutenant, six Cornets, one Chaplain, one Adjutant, one Surgeon, six Quartermasters, six Sergeants, twelve Corporals, six Hautboys, six Drummers, and 120 private effective men.[2]

The problem of the purchase of commissions was raised in 1765, and George III appointed a board of general officers to consider it. It was quite possible then for a father to purchase in the course of a fortnight all the different steps from cornet to lieutenant-colonel for his son, a lad at school, who might leave the playground to

[1] *Ireland, Entry Books,* 13.   [2] *W.O.,* 8/5.

command a regiment. The age of sixteen was fixed as the minimum age to enter the service as cornet or ensign, the age that had been laid down in the 1711 regulations. The sum for either commission was fixed for time of war as well as peace, adding about one hundred pounds for every additional shilling the higher rank would receive in pay. Besides this, a small and fixed sum was added to each superior rank, as the value of the rank itself, exclusive of the value of the higher pay. The rules provided that commissions might sell for less and not for more, and that the loss was to fall on the sale of the lowest commission. This, however, was a condition of affairs more to be hoped for than to be realised. More practicable was the regulation on the line of promotion, which ordered that the senior of any rank in the regiment, who offered the regulated price, should exclusively be entitled to purchase the vacant step.

The rules scarcely contemplated the difference between a regiment whose commissions were in keen demand and a regiment whose commissions were not in such demand. Just as privates sought to enter the rank of the 8th Dragoons, so officers sought. In fact, there was such lively competition to enter it that candidates for the cornetcy offered five to six hundred guineas above the regulation price. The gap between promise and performance in these rules is grasped when we turn to the prices of commissions in the Dragoon Guards and the Dragoons, on the 10th of February, 1766:

Commissions.	Prices.	Difference.
	£	£
Lieutenant Colonel	4700	1100
Major	3600	1100
Captain	2500	1100
Captain Lieutenant	1400	250
Lieutenant	1150	150
Cornet	1000	1000
		————
		4700[1]

That is to say, the cornet offered one thousand pounds for his commission only to find that it cost him two thousand pounds.

[1] *S.P., Entry Books,* 14.

The state of the commission market on the 3rd of February, 1767, proves that the rules of 1765 were beginning to tell:

Commissions.	Prices.	Difference.
	£	£
Lieutenant Colonel	4365	959
Major	3406	1150
Captain	2256	1013
Captain Lieutenant	1243	271
Lieutenant	972	155
Cornet	817	817
		4365

Major-General Lord Blayney reviewed the regiment on the 5th of June, 1767, and a most exhaustive report on its state was drawn up. We are given the officers' names according to their seniority in the regiment:

	Country.			Years of	
	English.	Scotch.	Irish.	Age.	Service.
Col., Major General John Severne	I			65	51
Lt.-Col., William Lushington	I			52	35
Major, Francis Lascelles	I			23	7
Capts. William Wolseley			I	34	12
Capts. Hon. William Moore			I	28	8
Capts. William Stuart		I		30	12
Capt. Lt., Arthur Johnston			I	51	25
Lts. Edward FitzGerald			I	46	16
Lts. Nathaniel Cook	I			54	13
Lts. Edward Wall			I	33	10
Lts. John Green			I	25	7
Lts. John Colthurst			I	25	7
Cornets St. George Hatfield			I	37	7
Cornets John Hunt			I	33	6
Cornets Robert Saunderson			I	24	6
Cornets St. George Conyers			I	29	4
Cornets Hon. B. N. Stratford			I	19	3
Cornets Charles Newman			I	21	3[1]
	4	I	13		

[1] I omit details of the former ranks of these officers, the only matter I omit.

Staff Officers	Country. English.	Scotch.	Irish.	Years of Age.	Service.
James Stephen Lushington, Chaplain	I				7
John Hunt, Adjutant			I	33	I
St. Leger Hinchley, Surgeon			I		3
	I		2		

Warrant Officers	English.	Scotch.	Irish.	Age.	Service.
Quarter-Masters { John Smyth			I	55	10
William Harvey	I			28	8
James Quin			I	42	2
Robert Stanford			I	44	I
James Shanly			I	28	I
Henry Townly			I	—	—
	I		5		

According to this report, Charleville Barracks are "not habitable" and Nenagh Barracks "the same."

THE NATIONALITY OF THE MEN IN THE SIX TROOPS IS:

	English.	Scotch.	Irish.	Total.
Col., Major General Severne	I		22	23
Lt.-Col., Lushington	I		22	23
Major Lascelles	I		22	23
Capt. Wolseley		I	22	23
Capt. Moore			21	21
Capt. Stuart		4	19	23
				136

THE AGES OF THE MEN IN THE DIFFERENT TROOPS ARE:

Age.							Total.
55							
50		I	I		2		4
45	I	I	I	I	I		5
40	2	4	I	I	I	4	13
35	I	2	I			I	5
30	3	2	4	2	2	3	16
25	10	8	4	3	7	7	39
20	5	3	5	10	7	7	37
18		2	5	5	I	I	14
15	I		I	I			3
	23	23	23	23	21	23	136

SIZES FROM 5FT. 1 AND UNDER TO 6FT. 1 AND UPWARDS.

Upwards of	Troops as above.						Total.
6 2		I					I
6 2							
6 ½							
6 1							
6 ½							
6						I	I
5 11½			I		I		2
5 11	1			3	3	1	8
5 10½	4	4	2	1	9	4	24
5 10	3	2	4	6	4	9	28
5 9½	6	8	9	5	1	5	34
5 9	7	6	5	4	2	2	26
5 8½	1	1	1	3			6
5 8							
5 7½					1		1
5 7	1	1		1			3
5 6½			1				1
5 6							
Under 5 6						1	1
	23	23	23	23	21	23	136

LENGTH OF SERVICE.

Years.	Troops as above.						Total.
35		I			I		2
30			I		I		2
25	I						I
20	1	4	3	2	1	2	13
15	2	1				1	4
10	4	5	1	2	1	3	16
8	2	3	2		2	1	10
7	3			1		6	10
6	1	1	5	3	1	2	13
5			1			1	2
4			2	1	5	1	9
3	1		1	4			6
2	1	1			3	2	7
1	3	3	2	4	3	1	16
R	4	4	5	6	3	3	25
	23	23	23	23	21	23	136

Longtailed Horses when Received.

1765 recruited	18
1766	12
1767	16
Total Long Tails	46

Ages of Horses from 3 Years to 15.

Age.	Troops as above.						Total.
15	1	3	3	2	1	2	12
14	1	2	1	3		2	9
13	1	1	2	1	3	2	10
12	1	2	4	3	2	2	14
11	4	4	2	5	4	1	20
10	3	3	2	4	1	2	15
9	3		1		1	2	7
8	2					1	3
7						1	1
$6\frac{1}{2}$							
6	2		2	1	3	1	9
$5\frac{1}{2}$							
5	2	5	4	2	4	3	20
$4\frac{1}{2}$							
4	3	3	2	2	2	4	16
$3\frac{1}{2}$							
3							
	23	23	23	23	21	23	136

Size of Horses in each Troop.

Hands.							Total.
16							
15 3						1	1
15 $2\frac{1}{2}$	1					1	2
15 2	1				1	1	3
15 $1\frac{1}{2}$	1				3	4	8
15 1	5	3	11	13	9	11	52
15 $\frac{1}{2}$	10	17	7	4	4	3	45
15	5	3	5	6	4	2	25
14 3							
	23	23	23	23	21	23	136

Troops	Commissioned Officers present						Non-commissioned Officers present (Staff)							Effectives — Men Rank and File						Effectives — Horses			Wanting to complete the allowance — Men				Wanting to complete the allowance — Horse				Since last Review — Men					Since last Review — Horses		
	Col.	Lt.-Col.	Major	Capts.	Lts.	Cornets	Chap.	Adj.	Surg.	Q.M.s	Serg.s	Hautbois	Drummers	Fit for duty	Sick present	Sick in Hosp.	Recruiting	Furlough	Total	Total	Fit for duty	Sick or Leave	Serg.s	Drummers	Hautbois	Rank & File	Serg.s	Drummers	Hautbois	Rank & File	Recruited	Dead	Discharged	Deserted	Recommended to Royal Hosp.	Recruited	Dead	Cart
Col. Severne	1				1	1	1	1	1	1	1		1	19	2				21	24	23	1		1		1		1		1	5		4			3		3
Lt.-Col. Lushington		1			1	1				1	1		1	21					21	22	22			1		1		1		1	4		4		1	3		3
Major Lascelles			1		1	1				1	1		1	18	3				21	23	23			1		1		1		1	5		3	1	1	2		2
Capt. Wolseley				1	1	1				1	1		1	19	2				21	23	23			1		1		1		1	6		2		4	2	1	2
„ Moore				1	1	1				1	1		1	19					19	21	21			1		3		1		3	3		3	2	1	2	2	2
„ Stuart				1	1	1				1	1		1	21					21	23	23			1		1		1		1	3		1		2	4	1	2
Totals	1	1	1	3	5	5	1	1	1	6	6		6	117	7				124	136	135	1		6		8		6		8	26		16	3	9	16	4	14

Absent Officers.

Names.	Since what time.	By whose leave and for what time.	Months.
Gen. Severne	April 25, '67	Government Licence	
Lt. Colthurst	„ 15, '67	„ „ till Nov. 1	4
Cornet Hatfield	Left behind	Sick at Limerick on his march to the Review at Birr	
Chapl. Lushington	April 25, '67	Government Licence	4

	Commissioned Officers present.						Staff Officers.			Non-Commissioned Officers and Private Men.					Horses.			
	Col.	Lt.-Col.	Major	Capts.	Lt.s	Cornets	Chap.	Adjut.	Surg.	Q.M.s	Serj.s	Corporals	Drummers & Hautbois	Privates	Serj's	Corporals	Drummers & Hautbois	Privates
In the Field	1	1	1	3	5	5		1	1	6	6	12	6	105	6	12	6	112
On Duty						1												
Sick in Quarters																		
Prisoners														7				
Absent by leave					1		1											
Total effective	1	1	1	3	6	6	1	1	1	6	6	12	6	112	6	12	6	112
Wanting to complete total establishment of the Regiment														2				2
	1	1	1	3	6	6	1	1	1	6	6	12	6	114	6	12	6	114

RETURN OF ARMS.

	Drums.	Firelocks.	Pairs of Pistols.	Bayonets.	Swords.
Good	6			126	132
Bad		126	132		
Wanting					
	6	126	132	126	132

When Received.

48	Firelocks	and	Bayonets	in	1756
46	,,	,, 54	,,	,,	1758
71	,,	,,	,,	,,	1761
	Drums	,,	,,	,,	1758[1]
	Swords	,,	,,	,,	1747
48	,,	,,	,,	,,	1757
12	,,	,,	,,	,,	1759
42	,,	,,	,,	,,	1762

RETURN OF ACCOUTREMENTS.

	Standards.	Standard Belts.	Serjeants' Sashes.	Pouches and Belts.	Waist Belts.	Slings.	Saddles.	Bridles.	Housing and Caps.
Good	2	2	6	126	126	126	138	138	138
Bad									
Wanting									
	2	2	6	126	126	126	138	138	138

When Received.

Standards and Belts in   1754
Cross Belts and Slings in   1746
48   ,,   ,,   ,,   ,,   ,,   1756
60 Pouch Belts } no dates given
22 Spring Belts }
116 Waist Belts and 156 Slings in 1759
Housings and Caps an entire set for
    the Regt. this present year 1767
18 Saddles with each clothing.

[1] The number is not given.

RETURN OF CLOTHING.

	Sergeants.										Drummers.												Rank and File.										
	Coats	Waistcoats	Breeches	Shirts	Rollers	Hats	Gloves	Boots & Spurs	Horse Collars	Cloaks	Coats	Waistcoats	Breeches	Shirts	Rollers	Hats	Gloves	Boots & Spurs	Horse Collars	Cloaks	Drum Carriages		Coats	Waistcoats	Breeches	Shirts	Rollers	Hats	Gloves	Boots & Spurs	Horse Collars	Cloaks		
Full mounting delivered in 1767	6	6	6			6	6		6	6	6	6	6			6	6		6		6		126	126	126			126			126			
Half mounting delivered in 1766	6	6				6	6		6	6	6	6	6			6	6		6		6		126	126	126			126			126			
In Store																																		
Complement of the Regiment	6	6	6			6	6		6	6	6	6	6			6	6		6		6		126	126	126			126	126		126			

N.B. The half Mounting was delivered to the Regiment in 1766.

ABSTRACT OF THE STOCK PURSE OR RECRUITING ACCOUNT

Dr.		FROM 17– TO 17–			Cr.

	£	s.	d.			£	s.	d.
To Stock Purse and Warrant				By the expense of 16 Recruit				
Men	490	9	4½	Horses	459	18	0
„ Vacancies of Men & Horses	39	6	0	„ the deposit of this year ..	400	0	0
„ Deposit of Last Year ..	400	0	0	„ Regimental Contingencies..	28	6	0
				„ Balance remaining ..	40	19	4½
	929	15	4½		929	3	4½

We have given this as it is the earliest detailed review of the regiment we have been able to find. Year after year such an account is presented to anyone who cares to inspect it in the Record Office, London. The end of Lord Blayney's report is: "The 8th Dragoons are a very well made body of men, their Horses a very active Horse in exceeding good order, but not thoroughly steady, their long tailed Horses were better than the other Regiments. They preferred their exercise on foot, and mounted very well. They are well clothed and well appointed."[1]

In the inspection returns of the regiment of the 24th of May, 1768, there is an entry of "Silver Epaulettes and Silver laced Hatts," and this is a very early mention of epaulets as an ornamental part of army uniform.[2] Epaulets were authorised as part of the dress of an officer in 1764.[3] This year the War Office decreed that the tails of the horses of the regiment were to be docked.[4]

[1] *Irish Review Returns*, 1767.
[2] *The Journal of the Society of Army Historical Research*, Vol. 2, p. 152.
[3] *The Journal of the Society of Army Historical Research*, Vol. 4, p. 19.
[4] *Cf. The Discipline of the Light Horse*, by Capt. R. Hinde.

Chapter VI

Life in the Regiment

JOHN FRANCIS SMET served as surgeon for more than thirty years with the Eighth, joining it in 1794, and his *Historical Record of the Eighth King's Royal Irish Hussars from its being raised to* 1803 constitutes an invaluable piece of work. In the regiment when he joined it he tells us that he still found some officers who had entered it at the close of the Seven Years' War. His own words are: "The subject of the early services in which the Regiment had been engaged was so often adverted to by those gentlemen, that I became interested in them, but I never contemplated bringing together some memoranda I had written on that score until 1806, when the Corps was quietly in quarters; it was then I wrote, in a connected form, what I had noted down formerly, and showed the paper to the late Captain Williams of the 8th Light Dragoons, whose father possessed a good deal of information on that subject. Captain Williams begged of me to allow time to send this paper to his old father (an officer of invalids), who returned it to his son with notes in red ink, and adding for my guidance on four pages of foolscap paper, a detail of what he knew about the Corps, with which Captain Williams' grandfather had served during the rebellion in Scotland."[1] Plainly, we are dealing with a narrative based on old tradition that has been pretty carefully checked.

The tradition contained in Smet's book goes back to the " sixties " of the eighteenth century, and accordingly we give a quotation from it as illustrative of the " sixties " :

> About this period, the Regimental Freemason Lodge was formed, an institution to which Colonel Severn was extremely partial ; and to which nearly all the commissioned and warrant officers belonged ; it continued to flourish for a number of years after the Colonel's death, but gradually decayed afterwards when the regiment left Ireland, and many of the old officers, by being promoted in other corps, or by

[1] Smet, pp. v-vi.

retiring, quitted the regiment. Such an institution was probably very useful at that time, when the cavalry corps in Ireland were extremely select ; as, from the very low establishment, it was in the power of the Colonels of choosing among a number of young gentlemen of distinction who might wish to get a commission, and who all could easily afford to add a hundred pounds a year to their pay, without which no candidate was ever considered as qualified to enter the regiment.   The warrants were also purchased at a high price, often by the sons of gentlemen for as much as five hundred guineas.   The privates were always young men well recommended and whose connections were known.   Indeed the dragoon service was at that time extremely easy and pleasant, so much so, that when a vacancy happened, several desirable recruits always offered, and the man selected in general, got no more than one shilling bounty.   The corps was divided into six small troops of twenty-three men each, and had twenty commissioned officers, viz.:—one colonel, one lieutenant-colonel and one major ; three captains, one captain-lieutenant, five lieutenants, six cornets, one adjutant and a surgeon.   Each troop had a quarter-master, a sergeant, a farrier, a trumpeter, two corporals and eighteen dragoons, which made the entire regiment only consist of 138 men, exclusive of officers and warrant officers, and was usually so much divided as to have hardly more than fifty men at one quarter.

Two-thirds of the officers had in general leave of absence for the greater part of the year.   Many of the dragoons were often on furlough, who were sometimes allowed to take their horses with them to their parents' houses, and generally wore their own clothes while with their friends.   The horses were, a considerable time of the year, at grass, when the proportion of furlough men was usually greater than at other times ; but the whole corps assembled at head quarters once a year and were kept together for a couple of months to perfect themselves in its evolutions preparatory to its being reviewed, after which most of the officers were again indulged with leave of absence, many of the men allowed to go on furlough and several troops detached to out quarters.

Such a service had many attractions.   While detached, everybody had an opportunity of amusing himself ; the officers with the gentlemen whose estates were in the neighbourhood, and the men among the farmers, having hardly any duty to do ; but when the regiments prepared to be reviewed, then was fashionable dissipation carried to a great length. The Royal Irish regiment, small as it was, had an excellent band, and even some scenes and theatrical decorations. Concerts, private plays, balls, dinners, and suppers, in the evening, gave the country towns, where headquarters happened to be, an air of life and gaiety which they only possessed in an inferior degree at other times. The officers now meeting again, after such long separation from each other, in affluent circumstances, which they had improved while they had lived with their friends, justly looked on the time of the year they were to be reviewed in as the pleasantest season. The mornings were spent at exercise and the remainder of the time in festivity. This lasted, with an occasional interruption, till some years after General Severn's death, which happened in 1787, when the regiment was given to Sir Charles Grey (since Lord Grey), who held the colonelcy until 1789, when General Lascelles, who had been lieutenant-colonel, was appointed to the command of it in the room of Sir Charles Grey, who was then unaccountably removed from it.[1]

Charles Lever, we regret to say, devoted his attention to the 14th Hussars, not the Eighth. His novel, *Charles O'Malley, the Irish Dragoon*, emphasises the gay side of cavalry life at the expense of the grave. All who care for Light Dragoons should read *Charles O'Malley*, which depicts the career of the soldier as it actually was in Smet's own day. Captain Richard Power sang the well-known song at the mess in Dublin when the officers were successfully trying to induce Charles O'Malley to join their corps :

THE IRISH DRAGOON.

(*Air*—"Love is the soul of a gay Irishman.")

Oh love is the soul of an Irish Dragoon,
In battle, in bivouac, or in saloon—
　From the tip of his spur to his bright sabretache.
With his soldierly gait and his bearing so high,
His gay laughing look and his light-speaking eye,
He frowns at his rival, he ogles his wench,
He springs in his saddle and "chassés" the French—
　With his jingling spur and his bright sabretache.

[1] Smet, pp. 38–40.

His spirits are high and he little knows care,
Whether sipping his claret or charging a square—
  With his jingling spur and his bright sabretache.
As ready to sing or to skirmish he's found,
To take off his wine or to take up his ground ;
When the bugle may call him, how little he fears
To charge forth in column, and beat the Mounseers—
  With his jingling spur and his bright sabretache.

When the battle is over, he gaily rides back
To cheer every soul in the night bivouac—
  With his jingling spur and his bright sabretache.
Oh ! there you may see him in full glory crowned,
As he sits 'mid his friends on the hardly-won ground,
And hear with what feeling the toast he will give,
As he drinks to the land where all Irishmen live—
  With his jingling spur and his bright sabretache.

Francis Smet and Charles Lever draw a fairly faithful picture of life in a dragoon regiment during the middle and at the end of the eighteenth century respectively. It is perfectly possible for a scientific soldier to-day to read the record of Smet and the novel of Lever, and to turn away and wonder how the British Army survived when such was the spirit actuating the dragoon of those days. No doubt the pendulum swung too much to the side of sport, yet the testimony of the enemy the dragoon met is emphatic in praise of our corps. The invaluable qualities produced by the sporting type requires but little justification at our hands, for the battle honours of the Eighth amply attest what splendid service it has rendered in our defence. There is a remarkable saying in the *Memoirs* of Admiral von Tirpitz when he pronounced that "the most formidable element Germany had to contend with was the spirit of the polo-playing Englishman." With a slight change in this quotation we may write that the most formidable element France had to contend with was the spirit of the racing and hunting Englishman, Irishman and Scotsman. Nor is it altogether wise to take the pages of Lever at their face valuation. There were beyond question Charles O'Malleys in the Dragoons : there were also Henry Conynghams. Perhaps the ideal Irishman—using the word ideal in its Platonic sense—exists only in English fancy. Certainly the real Irishman whom one meets, or even one hears of as achieving fame, is seldom recognisable as an even imperfect adumbration of that ideal. The Duke of Wellington, John Nicholson, Lord Kelvin—all these are Irishmen, and between none of them and Lever is there any profitable parallel to be drawn. Their careers strike the practical note which is so conspicuously absent in Lever's life. Other representatives of Ireland, of whom Tom Moore may be taken as the type, have been distinguished by a sentimental melancholy, entirely alien from Lever's nature. But the Englishman, when he generalises about Ireland, forgets all that. He has it firmly fixed in his mind that the natural Irishman is a dare-devil who rides hard and drinks hard, living from hand to mouth, outrunning the constable, harassed by duns, equally ready to borrow and to lend, to fight a duel, or to take a hand at whist, lengthen his days by the theft of hours from the night, quarrelsome in his cups, yet always bubbling over with good humour and good stories, incapable of "dirty" conduct, yet equally incapable of keeping a good resolution—a man whose weaknesses must be pitied rather than censured, because he is such excellent company. Lever was pretty much that sort of man: Lever, therefore, argues the Englishman, was typically Irish. What the Englishman fails to perceive is that Lever, in a large measure, created the type which he is declared to have exemplified in his life, and that the train of reasoning which ends by demonstrating his typically Hibernian character is really an argument which returns by a vicious circle to its starting point. Had the Eighth been largely composed of either Charles O'Malleys or Charles Levers, it is quite certain that when it was once disbanded, say, in 1697 or 1713, it would never have been restored.

On the 30th of January, 1768, Lord Shelburne informed the Lord Lieutenant, the first Marquess Townshend, of his views on the retirement of officers:

As to Lt. Col. Lushington, Lt. Col. Pepper, Capt. Hill and Capt. Grant, who all desire to retire upon more or less pay, His Majesty doth not relish that mode of retiring, which, in many instances, as experience has shewn, hath been attended with great inconveniences to the service and hath left a long and heavy incumbrance upon Regiments under those circumstances.

It may not be improper to mention to your Excellency that the King did not seem to understand the meaning of the elder captains of the 8th Royal Dragoons having declined the purchase, and quitted to Captain Stewart their pretensions to their succession, as if Col. Lushington was not only to retire upon a Major's pay, but, at the same time, to receive money from the captain for his promotion to the majority.

His Majesty observed in the succession to Captain Hill, that Ensign Engel is recommended to succeed Lt. French, but that no reason is assigned why Lt. Bishop, who seems to serve as an ensign, and on ensign's pay, should not be posted on the muster-rolls as Lt., by which means, if that succession had taken place the Regiment would have had its proper compliment of ensigns.

These points might have required some explanation if the King had approved of those officers retiring in the manner proposed ; but, as that is not the case, I have His Majesty's Commands to acquaint your Excellency that he is willing to Permit those respective officers to retire in any other manner that your Excellency shall propose, *agreeably to the Regulations*, which His Majesty hath thought proper to establish with respect to officers in His army in Ireland, who desire leave to quit the service.[1]

Lieutenant-General Michael O'B. Dilkes reviewed the regiment at the Phœnix Park, Dublin, on the 28th of May, 1768. No doubt there was the usual round of festivities and gaiety, yet behind these festivities and gaiety the life of the regiment was looked after. The observations of Lieutenant-General Dilkes are :

Officers : Made a good appearance. Well Dressed. Well Armed. Saluted well. Uniforms plain, with a slashed sleeve, small yellow cuff ; white lining ; white waistcoats and breeches ; silver buttons, not numbered ; silver epaulettes and silver laced hats. In general well mounted.

Non Commissioned Officers : Made a good appearance. Well mounted.

[1] *Ireland, Entry Books*, 13, f. 122.

Trumpeters : Young, but not yet perfect in their soundings.

Men : Of a good size. Young and well made. Clean under arms. Well dressed. Steady and attentive. Hats well cocked but small.

Horses : In good condition for service. Nimble. 54 with long tails. 9 purchased since last review. 3 not fit for the ranks having had the distemper.

Clothing : Old, but good, clean, well fitted and agreeable to His Majesty's regulation and the patterns sealed by the Board of General Officers.

Arms : Clean.

Accoutrements and Horse Furniture : Shoulder belts and swivel belts (which they wore cross ever since they were in Spain, at which time they were given them as a mark of honour and distinction) good. Waist belts extremely bad ; but new ones bespoke. Horse Furniture good and according to the King's Regulation.

Recruits : Good. 25 enlisted since last review. 21 in the ranks. 4 not fit for the ranks.

Complaints : None.

Accounts : Settled properly.

Manual Exercise : Well performed and executed according to His Majesty's last Regulation.

Movements, evolutions, and manœuvres : . . .[1]

General Observations : This Regiment performed its movements, evolutions, and manœuvres with great alertness, steadiness, and attention. Is in every respect a good regiment, and fit for immediate service.

Barracks : All good, except one floor in the officers' apartment: East Wing.[2]

The new lieutenant-colonel on the 31st of May, 1768, was Francis Lascelles. Major-General Richard Pierson reviewed the regiment at Mallow on the 29th of May, 1769. His report and that of Lieutenant-General Dilkes are in pretty precise agreement.

[1] These are of a complicated character.   [2] *Irish Review Returns*, 1768.

The trumpeters are now thought to be well taught and well mounted. The report on the men is the same, save that it is noted that the black spatterdashes are not according to order, having only half gaiters. The barracks for two troops at Tallaght and for one and a half troops at Cappoquin are in good order. The barracks for the half troop at Mallow are also in good order, but those for the entire troop are not habitable.[1]

During the middle of the eighteenth century it was quite common for cornets and ensigns to spend a year abroad at an academy for the improvement of their education. We have a case in the early part of 1770 where a cornet went to Turin, then a favourite resort for this purpose. On the 18th of September, 1772, leave of absence for twelve months was granted to Cornet Charles Brownlow of the Eighth "to attend an Academy abroad, not having yet finished his education; and to Lieutenant William Montgomery of the 40th Regiment to remain abroad to the 10th of April next for his further improvement."[2]

It is clear that in 1770 the tightening of discipline is a matter of concern to the authorities. There are shades as well as lights in Smet's picture, and there are evidences of the care taken to get rid of the shades. On the 9th of March Lord Weymouth informed the Lord Lieutenant, the Marquess Townshend, that the proceedings of Courts Martial at Limerick and Dublin showed that discipline leant to the lax side, a position that certainly did not underestimate the truth. The letter of Lord Weymouth proceeded to state: "His Majesty took notice of the great necessity there is for strict regulations in order to restore that discipline so much wanted in the army in Ireland, particularly among the Dragoons, as your Excellency observes, and is much pleased to see that matter taken up with proper spirit. The absolute necessity of exemplary punishment is too obvious, and I was sorry to see the reason given by the Court Martial for recommending Major Wrixon to favour, I mean the distress in which the loss of his commission would involve his sister; and I must inform your Excellency that such a reason given by a military *man* in such a case could not pass without

[1] *Irish Review Returns*, 1769.   [2] *Ireland, Entry Books*, 14.

animadversion. In short, His Majesty sees no good reason for mitigating the sentences of Courts Martial, unless farther circumstances appear to engage your Excellency to be of a different opinion on this head."[1]

Major-General Pierson again inspected the regiment at Loughrea on the 30th of May, 1771. Two years before he had been with the Eighth, and his present report is as favourable as his former one. The black spatterdashes are now quite in order. The horses, however, are not in good condition though nimble. The arms are clean and good, except the pistols, which are all bad. The tendency was for the movements and manœuvres, the evolutions and firings to become increasingly complicated, and if anyone turns to the review return he will feel amazed to see that the men were able to execute their intricacies. Yet Major-General Pierson finds that they were "well performed," and he pronounced the regiment "very fit for service."[2] The barracks at Loughrea are in good order, those at Portumna are in process of repair, while those at Gort are much out of order.

At Birr on the 12th of June, 1772, Lieutenant-General Lord Blayney inspected the regiment for the second time. Five years had elapsed since his first inspection, and he had had time to correct his impressions. Since then the general return of the inspecting officer had become much more elaborate, and it is gratifying to notice that he cordially commends the regiment in detail. The officers made a good appearance, and so did the non-commissioned officers. The appearance of the men also met with approval. The trumpeters, however, though pretty well taught, were but indifferently mounted. The movements and manœuvres are not nearly so complex as these Major-General Pierson witnessed. In truth, the regiment "performed very well, but rather slow in time."[3]

The attractions of life in the Eighth have been vividly portrayed by Francis Smet, and, accordingly, in spite of the rules on the purchase of commissions laid down in 1766, prices continued to

---

[1] *Ireland, Entry Books*, 13.   [2] *Irish Review Returns*, 1771.
[3] *Irish Review Returns*, 1772.   This return is in the Mess of the Eighth.

soar.   On the 9th of February, 1773, it was ordered that the sum paid for commissions in the Dragoons Guards and Dragoons be:

Commissions.	Prices.		Difference.	
	£	s.	£	s.
Lieutenant Colonel	5350		1100	
Major	4250		1100	
Captain	3150		1050	
Captain Lieutenant	2100		735	
Lieutenant	1365		262	10
Cornet	1102	10	1102	10
			5350[1]	

Fresh regulations on the state of prices at which the several commissions in Dragoon Regiments in Ireland should be sold were proposed on the 26th of June, 1773.   We are not told how far these proposals came to the stage of performance.   We are afraid that they simply remained in the stage of proposals, and the reason for this is obvious.   The problem of wages, apart from Trades Union ukases, resolves itself into the fact that when two employers run after one working man wages rise, and when two working men run after one employer wages fall.   Similarly, when the demand for a cornetcy is keen, prices rise, and, when the demand is less keen, they fall.   If a lad enjoyed hunting and racing, theatricals and concerts, and if the Eighth promised him a life of pleasure, what could prevent prices soaring?   The regulations of 1773 tried to do so, and this is their scale:

Commissions.	Prices.	Difference.
	£	£
Lieutenant Colonel	5069	959
Major	4110	1150
Captain	2960	958
Captain Lieutenant	2002	797
Lieutenant	1205	277
Cornet	928	928
	5069[2]	

[1] *Ireland, Entry Books*, 14.   [2] *Ireland, Entry Books*, 14, f. 190.

The matter of the exchange of officers lent itself more readily to control than the purchase of commissions. On the 17th of May, 1773, Lieutenant St. George Hatfield of the Eighth obtained grudging permission to exchange with Lieutenant Edward Willey of the Battle Axe Guards, "which is no more a military corps than the Yeomen of the Guard." Such an exchange was not to form a precedent, for neither Hatfield nor "any other officer in the Battle Ax Guards will ever be permitted in future to purchase or exchange in the army."[1] On the 18th of September, 1773, Cornet Charles Brownlow, who was at an academy abroad, was given permission to continue there for another six months "in order to finish his education."[2] There was a muster of the regiment at Cavan on the 13th of October, 1773, for ninety days and another at Belturbet for the same period.[3] The next year, on the 21st of May, Major-General J. A. Gisborne reviewed the regiment at Belturbet. His general return bestows ample praise. The officers and men still make a good appearance. The trumpeters are pretty well taught, and are mounted on grey horses. The horse furniture is generally good save the pouches, belts, and cross belts, which are all bad. The barracks at Belturbet and Navan are in good condition, and the general remarks are: "This regiment went through its business with a good deal of steadiness and exactness. Appears to me to be well taken care of, and is fit for service."[4] Major-General Gisborne inspected the Eighth at Athlone on the 3rd of June, 1775, and his return still continues cordial. He notes that seventeen pretty good horses have been purchased since his last review, though none of them are fit for the ranks. There are nine fresh recruits, and of them eight are fit for the ranks. The movements and manœuvres, the evolutions and firings are more involved than those of the preceding year. Still, "this Regiment appears to me to be in great order and very fit for service."[5]

The experiences of the Seven Years' War combined with the beginnings of the American in 1775 demonstrated the value of light cavalry. The services of the 15th and 16th Dragoons operated

---

[1] *Ireland, Entry Books*, 14, f. 192. [2] *S.P., Entry Books, Ireland*, 14, f. 208.
[3] *Ireland, Entry Books*, 16. [4] *Irish Review Returns*, 1774. [5] *Irish Review Returns*, 1775.

in the direction of augmenting light horse at the expense of heavy. The light horse then consisted of the 15th, 16th, 17th, and 18th Dragoons, and to these it was proposed to add all the heavy dragoon regiments from the 7th to the 14th. With the worth of light cavalry, we can combine another reason for the conversion of heavy horse into light. Military aid was granted to the civil officers appointed to collect the revenue in Ireland, and many applications for such aid were received from the magistrates in the execution of their duty. As these applications had lately become more frequent, and as the civil power found itself not sufficient "to quell the licentious Spirit of the lower class of People in Ireland, particularly of the Persons associated under the name of White Boys," the first Earl Harcourt on the 3rd of June, 1775, made a proposal to the Earl of Rochford. This was that as one Regiment of Light Dragoons had gone to North America, and the other two were being weakened by drafts—we meet this plague again—taken from them, that two or more Regiments of Heavy Dragoons be converted into Light Dragoons. Indeed "this measure will be considered by all Ranks of People as a particular Mark of His Majesty's gracious attention to the Peace and Welfare of this Kingdom."[1]

When Pitt was asked when the Napoleonic Wars would cease, he gave the reply that this would happen when we achieved security. Security means not only immunity from enemies abroad : it means immunity from them at home. For security is the basis of all prosperity. Not a little of the exertions of the Eighth were spent in putting down the Whiteboys. Just as they had assisted in the putting down of the rapparees during the seventeenth century, so they assisted in putting down the Whiteboys during the eighteenth. The origin of the Whiteboys is to be found in the fact that the long-continued murrain among cattle in England and on the Continent increased enormously the value of pasturage as compared with tillage. This meant evictions, and this also meant that the peasants formed themselves into organisations in order to resist evictions. In 1775 the Whiteboy organisation was sufficiently formidable for officials like Harcourt

[1] *S.P., Ir.,* 447, f. 57.

to take alarm. By a system of intimidation the peasant was forced to the conclusion that it was safer to disobey the law than to obey it. The Whiteboys marched about the country, often in broad daylight, wearing white cockades and blowing horns. Nor did they fly before the soldiers. As early as 1762 an observer writes from the county of Tipperary that "above 500 men frequently assemble with shirts over their clothes doing whatever mischief they please by night, under the sanction of being fairies, as they call themselves." He drily adds that "the fairies are composed of all the able young fellows from Clonmel to Mitchelstown." A letter in 1778 tells how a single person passing from Ballinasloe fair to Clara had 760 sheep killed in one night, and next morning no one dared to send him a horse to carry away the carcasses, or to bid more for them than 3s. 6d. a sheep, that being the rate the Whiteboy proclamations had prescribed.

The outrages of the Whiteboys lay at the back of the mind of Lord Rochford when he wrote to the Lord Lieutenant, Earl Harcourt, on the 26th of June, 1775:

Having laid before the King your Excellency's letter of the 3rd instant in which you humbly propose for his Royal consideration the great benefit that would arise for the service of the revenue and for the preservation of the public peace, if more Dragoon corps in Ireland should be converted into Light Dragoons, I have the honour of acquainting your Excellency that His Majesty is not only convinced of the propriety of such a measure, but considers that species of cavalry may be in other respects of infinite use ; His Majesty is therefore pleased to approve that two regiments should be at present converted from heavy to light Dragoons each regiment to part with the horses of two troops in the first instance and not to cast any more until the said two troops be complete with horses agreeably to the service of light cavalry. Colonel Warde has distinguished himself as an officer of light cavalry, the 14th Regiment of Dragoons at once appears to His Majesty the most eligible. The 8th is the other His Majesty pitches upon, as the Lieutenant Colonel is a young man and therefore most likely to do his utmost to get that corps on as good a foot as the 14th undoubtedly will be. His Majesty chuses to leave the 9th commanded by Colonel Mocher for the present on the heavy establishment, that the three other regiments of dragoons may have one to set them example for improvement.

Your Excellency will undoubtedly give the necessary directions to the several departments in Ireland that they may make such interior arrangements as will avoid the inconveniences that attended the converting the 12th Regiment.

Such horses as are unfit for service and are to be parted with ought to be bought by the Corps that have vacancies, and great care ought to be taken of the Stock Purse during the change, as the funds for remounting and recruiting must be appropriated with the greatest economy for the intended purpose.

These are the general instructions I have in command from the King to convey to your Excellency, and His Majesty entirely relies upon your zeal and diligence for carrying this service into execution.[1]

The Lieutenant-Colonel was Francis Lascelles, who had filled that position since 1764. As the Lord Lieutenant, Earl Harcourt, informed the Earl of Rochford on the 7th of July, 1775, that "the said Commander in chief representing that as it appears by the reports of the Reviewing Generals that these two Regiments (*i.e.* the 8th and the 14th) are the best mounted, and in every other respect the best Heavy Dragoons on this Establishment, He would humbly submit it to His Majesty's Consideration whether His Majesty might not be induced for the good of the Service to make choice of two other Regiments of the Heavy Dragoons on this Establishment."[2]   The Commander-in-Chief would have proposed the 9th and the 13th Regiments of Dragoons, "knowing that the former and being very credibly informed that the other are the worst Regiments of Heavy Dragoons in Ireland."

As the change from heavy to light horse might involve the loss of some of the distinctions of the Eighth, the Lieutenant-Colonel, Francis Lascelles, memorialised Earl Harcourt on the 10th of November, 1775:

Sheweth

That the aforesaid Regiment has for many years enjoy'd the Honourable distinction of wearing Cross Belts, which Badge was given

[1] *S.P., Ir.,* 447, f. 68.   [2] *S.P., Ir.,* 447, f. 77.

them soon after their being Raised in the year 1693, in Consequence of their obtaining a Compleat Victory over a Regiment of Horse in Spain, and as on the present change of the aforesaid Regiment from Heavy to Light Dragoons, that Honourable distinction will be lost.

Your memorialist prays Your Excellency will please to move His Majesty that in Lieu thereoff the 8th: Regiment may be Faced with Blue, and call'd the Kings Royal Irish Light Dragoons.[1]

George III, we learn, was on the 28th of November, 1775, graciously pleased to condescend to the above request. The cocked hats were exchanged for helmets with red horse-hair crests; arms and accoutrements of a lighter description were adopted, and the standard height for men and horses was reduced. From 1776 the Regiment was styled the 8th King's Royal Irish Light Dragoons.

The increasing influence of the American War is obvious in the letter Lord Weymouth wrote to the Lord Lieutenant, Earl Harcourt, on the 1st of January, 1776, in the course of which immediate orders were given for the augmentation by recruits of the four Regiments of Horse and the seven Regiments of Light Dragoons now in Ireland with one corporal and ten private dismounted men to each troop of horse and dragoons.[2] Nor was Lord Weymouth content with issuing this order, for on the 2nd of May he wished to know if it had been executed.[3] On the 23rd of January, 1776, Lord Weymouth authorised the Lord Lieutenant to employ a certain proportion of horses in drawing carriages and as bat horses.[4] Lord Weymouth discussed on the 23rd of February the desirability of granting pardons for deserters and of lowering the size of recruits. The latter, he perceives, is "detrimental to the service, experience having shewn that it is very dangerous to give too great latitude to officers on that head." Still, pardon was to be given to deserters if they surrendered before the 10th of April, and forty shillings, not twenty, was to be allowed to anyone apprehending a deserter.[5] Reviews of cavalry this year, so we are informed on the 23rd of March, 1776, are to be postponed.[6]

[1] *S.P., Ir.*, 449, f. 74. *Cf.* Harcourt's order, December 9, 1775.
[2] *Ireland, Entry Books*, 15, f. 54.   [3] *Ireland, Entry Books*, 15, f. 243.
[4] *Ireland, Entry Books*, 15, f. 174.   [5] *Ireland, Entry Books*, 15, f. 199.
[6] *Ireland, Entry Books*, 15, f. 221.

At this stage in regimental history we are fortunate in possessing a series of letters written to and from Lieutenant-Colonel Francis Lascelles and Captain-Lieutenant Hunt, who was in temporary command after Colonel Lascelles left till Lieutenant-Colonel Lyon was appointed in May, 1780. Lascelles retired in 1780, and the new major was Robert Henry Southwell, an Irishman not unproficient in the national art of blarney. This series of letters runs from the 22nd of October, 1775, to the 4th of May, 1787. The first letter in this series is from John Severne, and is of the date of the 22nd of October, 1776. It is written to Sir John Irwine, the Irish Commander-in-Chief:

Sir,

Permit me to apply to you in relation to the Regiment The King honors me with the Command of. The 8th Dragoons, early in this centry, acquired Cross Belts in Spain by making a Regiment of Spanish Horse prisoners, which they were then permitted, and continued to wear, and which was confirmed to them by The Kings Order of Regulations issued I think in the year 1769.

When His Majesty was pleased to change the Regiment to the Light Establishment, in Lieu of their Cross Belts (which they had so honorably obtained) he was graciously pleased to distinguish the Regiment with the Title of Royal.

My health at that time rendered it necessary that the Field Officer Commanding should transact all affairs of the Regiment and it is very lately I learn from Major Stewart that a Badge and Motto was not adverted to, and was omited in the application when the title of "Royal" was granted ; and, not being included in the order, the Board of General Officers could not approve of a pattern Housing shewn to them whereon was the Harp and Crown.

I beg leave to make my application thro you as the Commander in Chieff and as every Royal Regiment is dignified with a badge and motto I humbly propose for the Royal Irish Light Dragoons

The Harp and Crown.
Pristinae Virtutis Memores.

If you approve thereof and pleas to promote with your infuence you will very much oblige the Regiment and me.

My agent will wait upon your aid-de-camp to know in what mode to apply, by memorial in my name or other ways, and receive his directions therein.[1]

Sir John Irwine wrote on the 28th of October, 1776, from the Royal Hospital, telling Lieutenant-General Severne that the method to set right the omission is to deliver to him a memorial. Sir John will then present it to the Lord Lieutenant.[2] The end of Sir John's letter is, "I hope you keep your health; no man wishes it more sincerely than I do, nor is with more truth and regard than I have the honour to be, Sir, your most obedient humble Servant." The Eighth had never proved itself unmindful of former glory, and it was peculiarly appropriate that such a motto as *Pristinae Virtutis Memores* should have been selected. Tradition is naturally strong in all regiments, and it certainly loses none of its strength in Severne's Dragoons. The honour of "Royal" was then unique, for the Eighth was the only corps of light dragoons so denominated.

The Lord Lieutenant, the Earl of Buckinghamshire, laid down on the 29th of January, 1777, that "Lord Viscount Weymouth, His Majesty's Principal Secretary of State, having by His Letter of the Twenty-First Instant, signified unto the late Lord Lieutenant of this Kingdom, that His Majesty had been graciously pleased to grant to the VIIIth, or Royal Irish Regiment of Light Dragoons in Ireland, the Badge of the Harp and Crown, and the Motto 'Pristinae Virtutis Memores.' We do hereby direct and require you to take care that in viewing and approving the Patterns of Clothing and Accoutrements for the said Regiment, His Majesty's Pleasure therein signified be punctually and duly observed."[3]

The new title of the Regiment, its badge, and its motto take the place of the old distinction of cross belts which now disappears. The facing was changed from yellow to blue, and the waistcoats,

---

[1] Mr. E. C. Severne kindly lent me these letters, and I compared them with the useful type-written copy Lieutenant-Colonel H. N. M. Thoyts made of them in November, 1906. This copy is with the regiment, and I call it the *Severne MSS*. This first reference is *Severne MSS.*, pp. 1–2.

[2] *Severne MSS.*, p. 3.

[3] *Regimental MSS*. There are a few eighteenth century letters in the Mess.

breeches, and belts to white. In 1784 the uniform was changed from scarlet to blue, and the facing from blue to scarlet. Sir John Irwine indicated in his letter of the 26th of February, 1777, to Severne that the menace of the Whiteboys had not altogether disappeared. He writes:

> I was happy to be the instrument of forwarding any wish of yours, and rejoice that His Majesty was graciously pleased to comply so cheerfully and readily with your request.
>
> I am extremely concerned to hear you are tormented with the gout. No man wishes you health more sincerely than I do, and a long continuance of it.
>
> The Quarters of your Regiment were fixed before I had the honour to receive your last letter. I hope they are not bad. You will have three quarters, two troops in each. Every Regiment of Cavalry and Dragoons is dispersed about in different detachments either to protect the quiet subject or the revenue officer. I should be glad to oblige everybody but as there are many Regiments now converting from heavy to light Dragoons, all claim particular favour and all plead the difficulties they are under, of course some must be disappointed ; however, Sir, if you should not like your quarters this year from the report of your commanding officer, I will do my best for your satisfaction in the disposition of quarters the following year. As I shall always have great pleasure in giving every attention to your commands and proofs of the sincere esteem and respect with which I have the honour to be.[1]

General J. A. Johnston reviewed the regiment at Clonmel on the 4th of June, 1777, and his general report bestowed hearty praise. The officers present a good and proper appearance and are well mounted. The men are of "small size but growing. Age, very young. Made well. Ride pretty well. Dressed well. Steady and attentive." The horses are in good condition, though the clothing is indifferent. The barracks at Clonmel and Clogheen are good, and so are the firing and furniture. At Ross, however, the gable is cracked, though the firing and furniture are sufficient. There is not sufficient accommodation at these barracks for the number of augmented men. Seventy-two men had been enlisted

---

[1] *Severne MSS.*, p. 4.

since the last review, and of the soldiers 30 were only 17, 79 were 18, and 54 were 20 years old. The general remarks are: "This Regiment is at this time complete, man and horse, and for the first time since it was reformed. Well advanced as a new Light Regiment, October 10, 1777. The dismounted augmentation a very good recruit."[1]

The details of General Johnston's review we can supplement by a letter Lascelles wrote from Dublin on the 10th of August, 1777, to Severne, who was then at Clifton, near Tamworth, in Staffordshire. It runs thus:

> The Receipt of your very obliging letter of the 5th inst. should have been acknowledged by return of post, but I waited a few day's to acquaint you that I had Received from Mr. Wybrants agreeable to your directions £137 13s. 11½d. and that, with that sum and what the old appointments sold for I have paid Mr Nixon and Mr Stanley's demand for Jackets, watering Caps and Snaffle Bridles, as also the Bill for watering caps which were made at Quarters: and must beg leave to say your Regiment is much obliged to you for, and make no doubt will be mindfull of your goodness towards them.
>
> All the appointments are regularly Booked as the Regiment Receives them; therefore no mistakes can happen.
>
> Since the Review I have bought Twenty Horses and Recruited Several men, so that we want 13 Horses and 12 men to compleat: our Funds at present will not allow me to buy many more; but there can be no doubt of our having our full numbers by next Spring.
>
> I return to Longford in a few days with Mr Warde who goes down as a Commissioner of the Board to examine into the state and condition of our Barracks which tho' a new one is the most inconvenient building for the purpose I ever Inhabited. It will give me pleasure at all times to execute any commands you may have.[2]

Bread is considered better than biscuit for the troops in camp, so Lord Weymouth told the Lord Lieutenant, the Earl of Buckinghamshire, on the 23rd of May, 1778, and a loaf of bread costs

---

[1] *Irish Review Returns*, 1777.   [2] *Severne MSS.*, p. 5.

sixpence.[1]   Lascelles, who was now in Cork, wrote to Severne on the 17th of June, 1778 :

We arrived in this Town the 9th, 10th and 11th Inst. the Troops intended for Bandon were detained here by order of Genrl. Mocher (Commanding in this Province) on account of the very Extravagant price they demanded for forage about that Country : I waited on the General to know his further pleasure which was that this Regt. Should remain here untill they marched into Camp the Middle of next Month, but since then He has informed me that his private Letters signify a Doubt whether any of the Cavalry will Encamp or not ; but that He has not as yet Received any official Information : Should this alteration take place it is not in my power to Guess where we shall be stationed as almost all the Barracks in this province are occupied.

In consequence of your favour of the 2nd June I have given Sergt. Molone in orders as Quarter Master in the room of Qr. Mr. Wall resigned and desired the Agent to date the Warrant the 1st May and enter it and send it down to me—but his answer of the 13th Just mentions that he had not at that time Received it from you, and by which I am fearfull it must have miscarried in some of the post-offices.

I am glad to acquaint you that the Commander in Chief in consequence of my application has consented to Chaplain Lushington being absent, provided that I will procure a Deputy to officiate for him, which I shall accordingly do : and have wrote to him that he need not join the Regiment.

I have not yet heard a syllable about the Reviews when it is fixed your commands concerning the returns shall be obeyed. We are present compleat in horses and only want Two men, one of which vacancies was occasioned by Sergeant Molone's preferment and the other by discharging a consumptive man.

We are in very great want of new Saddle Bags, our old ones are quite worn out and I have agreed with a Sadler here to make 138 upon a new construction for Seven shillings each and as our Captains are almost

[1] *Ireland, Entry Books*, 16, f. 55.

ruined with the sums they are continually advancing for their Troops and the very great Doubt there is of any allowance being made for it notwithstanding the Kings Warrant I must beg to solicit your further assistance towards

> paying for the bags
> or any part thereoff-
> whatever you think
> proper to allow shall
> be as usual notified
> to the men and deducted
> from the first cost.[1]

Major-General F. Mocher reviewed the Regiment at Kinsale Camp on the 5th of October, 1778, and the tone of his general return is most laudatory. The appearance of the officers, non-commissioned officers, and men receives cordial commendation, but the trumpeters are taught but indifferently and are mounted indifferently. The horses are in good working order, if not remarkably nimble. There are 51 good recruits, 13 deserters, and 8 discharges. Since the last review there are 72 enlistments, and of these 42 are in the ranks with 9 unfit for the ranks. The firing, however, is merely tolerably well, and the manœuvres are not so rapid as they ought to be. Nevertheless, the general remarks are: "The regiment well appointed ; a fine body of men, of a good size. Exercise well, but not so steady on horseback as could be wished. Several bad horses, but the Stockpurse not in a state to admit of an effective change. About 30 properly bought would be requisite, if ordered on immediate service. No order or regulation of exercise for the Light Dragoons in this Kingdom has been received. Great want of uniformity consequently prevails. In the wheelings, some corps look to, others from, the hand they wheel to."[2]

Orders were issued on the 4th of February, 1779, for an allowance of ten pounds for an additional horse to carry the blankets of each

---

[1] *Severne MSS.,* pp. 6–7.   [2] *Irish Review Returns,* 1778.

troop in camp, and also for an allowance of one hundred days' forage money to the regiments of cavalry and infantry, which had been in camp, in aid of their expense of keeping their horses during the winter.[1] Lascelles wrote from Mallow on the 12th of March, 1779:

> By this last post I sent notice of Quarter Masr. Walkers resignation and have now the necessity of troubling you on the affairs of our Adjutant,[2] whose large Family and other circumstances obliges to resolve on asking your permission and mine to quite the Service ; for my own part as I know he cannot continue to support himself on the pay (or indeed cou'd he have done it so long, but for helps he has received through me) I do very readily agree to it ; and at the same time recommend as a successor our (pres.) Quarter Master Hunt, who was drill ser-geant in the 14th Dragoons, writes a good hand and had been used to the keeping of accounts and papers of a Regiment and was besides as Colonel Burgoyne represents not a bad riding-master ; in short he has promised to exert himself in the employment and by so doing endeavour to recommend himself to you, and me, and having been a long time bred in the school of obedience, it is to be supposed He cannot have conceived any notions repugnant to the duties of an Adjutant.
>
> Our (present) Adjutant Burgess informs me He gave to Captain Hunt £350 for the commission and I have required a letter from the Quarter Master (of which the enclosed is a copy) concerning the Terms and conditions of his Bargain with Mr Burgess etc. etc. and as I am of opinion the Regiment cannot suffer by the change I hope it will meet with your approbation. I must beg the favour of your answer by return of post.[3]

Major-General Massey reviewed the regiment at Aghada camp on the 27th of September, 1779. His general report runs on the usual lines. The description of the officers' dress is "coats laced with silver. Laced epaulets. Lapelled with blue, white waist-coats and breeches. Silver buttons with a lion, harp and crown and number of the regiment, helmets, etc." The debtor side of

---

[1] *S.P., Dom., Mil.*, 28.   [2] He was Thomas Burgess.   [3] *Severne MSS.*, p. 8.

the Stock Purse account is worth giving from the 1st of July, 1778, to the 30th of June, 1779:

		£	s.	d.
To Balance due in last account		87	4	7
„ nine horses recruited at 20 guineas each ..		204	15	0
„ 27 men recruited at £3 13 8 each		99	9	0
„ subsistence given before they joined		24	4	8
„ bounty money given discharged men ..		2	14	8
„ expenses attending deserters		17	13	8½
„ the agent's charge for Muster Office fees, clearing warrants, etc., to December 31, 1777 ..		6	12	1
„ 7 horses wanting February 1 at 20 guineas each		157	5	0
„ 7 men wanting at £5 English each		37	18	4
„ balance remaining		68	6	1
		708	2	7½[1]

In General Massey's eyes the appearance of the officers, non-commissioned officers, and men left nothing to be desired, and even the trumpeters sounded well and were mounted well. There is not a single example of fault-finding throughout the whole report. Most reviewing officers hint at least a fault or two, but General Massey does nothing of the kind. His concluding general observations are: "This Regiment performed their movements and evolutions, etc., with the greatest exactness and rapidity, and is fit for immediate service."[2]

On Christmas eve, 1779, Lascelles wrote from Doneraile to Severne:

Two days ago I received a Letter from Tallow acquainting me that Quarter Master Quinn who has been sick there several Months Died on the 15th inst. In consequence of which and of your former declaration that in case of Vacancies of this Kind you should receive my recommendation for filling them up.

I am not above saying that the sale of this Warrant would at this time be a great object to me, and Shall therefore esteem it a particular favour if you would let me dispose of it, in the doing of which I must

[1] The total is wrong.   [2] *Irish Review Returns*, 1779.

acquaint you that I mean to give the preference to a Sergeant at a very moderate rate ; there being no man of that degree of merit in the Regiment to entitle him to the intire Gift and my attention on all occasions to your interest are the inducements I have for asking this first, and only favour.

We marched to our winter Quarters the beginning of this month viz. 3 Troops at this place and 3 at Charleville.   Our new Clothing for the present Year is now on the road, the General officers being all employed at the Camps during the Summer, was the cause of its not passing the Board till lately : Nixon informs me by this days post that I shall find they are the best I have received for many years.

We want 4 men and 9 Horses ; by the first of February I hope the Regiment will be compleat.   The last two Campaigns has occasioned an Extraordinary wear

and tear of the appointments
but everything shall
be put to rights
with all the economy I
possibly can.[1]

For the whole of 1780 we have no other information save that given in eight letters among the Severne manuscripts.   They, however, are so interesting that we give most of them.   Lascelles is in 115 Jermyn Street, London, on the 12th of February, and he feels overjoyed by the news of Sir George Rodney's victory over the Spanish fleet.   Plainly, Severne had granted him his first favour, and Lascelles had given the vacancy to Sergt. Cochran if he can find two hundred pounds for its purchase.   If he cannot, the offer is to be passed on to another Sergeant in the Regiment "whose circumstances I know better and whose merit is fully equal, tho' not so old a Sergeant in the Corps as Cochran."[1]   On the 19th of April, however, we find that "the Sergeants cou'd not raise above £100 Irish for the Warrant rather than have it go out of the Regt."   Under these circumstances Lascelles still offered

[1] *Severne MSS.*, p. 9.   [2] *Severne MSS.*, p. 11.

the vacancy to Cochran, and he accordingly wrote to Severne to sign the warrant with Cochran's name.[1]

Lascelles announced on the 4th of May that he has just been appointed Lieutenant-Colonel of the 3rd Regiment of Dragoons, "which circumstance however I trust will not prevent my enjoying a continuation of your Friendship."[2] John Hunt is put in temporary command, and he writes less attractive letters to Severne. Still, they have the merit of showing the manner of life as it actually was. The new lieutenant-colonel on the 8th of May, 1780, was Andrew Lyon. Hunt wrote from Charleville on the 13th of June:

I was favoured with yours of the 6th inst. and herewith send you the Stockpurse-account of the Regiment for the last two years, during which time the Captains did not receive any Stockpurse, the last dividend being made on leaving Longford before the new regulations commenced when each Captn. received £35 16s. 7½d.

The reason why there has been no dividend since then will appear by the enclosed account to be owing to the great Number of Horses bought and men recruited during the last Two years Vizt. 48 Horses which cost £1092 and 98 men who cost £360 19s. 4d., amounting in all to the sum of £1452 19s. 4d.

You will observe in the last year's Acct. ending 30th June, 1779 there is a Ballance remaining of £68 6s. 1d. which Col. Lascelles deferred dividing being in Expectation of getting leave, and having applied to Genl. Cunningham to omit giving credit for 7 Horses and 7 men wanting to compleate the Regiment the 1st Feby. 79 as they were compleated immediately after, but there was no getting over the Kings Order, and so that sum was ordered to remain for the Credit of this present year by wch. means we lost so much and this year we shall have more than enough to pay the £30 to each Captain and the Overplus be carried on to the next year's credit for such is the King's Order, the £68 6s. 1d. will be divided along with the £30 in next abstract to each Captain.

This is the clearest Acct. I can give of the Non-division for 2 yrs. past and if you choose to se the Accounts from the change of the Regimt. to this present period I can furnish you with it and not think it the least trouble.

[1] *Severne MSS.*, p. 12.   [2] *Severne MSS.*, p. 13.

The Doneraile Troops march yesterday Two to Bruff and one to this town, your troop and Capt. Saundersons are gone to Bruff where they have excellent Quarters and the Colonels come here as I judged he would choose to have his Troop here when he joyns.[1]

Captain-Lieutenant John Hunt wrote to Major Southwell from Charleville about the case of a namesake, Thomas Hunt, who was Adjutant, on the 28th of July :

This morning I was favoured with yours enclosing General Severnes Letter and am much obliged to you for the Trouble you have taken about Hunts Warrant ; the Reason why he wishes to sell is as follows.

When Colonel Lascelles I may say forced Burgess to sell the Adjutancy and that Hunt was looked upon as fit to succeed to that post, there was £300 of the purchase money borrowed from a Mr Bury near Birr, this Mr Bury is since Dead and his Executors are very pressing in their demand to have this money paid, which Hunt has no other method of doing than by the sale of one or other of his Employmts. and as a purchaser for an Adjutancy cannot be so readily found out as for a warrant the latter was thought best to be disposed off, as so proper a person was found to succeed ; this is the real and Genuine Cause why he requested permission to sell the Warrant which he is to sell at a loss of £50 having given Drewit £350 for it and is only to receive 300 from Dawson.

I hope when you are so good as to convey these urgent reasons to the General it will satisfie him that there is not the Smallest degree of Deception Intended and I give my Honor Hunt is this minute in as aparent good Health as I am or any man in the Regimt. and nothing but Necessity prompts him to wish parting with the Warrant. Last post I took the liberty of Inclosing you *my Forlorn Hope* to be presented to Sir John Irwine after you have perused it. I must confess my expectations from it are not very sanguine, however I am sure you'l give it what assistance you can. Last post I got official notice that Col. Lyon had leave of absence till 31st Aug. . . .

P.S. I have by this post wrote to Genl. Severne to know his pleasure about his Dividend of the Stock Purse and mentioned to him that I had wrote to you about the reasons that induced Hunt to ask leave to sell the Warrant.

[1] *Severne MSS.*, p. 14.   [2] *Severne MSS.*, p. 15.

The same day Hunt wrote a more formal letter to General Severne :

The last time I had the Honor to adress you was from Athlone in the year 1775 when I was promoted to be Captain-Lieut. and not having since been favoured with your notice conceived I might unfortunately have fallen under your displeasure tho' totally ignorant of the Cause having ever considered General Severne as a benefactor both to me and my Family and shall always retain a grateful remembrance of the favour done to me and my Father.

I have now had the Honour of Commanding your Regiment for Seven months Since Colonel Lascelles left us and will be bold to assert that His Majesty has not a finer Regt. in his Service both for Men and Horses or a regimt. that knows their business better. There are 4 Troops quartered in this Town and 2 at Bruff about 8 miles distant ; we frequently meet midway to go thro' our Manouvrs and should not be ashamed if His Majesty was to be present. Last post I got official notice from the Commander in Chief that Lt. Col. Lyon had leave of absence untill the 31st of August.

Some time ago I sent Major Southwell, in order to be transmitted to you, the State of our Stockpurse for three years past by which you'll perceive the fund would not admit of the Dividend to the Captains agreeable to the Kings regulation and that they had the contingent expenses attending their Troops to pay out of their own pocketts. This was owing to the number of Men and Horses recruited to compleate the Regiment on the change from Heavy to Light. This year we have immerged from that difficulty and there is a fund sufficient to pay each Captain his £30 and a Ballance remaining to be placed to the Credit of next year.

For these five years past I have had the Command of your Troop I kept it in as complete Order as any Troop in the Regimt. Paid 6 Guineas a Year since the regulations came out to The Troop Clerk, had several losses by men who deserted and were in debt. et. the Amount of which I cannot Ascertain as I was not particular in keeping an exact Account. I take the liberty of mentioning these particulars to you as I am now Crediting each Captain his Stockpurse dividend and I would by no means presume to medle with yours but wait to know your Pleasure on that head which when known shall be strictly obey'd.

At the request of Adjutant Hunt I wrote some time ago to Major Southwell to beg he would Apply to you for permission for him to dispose of his Warrant ; this day I received a letter from

the major to know the
reasons he wishes to
sell of which I have informed
him and hope they will appear

satisfactory to you which is a Debt of £300 he owes for the purchase of the Adjutancy, the person the money was borrow'd from being Dead and his Executors pressing him for the Money which he has no other way to pay than by selling one of his Employments.[1]

In Dublin Major Southwell heard from Captain-Lieutenant John Hunt on the question of the warrant for Adjutant Thomas Hunt, strongly supporting the line taken by the captain in a letter of the 1st of August.   On the 18th of August, 1780, John Hunt wrote to General Severne from Charleville :

I take the earliest Opportunity of returning you my Thanks for the contents of your Letter of the 9th Inst. which I was honored with by last post.

As I constantly reported to Major Southwell everything concerning the Regiment since I had the honour to command it and believing he corresponded with you, would not doubt but you were informed of everything relative thereto, Otherwise I should have been regular and particular in reporting to you.   The Only change in our Quarters since we marched in here last December was Sending Two Troops from Doneraile to Bruff and bringing the 3rd Troop here on Account of the Exorbitant price demanded for Hay at Doneraile Vizt. 3 Guineas p. Ton, and I procured it at Bruff for a Guinea and a half.   Every Horse in the Regiment has been recruited either by Col. Lascelles or Lt.-Col. Stewart (late Major) except One that I bought some time ago to replace one that Died.   Some were bought at Fairs and some from the dealers in Dublin and picked up wherever they could be had, they came at a very high price but this was Owing in a great Measure to the Great Demand there was for Light Dragoon Horses at that time as the 13th and 14th were changed to Light about the same time we

[1] *Severne MSS.*, pp. 16–7.

were and every Commanding Officer was trying to get the best for his Own regiment to this may be added the Anual Recruit of the 12 and 18th so that for some Years past the Kind of Horses we Use were never known to be so dear owing to the foregoing reasons.

The High Expence of recruiting the Men may be accounted for in the same manner as the Horses and were it not that Government leave was obtained to Draw the £400 Deposit from the Agent The Regiment would not yet have been complete from the Ordinary funds Appropriated for Recruiting etc: We are now Complete in Horses and want but one man, and I have no doubt but that Col. Lyon when he joyns us will Coroborate the Report I did myself the Honor to make you in my last letter.[1]

In 1781 the American War of Independence forced the Government to note the necessity for fresh soldiers. On the 19th of January we have an abstract of the names of lieutenants, with the regiments to which they belong, who are engaged in the task of raising new companies.[2] One of these is Lieutenant Henry Saunders of the Eighth who is so employed. Such a man, we learn, ought to have been a lieutenant of two years' standing,[3] whereas Saunders was one of six years' standing.

In the Severne manuscripts we have our first letter from Andrew Lyon, the new lieutenant-colonel. On the 13th of February, 1781, he writes to Severne:

I have the honor to acknowledge the receipt of your Letter of the 26th of January wherein you approve of Corporal Davis's Succeeding Quarter Master Simple and I ordered him to send you last post his Resignation and an acknowledgement that money matters were settled between them.

I beg leave now Sir to trouble you with what is of the greatest consequence to me—and wherein I must crave your approbation, as my family affairs require my quitting the Service immediately which with reluctance I communicate to you who has shown me every part of polite attention since I have had the honor to be under your command

---

[1] *Severne MSS.*, pp. 19–20.   [2] *Ireland*, 472, f. 76.
[3] *Ireland*, 472, f. 81, February 3, 1781; f. 96, February 13, 1781.

but the large Sums my Commissions have cost me since I came into the Service and having those to provide for, for whom I ought to make every sacrifice, obliges me to embrace an offer that I think is to my advantage ; as an only Son I have would be left intierly unprovided for in case I should die before I had quitted the Service, and it is a scheme I have thought of for some time but always wished first to obtain rank of Lt. Colonel.

Major Southwell and I have corresponded upon the above subject and I believe with your approbation and recommendation of him for the Succession matters between us would soon be settled.   I have applied for leave to go to Dublin which I expect will be granted me— and am therefore to beg when you do me the honor to answer my Letter to direct it to Messrs. Wybrants the Agent.

Your Regiment just now looks clean and well, the Jackets made of the old Cloaks are finished and I have contrived to give them (from some savings) New Waistcoats and Britches so that they will be smartly cloathed till the end of the Summer.[1]

The Eighth had on the 5th of April, 1781, 192 men, 135 horses, and 3 horses were wanting to complete the establishment.[2] There were six troops stationed at Charleville and Bruff.   All the cavalry, except the 1st and 4th Horse, were in possession of the camp equipage used in 1779.   Incidentally we learn that the lieutenants had raised no less than 1300 recruits.[3]   On the 12th of September we have another return, and by it it appears that the effective rank and file are 174 men, and 123 horses, while the rank and file fit for duty are 148 men and 123 horses.   One troop of the Regiment is stationed at Middleton and one at Castle Martyr, and two apiece at Tallaght and Cloyne.

The moment Major R. H. Southwell is in office as lieutenant-colonel on the 4th of April, 1781, he seizes the opportunity to raise real questions on the past history of the Eighth.   Naturally he turns to Lieutenant-General Severne, who boasted in 1783 of no less than over sixty-seven years' service.   Accordingly from

Kilkenny on the 2nd of December Southwell asked the commanding officer nine questions :

Dear General

I have the pleasure to acquaint you the Agents have sent down the half-Mounting Acct. to 1782 inclusive of which a particular explanation shall be kept.   I am in hopes it will afford Leather (Buckskin) Breeches for the men, which will be one of the best appointments they could possibly have.

I am now busily employed in Adjusting—Enlarging and Regulating a thing much wanted, the *Regimental Book* for the careful and exact entry of all clothing appointments, etc. etc., delivered to the Regt. This you will, as Colonel, find the infinite advantage of, and indeed the Corps in general will be greatly benefitted thereby, it has already cost me much pains and no small trouble to attempt this most necessary work from the great want of Information of many things I hope before I quit it I shall make it as perfect a thing of the Kind as perhaps is in any Corps, either of Cavalry or Infantry, I am much at a loss for the antient Records of the Regiment which I request you will have the Goodness to assist me ; which no doubt from your extensive knowledge of the Regiment you can easily do.   I beg many pardons for this trouble but as it proceeds from my Zeal for your Regiment am in hope you will pardon my making the following Query's.

1st. Had not the 8th Dns. been raised much sooner than is mentioned in the Army List (1693) and had it not been reduced long before that period and then Regimented again ?   (viz. 1693).

2. Had it not been employed with credit in K. Williams time in Ireland (agst. James 2nd and the French) then went to England and afterwards to Flanders in that K's Campaigns against Lewis 14th ?

3. Did it not Return after those Campgns. to Ireland and when ? and was it not sent to Flanders again in Q. Annes' time when Genl. Bowles was Colonel in the Command of the great D. of Marlborough?

4. At what particular time and place and action and under whose command did the Regt. defeat a Regt. of Spanish Horse in Spain whereby the honor of wearing *Cross Belts* was conferred ?   Did not the famous Earl of Peterboro Command the B. Army in Spain at that time ?

5. Did not the Regt. obtain great honor in this Engagement and much signalized thereby so as to be esteemed a favorite Corps?

6. When did the Regt. return to Ireland afterwards, and did it continue there till the Rebellion of 1715 and was it employed in Scotland or England then?

7. Did not the Regt. gain great Renown in Scotland in the year 1745 when it was ordered over there from Ireland and was it not augmented to 63 p. troop nine troops (3 Sqdns.) and did not his late R. Highness *Wm. Duke of Cumberland* take Distinguished notice of the 8th Dns. when other Corps from Ireland had not behaved well? And was there not afterwards a particular exception to the 8th Dns. still to continue their Cross Belts when the Regulations of the Clothing etc., etc. of the Army was at that time settled?

8. How long did the Regt. remain in Gt. Britain after the Rebellion? and what reduction was made when it came back from Ireland?

9. Was it not from your knowledge of the good Conduct of the Corps at all times you did them the honour to have it made *Royal* when reformed to Light and chose the Motto yourself—"Pristinae Virtutis Memores"—?

Southwell's letter is interesting because it suggests *inter alia* that the Eighth were quite conscious that their history did not begin with the formal raising of the regiment in 1693. General Severne wrote from Shrewsbury to Southwell on the 16th of December, 1783:

Dear Colonel,

I am very glad the account of half-mounting is at length settled to your satisfaction (the agents have not favoured me with the state of it) I am very sure you will employ the Ballance thereof to the very best advantage for the benefit and service of the Regt. As Capt. Hunt was very capable I hope you found the Regimental Book regularly kept during his time I doubt the succeeding Adjts. were defficient therein and you will give great satisfaction to the Colonel and the greatest service to the Regiment by adjusting and regulating thereof as that is the only Record to apply unto not only of Men Horses Clothing and accoutrements and every particular what has been recorded and delivered to the Regiment, but every movement and conduct of the Regt. worthy Remembrance should be entered therein and not trust to verbal tradition.

When I became Lieut. Colonel early in 1750 there was not any officer in the Regt. that had been in Service earlier than the year 1745 or could give me but little information of their achievements from what I could obtain from them or others I will endeavour to answer your Querys to the best of my recollection.

1st. The Regt. was I conceive raised in 1693.

2. Served during the War in Ireland with applause.

3. The Regt. was sent to Spain the beginning of that War but whether from England Ireland or Flanders could not learn.

4th and 5th. Marshall Staninburgh[1] commanded the allied armies in Spain at the Battle of believe[2] Estepana (I cannot at present recollect the name but think it was not Saragossa ; the great battle he fought) where they defeated and took a Regiment of Spanish Horse Prisoners when the men exulting in victory took from their Prisoners their Cross Belts and wore them which as a mark of the honour they had thereby gained in Battle the Marshall permitted them to wear which they continued to do from that time.

6. When the Regt. returned from Spain I know not but think I have heard it was reduced in that Kingdom probably was with most or all of the English Cavalry taken with Genl. Stanhope at Bevago[3] and probably but few men remaining in it for it was broke after the Peace of Utrecht by the Ministry then prevailing out of its turn but soon after the Accession of King George the 1st was Raised again under its famous Colonel Pepper and officers and restored to its former Rank in the Army. I know not where employed in the Rebellion 1715.

7. After the Year 1715 they were sent to Ireland and in the year 1745 returned to England and each of the 6 Troops were augmented to 70 and formed 3 Sqdns.

8. In the year 1745 they joyned the Army when commanded by Marshall Wade at the Camp near Newcastle afterwards with the Duke of Cumberland on the advance under Oglethorp and served in Scotland till his Royal Highness put an end to that Rebellion it was on the Peace of 1748 reduced to the new establishment and the beginning of 1749 returned to Ireland.

[1] Staremberg.   [2] Estevan de Litera.   [3] *Brihuega*.

9. In the year 1769 by the Kings Order of Regulation of the clothing and accoutrements The Cross Belts are expressly confirmed to the 8th Dragoons with the addition of carrying their swords like the Regt. of Horse by the Cross Belt which before they carried in waist belts.

10. When Colonel now Lord Waldegrave became Colonel he had the Late Duke of Cumberlands (order) to take the Cross Belts from the Regt. I then remonstrated against it and submitted my reason in writing to his Royal Highness and we were permitted to continue them.

11. When the Regt. was made Light in commemoration of the honor they had gained of which the Cross Belts were the Badge the King was graciously pleased to make them Royal.[1]

We have no reply from Southwell till the 13th of February, 1784, when he wrote to Severne from Kilkenny. He had been confined to his room for a considerable time with a feverish cold. The information he had gained he added to the Regimental Book. He enclosed an account of the state of the Charitable Fund settled last year as an annual fixed establishment in the corps, and he also enclosed a return of the regiment, daily hoping to receive the order for the reduction of the dismounted men,

which however is not given out as yet in the present unsettled and distracted State of both Countrys no public business usually transacted by Ministers is done. The Clothing is going on very well. I don't mean to go to a Single man Beyond the old establishment unless Orders come to the Contrary.

As most Regts. here have a Band of Musick which is a very great Sett-off to a Corps I beg leave to propose such an Idea to you—the expence would be but a trifle for Musical Instruments Books etc. and for about *thirty* guineas I think I could defray them I am very delicate of mentioning anything that could be an expence to you but humbly conceive you would not be displeased for a small matter to sett off your Regiment in so very great a degree as all the Corps in the Kingdom who wish to make a good figure have a Band of Musick.

[1] *Severne MSS.*, pp. 25-7.

There is nothing settled here as yet. We expect daily a new Vicer Roy[1] Secretary and Commander in Chief.

The weather in Ireland has been severe in a degree unknown since the Great Frost of '39–40 it has been more than two Months and no sort of likelyhood of its changing.[2]

Severne wrote from Shrewsbury on the 16th of March, 1784:

Dear Colonel,

I hope this will find you perfectly recovered of the indisposition your last complained had for some time confined you.

If the imperfect information I was able to give you relating to the Regiment has been of any use I shall be very glad in any respect to have contribute to your very Laudable undertaking in making a perfect Regimental Book and therein registering the conduct and services of the Regiment which should be carefully kept in every Corps whose behaviour has obtained honor or been serviceable to their country.

I am very glad your benevolent proposal of the Subscription to a Charitable Fund has by the Acct. answered your good intention in relieving Several distressed objects and which I hope has the approbation and assent of all the officers and men to continue annually. By the last Monthly Return you favored me with I find is several alterations of Officers, I wish therefore and desire you will please to direct a Return to be made out for me of all the Officers, dates of their Commissions and whom they succeeded in their promotions on coming into the Regt. whether by purchase or otherways. I wish to comply with every desire you have in relation to the Regt. What you mention of a Band of Musick you do not seem to have formed the scheme and estimated the expence thereof which in every Corps that have them is supported by the Captains and their unanimous consent.

The Regts. of Mallitia in this kingdom in general had good Bands of Musick but few of the Regulars, the former erected funds for their Support which the latter knew not of nor could do. The expence I am informed by the Officers of Mallitia were great, the instruments between £80 and £90 the first year. Near the same the second having

[1] The Earl of Northington was leaving and the Duke of Rutland coming.
[2] *Severne MSS.*, pp. 28–9.

been spoiled by the young Learners in teeching the others. The Mallitia were generally in Quarters in Capital Towns alltogether the Gayety and Musick made the Officers more acceptable, but did not add to their appearance as Soldiers. A Regt. of Cavalry in Ireland is never Quartered together but in Dublin Duty, at Coll. Lascelles request I formerly gave a set of instruments cost £40 or £50 but know not if they answered to any purpose. I give you my thoughts but shall acquiesce and submit to the joyful desire of the Field Officers and other Captains.

I most truly hope your Lord Lieut. will be perfectly acceptable to the Kingdom ; your establishment of the army settled soon and the great busyness of the Nation arranged to the mutual satisfaction and happyness.

I hope the clothing is not only in forwardness but nearly completed and everything necessary wanting (when our musters are great) furnished soon after.

I hear you may expect the Commander in Chieff daily and that he is to lay before the King a schem for altering the clothing arms and accoutrements of the Light Cavalry, although we have had a long continued frost and still cold weather the Lands appear well and promising. Let us hope an end to the distressing state of our country's and a prosperous year and unanimity.[1]

Severne clearly thought the band an innovation for the regular army. Southwell no less clearly desired to be ahead of the times. His regiment was to him what it has been to not a few who have had the honour of belonging to it. It was his wife and his family, to be cared for as a beloved object. It is, therefore, important to notice that he cared for all that really concerned the welfare of his men. Indeed in 1785 we find that the Eighth is, according to Lord Luttrell, the "only corps I know of in which a schoolmaster is kept."[2] The schoolmaster was supposed to be abroad in the land in the seventies of the nineteenth century. He was abroad

---

[1] *Severne MSS.*, pp. 30–1.

[2] *Journal of the Society of Army Historical Research*, III, No. 14, p. 249. *Cf. Irish Review Returns*, 1785.

in the eighties of the eighteenth century in the Eighth. Southwell also had a gymnasium for the men, and they were constantly exercised at the leaping bar.

From Nenagh Southwell wrote to Severne on the 5th of May, 1784:

Dear General,

I do myself the honour of Inclosing a Return of the Regt. for this month by which you will perceive we are quite compleat in both men and Horses, the good of the Regiment required many Horses to be cast, two or three years back, which had been ruined at the Camps and many sunblind, of course totally useless and were obliged to be cast, however I have great satisfaction in being able to assure you that at this moment I believe you have as good Horses in your Regiment as any in the Service, and as fit for any Kind of service. I have trained every man and Horse in the Corps to go across a Country *a l'Houssard* in the true Prussian style of Hussar, and to leap ditches drains walls bars etc. which I must say the Regt. performs in such a manner as to gain the approbation and applause of the publick I really do wish I could have the honor of seeing you at the head of your own Regiment and I flatter myself your approbation would follow as well as that of the publick voice I must say and I think here Justice to express my most perfect approbation of the behaviour of the Non-Commissioned Officers and private men, among whom there exists an *Esprit de Corps* that really does them great credit and which I do all in my power to applaud and keep alive. I leave you to Judge of all this when I assure you that for more than Twelve Months past we have not had *a single punishment* I believe there are not many Regiments in any Service can say as much and I can with truth assure you that at the same time no single point of Discipline is infringed nor Duty omitted and you know the Cavalry Service too well not to be perfectly sensible How many and how various are the different Branches of Duty a Dragoon Regiment has to do and particularly so a *Light* Dragoon Regt.

I can also with truth assure you the Arms, accoutrements, saddles, etc. of most Kinds are now all *excellent* in their Several kinds and by the Inspections I have established nearly four years back in your Regt. Daily, Weekly, fortnightly monthly, every two months and annually

T

absolutely *nothing* is lost or destroyed, and every article being booked as well in the Several Troops as by the Adjutant in his Regtl. Book it is morally impossible that any thing should be lost or spoiled thro' the neglect of any person and I must say in Justice to myself and to *Truth* all these Inspections Entrys and Regularity have been of essential benefit to your Regt. and it is *notorious* did not exist in the Corps till I established them : therefore I think it my duty to say to you as my worthy and much esteemed colonel, and it will be no small satisfaction to me to have the honour of your approbation as a pleasing reward after the continued and I may say unremitting pains, with which I have laboured these four years past, three whereof I have been a President in establishing Regularity, System, and Cavly. appointments in short all the branches of the Lt. Dragoon Service in your Regiment, it is not *now*, it is not at the *present moment* the good effect of these Regulations and so much care will appear—you as Colonel of the Regiment will, I am certain experience in the end by the great care taken of all appointments whatsoever which must in the end prove so highly advantageous : and I believe a worse appointed Corps when I came to be Lt. Col. thereof could not be seen, which I attribute to neglect intirely and the Consequent ruin of all appointments which you Sir I am certain for I know it to be the Case were ever willing to give your Regt. but without care what can last ?

I beg leave to mention that last year on my representation of the establishment of a Band in your Regt. and the consequent unavoidable expence, you were so good as to say, in your letter dated May 5 which I had the honour of receiving on the 20th and answering on the 2 of June ; that you would Contribute towards Instruments and other unavoidable and necessary things for that purpose ; since that time I have not troubled you in hopes of being able to effect matters without it, but I now find our little fund run out, which necessity requires me to remind you of your letter—the sum I would beg to mention is *twenty guineas* which, if agreeable to you to direct the Agents to send to the Pay master, will be I promise you, the only time I will ever again trouble you on that Account : I can with truth assure you the Band has cost myself out of my own pocket more than that, but now the thing is finally established and settled there will be an end to any extraordinary expence.

Agreeable to former orders I will take care to have a Return of the Regt. for you every Month or at any other time you chuse.

Mrs. S. tho unknown, desires her Compts. and your little godson his duty.[1]

No doubt Southwell had done much for the regiment, especially on his own showing. There are many review returns, and we have quoted those of Lord Blayney for the 5th of June, 1767; of General Dilkes for the 28th of May, 1768; of General Pierson for the 29th of May, 1769, and for the 30th of May, 1771; of Lord Blayney for the 12th of June, 1772; of General Gisborne for the 21st of May, 1774, and for the 3rd of June, 1775; of General Johnston for the 4th of June, 1777; of General Mocher for the 5th of October, 1778; and of General Massey for the 27th of September, 1779. In not one of these reports is there a breath of real censure of the Eighth, and they all contain warm praise of its condition. The last five in no wise bear out Southwell's strictures on the appointments. Talleyrand indeed put his finger on the weak spot in the character of men of the Southwell type when he urged them to beware of *trop de zèle*.

Major-General Lord Luttrell reviewed the regiment at Nenagh on the 6th of June, 1785. His report is quite as eulogistic as General Massey's, and that is saying much. Southwell's work no doubt is plain in the entry on the Orderly Books which, we are told, were particularly inspected. "The Orders of the army regularly entered. The Regimental and Standing Orders are proper, minute and accurate." When, however, we come to the appointments, this note of commendation is not struck, and this is the department on which Southwell prided himself. For though the accoutrements and horse furniture are agreeable to the King's Regulations, there is a "but." We learn that 80 bridles and 138 housings and caps are wanting. Lord Luttrell's general observations are: "This Regiment is remarkably quiet and well behaved in quarters. Punishments are very rarely inflicted 'tis the only Corps I know of in which a schoolmaster is kept. The soldiers regularly attend him at sett hours."[2]

[1] *Severne MSS.*, pp. 32–4.   [2] *Irish Review Returns*, 1785.

Southwell dots the i's and crosses the t's in Lord Luttrell's report in his letter written from Nenagh to Severne on the 11th of June, 1785:

Dear General,

I have to return my hearty thanks for the honour of your last letter of 22 ulto which I should have sooner answered but for the hurry of the Review.

I am exceedingly happy to tell you that Gen. Luttrell reviewed your Regt. Monday last 6th inst and was pleased *in the most particular manner* to approve of the Corps in every Respect and returned his thanks to the whole in the most polite manner possible. The leap of the Horses and manœuvring of the Regt. over Several very large Ditches and preserving the Ranks the whole time attracted the Generals most particularly and drew the applause of all the numerous crowd of Spectators. The general told me he had often seen a *Skirmishing party* of a few trained Horses attempt a ditch now and then but never yet seen an entire Regiment do the like before. The Interior Œconomy of every Troop and the books of Inspection established in each Troop— beside the Adjutant's book for the entry of *Everything* were the first things I shewed the Reviewing General and he assured me that he never yet saw such Books in any Regt. and that attention so manifestly shown to the care of all appointments and preservation thereof surprized him and did all those who planned and took care of them infinite credit. In short General were I to tell you all He said it would surpass the bounds of a letter but I confess to you I feel an *honest* pride in the character of the Regt. has acquired and think it the honorable and well earned reward of all our Care and pains.

Be assured Sir Nothing can add to the satisfaction I feel from the honor of your approbation so warmly expressed in your letter I am now answering it will always in future as it hereto has been my principal object to prove how much I have your interests and those of your Regt., which I look upon as one and the same at heart.

We are now a good deal hurryd on our leaving this Quarter—we march this day to Carlow 4 Troops Athy 1 Troop Ross 1 Troop as soon as the Regt. gets to settled Quarters I shall have the honour of transmitting you the Stock Purse Acct. etc. but must now go to the Mallow waters on account of Mrs S's health where I mean to stay only so long as her health may absolutely require.[1]

Major-General Charles O'Hara inspected the regiment at Cashel on the 12th of June, 1786. He appreciated the appearance of the officers, non-commissioned officers, and 135 men, while he depreciated that of the 137 horses, accoutrements, and horse furniture. No doubt it afforded Southwell satisfaction to know that the Regimental and Orderly Books were properly kept. O'Hara's general observations were: "The Commanding Officer of this regiment has introduced a frequent shouting of the whole corps which he calls a war-whoop, destructive of all attention in the men, the cause of much confusion. N.B.—There are 2 grey horses more in this regiment than the Establishment."

Southwell was an enthusiastic Irishman of 37 with 16 years' service behind him. In his boyhood he was, no doubt, familiar with the story of the Battle of Dettingen. There the French Guards staggered under the deadly and unceasing fire, and as they staggered the British raised an irregular cheer. "Silence," shouted Lord Stair imperiously, galloping up. "Now one and all together when I give the signal." As he raised his hat, the British broke into the stern and appalling shout which was to become so famous on the fields of the Peninsula. The Irish officer had Dettingen in mind, and his inspecting officer simply thought of propriety. We are afraid that this report exercised an unfavourable influence on the prospects of Southwell, who was not destined to succeed Severne.

The last three letters shed much light on the working of the regiment, and, as it is difficult to obtain letters of this class, we give them. They are all written in 1787. On the 2nd of February, 1787, Southwell wrote from Mallow:

Dear General,

Last post I had the honour of yours of the 22 Jany. and to save postage send you on other side an order[2] lately received from Government.

---

[1] *Severne MSS.*, pp. 35–6.   [2] This order is of no interest to the regiment.

As to clothing for a few of the Musick when I first mentioned it to you it was only in the nature of a proposal, by no means a demand as you term it for I did suppose you would have been happy to have done so much for the good appearance of your Regt. however should you think otherwise I have no more to say.

Last September the first thing I did on joining was to send the Agents a most exact clear and most particular Acct. of the Clothing leather breeches frize (freize) etc. which the new Kings regulations prescribe for the Lt. Dragoons which you say you have received and am happy to find you are pleased there with as to the other accounts you speak of desiring to have them sent you there is no account but *one* namely for the *new Horse furniture* the old having been cast more than three years and I deferred as long as I could with any propriety to get the new, which however I expect every day to receive, the £150 you allude to was credited by the Agents in order to enable the sadler to go on with the work *on account* ; the reason why the account of this £150 has not been sent by the Paymaster to the agents is, that till the actual delivery of the *new furniture* it could not have been made up and so the Agents were informed to my knowledge and by my particular direction and I am much surprized they did not tell you so—but as soon as the furniture is delivered, which as I said I daily expect that moment the account of the whole shall be made up and sent to you.

And now I beg to repeat what I before said to you in a former letter, my *fixed* resolution never to be concerned either directly or indirectly in any Accounts whatsoever respecting the appointments of your Regt. it certainly is no part of my duty, all that I have to do is to take care of the appointments et. be of the proper quality as ordered by the Kings new regulations the whole of what regards the *Light* Dragoons being by those regulations totally altered from what they were heretofore —I know no office more troublesome and often more thankless than that of being concerned in accounts unless Duty absolutely require it.

The annual Inspection made agreeable to the Kings Regulations by the Major and myself, the abstract whereof as soon as made out in the Regimental Book, I shall send you, and a Copy to the Agents— the most material thing I recollect necessary to be got is a *set of new bitts*, the old having been cast and are in truth very bad and unfit for service.   When new cloaks are got they are by the Kings Regulations to be *blue* instead of *Red*—you will therefore be good enough to give your directions to the Agents relative to the *bitts* and they will bespeak them accordingly of quality and pattern agreable to the new Regulations, the new blue clothing due in June 8 7 is I suppose now getting on, please to recollect that a Sete of *Buckskin breeches* will be wanting by Kings regulations.

I have directed a pattern pair to be made and the lowest price charged, by the man who made the last, but the agents will I presume get your directions on this head, and if they can get the same quality cheaper they will do it.

I beg leave to repeat that I know of *no* tradesmens bills whatever— new boots were got last year and the accounts thereof long since sent to the Agents after the delivery of the boots to the Regiment : the *Horse furniture* will make the last and only account I know of excepting that for Clothing which Deserters have taken with them and which of course must be replaced to their successors every Soldier being (entitled) to clothing on joining the Regiment in place of those Deserters. This account I beg to repeat should have been sent sooner but for the very obvious empractibility of making it up till the Delivery of the Furniture on acct. of which the £150 was principally sent by the Agents.[1]

Southwell still wrote from Mallow on the 9th of March :

Dear General

I have the honor of yours of the 2 1 ulto and beg leave to assure you how anxious I have been to have your Acct. drawn out and settled which owing to the difficulty of getting the Tradesmens bills etc. I have not been able to do till yesterday and I now enclose you as follows,

> A monthly return as usual.
> Your acct. with all the tradesmens bills charged
> Copy of the Yearly Inspection per Kings Order.

I also send to the Agents an exact Copy of the two last and the bills of those tradesmen marked in *Red Ink*.

I have great pleasure in acquainting you the new Horse furniture is at last arrived and I will venture to say handsomer and better were

[1] *Severne MSS.*, pp. 37–9.

never seen, as everybody allows and, what is more I will venture to say they will *outlast* any two setts the Regiment has had and look at all times so as to do credit to your Corps and I trust you will approve of this as tending to keep up that character and reputation the Regiment is now and I flatter myself not undeservedly, held in.

As to the *Band* agreable to your desire I beg leave to acquaint you, it consists in fact only of six trumpeters tho' occasionally Six other Lads perform all of whom are sufficiently Masters of their several parts as to make up a very handsome band but not one of them are inlisted either as Trumpeters or Musicians but as *privates* the benefit of this to the Service is obvious and great for as these boys grow up they will be put into the Ranks and prove a Nursery of the best Non commissioned Officers, as I have taken special care to Educate them properly and established *a School* where they are taught to read and write etc. and on Sundays they always sing the Psalms whilst some of the others perform them on the Clarionets and Bassoons etc. it was for the six additional hands that I ventured to propose to you the clothing as I supposed you would not be unwilling to grant it amounting to about £15 but I beg you will be persuaded I am far from wishing you to do anything that might not be perfectly to your mind.

I have to remark that your Regiment has been a good deal harassed by frequent marches backwards and forward these two years past owing to the unusual disturbances of the Insurgents in various parts of the South : these marches not only harass both men officers and Horses but wear out appointments considerably as I believe I have mentioned before, but there is no help for these Marches Night partys et. et. which I fear will continue till the Country is somewhat more settled than it is now—and when that will be is what all good men ardently wish, but few can pretend to guess at.

In respect to the General Yearly Inspection you will please to remark the articles cast by the Major (Gen.) and myself, but my present intention is to make that matter come as light as possible tho the Kings Order positively states that the several articles wanting etc. to be provided against the ensuing Spring Review and I trust you will do me the Justice to be persuaded that in every circumstance I have equally at heart your interests as well as of the Corps I have the honor to command—tho I must confess how happy I am that you have exonerated me from the very unpleasant task of having any more to do with Trades-men as I could wish you will please to order the Agents to do all that comes under that description.

I beg to conclude by assuring you that I attentively considered the account I send you which I do believe to be regular and just in every particular—and that I have only one object in the discharge of my duty, the good of the Kings Service and in performance of that to merit the good opinion of you Sir as my Colonel.[1]

From 1760 to 1778 the south of Ireland had never been free from the movements of the Whiteboys, and Southwell merely draws attention to one of the deadly foes of security and therefore of prosperity. Moving occasionally in day time, for the most part they marched silently in dead of night, committing depredations which reduced the country to a condition of absolute anarchy. Sometimes they dragged a man at midnight from his bed, beat him and left him bound and naked in the ditch, by the roadside. Sometimes they carried a man to a newly-dug grave and left him, with his ears cut off, buried up to the chin in earth, or in thorns or furze. One man appropriated two pounds of powder concealed for the benefit of the Whiteboys. They discovered him, obliged him to pour the powder into his hat, placed it beneath him, ignited it, and blew him to pieces. The outcome of such deeds was the paralysis of law. The Whiteboy Act of 1787 aimed at the forcible suppression of this organisation, and in this suppression the Eighth assisted.

The last letter we have of Southwell's is dated the 4th of May, 1787:

Dear General,

I am to acknowledge the honor of your last letter and beg leave to repeat the assurance so often made which I hope you will do me the Justice to be persuaded of the sincerity of that there is no care on my part or attention to your Regiment and to your personal interests as Colonel, that I shall not always make the most particular objects of my Study as I trust I have always hitherto done.

[1] *Severne MSS.*, pp. 40–1.

Your directions relative to any appointments that may be necessary in future shall be attended to—as to this year I beg leave to repeat my intention not to call for any tho' the *bitts* have been cast yet I will contrive to make them do another year.

I am perfectly sensible of your goodness to the Regt. by your generous offer of providing Coats for the Band but so far am I from an idea of putting you to any expence that I can perfectly avoid, that I do not mean to trouble you.   My idea is, if you approve it, to save the six trumpeters suits due this clothing whereby I shall contrive a saving to you without injuring the Regiment—and the six Lads of the band who are all now fit for the Ranks will *not* require any other cloathing than merely their *private* clothing—thus I do not mean to trouble you for what you are so good to offer, as I really think by this scheme it will *not* be necessary.

You will please to recollect that by the late Order of His Majesty the *intire* clothing, appointments et. et. of the Light Dragoons are totally changed to the *Hussar* pattern of course the Horse furniture must be of that description as also the Cloaks—to be *blue* and of a different shape from the last.   The new horse furniture therefore is of white goat skin and the G.R. and Harp and Crown and device instead of a nasty embroidered worsted and silk which was very costly and would not last any time or appear creditable, are now made of *brass* which will last these twenty years (or longer) can be taken off and cleaned whenever necessary and will look as well the last day as the first.

The Officers' Court Dress is not as yet exactly settled.   You may recollect I wished to be honoured with your Commands relative to it and you desired to consult me and please everybody as to the pattern etc.   I therefore waited till the Regt. should assemble for that purpose but if you have any commands relative to that business I beg you will please to acquaint me and they shall immediately be executed.

Any directions you are pleased to communicate to the Adjutant or to your humble servant relative to the mode you direct for keeping the accounts shall be punctually observed.   I conclude by assuring you of my very earnest wishes at all times to comply with the smallest of your commands on being made acquainted therewith.[1]

[1] *Severne MSS.*, pp. 42–3.

Lord Luttrell had become, since his inspection in June, 1785, Earl Carhampton, and he reviewed the regiment at Mallow on the 8th of June, 1787. Lieutenant-General Severne was present for what proved to be his last inspection. In spite of the vigorous exertions of Colonel Southwell, the report now is not nearly so flattering as that of 1785. Lord Carhampton plainly was satisfied with the very good appearance of the officers, non-commissioned officers and men. The men were "of a proper size. Young and well made. Clean under arms. Well dressed. Steady and attentive. Helmets and black spatter dashes according to order." The horses were "in good condition. Nimble. 10 purchased since last review." Though the arms were clean, there were 6 firelocks, 3 bayonets, $16\frac{1}{2}$ pairs of pistols, and 1 sword wanting. The accoutrements were agreeable to the King's regulations. But the bridles were bad, and 6 pouches and 2 sword belts were wanting. The Orderly Books were particularly inspected, and this of course gave Southwell keen joy. They were properly kept, and the C.O. certified that each officer had a copy. The manœuvres, evolutions, and firings were agreeable to the King's regulations, yet Lord Carhampton was not satisfied with the state of the accoutrements. The trumpets were received in 1783, the carbines, bayonets and hilts for swords in the following year. His report was :

	Trumpets.	Firelocks & Carbines.	Bayonets.	Pairs of Pistols.	Swords.
Good	6	132	135	$121\frac{1}{2}$	137
Bad					
Wanting		6	3	$16\frac{1}{2}$	1
	6	138	138	138	138

Lord Carhampton's general observations are : "I cannot say this regiment is equal to some others notwithstanding the constant attention of Colonel Southwell. The new furniture does not seem to me to be well adapted to Light Cavalry. Colonel Southwell practices the regiment constantly at the leaping bar. The regiment was not assembled this year.   Inspected 4 troops at Charleville and 2 at Mallow."[1]

Shortly after this inspection, on the 6th of July, 1787, John Severne's long connection with the Eighth was severed by the hand of death.   For over three score years and ten he had served the Army.   He was succeeded on the 13th of July by Lieutenant-General Sir Charles Grey, from the 28th Foot.   The second son of Sir Henry Grey, first baronet of Howick, Northumberland, he obtained at the age of nineteen an ensigncy of foot.   He was a lieutenant in 1752 in Guise's (the 6th) Foot, then at Gibraltar. His name appears in the "Annual Army List" for 1754, the first published officially.   In 1755 he was captain of the 20th Foot, of which Wolfe was lieutenant-colonel.   He served with his regiment in the Rochefort expedition of 1757, and at the Battle of Minden, where his regiment acquired great fame.   He was wounded at Minden in 1759 and at Campen in 1760.   In 1761 he was promoted to lieutenant-colonel commandant of the newly-raised 98th Foot, the earliest of several regiments so numbered in succession.   He became colonel in the army and king's aide-de-camp in 1772.

In 1776 he set out with the reinforcements under General Howe, and received the local rank of major-general in America, which was made substantive two years later.   Had the other English leaders displayed his vigour and activity the war would have led to a different issue.   In 1777 he decisively routed a force under the American general, Wayne.   Grey had taken the precaution of removing the flints from his men's muskets in order to prevent any possible betrayal of their advance, and from this incident he acquired the name of "No-flint Grey."   He commanded the third brigade of the army at the Battle of Germantown, 1777.   In the autumn of the following year he crippled the enemy by the capture and destruction of stores at New Bedford and Martha's Vineyard. On his return home in 1782, Grey, who had been appointed major-general and colonel of the 28th Foot in 1778, was promoted to

[1] *Irish Review Returns*, 1787.

lieutenant-general and made K.B. He was also appointed commander-in-chief in America, but the war terminated before he took up his command. In 1785 he was one of a board of land and sea officers nominated by George III, under the presidency of the Duke of Richmond, to investigate the question of the defenceless state of the dockyards.

In 1787 he was transferred to the colonelcy of the 8th Dragoons, and in 1789 to that of the 7th Dragoon Guards. In common with Ralph Abercromby and Charles Stuart, Thomas Maitland, and John Moore, Charles Grey was a stern disciplinarian, but a disciplinarian who cared for the soldier's comfort. In 1793, Grey and Jervis, afterwards Earl St. Vincent, were appointed to command a joint expedition against the revolted French West India Islands. Before it sailed the Duke of York had retired from before Dunkirk, and the ports of Nieuport and Ostend stood in grave danger. With a small force Grey relieved Nieuport, and the relief was marked by the hearty agreement between the two services. He set out for the West Indies in November, 1793, and captured during the following year Martinique, St. Lucia, the Saints, and Guadeloupe. Grey returned home in H.M.S. *Boyne* in November, 1794. On his return he was promoted to general, made a privy councillor, and transferred to the colonelcy of the 20th Jamaica Light Dragoons. In 1799 he was removed to the colonelcy of the 3rd Dragoons (now the 3rd Hussars). In 1798 and 1799 he commanded the southern district in order to repel the threatened French invasion. In 1801 he was created Baron Grey de Howick, and in 1806 he was advanced to the dignities of Viscount Howick and Earl Grey. He also had the governorship of Guernsey in the place of Dumbarton, previously held by him. Full of honour and of honours, he passed away on the 14th of November, 1807, at his seat Fallodon, near Alnwick. Wherever the English language is spoken he and his family are renowned for their faithful services to the public weal, services that still continue to be rendered. For if it fell to the eighteenth century Lord Grey to repel the might of Napoleon by arms, it also fell to the twentieth century Lord Grey to repel the might of William II by diplomacy.

Francis Lascelles became colonel on the 19th of March, 1789. A captain of a troop in the 17th Light Dragoons in 1761, he was major in the Eighth in 1764, and lieutenant-colonel in 1768. He was promoted colonel in 1777, and removed to the lieutenant-colonelcy of the 3rd Dragoons in 1780. He was major-general in 1782, lieutenant-general in 1793, and general in 1798. He removed to the 3rd Dragoons in 1797, when on the 23rd of March Sir Charles Grey was re-appointed to the Eighth. Richard St. George was appointed the new lieutenant-colonel on the 31st of March, 1788, to be succeeded by Richard Rich Wilford on the 31st of October, 1789.

Major-General J. Patterson reviewed the regiment at the Curragh on the 4th of June, 1788. His report follows on orthodox lines, and bestows praise mingled with blame. It is obvious that the officers, non-commissioned officers, and men presented a really good appearance. On the other hand, the horses are in bad condition and 138 stirrup irons will be unserviceable by the next assignment.[1] Major-General Robert Prescott reviewed the regiment at Ballinrobe on the 14th of June, 1790. It is clear that the Eighth had attained the standard it had reached before 1786. Practically everything now receives praise, and many of the horses, we learn, are in good order. True, some of the horses are indifferent, yet they are "well rode." The report concludes with the emphatic words that "this Regiment appeared well disciplined."[2]

At Longford Major-General John Leland reviewed the troops on the 5th of June, 1792. He noted the absence of the Stock Purse Account. His conclusion is that this is "a fine regiment, uniform in its appearance. The Horses of a good mould, in equal conditions, and well trained. The men very well set up in their saddles, and performed the different manœuvres with celerity and precision."[3]

[1] *Irish Review Returns*, 1788.
[2] *Irish Review Returns*, 1790. " Appeared " meant much more then than to-day.
[3] *Irish Review Returns*, 1792.

By warrant of the 14th of June, 1792, the contingent men were made effective, which practically resolved itself into a form of augmentation. The colonel of course received an allowance in the place of the annual off-reckonings and agency of these men. In the warrant of the 14th of June the matter is worked out precisely in a form that would have endeared itself to Southwell. The expense of first clothing and accoutrements for six dismounted men in each regiment of Dragoon Guards and Dragoons, considering them as an augmentation, is:

6 cloaks	at £1	19	6 each	£11	17	0
6 coats, waistcoats and breeches	,, 3	1	10 ,,	18	11	0
12 pairs of gloves	,, 0	2	2 ,,	1	6	0
6 sets of buff accoutrements	,, 1	11	3 ,,	9	7	6
6 swords	,, 1	2	9 ,,	6	16	6
6 pairs of boots and spurs	,, 1	7	3 ,,	8	3	6
For each Regiment				65	12	6 [1]

The off-reckonings for one dismounted man for one year	5	9	10.84
Agency for Do.	3		2.02
	5	13	0.86
For six men in one Regiment annually	33	18	5.20 [1]

By the warrant of the 15th of September, 1792, an extra allowance of bread money was granted. For 12 Corporals, 6 Trumpeters, and 120 Private Men an allowance of £2 5s. 7½d. was given at the cost of £314 16s. 3d. a year. Six Serjeants also received nine shillings a year at the cost of £2 14s. Men who were absent, unless they were really and *bona fide* detached upon duty, were to forfeit this bread allowance.[2]

---

[1] *King's Letters*, 1787 (8 *W.O.* 8). The total £65 12s. 6d. is wrong.
[2] *King's Letters*, 1787 (8 *W.O.* 8), f. 285.

An augmentation of cavalry and infantry was decreed on the 8th of May, 1793, and a regiment of dragoons was to be composed of :

        1 Colonel and Captain
        1 Lieutenant Colonel and Captain
        1 Major and Captain
        3 Captains
        6 Lieutenants
        6 Cornets
        6 Quartermasters
        1 Chaplain
        1 Adjutant
        1 Surgeon
       12 Sergeants
       12 Corporals
        6 Trumpeters
        6 Hautboys
      120 Privates mounted
       48   „   dismounted
       ———
      231

The colonel was to receive £572 12s. 5d. in order to provide his men with full clothing and accoutrements combined with the accruing off-reckonings.

The question of stoppages received attention on the 6th of July, 1793.   None of the following were to be defrayed out of stoppages :

One pair of leather breeches or two pair of shag breeches in
    two years value £1 6 per annum £0 13   0
To stable jacket and trousers and foraging cap in two
    years 15s. per ann.   0   7   6
Horse cloth 6/6 Sersingle 3/6 in 6 years 10/ per ann.   ..   0   1   8
Feeding bag 1/ Watering bridle 3/6 Collar and log 6d in
    6 years. 5/ per ann.   0   0   10
                                                   —————
                                                    1   3   10[1]

[1] *King's Letters*, 1787 (8 *W.O.* 8), f. 330.   The total £1 3s. 10d. is wrong.

On the other hand, the soldier was scarcely so thankful for this sum of twenty-three shillings when he was faced with the following which must come out of his scanty pay:

3 shirts and trousers at 6/6 each p. ann.	0	19	6
1 stock and clasp Do	0	1	0
2 pairs of worsted stockings 2/5 each Do	0	4	10
2 pairs of thread or cotton Do 3/ each and 2 pairs of short gaiters 4/8 each	0	9	4
2 pairs of shoes 7/ each p. ann.	0	14	0
Mending Do Do	0	3	0
2 shoe brushes 6d each Do	0	1	0
Powder, pomatum, soap, combs and razors Do ..	0	12	0
3 buckles Do	0	0	6
Cloth brush, worm, picker emery, oil pipe clay, whiting and blacking	0	16	9
Washing and mending	1	6	0
Mane comb 6d Curry comb and brush 3/8 in 2 years	0	2	1
Tailor's bill	0	2	$9\frac{1}{2}$
	5	12	$9\frac{1}{2}$ [1]

The soldier of those days felt as we ourselves feel when we stop at a hotel where almost everything outside food is an extra. We prefer to pay a sum down to cover everything, and we detest to be obliged to pay one sum plus a whole series of tiny sums. The system of deductions and the system of drafting were then two of the greatest curses of the British Army.

It was always a source of temptation to the colonel to sacrifice sound practical training to a love of display, and if any one gazes at the list of movements, and manœuvres, evolutions and firings in, say, the year 1775, he will think the whole system mad. David Dundas watched the last manœuvres carried out in 1785, under the eye of Frederick the Great. "Old Pivot," as Dundas came to be called, saw his way to modify these amazingly complex movements. No doubt he carried his modifications too far when he

[1] *King's Letters*, 1787 (8 *W.O.* 8), f. 330.

distributed the whole science of military evolution into eighteen manœuvres. "General," remarked Sir John Moore to him in 1804, "that book of yours has done a great deal of good, and would be of great value if it were not for those damned eighteen manœuvres." "Why-ay," answered Dundas slowly in broad Scots, "blockheads don't understand." His teaching was applied to the cavalry as well as to the infantry. Officers came, after a long time, to think it not quite sufficient if their squadrons could execute a certain number of evolutions with rapidity, and charge at headlong speed. The test really was, Can the regiment rally after the charge?

Chapter VII

The Napoleonic Wars

THERE is no war into which we plunged with greater reluctance than that which began with France in 1793, and lasted, with the interlude of the Peace of Amiens, to 1815. Yet from 1689 we had been fighting with France. There were intervals in the contest in Europe from 1697 to 1701, from 1713 to 1740, from 1748 to 1756, and from 1763 to 1793. There were, however, no such intervals in North America and India, where war was waged tolerably continuously. The prize for which France and England fought was no less than the colonial headship of the world, and the outcome of the Napoleonic Wars was to award that prize to ourselves. Our struggles with Louis XIV had been largely European ones: our struggles with Napoleon were world-wide. The Eighth were destined to meet his forces, in different shapes, at the Cape of Good Hope, in Egypt and in India. It would almost seem as if century after century we were destined to meet a sovereign who aimed at supremacy. At the end of the sixteenth century we encountered Philip II of Spain, at the end of the seventeenth century we encountered Louis XIV of France, at the end of the eighteenth century we encountered Napoleon I of France, and at the beginning of the twentieth century we encountered William II of Prussia.

In 1793 we had a regular army of about 50,000 men, with about 30,000 militia behind it; we had about 75 ships of the line fit for sea and 25,000 sailors to man them. We formed coalition after coalition during the twenty-two years of war, but coalition after coalition broke to pieces in our hands. As Pitt put it, England would save herself by her own exertions and Europe by her example. What prospects of success were there? Nelson used to declare that one Englishman could beat three French, and he pretty well was obliged to do so. Forty-five millions of French, Napoleon once declared, must prevail over sixteen millions of

English, and of course he was able to coerce many more millions to support his policy. No wonder he insisted that his victory was certain.

There were men, then as in the World War, who thought the prolongation of the struggle impossible. *Peter Plymley's Letters*, ten in number, appeared in 1807, and passed through sixteen editions in a single year. In them Sydney Smith argued for the removal of Roman Catholic disabilities, because it was absurd to weaken England by keeping four million Irishmen enemies when they might be made friends. Incidentally he asserted that success in the war was impossible. Our allies were worthless, except those "ancient and unsubsidised allies of England," the winds. Our blockade of France was useless. Invasion was likely to come immediately, and sure to be successful. He denounced the optimism of the British nation: "We do not appear to me half alarmed enough." He condemned the continuation of the struggle. "The war is carried on without it being possible to conceive a single object which a rational being can propose to itself by its continuance." Nor was Sydney Smith untypical, for it would be quite easy to multiply utterances of this kind from many sources. The truth is that we are a grumbling nation, yet a nation that has always risen to a glorious height when exertion was genuinely demanded. We expressed distrust of our government as freely in 1814 as in 1914. Ministry after ministry fell, and it was not until the late date of June, 1812, that we had the stable and lasting Liverpool ministry. Few there were who were inspired by the same feeling of confidence as William Wordsworth. "We are left alone," so he wrote on the news of the overthrow of Prussia,

> We are left, or shall be left, alone,
> The last that dare to struggle with the foe.
> 'Tis well ! from this day forward we shall know
> That in ourselves our safety must be wrought ;
> That we must stand unpropped, or be laid low.
> O dastard whom such foretaste doth not cheer !
> We shall exult, if they who rule the land,
> Be men who hold its many blessings dear,
> Wise, upright, valiant : not a servile band
> Who are to judge of danger, while they fear,
> And honour, which they do not understand.

The intrigues and the dissensions of the ministers rendered the nation aghast. A sailor, writing to a member of Parliament, summed up his view of them: "What a cursed set you all are."[1] Nor were the newspapers helpful. There was no censorship, and editors continually published information of the utmost value to the enemy. The Sunday papers were full of it. Wellington also complained that their dogmatic comments on military operations, by their alternate optimism and pessimism, perturbed the minds of the people with groundless hopes and needless fears.

The weight of the National Debt was then appalling for such a tiny population as sixteen millions. In 1792 it amounted to 237 millions and the annual interest to 9 millions. In 1815 it amounted to 885 millions and the annual charge to 32 millions. There is no difficulty in agreeing with the opinion that the costliest monument ever erected to Napoleon is the British National Debt, for we expended no less a sum than over six hundred millions in beating him.

What did our arms achieve in Europe? Our record down to the Battle of Maida is defeat after defeat. Nor does Wellington win the victory of Vimiero till 1808. In fact, our military bead-roll from 1793 to 1808 consists of losses in the field. How could we, so men felt, contend with the genius of Napoleon? "Alas," wrote even such a patriot as Sir Walter Scott, "we want everything but courage and virtue in this desperate contest. Skill, knowledge of mankind, ineffable, unhesitating villany, combination of movements and combination of means are with the adversary. We can only fight like mastiffs, boldly, blindly and faithfully." So much was this the case that Wellington informed Lord Stanhope, "It is quite certain that my opinion alone was the cause of the continuance of the war in the Peninsula." It was not without reason that a young officer wrote to his mother, when the campaign of 1812 was about to begin, "all the croakers are in England."[2] It is startling to learn that the Corporation of London repeatedly demanded the dismissal of Wellington.

[1] *Creevey Papers*, I, pp. 92, 95, 98.
[2] Granville, *Private Correspondence*, II, p. 433.

Ireland had been dragged into the contests which Philip II and Louis XIV had waged, and she was now to be dragged into the contest which Napoleon was beginning to wage. In the two former wars she had thrown in her lot with the foes of freedom; now she threw in her lot with the friends of freedom. In the Irish metropolis there stands a monument erected to Nelson, the greatest sailor we ever possessed, and another to Wellington, who ranks next to Marlborough. It is right that these two monuments should stand in Dublin, despite the Rebellion of 1798, for Ireland gave of her best in the twenty-two years' practically ceaseless struggle with the greatest genius in war the earth has ever known.

It is right that we should commemorate our Nelsons and our Wellingtons. It is, however, certain that they could not have carried on their war for well-nigh a generation had it not been for the inventors who made the Industrial Revolution possible, thereby supplying the sinews of war. The roll of honour from 1760 to 1785 in the world of business includes men like Brindley, Watt, Roebuck, Hargreaves, Crompton, Arkwright, Cartwright, and Wedgwood. They turned England into the great industrial nation she is. As she turned so decisively to manufactures, she wanted bread. In the days before the application of steam to transport, she had to apply to Ireland. From this point of view a modest place on the roll of honour of the men who won the Napoleonic Wars may be accorded to John Foster.

The early part of the eighteenth century changed Irish agriculture from the tillage stage to the pasturage, thereby giving rise to the Whiteboys. Now this whole process was reversed. For in 1784 Foster passed his Corn Law, a measure which vitally affected the destinies of Ireland from that day to this. It was this law which called into being the stately Custom House which until the other day adorned Dublin. It was this law which called into being the mills which dot the land, ruined through the passing of Free Trade in 1846. It was this law which called into being a large population for the first time in Ireland. In 1784 the population was two millions, and in 1800 it was four millions. That is, population doubled in less than a generation. Tribal contests at home, wars abroad, disease and famine had always reduced Irish numbers to small proportions. Now there were no tribal contests at home, and disease and famine tended to become much less than they had been.

Foster's great Corn Law granted a bounty of 3s. 4d. a barrel on the export of wheat as long as the home price was not above 27s. a barrel, and it imposed a duty of 10s. on imported wheat when the home price was less than 30s. It also granted bounties on the exportation of flour, barley, rye, oats and peas. The result of this measure was that the bullock disappeared in large measure, and was replaced by the plough. Vast pasture-lands were converted into innumerable small tillage-farms. Beside every stream there was a corn-mill, and the air hummed with the motion of the mill-wheel.

Wellington's men in the Peninsula benefited by Foster's Corn Law, for cargoes of corn, oats for the cavalry and transport horses, salt meat for the men, shoes for their feet, all came from Ireland. Nor did Ulster lag behind. She was to the front with her contribution of men and material. In the Napoleonic Wars she supplied the linen for the use of the soldier just as she did in the World War. It is noteworthy that in the war just over the fine linen of Belfast went to the perfecting of the wings of the aeroplane. The Irish share in the conflict waged at the end of the eighteenth century was in no wise confined to material. In 1793 the Penal Laws had at last been relaxed, and Roman Catholics could join the army. The Irish population was no more than two millions in 1793 and was barely over four in 1815, yet out of these small numbers she sent from 1793 to 1815 no less than a hundred and fifty thousand Irishmen to the front, and she also sent the greatest of them all, the Duke of Wellington. From 1793 to 1815 from one-third to one-half of the total forces raised by the United Kingdom were Irish. As for the fame they achieved, let the battlefields of the Napoleonic Wars speak for them.

The first fashion in which the war made its presence felt was in the augmentation of the troops. On the 20th of November, 1793, an augmentation of 6 Sergeants, 6 Corporals, and 108

Private Men was ordered in the following regiments of Dragoon
Guards and Dragoons, viz. the 4th, 5th, 6th, and 7th Regiments
of Dragoon Guards, and the 5th, 8th, 9th, 12th, 13th, 14th, 17th,
and 18th Regiments of Dragoons, to commence on the 9th of
April last inclusive.[1]   In the Eighth, then at Longford, there
were to be:

1	Colonel and Captain
1	Lieutenant Colonel and Captain
1	Major and Captain
3	Captains
6	Lieutenants
6	Cornets
6	Quartermasters
1	Chaplain
1	Adjutant
1	Surgeon
18	Sergeants
18	Corporals
6	Trumpeters
6	Hautboys
228	Private Men mounted
48	Do dismounted

351

William Pitt signed the proclamation, ordering Lord Westmore-
land on the 24th of December, 1793, to provide an augmentation
of 6 Corporals and 90 Privates dismounted to each of the following
Regiments of Dragoon Guards and Dragoons, viz. the 7th Dragoon
Guards, the 5th, 8th, 9th, 13th, 14th, 17th, and 18th Dragoons
to commence from the 7th of August last inclusive.[2]   All told,
this raised the strength of the Eighth to 447 men.   In addition to
the numbers of the November proclamation there were 6 dismounted corporals, 48 mounted privates, and 42 dismounted
privates.   Perhaps one-third of them had not been six months in

[1] *King's Letters*, 1797 (8 *W.O.* 8), f. 350.
[2] *King's Letters*, 1797 (8 *W.O.* 8), f. 370.

the service. The regiment embarked at Dublin on the 5th of March, 1794, on board the following ships:

William and Mary	The Lt. Col., 1 Capt.,	1 Q.M., &	N.C.O.'s & men
Grace of Salt Coats		1 ,,	,,
James	1 Major		,,
Irene	1 Capt.	1 ,,	,,
Friendship	1 Lieut. and 1 Cornet		,,
John and Eleanor	1 Capt.	2 ,,	,,
Betsey of Liverpool	1 Lieut.		,,
Seaton	1 Capt., Adjut., Surg., & 2 ,,		,,
Jane of Harrington	1 ,, 1 Cornet		,,
Dolphin			,,
Hibernia	1 Cornet	1 ,,	,,
Elizabeth	1 Lieut.	1 ,,	,,

In all there were one lieutenant colonel, one major, five captains, three lieutenants, three cornets, one adjutant, one surgeon, nine quartermasters, twenty-six sergeants, twenty-seven corporals, nine trumpeters, three hundred and ninety privates, twelve women, and four children. The Colonel, Lieutenant-General Francis Lascelles, and the Chaplain, Francis Ellis, were absent on leave.[1] The regiment landed at Liverpool in March, marched to London, and embarked at Blackwall in April in obedience to the following order of the 15th of April, 1794:

I am directed by Lord A. to signify to you H.M.'s P. that the 8th Lt. Drs. under your Command are to be embarked on Friday morng. next the 18th for Flanders. The whole Regt. will accordingly march from their Quarters early enough on that Morning, to be able to arrive at the said Place of Embarkation, by 7 o'clock at the latest. It is recommended to the Commg. Offr. to send the Regtal. Baggage forwards, so as to get it embarked the day before, if possible, or at least before the embarkation of the Horses and Men takes place, if it can be done without too much inconvenience.

A party of the Foot Guards will be ordered to attend upon the occasion to assist in preserving good order, and in preventing Disturbances of any kind during the Embarkation. An Embarkation Return of the Regt. to be sent to the S. at War and the Adjutant General.[2]

[1] *Home Office*, 100/48.   [2] *W.O.*, 3/12, *War Office, Out Letters.*

At Ostend on the 26th of April, 1794, the regiment arrived. With them were the 12th, 38th and 55th Regiments of Foot, finding recruits for the 14th, 37th and 53rd there.[1] The allied army had taken the field under Francis II. The British and the Hanoverians under the Duke of York lay before Tournai. The corps under the Prince of Orange were at Landrecies. The Eighth were directed to join the Austrians under General Count Clerfaye, who commanded an army in West Flanders, and had just been forced to evacuate Courtrai. On their arrival at Clerfaye's camp, the Eighth were attached to the Hanoverian division under Major-General Hamerstein. The lieutenant-colonel, Richard Rich Wilford, and the major, Thomas Pakenham Vandeleur, were sent to other regiments, and Vandeleur rejoined his old corps as lieutenant-colonel three weeks after their landing in Flanders.

James Craig was appointed Chief of Staff of the Duke of York's Staff, and in his official capacity he mixed much with the Austrians, and came to distrust them deeply. How much he loathed their cordon system is evident in his words: "It is impossible to bring the Austrians to act except in small corps. I lament that we should be destined as victims of their folly and ignorance. Do not be surprised at the word ignorance: I am every day more and more convinced that they have not an officer among them." The pity is that these words, severe as they are, were absolutely true. In the days to come the Archduke Charles was to show that he was a commander of the highest class, but it was quite clear that Clerfaye would never belong to it. With other regiments the Eighth were to suffer from the cordon system. They also suffered from the lack of knowledge of German in spite of the fact that some of them had been at Turin and other centres for the improvement of their education. Major Hart of the 6th Dragoons, who was a brevet lieutenant-colonel, had been appointed to the temporary command, and he sent out a patrol of young dragoons. They encountered an escort of Hanoverians who were in charge of two field pieces, taken from the French, which they were bringing to Ostend. The Hanoverians, struck by the unfamiliar dress and

---

[1] *W.O.*, 1/169. There are details on all this campaign in the *Dietz MSS.*, pp. 9–25.

language, felt that here was the foe. The Eighth, struck in their turn by the unfamiliar dress and language, also felt that here was the foe. After considerable trouble the Germans induced the Eighth to believe that they were friends. The bargain was somehow arranged that the Germans should escort their guns and that the Royal Irish should escort the Germans until an explanation could take place at the first British post, which was accordingly done, as Smet tells us, to the entertainment of everybody.[1]

In the vain hope of forcing the French to evacuate Flanders, a combined movement was undertaken. With Clerfaye's army the Eighth advanced, and crossed the river Lys successfully at seven o'clock on the morning of the 18th of May. Turning eastward, he met between Bousbecque and Linselles Vandamme's brigade, numbering eight thousand men against his sixteen thousand. The two columns under the Duke of York were in the meantime undergoing the process of annihilation, and neither Kinsky nor the Archduke Charles made the faintest attempt to save them from their doom. Clerfaye, for instance, engaged the French, overthrew their right wing, took eight guns, and then—remained quite stationary. Major-General White ordered the Eighth to clear the village of Bousbecque before the infantry could efficiently support them. Lieutenant-Colonel Hart with four-and-a-half troops and Captain Newman with the other four-and-a-half moved on towards the village. An aide-de-camp of General Count Clerfaye's, seeing the movement from a windmill where he was observing the enemy, tried to countermand it, but in vain. Hart and his men had entered the village. Again, we meet with the trouble arising from lack of linguistic skill, for the aide-de-camp could scarcely make himself understood.

The sharp fire of the infantry and of four field pieces, levelled over the churchyard wall, galled our men considerably. In spite of the loss of such officers as Captain the Hon. Henry Howard and Lieutenant John Henry Browne, and in spite of the loss of men, the troops persisted in their heroic advance. The dash of the regiment carried it up the village street, and, leaping the

[1] Smet, p. 45.

churchyard wall, the men cut down the French artillerymen, capturing the guns. At the head of his squadron, with his horse streaming with blood, Lieutenant-Colonel Hart was the first to leap the wall, his men emulating his fine example. Private Michael Manelly particularly distinguished himself. He received several wounds in defence of a standard of which he had gained possession. Though his horse was killed under him and his strength began to fail from loss of blood, yet he bore off the standard, burying it in the ground before he was taken prisoner. Taking refuge in the houses of the village, the French continued to pour in an incessant fire. Captain Cooke had been pursuing fugitives, but after the first shock of surprise the enemy came forward with fresh numbers. Hart had to call his men out of the village in order to rescue them. At that moment, his horse, pierced with a ninth ball, was staggering from loss of blood. As Robespierre had issued an order for the destruction of all British prisoners, Cornet Sherlock insisted on giving his horse to his commanding officer, as his country would benefit more by his services than by any he himself could render. With equal insistence Hart refused the offer, leading his men on his bleeding horse into the plain, when by a circuitous sweep he at last reached Clerfaye's advancing line.

Repulsed as they were in their first engagement, nevertheless the Eighth covered themselves with honour. The honour, however, cost them a heavy price. Out of two hundred engaged, no less than 186 were killed, wounded, or captured. Out of two squadrons the survivors were Colonel Hart, Cornet Sherlock and fourteen men. Captain Cooke and the bulk of his detachment were prisoners.

The following orders were issued on this occasion:

Major-General Whyte laments the loss sustained by the Eighth light dragoons, whose spirited and distinguished gallantry, led on by Lieutenant-Colonel Hart, has gained them the highest honor. He desires that his thanks may be accepted by the commanding officers, and all the officers and men of the thirty-eighth and fifty-fifth regiments, also by Major Bowes and the officers and men of the twelfth regiment, whose conduct has been highly approved of by Major-General

Hamerstein, under whose command they immediately were. To Lieutenant-Colonel Hart, who led on the squadron of the Eighth light dragoons to the attack at Rousbeck, his best and distinguished thanks are due ; also to Lieutenant-Colonel McDonald, who led on the fifty-fifth regiment with such marked propriety and discipline, to support the attack on the front. He is perfectly convinced the same praise would have been due to Lieutenant-Colonel Pitcairn, of the thirty-eighth, had they been called into action.

General Count Clerfaye also expressed his approbation of the conduct of Lieutenant-Colonel Hart and Cornet Sherlock, and directed it to be inserted in orders on the 20th of May.

The Eighth had received their baptism of fire in the Napoleonic Wars, and we feel glad to be able to supplement the account of it with the letters written by Dodwell Browne, whose younger brother, John Henry, was serving as a lieutenant. Dodwell Browne, then a lieutenant in the Navy, wrote on the 27th of May to his father, living at Castlebar :

In order to prevent your being in suspence I sent you an account of the last Battle the moment it arrived here. I also in a few days after sent you the newspaper with the Duke of York's official letter by which you see that so far Henry is safe. Now I must tell you to be on your guard against a report circulated in the papers ; it is I hope void of any foundation. It says that Clayrfait had with him on the 17th and 18th a detachment of the 8th Dragoons consisting of 120 men under Major Hart and that only 12 of them remained after the Battle. I must again tell you that it amounts to a certainty that the above statement of the loss of the 8th is false although they were certainly under the command of Clayrfait on 17th and 18th yet it appears by his official letter to the Emperor that he sustained hardly any loss, and that the most brilliant success attended all his movements on the above days. This letter only made its appearance this day. I shall write to Harry every word you mentioned in your letter. We must not expect regular answers from him as the vicinity of the Enemy employs him otherwise than writing letters. It certainly must be a matter of delight to him to be an eyewitness of the incomparable movements of Clayrfait who is in general estimation the first officer of the Allied army. In mine he's only the 2nd, Coburg being my favourite. . . . I thought you knew that Wilford had left Harry's regiment when at Chester : young Vandeleur is now their Colonel.[1]

Writing again to his father on the 4th of June he said :

I am in hopes of hearing from Harry every day. I fear the poor fellow has no time to write as there are hardly any Cornets in the Regt., the whole subaltern duty falls on him and one or two more. It is very vexatious to me to find that our hopes of his getting forward by death vacancies are without foundation, the vacancy occasioned by Capt. Howard who was killed on the 18th was bestowed on a stranger to the regiment. We may guess what must have been the feelings of Harry on the occasion as this is the way in which seniority and merit are rewarded. I wish we had him out of the army. . . . I am to be 1st Lieut. of the *Seahorse*: if I have as much luck in her as I had in the *Sphinx*, I shall be very well. You hear no such thing as a prize taken by us. The reason is that the French have no trade.

Alas ! the hopes of Harry's promotion were all dashed to the ground by the letter William Ouseley, a lieutenant in the Eighth, wrote on the 19th of May from the camp near Wervick to the father :

It is with tears and heartfelt regret that I take upon myself the dreadful task of announcing to you the death of your son—my most particular friend—who was shot yesterday near this place, along with near 100 of our men and two other officers. His gallantry and noble spirit are the subject of everyone's praise, and will, I hope, afford you some consolation.

The next letter seems to have been from one of the Eighth, who wrote it at Ostend on the 22nd of May to his brother :

Dr. Brother. Thanks be to God that I can send you the happy tidings of our Father's recovery, he is so well recovered that he is able to work and has taken the Troop in Charge Again, he is now with the Regiment at Rhuseland and My Mother is with the baggage at turin[2]

---

[1] I owe these letters to Mr. Dodwell F. Browne, of Rahins, Castlebar, who kindly gave copies of them to the regiment.

[2] Turcoing (?).

9 miles from the Regiment and I was sent there with the Colonels horse that was wounded in 5 places in the last Engagement but the Colonel Escaped Unhurt, it was the Blodies Battle that was Faught for the time. Since the war began we lost 115 men and 118 horses beside Capn. Cooke, Capn. Howard and Lieutenant Brown that was killed. Lieut. Brown killed 22 Men after his Horse was Shot and at last a Great Number of the French came up and he would have fought his way through them in like Manner until one of them came behind him and Stabd. him through the Body, the Austrians began the Attack at half past ten in the Morning and Continued till dark Night, the Loss of the French is Innumerable and in the Night they Run away like a flock of Mad sheep.

Dr. Brother this is the 3rd Engagement that I have been at and Escaped all unhurt, thanks be to God we are all very well in our health though being very much Harrished, we cannot take a saddle of (off) a Horse for fear of being Called up and Not have time to put them on, I was for 3 days and 2 nights and Never lit of the horse only to feed him and the Horses are like Spiders they are so poor, when you receive this Make no Delay to write to me as I Expect to Remain here this while to Come and let me Know how my Dr. brother[1] sister is. Dr. Brother Do not be Uneasy about the promise that I made you when I was in Liverpool, I had not time to perform It Since but I hope I Soon will, Give my Blessing to the Children and our love to the whole Family. No more at present from your loving and Dutiful Brother untill Life Departs. Willm. Dunn.

P.S. when you direct your Letter direct it to be Immediately Forwarded to Wm. Dunn 8th Lt. Dragoons Ostend or Else where, I remain as before Wm Dunn, Excuse haste and my sore finger.

Ouseley wrote again from Ostend on the 14th of June:
Dear Sir

I was favoured with your letter in due time—and as my esteem for your late brother amounted nearly to fraternal regard, you may be sure that whatever I can do for poor Cusac shall be most cheerfully done—having been laid up here for some days with a pleuritick Complaint. I have seen but little of the Regiment which has been constantly engaged —but I know that Cusac is safe and attends his 2 horses of our late

[1] Brother's.

friends—on the subject of those horses I should wish to know your pleasure—but as I am on the Eve of leaving the Service and returning to England I think a letter directed to Quarter Master Wood—who belonged to the same troop—or indeed to the Commanding Officer, containing your instructions as to the sale of disposal of the horses would be the surest method of having the business settled.

I cannot withhold from you the melancholy consolation which the tale of your brother's Gallant behaviour may afford—altho' the recapitulation of such circumstances will distress and afflict—as I feel this moment myself.   On receiving a Wound with a bayonet he rushed more furiously among the Enemy—and sabred several—Cutting them with the Strength and rage of a Giant—till alas ! a ball thro' the head put a period to the noble Career of my dear unfortunate gallant friend—He, like every other person who fell was strip'd and plundered by the infamous followers of the Army—and buried in a field near the place where he dropt—the Village of Roosbeck—situation on the River Lys, a fatal stream which we had crossed the day before and were compelled to recross the day after.

If I can judge from my own feelings I have said enough—perhaps too much—Providence will, I trust, assuage by your presence the just affliction of your Father for whom I feel from my very Soul.

Adieu my dear Sir and believe me very truly yours

WM. OUSELEY.

P.S.   If it be possible I will procure the discharge of Cusac and take him with me to England.   Direct to me at the Hotel de York Ostend.

Writing from Holland on the 28th of December, Quartermaster Isaac Bond, *per* one Walter Screen, advised that he had by order of Colonel Vandeleur paid the bearer the balance of Browne's account, and added : "Permit me to say that His Majesty and the 8th Drags. has lost a Brave and Worthy soldier by the death of Lt. Browne ; he fought and died valiantly."   The phraseology of these letters is old-fashioned.   The hearts beating behind them are in no wise old-fashioned.   Browne died like a hero, and all men of his spirit then regretted the loss they keenly realised that they had sustained.

Clerfaye attempted to relieve Ypres, and failed in the attempt. The Duke of York deemed it of such importance that, if possible, another attack should be made, but his opinion was overruled. He expressed to the Prince of Coburg the absolute necessity of saving Ostend and covering the frontiers of Holland. Sluggish throughout the campaign, Clerfaye displayed his sluggishness to the end. He attacked Souham with five columns, gained some advantage, captured ten guns, and then did nothing—until Souham gathered fresh troops when Clerfaye retired. With his retirement all was over with Ypres, the key of maritime Flanders, the main support of the right flank of the Allies, the bulwark protecting the British communications with Ostend.

On the 8th of June at Langemark the regiment was ordered to carry the bridge, defended by two guns, covered by a parapet, and supported by a battalion of infantry. Rapidly the attack was made, the battery taken and the French battalion cut to pieces with the loss of only two men killed, though the loss in horses was very severe. In order to cover Ostend and the Dutch frontier, it was at last decided that Clerfaye should take up a position between the Lys and the Scheldt about Deynse, some ten miles to the south-west of Ghent; keeping half his force between Bruges and Ostend, and sending the Eighth, the Thirty-eighth and Fifty-fifth, to Ostend.[1] "We are too weak by ten thousand men to hold this defensive position," wrote the clear-sighted Craig, "if the French see their chance and push Clerfaye, they will force us to abandon this position about Tournai, and will pass the Scheldt in spite of us; and then ten to one we shall find ourselves separated from him and beaten in detail. . . . Sooner than hold the defensive position I would concentrate the whole army, eighty thousand men, march to the Sambre, attack them at any risk and march back again. . . . You may expect to hear from us soon in Holland."[2]

With the Eighth, the Thirty-eighth and the Fifty-fifth, Hamerstein attacked a superior force of the enemy at Ghits on the 14th

---

[1] *W.O.*, 1/169.

[2] *Cf.* the Duke of York to Dundas, June 10, 13, 14, 1794; Craig to Nepean, June 10, 13, 14, 1794; Calvert, pp. 238–53.

of June, and failed in his attack.   After the action he retreated to
Thoront, and, in the night, falling back with the Hanoverians,
he ordered the British troops to Ostend.[1]   Arriving at Ostend on
the 14th, a detachment of the Eighth was subsequently stationed
at Nieuport, where General Diepenbrock was posted with a
garrison of the Hanoverians.   On the 21st of June Lieutenant-
General the Earl of Moira arrived at Ostend with a reinforcement
of about ten thousand men.   The Eighth joined this force which
rejoiced in a young Colonel, Arthur Wellesley by name.   Then
he was simply an impecunious younger son who had given pleasure
in Dublin social circles by his skill in playing the violin.   The
advance of the French forced the Eighth to leave Nieuport in
haste.   All the regimental baggage was lost, as the enemy took it
while it was on its way to Ghent.   This baggage included stores
and regimental papers and registers.   The capture of the stores
inflicted loss at the time : the capture of the regimental papers and
registers inflicted loss for all time.   The plate chest with an ancient
account of the corps was also lost in its transmission from Ireland
to England.

Lord Moira commenced his difficult march through Flanders
in order to join the Duke of York's army, taking with him the Royal
Irish.   On the 6th of July four hundred French dragoons entered
Alost, driving in the picquets of the regiment.[2]   As they approached the market-place Colonel Doyle, taking them for
Hessians, rode up to a French officer to ask him for the news of
the day, and received for an answer a wound on the head.   Without
a second's delay he rode off to a picquet of the regiment of less
than forty men under Lieutenant-Colonel T. Pakenham Vandeleur.
The spirit of the men of Balaclava was present, for the less than
forty charged the four hundred with that grim determination that
does not realise when it is beaten or in fact that it can be beaten.
Vandeleur, Lieutenant Kitson, two troop quartermasters, and
nine men were wounded.   The Adjutant Graham and two dragoons
were killed, and Riding-Master Marshal died of his wounds.[3]

[1] *Foreign Office*, 26/25.   [2] *W.O.*, 1/169.
[3] Smet has a good account, pp. 53–6.

On the 9th of July a junction with the Duke of York's army was effected at Malines.

In the meantime the French besieged Nieuport, and detachments of the Eighth and the Fourteenth in that fortress embarked on small vessels. As the vessels sailed along the shallow river, they were exposed to the fire of the French infantry on the banks. Two barks successfully escaped the fusilade. The third, however, was forced back, and when Nieuport surrendered twenty-two men and horses of the Eighth remained prisoners.

A force of nearly one hundred and fifty thousand French was pressing the Allies harder, and, had it not been for the interference of the Committee of Public Safety, the end must have been sheer disaster. The regiment, much reduced in number, bore its share of all the miseries, fatigues, and hardships consequent on the retreat out of Holland. At Duffel it was employed with a squadron of the 14th and four troops of 80 men each of the 7th, 11th, 15th, and 16th Light Dragoons for the purpose of alarming the French for the safety of their guns. Surprised by the onset of our men, the French dragoons broke before their attack. On the evacuation of Brabant the Eighth was joined by the detachment which had escaped by sea from Nieuport, and which landed at Antwerp. The British troops now consisted of four brigades of cavalry and seven of infantry, making altogether some twenty-five thousand men. According to Smet, the numbers were:

	Cavalry.		Infantry.
British	4742		21752
Hanoverian	1705		3913
Hesse-Cassel	1045		3727
Hesse-Darmstadt	346		1464
	7858	Infantry	30856
		Cavalry	7818
		Grand Total	38674[1]

[1] Smet, p. 59. Smet's total is incorrect. Fortescue agrees with these numbers. *Cf.* IV, Part I, p. 296.

There were four brigades of cavalry. These were David Dundas's Brigade—2nd and 6th Dragoon Guards; 2nd and 6th Dragoons. Ralph Dundas's Brigade consisted of the Blues; the 3rd and 5th Dragoon Guards, and the 1st Dragoons. Laurie's Brigade consisted of the 7th, 11th, 15th, and 16th Light Dragoons. Vyse's Brigade consisted of the 1st Dragoon Guards, the 8th and the 14th Light Dragoons.

The actions at Bousbecque, Langemark, Alost, and Duffel, combined with the loss of the detachment taken at Nieuport, had reduced the regiment to one-fifth of its original strength, and it formed a single squadron of about a hundred effective men. Nor had the horses suffered a whit less severely. On the arrival of the corps in Holland about a hundred horses were rendered unfit for service; and twenty-two of them were shot and the rest sent to the interior of Holland to graze. There was not even a second squadron, and the 14th Dragoons were attached to serve as such. Yet so recently as the 1st of July, 1794, there had been a monthly return that told a widely different tale. According to it there were: "1 Squadron, 1 Lt. Col., 3 Capts., 2 Lts., 1 Cornet, 3 Staff Officers, 8 Qr. Mrs., 26 Sergts., 6 Trumpeters. Present fit for Duty, 207. Sick, 61. On Command, 26. Prisoners of War, 3. Total rank and file, 297. Horses present fit for duty, 161. Sick or lame, 93. Total, 254. Wanting to complete Rank and File, 96. Horses, 132."[1]

In September the regiment was stationed at Boxtel. The French attacked this post on the 14th, and two detachments, under Captains Francis Sherlock and J. Ormsby Vandeleur, spent their energies in retarding the advance of the French hussars and chasseurs. The enemy succeeded in capturing Boxtel. The troops of Hesse Darmstadt lost many men, and the Eighth had several men wounded. Though Captain Vandeleur's horse was killed under him and one troop horse fell into the hands of the French, yet not a single man was left on the field. Dommel could not be maintained with the enemy in Boxtel, and Abercromby was sent to reconnoitre if it might be regained.[2] He found the enemy in

---

[1] *W.O.*, 1/169.   [2] *W.O.*, 1/170.

such strength that he retired. The enemy had been reinforced by the corps from West Flanders and by that from Valenciennes and Condé, and the column which had been marching towards Maestricht, making together scarcely less than 80,000 men. Accordingly, the Duke of York, recognising that he was not at liberty to risk in so unequal a contest his troops or those of the allies, determined on retreating across the Meuse.

There had been difficulty from the dissimilarity in language: there was difficulty from the similarity in uniform. During the retreat through Holland a squadron of the hussars of Salin, who had just joined the army, were taken by the Eighth for the French black hussars, and narrowly escaped a charge from them. It was the duty of the cavalry to cover the retreat, and accordingly the regiment had encounter after encounter with the advancing French squadrons of hussars. For instance, two parties of them, supported by the remainder of the regiment and the detachment of the 14th, kept several squadrons of French hussars completely at bay. The hussars retreated under the trees, where their riflemen were posted, whenever hard pressed. Despite this, the retreat pursued its melancholy way. In November, 1794, the British army was stationed behind the Waal. The regiment remained at the village of Rheinswonde for its headquarters. During December the French tried to cross the Waal, approaching under the cover of the fogs then prevalent. At the Waal a detachment of the Eighth was employed on one of these occasions in repelling the enemy. Lieutenant-General Bush was killed that day in driving the French back into the river. This was the last affair in which the regiment was actively engaged with the French in Europe.

In January, 1795, the retreat was still in process. The horses of Colonel Vandeleur and Captain Newman fell with them, and with difficulty did the intense frost allow them to be raised. Indeed a trooper of their regiment was actually frozen to death. Sir John Fortescue writes that "the days that followed are amongst the most tragical in the history of the Army. During November and December the discipline of the troops in Holland had greatly improved, but with the coming of the frost and the hardships that attended the constant alarms and marches on the Waal, it had once more broken down completely. Certain regiments of French emigrants, which had joined the army late in the year, were the worst offenders; but it seems certain that some of the British were not far behind them. The country to the north of Arnheim is at the best of times an inhospitable waste, and there were few dwellings and few trees to give shelter or fuel after a dreary march through dense and chilling mist over snow twice thawed and refrozen. Marauders from the regiments of every nationality swarmed round the columns; the drivers of the waggons freed themselves from all control, and the line of march was disorderly beyond description. When the day was ended, the troops of different nations fought for such scanty comforts as were to be found; and once there was a pitched battle between the Guards and the Hessians, who had been on bad terms with each other from the beginning of the campaign. Day after day the cold steadily increased; and those of the army that woke on the morning of the 17th of January saw about them such a sight as they never forgot. Far as the eye could reach over the whitened plain were scattered gun-limbers, waggons full of baggage, of stores, or of sick men, sutlers' carts and private carriages. Beside them lay the horses, dead; around them scores and hundreds of soldiers, dead; here a straggler who had staggered on to the bivouac and dropped to sleep in the arms of the frost; there a group of British and Germans round an empty rum-cask; here forty Guardsmen huddled together about a plundered waggon; there a pack-horse with a woman lying alongside it, and a baby, swathed in rags, peeping out of the pack, with its mother's milk turned to ice upon its lips,— one and all stark, frozen, dead. Had the retreat lasted but three or four days longer, not a man would have escaped; and the catastrophe would have found a place in history side by side with the destruction of the host of Sennacherib and with the still more terrible disaster of the retreat from Moscow."[1]

Smet, as surgeon, also discerned from his own angle the horrors of the retreat.[2] He describes how in 1795 the sickness had

[1] Fortescue, IV, Part I, pp. 320–1.   [2] Smet, p. 66.

increased to such an alarming pitch as to fill the hospitals with more than half of the British infantry. The mortality was absolutely appalling. At Rhenen, for example, we hear that there alone some thousands of our soldiers were buried. The surgeons, too, suffered from the infection, and the skill of their successors left very much indeed to be desired. The frost lasted, enabling the French to increase the pressure of their pursuit. The Eighth crossed the Ems in February, 1795, occupying villages until its removal to East Friesland in March. In May the regiment was quartered at Bremen, where several men joined from French prisons; and the squadrons of the 14th Dragoons were drafted to it. The Westphalian peasants treated our men with a kindness and a consideration that contrasted forcibly with the conduct of the Dutch. During the summer the regiment encamped on one of the plains of Westphalia, when Colonel Pakenham Vandeleur employed the time in re-establishing its order and discipline. All the horses of the infantry officers suitable for Light Dragoon service he could purchase he purchased, and also seventy horses of the 5th Dragoon Guards, which were deemed too light for their riders, were also acquired. Men also enlisted until the corps exceeded three hundred mounted men. To the re-invigorated regiment Lieutenant-General Lascelles brought the welcome news that George III had been graciously pleased to direct that the Royal Irish Dragoons should resume wearing buff accoutrements, as a special mark of royal favour and approbation of their conduct during the period of their arduous continental service.

Orders for home arrived, and in November, 1795, the regiment embarked. The stormy winds and the stormy passage prevented its arrival at Newcastle till the eve of Christmas Day. Their strength then was 350 men and 250 horses. How serious were the expenses of those days is evident from the fact that the transport of each horse cost the government about fifty pounds apiece. While at Manchester in January, 1796, a considerable alteration took place in the establishment of the regiment. A second lieutenant-colonel, Major James Hall, and two majors without troops, Captains Samuel Cooke and J. Ormsby Vandeleur, were added. The regiment was formed into eight troops of eighty men apiece. The 7th Dragoon Guards, the 5th, 9th, and 31st Light Dragoons, especially the last, contributed drafts with the result that the establishment in men and horses was quite complete.

Though the Eighth had left Holland, they were not quite finished with that country. The success of the armies of France in the retreat had inevitably increased the prestige of the Republic. The Dutch published a proclamation, announcing the rights of man and reconstituting the administration upon the principles of the Revolution. On the 15th of May France concluded an alliance, offensive and defensive, with the Dutch Republic. Holland, clearly, had left the side of the Allies. What about the Dutch colonies? They at least might be saved. As early as on the 4th of January, 1795, one of the house of Baring wrote to urge upon Dundas the importance of seizing the Cape of Good Hope and the other Dutch possessions before the French could lay their hands upon them. Our government was naturally apprehensive of the Cape of Good Hope falling under the control of the French, by which the sea route to India would be gravely menaced. A large proportion of the Dutch people at the Cape favoured the French, and clearly there was no time to be lost.

On the 11th of June, 1795, a fleet consisting of three ships of 74 guns, named the *Monarch*, *Arrogant* and *Victorious*, three of 64 guns, named the *America*, *Ruby* and *Stately*, a frigate of 24 guns named the *Sphinx*, and two sloops of war, the *Echo* and *Rattlesnake*, respectively of 18 and 16 guns, were off Simons Town. The admiral commanding was Sir George Keith Elphinstone, and there were troops on board under command of Major-General Sir James Craig, the acute critic of the cordon system of the Austrian army. In the afternoon of the 14th of June there arrived on shore Lieutenant-Colonel Mackenzie, of the 78th Regiment, Captain Hardy, of the *Elcho* sloop of war, and Mr. Ross, secretary to General Craig, who handed to Commissioner Sluysken a mandate from the Prince of Orange, dated at Kew on the 7th of February, 1795, ordering him to admit the troops of the King of England into the forts and elsewhere in the colony, also to admit British ships of war into the ports, and to consider such troops and ships of war as the forces of a friendly power sent to protect the colony against an invasion of the French. They also delivered to Sluysken a letter from Admiral Elphinstone and General Craig, in which an account of the condition of the Netherlands was given. The winter in Europe had been an excessively severe one, he was informed, and towards the close of January the rivers were frozen so hard that the French armies crossed into Utrecht and Gelderland, compelling the English forces to retire into Germany and the Dutch forces to surrender. In a few days the whole country fell into the possession of the French without any treaty of capitulation, and the Stadtholder was obliged to make his escape in a fishing boat, which conveyed him from Scheveningen to England. Great Britain and her allies were, however, raising large armies, and they were confident of being able to drive out the French in the next campaign.

On the 18th of June General Craig, attended by three officers and his secretary, arrived in Cape Town and had an interview with Commissioner Sluysken. On the following day the Dutch Council met, when the General communicated to the members the object of his mission and the manner in which he had been instructed to carry it out. The fleet and troops, he stated, had been sent by His Britannic Majesty to protect the colony until the restoration of the ancient form of government in the Netherlands, when it would be in His Majesty's power to restore it to its proper owner. No alterations would be made in the laws or the customs of the country without the expressed desire of the inhabitants, nor would any additional taxation be imposed. The people would be required to defray the cost of their government as it then existed, but nothing more. They would be at liberty to trade with England and the English possession in India in general. The troops would be paid by England, and would be required to take an oath of allegiance to His Britannic Majesty for the time that he should be in control of the colony. The civil servants would retain their offices until His Majesty's pleasure should be known.

The Council replied in writing, declining to entertain the proposal, and informing the General that they were determined to protect the colony with their own forces against any power that should attack them. Admiral Elphinstone and General Craig, upon the return of the latter to Simons Bay, issued a proclamation in which the government and inhabitants were invited to place themselves under His Britannic Majesty's protection, as the French would undoubtedly endeavour to obtain possession of the dependencies of the Netherlands.

Three days later the English officers issued an address, in which the offer of protection under the conditions named by General Craig were repeated, and a committee of the inhabitants was invited to come to Simons Town to confer with them. The address was printed in Dutch and German, and many copies were distributed. It put before the colonists the alternative of a French or an English occupation. The former was pictured as a government on Jacobin principles, with the tree of liberty and the guillotine in the foreground, freedom of slaves accompanied by such horrors as those which had laid waste the rich and beautiful islands of San Domingo and Guadeloupe, total cessation of intercourse with Europe and India, the annihilation of commerce, and the absence of money and the necessaries of life. Great Britain was indeed the only power in Europe able to assure the safety of person and property under the existing laws or others that the inhabitants might desire, free sale of all productions of the country at the best prices obtainable, release from imposts intended for the exclusive benefit of the Dutch East India Company, commerce by sea and land from one part of the colony to another, and better pay for such soldiers as might choose to enter the English service.

The Council broke off all communication with the British. On the 26th of June, however, the admiral and the general wrote a long letter, the keynote of which was that the Netherlands had been absorbed in France, and as the Cape Colony, if left to itself, would also be absorbed, His Britannic Majesty could not allow it to fall into the hands of his enemies. The Council not unnaturally replied that there was a great difference between offering assistance against an invader and requiring them to surrender the colony to the British government.

The supply of provisions to the British fleet was forbidden. Another detachment of burgher horsemen and pandours, a company of half-breeds and Hottentots, under Commandant Jan Gerhard Cloete strengthened the post at Muizenburg. The troops that had garrisoned the battery Boetselaar were also removed to Muizenburg, only one man being left behind to spike the guns in case the English should land. The moment the designs of the British were known, the burghers of the Cape and Stellenbosch, who had been opposing the Dutch government, declared themselves ready to assist in the defence of the colony to the utmost of their power. When the Commissioner announced that the country would not be surrendered, he was met with loud huzzas in the streets, and was hailed as Father Sluysken. As the great majority of the colonists were attached to the republican party in Europe, they were ready to offer a welcome to the French, if they could not be left to themselves. Fortunately for us, the high officials did not take this line of conduct. Colonel Gordon, the Dutch commandant, stated that he was prepared to admit the English troops if the Jacobins should threaten an attack. As he was of Scots descent and Orange proclivities, he was no more than half-hearted in his preparations. Most of the officials of lower grade and a few of the burghers were willing to welcome the English troops, believing that the object of the British government really was to hold the country in trust for the fugitive Stadtholder. On the 16th of September, 1795, Commissioner Sluysken and Colonel Gordon surrendered, and the Cape colony was in the hands of the British.

In the spring of 1796 the regiment received orders to march towards Coventry on their way to embarkation for the East Indies. There the 10th Light Dragoons selected 200 of the horses out of the 650 the Eighth owned, and the rest were divided among the other dragoon regiments then incomplete. The men marched on foot to Portsmouth, and they embarked 488 strong, divided into six troops. The seventh was kept incomplete and at home to recruit, and the Eighth was reduced, 130 men being transferred to the different regiments in India.[1] Their clothing was to be grey.[2] Two days before the sailing of the fleet, the destination of the regiment was altered for the Cape of Good Hope. On the 11th of August, 1796, it sailed with directions to place itself under the orders of General Craig. It arrived at the Cape on the 10th of November, and disembarked on the following day. As it lost only one man by sickness during the voyage of over ninety days, it landed close on five hundred strong. There were only ten privates above twenty-five years of age, and there were some under seventeen.

In a letter of the 20th of November, 1796, General Craig informed Henry Dundas:

> I have the honour to report to you the safe arrival of the fleet under convoy of *L'Oiseau*, having on board Major-General F. Dundas and the 8th Regiment of Light Dragoons. It came to an anchor the 18th instant, and the Regiment disembarked in a high state of health yesterday afternoon. . . . When I took upon myself the measure of detaining here one of the Regiments[3] destined for India, it was under circumstances which I conceived justified the apprehension that the attack which had been so lately defeated would be followed by another from that part of the enemy's force, which I expected must have been destined to co-operate with it, and which I believed would be both stronger in point of numbers and more formidable in point of activity and conduct. I was besides, Sir, actuated by the consideration that whatever inconvenience might arise to the service in India from the step for which I rendered myself responsible, it was not at any rate likely to be of long continuance, as the successive fleets of whose coming I had notice, would furnish the necessary opportunities for forwarding the Regiment, when the reasons for detaining it no longer existed.
>
> The very considerable period of time which has elapsed since the appearance of the Dutch force on this coast, although it does not entirely destroy it, certainly lessens in a very great degree the probability which then existed that it would be followed by another force destined to co-operate with it. And as this is the last fleet of this year which will touch here, and by which I could forward the Regiment to its

---

[1] *W.O.*, 3/28.   [2] *W.O.*, 40/8.   [3] The 80th Regiment.

original destination, I cannot think myself warranted to detain it any longer, for reasons the immediate proof of which now appears so slight.

At the same time, Sir, I think it a duty incumbent upon me, and a justice due to my successor in the command, to say that having spared no pains in the endeavour, and having had sufficient time to make myself thoroughly master of those circumstances which must influence the fate of the colony in the event of a serious and well directed attack upon it, I cannot consider the force which will remain after the departure of the 80th Regiment to be such as will warrant its future security.

By the departure of the 80th Regiment we shall lose, Sir, 810 of the most effective and very best men which we have, while by the arrival of the 8th Dragoons, we receive an accession of 444 to appearance very good men also, the difference is 366 men.

After the departure of the Regiment, our force will be

Artillery	179
Cavalry	899
Infantry	3609
	4687

I consider the Cavalry as a very great and useful addition, should we be able to employ them as such, and if not, that part of them which cannot be made use of as Cavalry, will be extremely serviceable on foot, but they will certainly not be so generally so as an equal number of infantry would be. These must form the real and effective force which can alone be depended upon. . . .

I consider the 8th Dragoons as a great and useful reinforcement, notwithstanding that I am under some doubt as to our being able to employ them as cavalry, not for any difficulty in mounting them, but from that of feeding their horses when mounted. As I had no previous intimation of their arrival, I have not yet made sufficient inquiry to enable me to form a decisive opinion upon it. I shall however exert every endeavour for this purpose, from a conviction of the great utility which may be derived from them.[1]

An attack of dysentery prostrated the newly-landed regiment, and a hundred were in hospital during the first two months after their arrival. Early in January a large detachment set out for the country, and this saved them. Major-General Dundas inspected

[1] *Cape of Good Hope,* 1796.

the troops at Rondybosh Camp on the 1st of January, 1797, and his report enables us to judge of the state of the regiment:

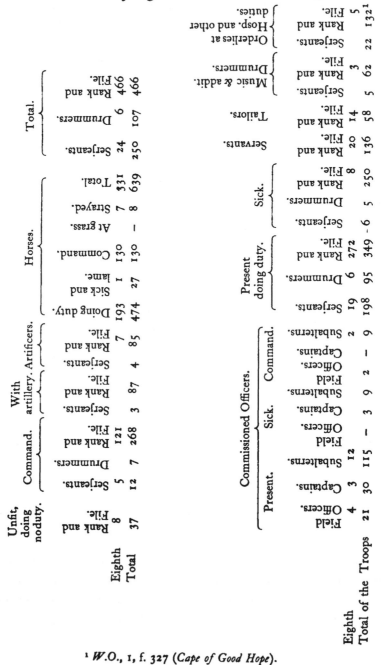

Prospects in January seemed to indicate a condition of quietness. The harvest had been very abundant and the vintage very favourable, and indeed the only complaint of the farmers was the plentifulness of the crops and the consequent difficulty of their storage.[1] There were two Dundases. The capable Francis Dundas was the General. The equally capable Henry Dundas was the Secretary of State for War, the closest friend of Pitt, who trusted him as he trusted no one else. A politician to the core, Henry Dundas was ignorant of war, and did not possess even that saving grace—knowledge of his ignorance. Craig told Henry Dundas in January, 1797:

> We have mounted about 150 of the 8th Dragoons, and are going on purchasing horses as fast as I can command the money to pay for them. My object with respect to the cavalry has always been to have the whole of them (except 100 or 150 reserved for the immediate service of the town) in the country stationed so as to form a line across from sea to sea cutting off every communication between the inhabitants of the interior part of the colony and the plain immediately about the Cape Town. For this purpose it was necessary to seek for a proper position as a quarter for the main body, detached from them to the right and left. I have taken a place exactly situated as I could wish. Every circumstance of this sort is at this moment attended with enormous expense, but it appeared to be inevitable. I have agreed to pay £50 a month for the land, which has the peculiar advantage, and which indeed next to its situation was my principal inducement for taking it, of furnishing very good summer pasture for almost any number of horses, so that we can never be at a loss for feeding them, and I have contracted for building temporary stables for 500 horses and huts for as many in proportion for 11,000 rix dollars. The whole to be finished by the middle of next month. On the right we have a place in the hands of the Government capable with a very little repair of containing a squadron of 160 horses.[2]

In March, 1797, General Lascelles was removed to the 3rd Dragoons, and General Sir Charles Grey was re-appointed to the colonelcy of the King's Royal Irish Dragoons. It was actively

---

[1] *Cape of Good Hope*, 1797.   [2] *Cape of Good Hope*, 1797, f. 326.

employed at the Cape, and one squadron was sent to the interior to preserve order among the Dutch colonists.

Smet describes an affray that arose between the infantry and dragoon barrack guards.[1]   Late in the evening a prisoner of the latter corps escaped out of the barrack room of the former, and the officer on duty sent to the dragoon quarters to inquire after him.   The dragoon sergeant, in charge of the barrack guard of that part of the Eighth, refused admission into his barrack without directions from the orderly officer of dragoons.   The stubbornness of the sergeant of the guard was supplemented by the imprudence of the infantry officer, who, without reporting the circumstance to the commanding officer of dragoons or the field officer of the day, peremptorily demanded admission for himself and his men. The sergeant maintained his ground, and an attempt was made to push through with levelled bayonets.   There was a nasty scuffle, in which fortunately no one was wounded.   The infantry barrack guard beat the alarm, which was taken up by the drums of the other guards.   At last the officers of the Eighth heard of the altercation, and, coming from the mess, made peace.   They seized the most forward, who were tried the next day by court martial; two were shot and some others were severely punished and turned out of the regiment.

Lord Macartney as Governor wrote anxiously to Henry Dundas on the 20th of October, 1797:

I flatter myself that you will excuse me for so strongly pressing the regular remittance of specie here for the payment of the private soldiers. I am the more solicitous on this point : I am apprehensive that an idea may be entertained of the probability of persuading them to take their subce. in paper, with the addition of the difference between it and specie.   I do not absolutely deny the possibility of it, but I know the nature of these gentry so well that I could have little hopes of their long remaining satisfied, for from their not well comprehending the fluctuation of exchequer, and from their suspicious nature they would be apt to complain of being cheated, and would bring forward the circumstance, in addition to other imaginable grievances.   I recollect

[1] Smet, p. 74.

when I was Secretary of Ireland, 2 artful soldiers of the 58th Regiment applied to My Lord Townshend for the redress of an injury, which they pretended to have suffered in being paid at Gibraltar, in Spanish money, at an exorbitant rate of exchange, and although their memorial was found on enquiry to have very little foundation, yet it occasioned a great deal of noise. Dr Lucas and other patriots were alarmed, and the affair might have made a serious sensation upon the garrison of Dublin, had it not been diverted by the prudence and address of the Lord Lieutenant.[1]

There had been trouble in the Eighth, and one way to avoid it was to pay its soldiers in currency of the old realm.

The influence of the mutiny at Spithead and the mutiny at the Nore was not without influence on the sailors under Admiral Pringle in the squadron in Simons Bay. As Lord Macartney eagerly desired to prevent the contagion of one corps from communicating itself to another, and, as he also wished to keep the soldiers in exercise and activity, in consultation with General Francis Dundas, he put the greater part of the troops under canvas in the neighbourhood of Capetown.[2] This he did on the 12th of November, 1797, when it incidentally appears that he had not received a single letter from England since the 6th of March. On the 15th of December he was still without letters. Naturally this meant that the Governor had not received specie in order to pay the soldiers.

Sir Charles Grey wrote from Barham Court to William Huskisson on the 10th of April, 1798, and his letter shows the activities of the commanding officer at home :

I have this Morning the honor of your Letter with the several papers of Intelligence enclosed, of yesterday, Together with Mr Dundas's Instructions to The Duke of Richmond and Lord Romney ; all which I think myself much obliged by—The Intelligence papers I return, They all agree on great preparations and efforts making at every Port, much exaggerated I doubt not, but let them come, they will only *once* repent of it, and their Telegraph scheme of starting all at once, from every Port, to overpower poor Old England, is so like a Frenchman,

---

[1] *Cape of Good Hope*, 1797, f. 821. [2] *Cape of Good Hope*, 1797, f. 865. *Cf.* f. 869.

x

that one must laugh at it—I beg you will inform Mr Dundas,[1] that ever ready and happy to obey his Commands, I shall most certainly give the Duke of Richmond the meeting at Brighton on the 19th to talk matters over on the 20th and be ready for the General Meeting on the 21st inst.   The Truth is, I have been a good deal indisposed for Ten days past with a complaint in my Stomack and Bowels, and was the only reason for my deputing Lt. Col. Taylor and Lieut. Genl. Hulse to meet the Duke of Richmond at Lewes in the fear I should not be able.   However the weather fine, the Jaunt may be the best prescription, and I shall certainly try it : I have therefore written an answer to a very Civil Letter I received this morning from his Grace, offering to come to Barham Court on the 15th, that I could not possibly think of his coming so far, particularly as his Grace complains of Gouty symptoms in his Stomack, but should have the Honor of awaiting his Commands at Brighton on the 19th inst.—I feel happy in the prospect you gave me, at the end of your Letter of an Alert near here, I pray they may be incessent, not at one but every Port.   It will strike a damp, and impede their preparations : This Leads me to talk *Treason*, but which I know is safe in Mr Dundas's hands and yours not to commit me should there not be a more active Commander at Deal than *Adml. Peyton*.   If there was, a great Deal might now be done, and every thing, with a proper Force, in case those Gasconaders should carry their long threats into execution.—Capt. Bowen now Commanding the *Argo*, stationed half seas over, is a most excellent Active Officer, and if he had the power would keep the Coast in a perpetual state of Alarm and security, not only that but be the means of considerable destruction by keeping barely out of Gun shot during the day, and in the Night stand close in for Bombardment and firing heavy guns : This was practised every Night upon Fort Royal Martinico during the siege of Bourbon, to their very great Annoyance and with great success.

In addition to the defence of the Coast, I have to mention that if two North Country Cutts[2] of 300 Tons each with heavy Cannon could be placed at Dengeness, It would be the greatest security to that approach—Captain Popham can moor them, who is a most active Dashing Officer, and has a scheme, which I shall send for Mr Dundas's Information of destroying the Port of Ostend, and the Interior Navigation by Bruges, by the destruction in a short space of time of the

---

[1] Henry Dundas.   [2] Cutters.

Sluices. He is now building at Dover Row Gallies with one or two heavy Cannon for the annoyance of the French Court and to keep at a respectable distance the French Row Boats which come very daringly close to Folkestone, Dengeness Seaford etc., and pick up straggling ships of our Trade. Had I regular Troops in Thanet with transports at Ramsgate and had the Liberty of Embarking Detachments I think great advantage might be taken of it, by a landing near Ostend and effectually destroying the Canals and their Interior Navigation, by which the french r . . . ve[1] great supplies at Dunkirk etc. : a few Hours would do it, and the risk trifling to the Object, which is always a consideration on an expedition—One Regular Regt.—the 18 Foot is arrived, I believe at Ramsgate, but Mr. Dundas promised me Three Regts. with Transports ready at Ramsgate to take advantage of every opportunity of offence and defence.

The Sea Fencibles do not enroll, so far from it that smugglers and Fishermen sent Boats along the coast to Apprise their Brethren and advise them against it : I have always suspected those People from their connection with France, and this confirms me they are Rascals, and will aid the Invaders, to prevent which I wish the Admiralty would make a sweep along the Coast, and send them all to the East or West Indies.[2]

Plainly, Sir Charles Grey had in his day plans akin to those meant for the sealing up of Zeebrugge in our day. With his wide experience of sea and land campaigns, we can readily grasp how keenly the influence of sea power appealed to him. As Sir Charles Grey at home had Henry Dundas in his mind, so Lord Macartney abroad also had him in his mind. With an optimism unshared by General Craig, Macartney informed Dundas on the 4th of February, 1798, that he believed that the Dutch were so reduced that he thought it questionable whether they can ever revive as a nation, dependent or independent.[3] From Parliament Street on the 1st of June, 1798, Lord Macartney heard that the King had been pleased to determine that the Eighth should be completed to the establishment of seven troops of seventy men apiece.[4] This number was to be obtained by resort to the abominable practice

---

[1] Receive. There is sealing wax over this word.   [2] *Add. MSS.*, 38735, f. 11.
[3] *W.O.* 1, 327 (*Cape of Good Hope*), f. 13.   [4] *Cape of Good Hope*, 1798, f. 821.

of drafting men from the 28th Light Dragoons. The remainder of the men of the 28th Light Dragoons were to be sent at the first opportunity to India, there to be incorporated into such regiments of light dragoons as the Commander-in-Chief might direct. The subsistence of the different regiments was fixed at :

	£	s.	d.
8th Regiment of Light Dragoons ..	5392	13	3
28th „ „ „ „ ..	5548	4	11
Scotch Brigade Foot	7455	7	1
84th Regiment „	9443	19	4
86th Regiment „	7903	10	3
98th Regiment „	3430	3	4
	39173	18	2[1]

There is an N.B. attached to this statement to the effect that this subsistence must all be paid in sterling money, a provision that illustrates the foresight of Lord Macartney.

The account of clothing and contingencies for the military establishment of the Eighth was :

	£	s.	d.
Clothing	3084	5	0
Contingencies	484	16	0
	3569	1	0[2]

The amount of full pay to the officers of the military establishment was £7163 2s. 6d. This full pay included subsistence and arrears, and did not go through the hands of the Deputy Paymaster General. It was drawn for on the Agent of the Regiment in England by the Regimental Paymasters at the Cape.

The quelling of the interior by the other regiments as well as the Eighth raised the question of loyalty. The oath which was required to be taken by all the officials and generally by the burghers of the Cape, Stellenbosch, and Swellendam districts was the following: "I swear to be true and faithful to his Majesty

[1] *Cape of Good Hope*, 1798, f. 829.   [2] *Cape of Good Hope*, 1798, f. 833.

George the third, by God's grace king of Great Britain, France, and Ireland, defender of the faith, etc., for so long time as his Majesty shall remain in possession of this colony." The people of Graaff Reinet did not submit. A letter explaining their conduct was written by the leaders of the Dutch forces to the British commanders, which led to the belief that they were ready to come to terms. General Craig appointed as landrost a colonist who had been an officer in De Lille's regiment, named Frans Reinhard Bresler, and gave him instructions to conciliate the farmers. Adriaan van Jaarsveld told Bresler that the Dutch intended to retain their own government, and would only agree to terms which he wished to be taken down in writing. These were:

1. That the people of Graaff Reinet were willing to take to Capetown for sale such articles as their land produced, according to the ancient custom.

2. That they would observe all reasonable orders and laws, provided the English governor would supply them with powder, lead, clothing, and such other articles as they needed.

Hendrik Krugel dictated two additional articles:

3. That the people of Graaff Reinet would not draw the sword against the English.

4. That their only reason for refusing to take the oath required was that when the states-general of the Netherlands should retake the country, they would not be able to justify themselves if they did so.[1]

On hearing of this practical rejection of his terms, General Craig sent Major King with three hundred men of the 84th Regiment to Stellenbosch, to be in readiness to move forward at short notice. Supplies of ammunition and goods of all kinds were cut off from the district of Graaff Reinet. A corps of Hottentots was raised for service in the interior. They were enlisted for a year, were provided with arms, clothing, and rations, and each man received sixpence a week in money. In September Major King left Stellenbosch with two hundred dragoons, including

---

[1] I use the convenient summary in Theal, *History of South Africa* (1795–1834), p. 12.

men of the Eighth, five companies of light infantry, one hundred and fifty pandours, and three field guns, to commence military operations in Graaff Reinet. The deputies declared their willingness to submit, and with this the matter rested for a time. Quartering dragoons upon offenders holding Jacobin principles was one method tried. There was a scale of diet, according to which the dragoons could insist upon being provided—if they were not provided with food to their liking.

In August, 1798, Mr. Hendrik Oostwald Eksteen of Bergvliet, between Wynberg and Muizenberg, invited a number of his friends to be present at his daughter's wedding, and he issued the invitations in the name of "Citizen Eksteen." On the day of the ceremony the governor ordered a party of dragoons to "proceed to the festive assembly of Citizens," and to remain there "to prevent any irregularity that might be apprehended from disaffected or suspected persons." "Citizen" Eksteen was required "without delay to retract and redress in the most public manner this wanton and petulant conduct, and to provide sufficient security for his good behaviour and dutiful deportment towards government in future, or to repair to that country where in the midst of confusion and medley his invitations would be better relished." Eksteen then came to headquarters, protesting that he had not meant to cause the slightest annoyance. His apology, however, was not accepted until he produced a bond for a thousand pounds, signed by two substantial persons, as "security that he would not in future be guilty of similar or any other offences against the government." As a matter of course the dragoons were then recalled.

In the meantime Bresler returned to Graaff Reinet and assumed duty as landrost. A guard of twelve dragoons accompanied him and remained at the drostdy as a garrison and to carry despatches. All arrears of land rents to the 16th of September, 1795, were remitted. The former inhabitants of the field cornetcies of Nieuwveld, Tarka, Sneeuwberg, Zuurveld, and Zwagershoek, who had been driven from their homes by Bushmen or Kaffirs, were to hold their farms rent free for the next six years, provided they would return home and resume occupation within four months. If the landrost should consider it necessary to call out a commando against Bushmen, the farmers were ordered by proclamation to obey. In dealing with the Kaffirs, the landrost was instructed that he must only employ force where he was sure of success. He was to report on the advisability of removing the drostdy from the village of Graaff Reinet to the neighbourhood of Zwartkops River. At first the farmers gave him a friendly reception. They stood, however, in awe of the strong body of troops kept at the Cape, and the moment the number of soldiers or their efficiency lessened, the danger-signal was hoisted.

During the night of the 22nd of November, 1798, a fire broke out in the dragoon stables at Capetown. A violent south-east wind enabled the flames to spread to the adjoining buildings, in spite of the vigorous efforts of the troopers to stop them. At length the fire was conquered by the process of destroying a row of houses in advance of it, and saturating the ruins and buildings beyond with water. Inevitably there was an immense destruction of government property. The coal sheds, the timber yard, the commissariat magazines, and the victuallers' warehouses were consumed with their contents. Seventy-two dragoon horses were burned to death. All the naval and military stores in the colony, except a very small quantity in Simons Town, were destroyed.[1]

The cause of the fire was conjectured to be due to the force of the wind carrying part of the wadding of the evening gun from the Castle, whence it lodged in the thatch. Lieutenant F. P. Rogers, of the Eighth, informed the Court of Inquiry that he was orderly officer on the evening of the 22nd, and visited the stables at twenty minutes past nine. He found everything quiet and saw no light whatever in or near the stables at that hour. There was a standing order in the regiment that lanthorns were not allowed, and that no light would be permitted in the stables. James Phillips, James Saunderson, Thomas Harper, and Richard Horton, privates in the Eighth, informed the Court that they were sentries in the stables on the evening of the 22nd, and they testified that there was no

---

[1] *W.O.* 1, 327 (*Cape of Good Hope*). Extract out of the Day Book of the Secretary's Office at the Cape of Good Hope, December 24.

light, and that they did not observe anyone with a light about or near the stables. Major-General Francis Dundas told Henry Dundas on the 2nd of December, 1798, of the gravity of the loss sustained by the service. "It is impossible," he continued, "to lament sufficiently this unfortunate accident which occasioned extreme regret in the breasts of all well-disposed persons in this colony." Yes, but what of the ill-disposed persons in the interior? Some of them supposed that the army was left defenceless in general and ammunitionless in particular.[1]

The arrest of the old commandant Adriann van Jaarsveld on a charge of forgery was the immediate occasion of the fresh outbreak at Graaff Reinet. He owed the orphan chamber £736, and for this amount he had given a bond on his farm. He paid the interest only to the 31st of December, 1791, and when he was asked in March, 1798, to pay the capital, he produced a receipt for the interest to the 31st of December, 1794. He was then summoned by the high court of justice to appear on the 29th of November to answer the charge of falsifying the receipt by changing the figure 1 into 4. As he did not appear, Landrost Bresler arrested him. A corporal and two dragoons strengthened the prisoner's guard. In the meantime Marthinus Prinsloo collected forty men for the rescue of van Jaarsveld. As the dragoons could not offer effective resistance to so many, rescued he was. Prinsloo now set forth that men like himself were afraid of being arrested, and accordingly the forty appeared in arms. The movement spread. Jan Botha and Coenraad du Bois joined. As these two men were living with the Kaffirs, they had influence with the young chief Gaika, influence which was magnified to be greater than it really was.

Prinsloo and Du Bois now sent out circulars, calling upon the farmers of the district to assemble in arms at the drostdy on the 12th of February, 1799. Five days later a hundred men assembled at the farm of Barend Burger. The Rev. H. W. Ballot, of Graaff Reinet, endeavoured to persuade them to return to their homes, but without much success. On the 20th of February

---

[1] *W.O.* 1, 327 (*Cape of Good Hope*), f. 475.

the thirty men who were blockading the drostdy entered the village of Graaff Reinet. Ballot this time persuaded them to withdraw, persuasions not unconnected with the firmness of the eight dragoons of the Eighth under Sergeant Maxwell Irvine, who all stood firm. They hoisted the English flag, and, drawing themselves up under it, announced that, if attacked, they would defend themselves to the last.

When the rescue of van Jaarsveld was reported to General Francis Dundas, on the morning of the 17th of February he sent Brigadier-General Thomas Vandeleur with a strong detachment of the regiment to march to Graaff Reinet. Two companies of the 98th Regiment and the Hottentot corps joined Vandeleur, who found the people in the eastern part of the district of Swellendam in strong sympathy with the insurgents of Graaff Reinet. He issued orders that every man should remain upon his own farm, under penalty of being treated as a traitor if found beyond it. He stationed some dragoons in a position that commanded the eastern road. Pushing on with his men, he reached the drostdy of Graaff Reinet only to find that the insurgents refused to make a stand there. The truth was that they felt discouraged by the farmers of Sneeuwberg, who joined Vandeleur, and by the number of Hottentots who also flocked to him. In fact, the natives treated the strife as one between colonists and Hottentots who had grievances of their own against the colonists.

Sergeant Maxwell Irvine in his letter to Acting Adjutant Dickson, of the 24th of February, 1799, from Graaff Reinet, gives his account of his operations, and Vandeleur thought that his letter "is worth reading." Hence we give it :

As this is the first opportunity I have to write to you, since Sergeant McGuires departure from this quarter, I intend to give you a full detail of the situation of the detachment now at Graaf Reinet. The 19th of January Sergeant McGuire left this quarter on his march to the Cape with an inhabitant of the Colony as prisoner with him, who was rescued from him and two Dragoons by a number of farmers amounting to seventy the 23rd of said month, and from that day to the 20th of February they lay encamped at 1 English mile distance from the town until they recruited their forces to the amount of 180 of them as near as could be reckoned by our spy. They were all well armed and had with them a great number of Hottentots and slaves likewise armed with muskets and ammunition. They all came into Graaf Reinet with an intention of hanging the Landrost and shooting every man of the detachment and have nothing more to do with English government and was it not that the Minister interceded and spoke agreeable to them, they would have been as good as their promise, and although their number was so great the small detachment under my command appeared ready and spirited. We formed under the English colours and was determined every man to die before the rebels should pull them down, which was intended by them to be their first assault, this being the second attack they have made since my arrival here and are determined the next time they come to complete their business. During all those troubles with our rebellious enemy the Landrost behaved with the greatest steadiness and was resolved to share the same fate of us, if they proceeded to attack. He has likewise informed me that he has wrote to General Dundas for more Dragoons to come to his assistance as the country is in such a rebellious situation, and I think it necessary to acquaint you of the situation of the rebels on the road as they have it lined with picquets for the immediate destruction of the troops that may be sent to this place.

Sir, you will be so good as to acquaint Brigadier General Vandeleur and Colonel Hall of the situation of this post in the same manner as I have to you.

The arms of every description are in very good repair, the horse appointments are all in bad repair except one kit. There has been no horses bought for the detachment as yet as this is the season that horses most commonly are unhealthy and subject to die.

We have but two horses here now but during the time of the disturbance the Landrost furnished us with a sufficient quantity of horses to mount the Detachment. . . .

P.S.

Sir, The farmers are all this time making alliance with the Caffres who are remarkably strong and quite convenient, and pay no regard to small arms or Dragoons or any thing except cannon or small mortars to throw shells, on which account nothing would be more necessary than to send some artillery here with such implements.

They have likewise obliged the Landrost to sign articles with them contrary to his inclination, as he thinking himself too weak at that time to continue disturbance with them.[1]

Brigadier-General Vandeleur told General Francis Dundas on the 26th of February, 1799, in his letter from Hemel Rod Rozet: "We are so far on our way to Swart Kops River. We arrived here at half past four this morning after a march of four hours and a half and proceeded on this way to the foot of Attiguas Cloof to remain for the night. The whole detachment, mounted and dismounted Dragoons, and Hottentots as well, and the horses considering the length of the march have kept up their condition wonderfully, not a single sore back or lame horse. I intend going on without a halt until we pass the Attiguas Cloof, where we shall arrive about daylight on Thursday morning, a march of 58 Dutch hours on horseback or 348 English miles in twelve days . . . it is with much pleasure I assure you we have been plentifully supplied all along the road and that there has not been the smallest complaint against any individual of the detachment. As the horses are getting rather weary, I intend halting one day in the Lang Cloof, but not without I find it absolutely necessary."[2]

The quick march of Vandeleur did its work, and the insurgents presented a petition, begging for pardon. The General laid down the condition that arms must first be surrendered before he would consent to have any dealings with them. On complying with this condition, he forgave ninety-three whom he considered least guilty on their paying a fine or furnishing one or two horses. The offer was gladly accepted, and these prisoners then released. The remaining twenty were sent to Algoa Bay. Van Jaarsveld and his son Zacharias were also arrested.

At Graaff Reinet General Vandeleur wrote to General Francis Dundas on the 21st of March, 1799, and in the course of his letter he said that the Landrost "speaks in the highest terms of the Dragoons, but particularly of the Serjeant." The writer asked

---

[1] *W.O.*, 1/231, f. 327.   [2] *W.O.*, 1/331, f. 331.

for a small howitzer, "which, I think, will be of infinite use in driving them out of their strong holds and fastnesses. . . . The troops have conducted themselves with great regularity through the whole march. . . .

"P.S.   Since I wrote the above, a most scandalous and barefaced robbery has been committed by a Drummer of the 98th Regiment. I have brought him to a Court-martial; and they have sentenced him 800 lashes; every one of which he shall get in the most public part of the village.   I wish, Sir, you would give me authority to hang the first man, caught plundering, as the most effectual means of completely stopping it."[1]

We give this episode of Graaff Reinet at some length, as it illustrates the services of the Eighth in restoring law and order among the Boers of South Africa just as they restored law and order in Ireland at the end of the seventeenth and of the eighteenth centuries.   This quiet and thankless work was gradually pursued by the dragoons from the time they landed in 1796 to their leaving in 1801.   Nor did Dundas omit to send presents to the men, Boers and Hottentots, who had stood by the Eighth at Graaff Reinet.[2]   He was particular to send guns to Commandants Vanderwald, Lambert, and Hendrik Reinsburg.   The gun of the first, for instance, was to be a double-barrelled with second sight, a very large bore calculated for killing elephants, long and strengthened at the stock with a thin plate of iron.   They were all packed in neat cases with cleaning ramrods, etc., and a brass plate on each case with the name of the respective Commandant to whom it belongs and the following inscription: "Given by Major-General Dundas as a reward for Services done to the British Government."

The Kaffirs received their presents.   The beads they got were small, black, blue, green, pale blue, pale green; in short, all colours but red and white.   The copper ornaments were of all sorts, but principally breast plates and wire for large rings for the arms. The copper was to be in sheet.   The cutlery consisted of coarse knives, which were to shut in cases, and tinder boxes and flints.

[1] *W.O.*, 1/331, f. 331.   [2] *W.O.*, 1/331, f. 699.

There were also small looking glasses. The chiefs were to receive a few dozen of large handsome copper breastplates with the British arms engraven on them.[1] The Kaffirs had been our friends. When, however, some of them gave trouble to the farmers we had to turn, much to their astonishment, against them. Though several hundreds of them were at the British camp, there were many of them roaming about the district, their hand against every one and every one's hand against them. Landrost Bresler reported that nearly the whole district of Graaff Reinet was in possession of the Hottentots and Kaffirs. Instead of acting in unison, the farmers were fighting in little parties, each on its own account. The situation indeed became so acute that Dundas set out for the frontier. A large burgher commando was called out in each of the districts of Stellenbosch and Swellendam, and fifty dragoons with some companies of the 61st and 81st regiments were ordered to the front. He patched up a kind of truce which was observed but indifferently, leaving a few dragoons in Graaff Reinet.

There were two hundred men, composed of detachments of the different corps, at Graaff Reinet. A blockhouse was erected near the landing place at Swart Kops, River Bay, commanding the spring of fresh water, and securing all the stores that might be landed from the Cape. A corps of a hundred men, including some of the Eighth, was posted there, and some men of the latter were stationed every ten or fifteen miles all the way to Capetown, so that the Royal Irish embraced in their charge a coast including the inland chain to Graaff Reinet, of about a thousand miles, with two hundred and forty of their men. "It will long be remembered," so Smet holds,[2] "that such was the confidence that General Dundas put in that corps as to make him repeatedly declare that he could not hold the colony safe without their services, which no other corps could have performed so well, from the thorough knowledge the 8th Dragoons had from experience acquired of all the roads, passes over the mountains, fords through the rivers, their address in swimming those with or without their horses, and their knowledge of the Dutch dialect spoken in that colony. The farmers trusted

[1] *W.O.*, 1/331, f. 699.　　　[2] Smet, pp. 81–2.

these men to such a degree as to leave their houses and cattle in their charge when they set out with their families and products to Cape Town; but nowhere were they more welcome guests than in the farms managed by widows: the activity and courage of the relay dragoons protected their houses from the runaway slaves, their cattle from beasts of prey which the dragoons delighted in hunting down, and repressed the insolence of the slaves and Hottentots employed."

Sir Charles Grey removed, like Francis Lascelles, to the 3rd Dragoons, and on the 4th of September, 1799, Lieutenant-General Sir Robert Laurie, Bart., succeeded him.   Laurie, of Maxweltown, in the county of Dumfries, served many years in the 7th Dragoons, rising to the rank of major.   In April, 1779, he was promoted lieutenant-colonel of the 19th Light Dragoons, removing the following October to the 16th Light Dragoons.   In the same year by the death of his father he succeeded to the dignity of Baronet. In 1782 he attained the brevet rank of colonel, and in 1793 he became major-general.   On the embodiment of the 28th Light Dragoons he was appointed colonel, three years later became lieutenant-general, and in 1803 general.   He sat for many years as member of parliament for the county of Dumfries, holding the high office of Knight Marshal of Scotland.   A regimental medal was "Presented by Colonel Sir Robert Laurie in 1803."   A later one had on the obverse a harp and crown, with the inscription, "VIII.L.D." above, and the regimental motto, "Pristinae Virtutis Memores," below.   The reverse was inscribed, "The King's Royal Irish Regiment, L.D. Reward of Merit: W. S. Rickwood, 1819."   In the Day Collection there is a gold engraved medal, one and a half inches in diameter.   It has on the obverse a harp, lion and crown, with the word "Laswaree" above, "Hindostan" and the motto "Pristinae Virtutis Memores" below.   It has on the reverse the inscription, "Presented by the non-commissioned officers and privates of Captain R. de Salis' troop, 8th Hussars, to Troop Sergeant-Major John Landers, on his leaving the regiment, as a mark of esteem for his exemplary conduct during the time he served in the above corps, 1838."[1]

[1] *The Cavalry Journal*, VII, p. 87.

The Kaffirs meanwhile continued their sudden swoops, and the Eighth continued their efforts to repress them.   The new Governor, Sir George Yonge, Bart., hoped on this and other accounts that the garrison would never be reduced to less than four thousand men.[1]   On the 8th of February, 1800, he perceives: "It appears, however, that neither the Hottentots nor the Caffres have been the aggressors, but the savage and oppressive conduct of the Dutch Boers, more uncivilised even than the others, have driven the one to despair, and irritated the others, to which may be added also that these Boers originally oppressed by the Dutch Government without hope of redress, and feeling their power being in reality, by the improvident grants of government possessed of the whole country, had actually become as it were more independent and knew no law but their own will.   Among them too were some evil-minded persons infected with Jacobinism and desperate in their characters, who were industrious in fomenting disturbances, in which they were but too much encouraged by certain persons in Cape Town who wished to unite them to France.   These seem to have been the source of the late troubles."[2]

There was a storm in a tea cup in which Sir George Yonge and General Vandeleur were involved.   As Governor Yonge was *ex-officio* Commander-in-Chief, accordingly he sent his A.D.C., J. C. Smyth to demand an escort of some of the Eighth who happened to be quartered at Stickland.   Captain Tucker conveyed the order in these words: "General Vandeleur, I am come from the Governor to inform you that it is his intention to have all the managers (of the rebellion) brought into town from Stickland. He therefore desires you will remove the Dragoons at Stickland at present there either to the Cape or some of your cantonments which ever may be found most convenient."[3]

Vandeleur brought the matter before Francis Dundas, the Commander-in-Chief, and he issued a general order that all commands must come from him.   Many letters passed between Yonge and Dundas, but the latter pertinaciously insisted upon his

[1] *W.O.*, 1/332.   [2] *W.O.*, 1/332, f. 59.
[3] *W.O.*, 1/332, April 8, 1800.

rights.[1] Tucker demanded on the 13th of April, 1800, a court-martial. Dundas drily replied that "as he does not consider you an officer of the garrison under his command, it is not in his power to comply with your request."[2]

The troubles at Graaff Reinet with the Boers were still giving rise to anxiety. For want of accommodation Dundas had quartered Hottentot soldiers in the church of Graaff Reinet, and this inevitably offended the Boers. Their view was that their sacred edifice was being polluted by rank heathen. Dundas pointed out that it was a necessity to have shelter for the Hottentot soldiers, and that there was no other building available; that it was cleaned out and the Hottentots withdrawn from it some time before the hour for divine service; and that he would have a proper barrack built as soon as possible. In order to quell the commotion General Dundas sent Captain Sherlock, of the Eighth, with three hundred men, selected from his own regiment, the 91st Foot, and the artillery corps, to Graaff Reinet. Though Bresler was still land-rost, Captain Sherlock, Captain Abercromby, and Lieutenant Smyth were appointed a civil commission to take over the chief civil authority in the disturbed district. Arriving at Graaff Reinet on the 29th of November, 1801, Captain Sherlock sent a dragoon to the farmers' camp, offering a full and free pardon to all who would return to their allegiance, with protection of their persons and properties, inviting them at the same time to make him acquainted with their real grievances, which would be redressed by the government. The farmers had fresh grievances, chiefly at the hands of an official, Maynier, who had not acted with much discretion. On the assurance that Maynier no longer occupied a post under the government, the farmers gave up their resistance. "Peace," so we are assured, "hath its victories no less renowned than those of war," and, if so, Captain Sherlock had gained a real victory. The Eighth had indeed done their duty.

General Francis Dundas had received orders to send a regiment of infantry, a troop of dragoons, and a company of artillery on a

---

[1] *W.O.*, 1/332, f. 275, etc.   [2] *W.O.*, 1/332, f. 313.

secret expedition, which was in fact destined to operate against the French troops in Egypt. He had always entertained a high opinion of the Eighth, and he refused to allow the supernumeraries of it to leave. He sent the established number of eighty only, though General Auchmuty declared that twenty-four additional dragoons would be a very material increase to the small detachment of cavalry he was to have with him. Indeed General Dundas had declared—and his actions prove that his declaration was more than merely official—his sense of the value and importance of the services of the Royal Irish Dragoons, realising that he could not permit the whole regiment to embark, as without its assistance he did not conceive that he could hold the colony.

Chapter VIII

The Continuance of the Napoleonic Wars

FROM South Africa the scene of action changed in 1801 to North Africa, when the 8th Light Dragoons were ordered to Egypt. Indirectly the regiment had met the schemes of Napoleon at one extreme of the continent, and directly it met the soldiers of Napoleon at its other extreme.

The elder Von Moltke used to say that he had twenty plans for the invasion of England, but he had not a single one for leaving the invaded island. Napoleon found it comparatively easy to enter Egypt, but he found it most difficult to leave it. As he was to leave his army in the days to come in Russia, so he left it in Egypt. His subordinate, the unfortunate Kléber, was a highly competent leader, but he was assassinated. The command devolved on Menou, who proved himself competent, yet his competency was quite thrown away through his egregious vanity and his culpable short-sightedness. The signal defeat of the French at Alexandria by Sir Ralph Abercromby left us in March, 1801, in a dominating position. An eminently thoughtful soldier if ever there was one, the victory was dearly bought by Abercromby's death. No matter what task he had been set, no matter what impossibility he had been asked to perform—and it is incredible what impossibilities politicians demand—Sir Ralph bent all the powers of his mind to its successful issue, leaving nothing to chance. Henry Dundas staked not his own reputation on the Egyptian expedition, and Abercromby, because he did his duty to his country and to such a desperate gambler, saved Dundas's reputation and added—if that were possible—to his own. The new commander was General Hely-Hutchinson, who was as close a student of his profession as Abercromby himself.   If it is not always well to take the book by the cover, it was by no means well to judge Hutchinson by his appearance, for there was scarcely a more ill-featured man in the whole army.

From India and from South Africa troops were coming to Egypt.   They were wanted, for on the 1st of January, 1801, Abercromby had had only 15,812 men.[1]   On the 24th of February one troop of the Eighth under Captain Hawkins, one company of Royal Artillery, with three companies of the 61st Regiment and eight pieces of artillery, embarked on board the squadron commanded by Sir Home Popham.[2]   In the *La Sensible* there were one captain, two lieutenants, one ensign, one quartermaster, four sergeants, seventy-five privates, with five women and three children, all belonging to the regiment.   The effective force ordered from the Cape to Egypt was to consist of about twelve hundred men. Richard Wellesley, brother of Arthur, of the India government, informed Sir George Yonge that he wanted the embarked troops to come to Bombay to be under the command of Major-General David Baird.[3]   This plan did not materialise.   On the 2nd of March, 1801, Wellesley informed Yonge that "it is not improbable that the state of the French power in Egypt may eventually render it necessary to make considerable additions to the armament which had proceeded to India to the Red Sea; and it is accordingly my intention to take immediate measures for strengthening the armament with such reinforcements as with the aid of the troops which I have solicited from your Excellency it may be in my power to provide."[4]

Henry Dundas had already ordered the shipment of a large Indian contingent, and Lord Wellesley had prepared a force of four British battalions and a few native troops.   Arthur Wellesley was to be second in command to Baird.   His illness at the last moment rendered this out of the question, nor is it to be regretted. For Arthur Wellesley was plainly reluctant to serve in such a capacity to Baird.   Exclusive of the forces from the Cape, Baird's

---

[1] *W.O.*, 1/345.
[2] *W.O.*, 1/334, f. 123.
[3] *W.O.*, 1/334, f. 275.
[4] *W.O.*, 1/334, f. 283.

army was composed of the 10th, 19th, 80th, 86th, and a detachment of the 36th, consisting of 3170 men. The native troops were one battalion of Bengal and two battalions of Bombay Native Infantry. On arriving at Mocha on the 25th of April, 1801, Baird found that two divisions of his army had left the place some days earlier, one for Jeddah, and the other he knew not whither; while he had fixed the rendezvous at Cosseir. On arriving at Jeddah, he found, to his dismay, that the two advanced divisions had not received his orders, and they had proceeded up the Gulf for Suez.

Baird's first object had been to land at Suez, and then to act as circumstances dictated. The pity was that the monsoon had commenced before his entrance into the Red Sea. The squadron of Sir Home Popham came into Jeddah in May. He reported that he had heard nothing of the fourth division of the army nor of the provision ships which were expected from India. Baird then sailed with Popham for Cosseir, which he reached on the 8th of June. According to the disembarkation return of the Eighth there were one captain, two lieutenants, one ensign, one quartermaster, four sergeants, one drummer, and seventy-five privates.[1] The East India Company bore the expenses of the transfer of the Eighth, but took right good care to bear them simply in part. The Company, inappropriately enough, dated its communication on this matter on the 1st of April, 1801.[2] The very next month it was discovered that Mr. Trayer, the contractor to the regiment, had been overpaid for clothing, and the Secretary of War instructed Messrs. Collyer, the Agents, to recover the amount as speedily as possible.[3]

Meanwhile the army of Baird had their march of one hundred miles of desert lying before them. The heat was intense, the thermometer at 96° and upwards[4]; the water was very bad, as it was impregnated with a saltpetre taste, causing violent vomiting

---

[1] R. T. Wilson, *History of the British Expedition to Egypt*, II, p. 143.
[2] *East India Letter Book*, No. 7.
[3] *East India Letter Book*, f. 41, May 20, 1801.
[4] 116° was reached.

and a species of dysentery. There were to be seven stages in the journey from Cosseir:

1.	To the New Wells	..	11 miles	Water
2.	Half-way to Moilah	..	17 ,,	No ,,
3.	Moilah	.. ..	17 ,,	Water and provisions
4.	Advanced Wells	..	9 ,,	,,
5.	Half-way to Segeta	..	19 ,,	No ,,
6.	Baromba	.. ..	18 ,,	Water
7.	Keneh	.. ..	10 ,,	The Nile

101

The Quartermaster-General, Colonel John Murray, preceded the soldiers with supplies of water and provisions, but in spite of these precautions there was much suffering from excessive thirst. Water alone, or water infused with a little vinegar, was found the best allayer of thirst. A very small quantity taken at a time, and kept as long as possible in the mouth, only occasionally wetting the throat, afforded the keenest relief. Baird's plan was to pass the army over the hundred miles in small divisions. The first, on reaching Keneh, was to send back its camels and water-bags to the fifth stage; the second, on reaching the fifth stage, was also to send its camels back to the third stage; and the third division, on reaching the third stage, was to send back its camels to the first stage, enabling the remaining divisions to come forward in succession on the same principle. The result was that the army arrived at Keneh with the loss of only three men.[1]

On arrival at Keneh on the Nile, the troops embarked for Cairo, which we had recently captured. At the same time Sir David Baird announced in general orders: "The war is not terminated; the enemy possesses the only harbour and strongest fortress in the country; and the services of the troops in the field are required in the execution of their duty." From Cairo the Eighth proceeded on their way down the Nile to Rosetta. Hutchinson assembled

[1] Hook, *Life of Sir David Baird*, I, pp. 289–386. According to Wilson only one drummer boy was lost.

sixteen thousand men for the siege of the French under Menou in Alexandria in August. With its fall French dominion in Egypt vanished.

Major-General Baird's troops were encamped near Rosetta on the 4th of September, 1801, and the Eighth then consisted of one captain, two lieutenants, one ensign, one quartermaster, one assistant surgeon, four sergeants, one drummer, and sixty-four privates.[1] On the 4th of September, 1801, Baird wrote to Lord Hobart from Rosetta:

On the 9th of July I had the honour of addressing The Right Honourable Mr Secretary Dundas, from Kennè in Upper Egypt, and of reporting that I was arrived there, with the advance of my army, waiting to know from Sir John Hutchinson if their services would be required in Egypt. On the 15th of that month, I had the honour of a letter from the General, acquainting me that as long as the French held the only harbour and the strongest position in the country, and that preparations to reinforce them were making in all parts, he could not consider Egypt as secured, or himself at liberty to dispense with the services of such a reinforcement. I determined in consequence to advance, and the remainder of my force was immediately ordered to cross the desert.

From the previous march of the large detachment with me, I was well aware of the difficulties to be encountered, but was better prepared to obviate them. The want of water, by great exertions, was no longer to be apprehended. Depots of wines, fresh provisions, and nourishment of different kinds, were formed at intermediate stations, and the men taken ill, or too weak to be removed, were conveyed to the next station, and there received medical assistance, until they were enabled to proceed. By these means the arduous undertaking was accomplished with little loss, the army was embarked, and sent down the Nile to Cairo, and on the 23rd of August the whole was assembled there. After leaving provisions in Coseir, on the desert at Kennè, at Giza near Cairo, and at Daimetta, the remainder of the corps reached this place on the 31st ultimo, on their route to Alexandria, but were halted by Sir John Hutchinson's orders, in consequence of the capitulation of

---

[1] *W.O.*, 1/345, f. 409.

that garrison.   As Sir John Hutchinson sends his despatches immediately home, I have not had time to be fully acquainted with his in-
tentions, respecting this army.   He has been pleased, however, to
inform me, that he is directed to leave us in Egypt, till orders respecting
us are received from home, and that he shall furnish me with instruments
for my guidance.

By the next conveyance I hope to have the honour of writing more
fully to your Lordship on that subject.   At present I must confine
myself to observe that having accompanied the troops that took possession of the French lines at Alexandria, I find them so extensive that
it will require a much larger force than I possess to occupy them.

I have the pleasure to report that the army under my orders is in
every respect fit for immediate and active service, and have the honour
to endorse a return of them.[1]

From this return it appears that Baird had 2271 British soldiers
fit and 773 sick.   Of these the Eighth numbered seventy-five.
He had also 2065 native soldiers.

A fresh field for Baird's men obviously lay before them.   Baird
wrote to Lieutenant-General Fox, the Commander-in-Chief, on the
10th of November, 1801 :

The army from India will be ordered to return with the least possible
delay.   The season for leaving the Red Sea generally commences in
March.   The route by Suez is I fear impracticable.   We must consequently go by way of Cosseir, a march of nearly 700 miles.   I have
experience to make me believe the whole of the army could not reach
their port of embarkation in less than three months.   Your Excellency
must be (aw)are therefore no time (is) to be lost in preparing for a
movement of so arduous and tedious a nature.   The enormous expense
(upwards of £40,000 sterling monthly) incurred by the East India
Company from the number of shipping necessarily retained in the
Red Sea for the re-embarking of this army is a consideration which
must weigh much with the Government and hasten our departure from
this country. . . .

We would thereby escape the Plague season which seldom is known,
even so high as Gorgi Genah, our place of general rendezvous (before

---

[1] *W.O.*, 1/345, f. 401.

crossing the desert) is about 130 miles further up the river. We have already lost several men and native followers by this destructive malady, and the months are fast approaching when it begins to rage in the Delta and Lower Egypt.[1]

For their services in Egypt the regiment received £52 as prize money[2], and they were to receive for their services in the Deccan no less a sum than over £1114.[3]

On their departure from Egypt, according to Smet, "the troop of the 8th Dragoons was as numerous as a squadron of the corps sent from England; that their horses which they had received from the Mamelukes were very superior to those furnished by the Turks to the corps who had landed from the Mediterranean, and that the dragoons dressed in French grey (the 8th) were no less distinguished thereby from those dressed in blue, than they were by their robust make, their clean appointments, and their steady conduct."[4] The men ascended the Nile, traversed the miles dreaded both by Baird and themselves and embarked for India at Suez on the 4th of June, 1802, bringing with them one hundred and fifty Arab horses which the East India Company had purchased. Grave as the hardships of the journey by land had been, graver still were those of the journey by sea. The weather was so untoward that two-thirds of the horses perished, and the men themselves suffered severely. On arrival at Madras the troop landed with fifty-one horses. From Madras the men passed on to Vellore, where their duty was to watch the sons of Tippu Sultan, who were residing in that fortress. There they remained till 1804, when they joined the body of the corps which had landed at Bengal from the Cape the year before. Three hundred and nine had embarked on the 11th of October, 1802, at the Cape for India. These consisted of one field officer, one captain, six subalterns, one surgeon, one veterinary surgeon, three quartermasters, eleven sergeants, three trumpeters, twenty-two women, twenty children, and two hundred and forty rank and file.[5] The War Office wrote to Sir Robert

---

[1] *W.O.*, 1/345, f. 530.   [2] Cox's Ledgers, Vol. A.   [3] Cox's Ledgers, Vol. B.
[4] Smet, p. 83.   The hair of all ranks was dressed in a queue measuring ten inches in length below the collar. *Cf.* Fortescue, IV, Part II, p. 911.
[5] *W.O.*, 1/894; *Bengal Military Consultations*, Range XX, f. 41.

Laurie on the 14th of December, 1802, raising the establishment of the Eighth to eight troops with 690 men. A recruiting troop of 24 and an additional quartermaster were afterwards added.[1]

The foe before us was the Marathas, the great military confederation of the Hindus. Since their rise to power in the seventeenth century on the ruins of the Mughal Empire, there were few parts of India that had not felt their sway. The general centre of the community lay at Poona, and there in the course of time the military head of the confederation sank into a mere chief, dominated by the Peshwas, whose position as mayors of the palace at Poona was much the same as that of the masters of the French Merovingians. Pitt, aware of the Napoleonic schemes for the extension of French dominion in India, realised that the best protection of our interests in the Orient lay in a series of brilliant conquests; and he determined on a forward policy. The agent he selected for this policy was Richard Colley, Baron Wellesley, who became Governor-General of India in 1798. He was a man who required large spaces for the unfolding of his plans. "You are dying of cramp," Addington once observed to him, when no opening appeared for his abilities in Europe. Wellesley's affections ran in a narrow channel, yet they ran all the more deeply on this account. As Clive's thoughts in his years of exile had turned to Manchester, as Hastings's thoughts had longed for Daylesford, so Wellesley's turned to his old school on the far-distant banks of the Thames. Sixty years of strenuous life in Asia and in England could not abate the strength of his feeling; and at his death, in 1842, he directed that he should be buried in the same Eton College chapel in which he had worshipped as a schoolboy. Calm, cool, and cold he pursued his forward policy throughout the years of his great career in the East. French influence was paramount in Europe through the splendid genius of Napoleon, and this influence was once more growing in India, basking in the light of this luminary. If the first and last attempt at Asiatic conquest on the part of Napoleon had been the abortive conquest of Egypt, yet the project of an expedition against British India was never out

[1] *East India Letter Book*, No. 7, f. 416.

of his mind.   Repeatedly he set out that his mission was that of "hunting the English out of all their Eastern possessions and cutting the Isthmus of Suez."   Naturally men like Wellesley watched with acute alarm the intrigues of Napoleon with the Marathas and the Sultan of Mysore, and the recruitment of French officers for the armies of those States.   Napoleon eagerly welcomed any opportunity of harassing the English in India, and also of resuscitating his favourite schemes of Asiatic conquest.

Wellesley had secured Mysore, Hyderabad, and Oudh from the sphere of French control, yet the Maratha States still remained under such influence.   The three leading Maratha chiefs were contending for supremacy.   If these three, Sindia, Holkar, and the Raja of Nagpore, persisted in this contention, surely Wellesley should offer his protection to the nominal head of the confederation, the Peshwa.   In 1803 Wellesley defined the situation thus: "To fix the peace of India on foundations of the utmost stability, and to preclude the intrusion of the French, it is necessary only that the British government should draw the Maratha powers under its protection."   As he had dealt with the Mohammedan rulers successfully, so would he deal with the Maratha rulers.

Baji Rao, the Peshwa, was threatened by Sindia, the most powerful of the Maratha chiefs,[1] and his adhesion to Wellesley's proposals would be of little advantage to him.   Indeed he would simply exchange one master for another.   Deeply to Wellesley's disgust, he refused the proffered treaty.   There was, however, a bitter feud between Baji Rao and Jeswant Rao Holkar, whose brother he had cruelly executed, and who marched on his capital. Sindia came to the Peshwa's assistance, but, after a desperate cavalry charge, Holkar won the day.   Flying for his life, the Peshwa was forced to crave our assistance.   The price exacted was the Treaty of Bassein, 1802, and by it he signed a general defensive alliance with Wellesley, under which he ceded districts yielding a revenue equivalent to the cost of a strong subsidiary force, to be permanently stationed in his territory; and all the Peshwa's foreign relations were to be subordinated to the policy of England.

---

[1] Mr. Boulger terms him the Murat of the Marathas.   *Cf. The Army Quarterly*, Vol. 5, p. 83.

Though neither Sindia nor Holkar would have anything to do with this treaty, nevertheless it formed the foundation of all our future dealings with the Marathas. Castlereagh, taken aback by this treaty, warned Wellesley against the dangers of interference with the turbulent Marathas. Wellesley took the line that the influence of the French was still to be feared, an argument of weighty import to a ministry engaged in that direct conflict with Napoleon which the Marathas were indirectly supporting.

The combination set on foot by Wellesley was met by a counter combination on the part of Sindia. He sought to form an alliance among the Marathas, securing the adherence of the Maratha chief of Nagpore, commonly called the Raja of Berar, who possessed wide influence over all the other leaders. Though Holkar agreed to a truce with Sindia, he refused to join him, and so did the Gaekwar of Baroda. It was a critical moment for Wellesley. The rupture of the Treaty of Amiens was imminent, and a French squadron was refitting at Brest for the East Indies. Fearing that Poona might be burnt down in the absence of the Peshwa, Arthur Wellesley hurried by forced marches through a wild and difficult mountainous country, at the last accomplishing sixty miles in thirty-two hours. He occupied the Maratha capital without opposition. An ultimatum was sent to Sindia, but he temporised. "After my interview with the Raja (of Berar) you shall be informed," such was the word he sent, "whether it will be peace or war." Henceforth war was inevitable.

The great moment for which the statesman in Wellesley had longed had at length arrived. Politically, he hoped to destroy the power of the Marathas over the Mughal at Delhi, and to bring him under British protection; and, in addition, he expected to expand his general scheme of tributary alliances. Militarily, in order to accomplish this, it was indispensable to conquer all those dominions between the Jumna and the Ganges which acknowledged Sindia; to root out the French force by which that district was protected; and to extend the East India Company's jurisdiction to the Jumna, including Delhi and Agra and a chain of forts in that region. At Delhi Monsieur Perron, one of Sindia's ablest

French officers, commanded a large body of regular troops, with which he held the fortress, keeping the Emperor Shah Alam in custody, and exercising authority in his name. This was the army Lord Wellesley dreaded, for it was well officered by Frenchmen who had trained the Marathas most ably.

Under Arthur Wellesley and Gerard Lake the war began in July, 1803, and in it the Eighth acquired their first battle honour.[1] John Sullivan Wood was its lieutenant-colonel, and he was appointed on the 16th of June, 1803. It had been stationed at Ghazepore, proceeding in July, 1803, towards Cawnpore, where Lake had collected the main body of the Bengal army. Lake was entrusted with the army of the north, just as Sir Arthur Wellesley was entrusted with the army of the south. Assaye was fought in September, 1803, to be followed by Laswari in November. The main army was under Lake, and it was the most powerful in point of numbers. The First Infantry Division was under Major-General Ware, and the Second under Major-General St. John, with the Cavalry Division under Colonel Vandeleur[2] of the Eighth, who commanded the First Brigade, consisting of the 8th Light Dragoons and the 1st and 3rd Bengal Cavalry. The Second Brigade was under Colonel St. Leger, consisting of the 27th Light Dragoons, the 2nd and 6th Bengal Cavalry; and the Third Brigade under Colonel Macan, consisting of the 29th Light Dragoons and the 4th Bengal Cavalry. The bulk of the artillery was distributed among units, two light, or galloper, guns being attached to each cavalry regiment, while each brigade of infantry had also a proportion of guns. The total of the whole of Lake's army amounted to 10,000.

What was the size of the Maratha army? According to Thorn, Sindia had about 40,000 regular troops, with 450 guns, and an immense number of irregulars. The French had looked after his artillery with considerable efficiency. The regular infantry, though

---

[1] Laswari, as a battle honour, has been awarded to the Eighth Hussars, the West Riding Regiment, 2nd Queen's Own Light Infantry, the 1st Brahmins, and the 4th Rajputs. *Cf.* that useful book, C. B. Norman, *Battle Honours of the British Army*, p. 150.

[2] The Mess possesses Vandeleur's *Duty of Officers Commanding Detachments in the Field*, London, 1801.

nominally Maratha, was really from Oudh, the Doab, and Rohilkhand. According to the high authority of Grant-Duff, the united armies of Sindia and the Raja of Berar totalled about 100,000 men, of whom 50,000 were horse, and about 30,000 were regular infantry and artillery. Those were the days when frontal attacks were delivered in close column, when there were point-blank volleys from Brown Bess, which barely carried straight up to one hundred yards, when the heaviest field-gun was a nine-pounder, and when the field batteries, of which there were far too few with our forces, were occasionally "horsed" by teams of oxen.

The Nabob Wazir of Oudh had furnished the Royal Irish Dragoons with white horses, and it had advanced from Cawnpore to join the army under General Lake. The commanding officer, Colonel Thomas Pakenham Vandeleur, obtained possession of the city of Muttra, which he garrisoned with his own regiment, the 29th Dragoons, the 1st and 4th Bengal Cavalry, with three battalions and nine companies of native infantry. On the 2nd of October Lake arrived with the main body. The next day Lake advanced to Agra. His work was to defeat that portion of the disciplined army created for Sindia by Count de Boigne and General Perron. In a word, he was to bring into subjection the region styled by Lord Wellesley as "the French state" *par excellence.* When De Boigne left in 1795, Perron efficiently took his place, and Perron was Commander-in-Chief of Sindia's army, and he was also the uncrowned king of the dominions of the King of Delhi. The base of his force was the strongly fortified cities of Delhi and Agra, and his arsenal lay in the great fortress of Aligarh.

Lake thought that no movement on Delhi was safe so long as Aligarh and Perron's regular army lay between himself and Allahabad. True, there was the risk, acutely noted by Lord Wellesley, that Sindia might slip past and raid the East India Company's territory. Still, some risk must be taken, and Lake was brilliantly to justify his boldness. Rough-and-ready in his methods, he displayed his surpassing powers in action, thinking more coolly on the battlefield than anywhere else. Utterly different from Abercromby, Lake could say, "Damn your writing—mind your fighting." Yet if he had this foible, he was as strict a disciplinarian as Charles Grey of the Eighth, Ralph Abercromby, Charles Stuart, John Moore, and Thomas Maitland. Like all these men, he shared their care for the comfort of the soldier. Lake was ever watchful of the health and the wants of his troops, and his popularity with them depended on this, not on fair words nor even on affable condescension. Nor did his acquaintance with his officers end on parade. He hunted with them, and in hunting with them he grew to know them as he never would have done in formal inspections. The hospitality dispensed by his four beautiful daughters also assisted in this knowledge. Fifty-eight as he was, Lake was as hard a rider as any officer of the Eighth could possibly desire. The commander headed every charge in manœuvre, as he headed every charge in war, and his popularity with the Light Dragoons was unbounded. He was a man indeed after their own heart.

The campaign opened with a simultaneous advance of four armies, Lake moving on Aligarh, Sir Arthur Wellesley on Ahmadnagar, Stevenson on Baroach, and Harcourt on Balasore. On the 3rd of September Lake stormed and carried the fortress of Aligarh. Perron offered a stout resistance at Aligarh, but the fortress with 280 guns and Perron all fell into the hands of Lake. Perron observed that the treachery and ingratitude of his own officers, as well as that of the Marathas, convinced him that further resistance to the British arms was hopeless, and indeed from the day of Dupleix nothing is more remarkable on the French side than the disloyalty of subordinates to their superior officer. Lake continued his march, steadily onwards. With the way now clear Lake pursued his march to Agra. The siege of the fortress was begun, and working parties were supplied by the Eighth, the Twenty-seventh, and the Twenty-ninth Light Dragoons. Agra, known to the natives as the key of Hindustan, fell, and keen was the rejoicing of Lord Wellesley, whose praise of Lake's matchless energy was unbounded.[1] The successes of the Commander secured

[1] Thorn, *Wellesley Despatches*, III, pp. 393–6, 407. *Cf.* p. 415.

the navigation of the Jumna, and by forced marches of the army he hastened in pursuit of the main body of the Mahratas. Weakened as he was by the actions he had fought, Lake resolved to push on with the remains of the 76th and the three cavalry brigades trained under his own eager eye.

The march of the 31st of October, 1803, brought our army close to the small town of Khatumbar but a few hours after the Marathas had left it. Leaving the camp at midnight, the cavalry rode on with haste and without rest, covering twenty-five miles in the darkness in six hours. They struck the retreating Maratha army near the village of Laswari about sunrise on the morning of the 1st of November.[1] The advance guard of the Eighth, commanded by Lieutenant Thomas Lindon, perceived the retreat of the enemy. At bay, Abaji, the commander, rested his force on the villages of Laswari and Malpur, in which he placed a number of guns.[2] His line of battle lay with its right at Laswari, with a small stream of the Barakri in its rear. Above this village the stream of the Barakri was dammed, and Abaji cut this dam with the object of flooding the slightly lower ground over which our cavalry would have to advance to attack the foe.

In his anxiety to force a battle, Lake ordered his advance guard and the 3rd Cavalry Brigade to cross the newly-created swamp forthwith. This flank movement was designed to clear the ground for the 1st Cavalry Brigade, ordered to attack the village of Laswari, and the right of the infantry. The inundation prevented at first the rapid progress of the advance guard, composed of one squadron of the Eighth, commanded by Major Griffiths of the 29th Light Dragoons, and the 1st Brigade, composed of the remainder of the Eighth with the 1st and 3rd Native Cavalry. With all these troops under him, Colonel Vandeleur advanced most rapidly. The skirmishers of the Eighth received a lively welcome from the

---

[1] Cf. Add. MSS., 23618, with a beautifully coloured plan of the Battle of Laswari, executed by or under the inspection of Lt.-Col. C. Hamilton Smith, July 22, 1830. Cf. the East India Military Calendar, I, p. 60. Cf. Thorn, p. 210 ff.; Notes of the Principal Transactions, p. 93; Wellesley Despatches, III, pp. 439–47, 449; Fortescue, V, pp. 59–67.

[2] Grant Duff, History of the Mahrattas, III, p. 179, for the number of the enemy. Contrast Wellesley Despatches, III, p. 450.

artillery. Lieutenant Lindon received a grape-shot in the knee and died within twenty-four hours. Lieutenant Willard, who succeeded Lindon, had his arm carried away by a grape-shot while he was in the very act of encouraging his men. Cornet Burrowes was severely wounded in the face and head. He indeed received his wound while engaged in single combat with an officer of the French artillery, captured during the day.[1] Three times this advance guard, consisting mainly of Captain Peter Abercromby's troop, was repulsed, and three times it was reinforced, returning gallantly to meet the foe.

The Eighth were mounted on grey Arabs, while their Colonel Vandeleur rode a favourite black charger, being thus as much singled out as a mark for a bullet as Nelson's decorations at Trafalgar singled him out.[2] Just before ordering the charge, he turned to address a few words to the men of his own regiment, appealing to them to bring honour to their standards, pointing to the harp and crown with which they were emblazoned. As he was about to take his place in front, he fell shot through the heart by a French artilleryman. The command of the regiment devolved on Major John Ormsby Vandeleur, and of the 1st Brigade on Lieutenant-Colonel Gordon. The Eighth, the Twenty-seventh and Twenty-ninth Dragoons, with the native cavalry, forced the flank of the enemy, but forced it at heavy cost. The Maratha artillerymen held their fire until our cavalry had arrived within twenty yards of the muzzles of their guns : then their effect was devastating. Meanwhile the 3rd Brigade distinguished itself in its attack on the right flank of the Marathas. Here too the fire was so galling that Lake commanded the brigade to retire, and gave a similar command to the 1st Brigade. This gave the Eighth time to re-form their broken ranks and to take some rest and scanty refreshment.

Napoleon never longed more anxiously for night or Grouchy than Lake longed to see the arrival of his infantry. From three

[1] *Cf. Narrative of the Battle of Leswaree*, by the late James Alexander Ure, Esq., Surgeon of the 62nd Regiment, and formerly Assistant-Surgeon of the 8th Hussars.

[2] According to Ure, Vandeleur's " horse kept his place with the regiment, and afterwards became the property of Cornet Burrowes, who took great care of him until the regiment left India, when he was shot, that he might not fall into unworthy hands."

in the morning they had been marching to cover the twenty-four miles that lay between them and the battlefield by eleven o'clock. Altogether they had covered sixty-five miles in forty-eight hours, a feat which rivals that so extolled by Napier at Talavera. The infantry attacked the Maratha right with vigour, supported by the 3rd Cavalry Brigade with the 1st and 2nd Cavalry Brigades in reserve. In spite of the heavy artillery fire, the infantry persisted in their advance. The Maratha cavalry charged, and did so feebly. The 76th particularly distinguished itself, repelling the determined onset of the enemy. Our cavalry now dashed forward, and at last the victory of Laswari was gained.[1] The army created by De Boigne and Perron lay defeated but not disgraced. No less than seven thousand of their men perished. Our killed and wounded were 822 out of our force of 8000 men. The casualties among regiments still borne on the Army List are:

Regiments.		Officers.		Men.	
		K.	W.	K.	W.
8th Light Dragoons ..	..	2	2[2]	16	34
76th West Riding Regiment		2	4	41	165
2nd Q.O. Light Infantry	..	1	1	11	26
Bengal Artillery	..	—	—	7	6
1st Brahmins	..	—	—	4	12
4th Rajputs	..	—	1	17	69

The Eighth mourned the loss of Lieutenant-Colonel Vandeleur, Captain George Story, sixteen rank and file, and one hundred and sixteen horses, while Lieutenant Lindon ultimately died of his wounds. Lieutenant Willard and Cornet Burrowes were also wounded. Lake's horse, "Old Port," the gift of Lord Wellesley, fell dead under him.[3] His son George at once offered his own charger. At first the father refused the gift, and at last reluctantly consented. He deplored the death of Vandeleur, whom he described as "a most valued officer." Lord Wellesley noted that

[1] *I.O., Home Series, Miscellaneous*, 485.

[2] There were three officers wounded.

[3] H. Pearse, *Life and Military Services of Viscount Lake*, pp. 255–6; *Wellesley Despatches*, III, p. 458.

"Colonel Vandeleur, who had manifested the greatest skill, judgment and gallantry, was killed in this charge. During his command . . . this brave and accomplished officer displayed considerable zeal and ability, and by his judicious movements compelled the enemy to make a precipitate retreat from the British territories. His death was universally deplored, and may justly be deemed a public loss."

The outcome of the Battles of Assaye and Laswari was to shatter to the very foundations the whole military organization built up by Sindia in conjunction with De Boigne and Perron. At the beginning of this second Maratha War Sindia had at least forty thousand highly disciplined men and a very large train of artillery, acting entirely under the control of a French commander, supported by the revenues of the finest provinces in India. Militarily, Sindia ceased to count for the simple reason that his army ceased to exist. His connection with the Mughal Court, his place as the most formidable member of the Maratha confederacy, nay, his very possessions—all were threatened with extinction. The Raja of Nagpore and himself were obliged to recognise the Treaty of Bassein and all that this treaty implied. Sindia had been tried in the balance, and had been found wanting.

The Royal Irish Light Dragoons returned to Cawnpore. Two of the Maratha chiefs, Sindia and the Raja of Nagpore, had submitted. Holkar, however, stood out. He hoped to take advantage of the discomfiture of Sindia, his rival and his enemy. He had been living at free quarters in Rajputana, and had put to death three English officers in his service who refused to act against their countrymen. Lake commanded Holkar to retire within his own country, but he evinced every sign of resorting to the traditional Maratha tactics of rapid cavalry movements, systematic pillaging, and sudden harassing incursions.[1] Sir Arthur Wellesley began the process of the reduction of the strong fortress of Chandore and the other possessions of Holkar, and the Eighth were also engaged against him. On the 2nd of October, 1804, the regiment left Cawnpore, and proceeded to Agra. At Secundra the Eighth

---

[1] *Wellington Despatches*, II, pp. 518–9.

were brigaded with the Second and Third Native Cavalry, under the command of Lieutenant-Colonel John Vandeleur of the Eighth.

Colonel Monson advanced against Holkar into central India, and Holkar drew him on by a pretended retreat, until Monson found himself face to face with a very superior force and with only two days' supplies. Attempting to retreat, Holkar turned upon Monson, and practically destroyed the whole of his force. On the approach of Lake to Delhi, Holkar's bands no doubt withdrew, but after the crushing defeat inflicted upon Monson they could well afford to do so. For eighteen days our men continued in pursuit, covering four hundred miles amid heat and privation with patience and perseverance. On the 17th of November the British dragoons approached the Maratha camp under the walls of Farakhabad.[1] Holkar and his men were sleeping, and were aroused from their slumbers by the shouts of the Royal Irish Light Dragoons. Holkar fled for his life, and his soldiers scattered in all directions for over ten miles. Thorn, who was present, says that many Marathas, whose horses were more exhausted than those of our cavalry, climbed for safety into the mango-trees. There they opened fire with their matchlocks on the rear squadrons of the dragoons as they rode up. They were discovered and pistolled,[2] and numbers of them tumbled lifeless from the trees. A small party of the regiment rode into the very middle of a crowd of Allygole musketeers, cutting them to pieces. The slaughter was absolutely appalling, and no less than three thousand of the foe were slain. Thorn calculated that by the time they had ridden back into camp at Farakhabad, the dragoons had covered considerably over seventy miles in twenty-four hours—an effort, as he believes, "probably unparalleled in the annals of military history, especially when it is remembered that it was made after a long and harassing march of 350 miles in the space of a fortnight."[3]

[1] *I.O., Home Series, Miscellaneous,* 626.

[2] Fortescue records this as the only instance where pistols proved useful to dragoons, V, p. 99.

[3] *Cf.* Major W. Thorn, *Memoirs of the War in India.* See *The Cavalry Journal,* II, p. 162, for G. F. MacMunn's article on General Lake's pursuit of Holkar.

The alarm of Holkar had been complete, and the work begun by such battles as those of Assaye and Laswari was continued by such surprises as that under the walls of Farakhabad. In his public despatch Lord Lake stated: "Lieutenant-Colonel Vandeleur (of the Eighth), who commanded the first brigade of cavalry, brought his corps into action with the utmost rapidity, and displayed the greatest judgment and gallantry in his repeated and vigorous charges of the enemy. His Majesty's Eighth Regiment of light dragoons, commanded by Captain Abercromby, and the first and sixth regiments of native cavalry, the former commanded by Captain Welsh and the latter by Captain Swinton, charged through the different bodies of the enemy's horse, with the greatest resolution and effect. A small party of the Eighth light dragoons totally destroyed a considerable body of Allygole infantry, which formed part of the enemy's force." The loss of the regiment on the last occasion was two men and eight horses killed; thirteen men and eleven horses wounded; and eight horses missing. Apart from the killed and wounded, the surprise cost Holkar no less than thirty thousand men. As rats desert the sinking ship, so the Marathas deserted their chief.

The British army halted two days at Fatehgarh to rest after their exertions, marching after their rest to Dig, the fortress to which the remnant of the Marathas and Holkar had retired. On the morning of the 23rd of December the breach was declared practicable, and Dig was carried after a brisk assault. Lord Lake expressed his thanks to the cavalry for the welcome aid rendered in the carrying on of the works against the fortress. He told Lord Wellesley on the 23rd of December, 1804: "Your Lordship will, I am confident, receive much pleasure in learning the highly exemplary conduct of the Three Corps of British Cavalry in Camp, the whole of whom volunteered their Services, as working Parties for the Trenches and Batteries, and assisted very materially in accelerating our Operations against this place; they have received my sincere Thanks for their exertions, and for a zeal so honourable to the British character."[1]   Yet the price the Eighth paid for their

[1] *I.O., Home Series, Miscellaneous*, 626.

share is evident, in some measure, in the return of the effective strength of the regiment on the 1st of December. There were 341 present for duty, but there were 198 sick. Thirty-one were wanting to complete the establishment.[1]

While the regiment was actively employed in India, Sir Robert Laurie died, and his place was taken by Lieutenant-General Sir John Floyd, Bart., of the 23rd Light Dragoons, on the 13th of September, 1804. Entering the army at the age of twelve as a cornet in Eliott's Light Horse, now the 15th Hussars, Floyd is said to have received his commission without purchase, as some recognition of the gallantry of his father, who was killed in Germany during the Seven Years' War. Floyd was made riding master to this regiment, and his skill in this capacity brought him under the notice of the authorities. General Eliott, afterwards Lord Heathfield, the heroic defender of Gibraltar, spoke cordially of his abilities, and he was lent to the 1st Dragoons, the Royals, in order to improve their riding. Under the patronage of Eliott, Floyd, without purchase, was promoted captain-lieutenant in 1770, captain in 1772, in the 15th Hussars, and major in 1779 in the newly-raised 21st Light Dragoons. In 1781 it was determined to raise a cavalry regiment expressly for service in India, and Floyd was gazetted lieutenant of this new regiment, the 23rd, and then the 19th Light Dragoons. He reached Madras in 1782, and in this year he was gazetted local colonel in the East Indies, and remained in that presidency for eighteen years. A competent authority pronounced that he then showed himself the most accomplished cavalry commander who ever served in the south of India.

In 1790 Floyd was promoted colonel, and that year Lord Cornwallis appointed him to command all the cavalry upon the Coromandel coast. In the three campaigns against Tippu Sultan he greatly distinguished himself. Before Lord Cornwallis assumed the command in person, he did his outstanding deed. In July, 1790, he had occupied Coimbatore with the van of the army, and, after leaving headquarters there, he established himself at Satyamangalam with a detachment of the 30th regiment and some of his

---

[1] *C.O.*, 77/33.

own troopers of the 19th Light Dragoons. Despite the overwhelming strength of the enemy's cavalry, he retreated in quite
good order. Cornwallis was so satisfied with this performance
that he gave Floyd the command of the vanguard. He was
wounded during the siege of Bangalore in March, 1791, distinguished himself on the left wing in the Battle of Arikera in May,
1791, and served in the general action in May, 1792, the action
that forced Tippu Sultan to sue for peace. At the capture of
Bangalore in 1793, he served as second in command to Colonel
Braithwaite, and was promoted major-general the following year.
On the renewal of the war with Tippu Sultan he again commanded
the cavalry, serving as second in command to General Harris.
He led the advance of the army into Mysore, and the charges of
his cavalry did not a little to win the Battle of Malavalli. At the
siege of Seringapatam it was the task of Floyd to command the
covering army, and this task he performed with all his ability.
The wealth he acquired from the booty of Seringapatam combined
with his savings in his lucrative employments enabled him to
retire from India. On arrival home he was received with great
distinction, was appointed colonel of the 23rd Light Dragoons in
1800, and was promoted lieutenant-general the following year.
He never saw active service again. Spending some years on the
staff in Ireland, he commanded the Limerick division from 1803
to 1806, and the Cork division from 1809 to 1812. Transferred
to the colonelcy of the Eighth in 1804, he was promoted general
in 1812, and next year received the honourable but sinecure post
of governor of Gravesend and Tilbury. In 1816 he was created
baronet, given a special crest of a lion rampant, bearing the standard
of Tippu Sultan in its paws.

Sir John Floyd came to the regiment when it was covering itself
with glory in the East. The reduction of Dig left Holkar in
parlous plight. Yet then his fortunes began for a time to amend.
For the Raja of Bhartpur, Ranjit Singh, to whom Dig belonged,
espoused his cause. He had concluded a treaty with the Government by which the possession of his territories had been guaranteed
to him. He had afterwards received other lands nearly equal in

value to one-third of his original possessions. Employing the discretionary powers entrusted to him by Lord Wellesley, Lake commenced immediate operations against the Raja by laying siege to Bhartpur. It was the business of the Eighth to cover the operations of this siege and to escort the convoys of provisions and military stores, and this they did in a manner that must have given pleasure to Sir John Floyd.

On the 18th of January, 1805, Major-General Smith joined Lake before Bhartpur. Amir Khan was harassing our camp with his cavalry, and Smith was detached with troops, including the Eighth, to set out in pursuit of him.[1] Amir Khan and his men marched towards Rohilkhand, of which he himself was a native. Smith followed him with three regiments of dragoons, three regiments of native cavalry, and a division of horse artillery. At Moradabad Amir Khan inflicted injury, but, fearing that his retreat might be cut off, he retraced his steps.[2] He was, however, intercepted, and brought to action on the 2nd of March at the foot of the high hills of Afzulgerh. The Twenty-seventh and Twenty-ninth Dragoons formed line, supported by the Eighth and the Sixth Bengal Cavalry. A nullah arrested the charge of the cavalry, and a body of Allygoles, concealed in the nullah, sprang forth, and attacked our men as warmly as Sindia's men had ever done. At this moment Captain George Deare, with the rear squadron of the Eighth, fell upon the right flank of the Allygoles, driving them off with the sternest determination. A simultaneous charge of the Twenty-seventh completed the triumph, and Amir Khan's horsemen fled in the utmost dismay. The fire of the galloper guns proved signally effective. Our loss was not more than forty killed and wounded, while the Amir Khan's force was severely punished. Abandoning Rohilkhand, Amir Khan recrossed the Ganges, making his way to Bhartpur. Major-General Smith followed him in close pursuit to Bhartpur, rejoining the army there on the 23rd of March, after a chase of over seven hundred miles in forty-four days. Above thirty of the enemy's colours fell into our hands, and among the number were two golden

[1] *I.O., Home Series, Miscellaneous,* 626.   [2] *I.O., Home Series, Miscellaneous,* 626.

standards which were carried by the Yekus, a number of chosen men who formed the body-guard of Amir Khan.[1]

Lord Lake was by no means impressed with the worth of the artillery he was forced to employ at the siege of Bhartpur.[2] Holkar, however, was so deeply impressed that he offered a lakh of rupees (£12,000) to any portion of his troops that would capture one of the guns. In the early hours of the 2nd of March, 1805, at Afzulgerh, a body of Marathas tried to surprise Captain Clement Browne's troop on the line of march. On one flank of the guns were the Royal Irish and on the other Skinner's irregular Horse. The moment he realised the situation, Captain Deare, who commanded the rear squadron of his regiment, gave the command, "Threes about,—gallop." Skinner did likewise, and the squadrons arrived in the nick of time to find the Allygoles cutting down the artillery-men, who barely had time to unlimber. The Eighth and Skinner's Horse did their work so well that the Marathas retired without the guns.

Alarmed by the activities of Major-General Smith and his men, the Raja of Bhartpur seized the opportunity of Lake's elevation to the peerage to offer his congratulations and to hint at negotiations. During the discussion of the terms, Lake, giving the cavalry a few days' rest, set out at their head in order to meet Raja Holkar as his means of bringing the negotiations to a straight issue. The dragoons rode quickly, yet Holkar, awake to the significance of this, also rode even more quickly, and on the 29th of March he succeeded in getting away. In the pursuit Holkar lost about two hundred men, together with elephants, camels, horses, and his camp. He then removed his headquarters a considerable distance south-west of Bhartpur, near Futtypore, where he deemed himself secure. The pursuit still continued briskly, and, guided by his camp fires, Lake effected a night march with much success. The re-numbered 24th and 25th Dragoons appeared under their new designation of the 27th and the 28th. They charged the demoralised troops of Holkar while the Eighth and the Second

---

[1] *I.O., Home Series, Miscellaneous*, 626.
[2] *The East India Military Calendar*, II, p. 224.

Native Cavalry charged the division of Amir Khan. The losses of the enemy were estimated at a thousand killed.

At last these warlike efforts persuaded the Raja of Bhartpur, Ranjit Singh, that success was not destined to crown his arms, and he signed the preliminaries of a treaty on the 10th of April. Bhartpur remained in the possession of Ranjit Singh, but we retained Dig until assured of the loyalty of the Raja, who pledged himself to hold no communication with the enemies of Great Britain and to employ no European in his service without the sanction of the Government. He also agreed to pay an indemnity of twenty lakhs of rupees. The tide of failure for Napoleon had not yet begun to flow in Europe, for the Battle of Trafalgar lay hidden in the womb of time.[1] He had transformed the Cisalpine Republic into a monarchy, and had crowned himself King of Italy in Milan. He was to incorporate the Ligurian Republic into France in June, and he was to win the dazzling victory of Austerlitz in December, 1805. Just as the sieges of Derry and Enniskillen, the Battles of the Boyne and Aughrim wrecked the carefully-calculated plans of Louis XIV, so men like Sir Arthur Wellesley and Lord Lake were wrecking the equally carefully-calculated plans of Napoleon. For the treaty signed by the Raja of Bhartpur marked the fall of " the French state," as Lord Wellesley termed it, in India. What the ancestors of the Eighth had executed in Ireland their descendants were executing in India. Fundamentally, France was the enemy, whether the Frenchman was called Louis XIV or Napoleon. Sir John Floyd had been the best cavalry commander who had served in the south of India, and he could reflect with pride that his spirit was to be found in his own regiment.

The British force had spent three months and twenty days lying before Bhartpur, and on the 21st of April they left it behind

---

[1] Sir John Floyd wrote to Lord Hardwicke, November 8, 1805, " I beg Leave to offer your Lordship my most cordial Congratulations on the Glorious Victory of the Glorious Nelson—greatest and happiest in his last Moments.

" I am infinitely obliged to your Excellency for your Goodness in communicating this great Event yourself.

" The Guns shall be fired conformably to your Excellency's desire, and the Intelligence shall be communicated to the Generals of Districts." *Add. MSS.*, 35763.

them. With the other cavalry the Royal Irish marched to Agra, taking up their quarters at the tomb of Akbar, at Secundra, seven miles from Agra. Apart from the long march from Cawnpore to Delhi, the cavalry had ridden five hundred miles in pursuit of Holkar, and seven hundred in pursuit of Amir Khan—records that testify eloquently to the exertions of the Eighth.

The loss of the fort and the armies of Bhartpur naturally removed the base for operations against the territories of the East India Company from Holkar. The immense host with which he had set out in the campaign of 1804 was now reduced to 13,000 men with 30 worn-out guns. Yet the fact that Lake had negotiated a peace with Ranjit Singh struck Sindia that the British raj was not all that it had been. Lake no doubt had won, but he had won through the magnificent manner in which his cavalry and infantry had invariably supported him. His artillery, however, was weak, and Sindia thought that the run of such miraculous success could not last much longer. He had written to the Raja of Bhartpur, exhorting him to hold out, and he had held out in a better fashion than some had expected. Even if he had given up Bhartpur, he had given it up by treaty, not by loss in battle or by the breaching of the walls of this fortress. If Ranjit Singh had signed peace, he might repudiate his signature. Sindia sounded Holkar also on the possibility of renewing the Maratha confederation. There were jealousies standing in the way of a thorough understanding between Holkar and Sindia, yet the former gathered his men for a renewal of the contest. With 3000 men, including 1000 cavalry and 20 guns, Holkar proceeded to harry the territory of the East India Company.

Lake gathered his forces at once, and on the 10th of October he marched from Muttra towards Delhi, disposing the bulk of his troops for the protection of the northern portion of the Doab against Holkar's infantry and that of any of the Sikh chiefs. Lake himself pursued Holkar with two brigades of cavalry, including our regiment, and the 3rd and 5th Bengal Cavalry, Captain Brown's battery of Horse Artillery, some field-guns, and the reserve infantry brigade. Lake arrived at Delhi on the 7th of November, and at

Panipat, where the Marathas had won their first outstanding victory, on the 17th of November. A week later our force arrived at Patiala, where Ranjit Singh told Lake that he had no intention of assisting Holkar with men or money. Ludhiana, a town on the river Sutlej, was the next stage in the pursuit of Holkar. On the 6th the whole army crossed the Sutlej, and, continuing on their journey, they encamped on the south bank of the Bias, opposite Amritsar. The long-drawn war at last came to an end when Holkar signed his second treaty of peace on the 7th of January, 1806. By it he was restored to his original position, losing his temporary acquisitions. Like Sindia, he was to engage no Europeans without the consent of the British Government. The dreams of Napoleon in India were vanishing. Egypt was to have been the road to India. Nelson had turned the invasion of Egypt into a disaster, and Sir Sidney Smith and Sir Ralph Abercromby had deepened this disaster into the humiliation of an acknowledged failure. The answer to his boastful letter to Tippu had been written in the storming of Seringapatam, where the Frenchman's i's were dotted and his t's stroked in a fashion he had never anticipated. The vision of the tricolour or the imperial eagle flying in the East Indies became less and less likely when the Battles of Assaye and Laswari declared themselves not on the side of the largest battalion.

Two days after the signing of this treaty the army began to retrace its steps. The Eighth arrived at their cantonments at Secundra in April, 1806, and remained there until the January of the following year, when it proceeded to Cawnpore. In 1806 the War Office issued a list of the regulation appointments supplied by the Colonel for each man in the regiment.[1] In April, 1807, Lieutenant-Colonel Robert Rollo Gillespie exchanged to the Eighth from the 19th Light Dragoons, and a more dazzling career than his there is not in the whole annals of the regiment.[2]

[1] *W.O.*, 30/44.
[2] The Mess owns *A Memoir of Major-General Sir R. R. Gillespie, Knight Commander of the Most Honorable Order of the Bath, etc.*, Lond., 1816. *Cf. The Cavalry Journal*, VI, p. 425.

As a lad Horatio Nelson wandered away for a solitary walk, and was found in a lonely place. "Were you not afraid?" he was asked, and his reply, "No, what is fear?" Such an answer Gillespie would have understood, for he never knew what fear was. Of Ulster parentage, he was destined for law, but at once evinced his decided preference for the army. When at the Curragh he acted as second in a duel between a brother officer, Mackenzie, and Barrington, brother of Sir Jonah. Both fired, and the fire of both proved ineffective twice. Gillespie urged that the matter should end. Barrington, a notorious duellist, objected forcibly to this procedure, and abused Gillespie's regiment, denouncing them as a pack of cowards. Gillespie took up the quarrel, and, knowing his opponent's skill with the pistol, drew a handkerchief from his pocket, challenging Barrington to fight across it. They fought, each holding an end of the handkerchief in one hand, a pistol in the other, with a second pistol at their feet. They fired, and Barrington's bullet carried away the hammer of Gillespie's pistol, slightly wounding him. Quick as lightning Gillespie stooped down, and, picking up the second pistol, shot Barrington dead.

A man of diminutive stature himself, Gillespie was angry at the theatre at Cork when a man of great size declined to take off his hat during the playing of the National Anthem the night before a brigade was about to embark. Gillespie remonstrated, and, on the remonstrance proving useless, he seized his opponent's nose between his finger and his thumb, twisting it completely out of shape. Vowing vengeance, the giant left the theatre holding his injured organ carefully. His fiancée, hearing of the fashion in which the injury had been sustained, broke off her engagement. A warrant was issued for the arrest of Gillespie, but he could not be found. A soldier's wife, however, was found, carrying twins along the gangway of the trooper, and she turned out to be the resourceful Gillespie.

The story of his exploit in San Domingo made him famous throughout the British Army. As adjutant-general the republicans stood in much awe of him, and resolved to murder him. Eight desperadoes were deputed to perform the task. They broke into his quarters, murdered his slave-boy, and proceeded to go upstairs to finish Gillespie. Awakened by the tumult, he met them on the stairs with sword in hand. He killed six of his assailants, when the two others, after firing at him and wounding him, fled. The report brought the patrol to the spot, and, though the two escaped at the time, they were captured in the end. With due medical attention the hero recovered. News, however, reached Ulster that he had been assassinated, and the shock hastened his mother's death. While he was attending a levée of George III soon afterwards, the King expressed his surprise at the small man with a singularly boyish appearance. "Eh, eh, what, what," exclaimed the King, "is this the little man who killed the brigands?"

In Madras Gillespie visited the Bangalore races. During the day a tiger broke out of a menagerie and set to work among the spectators. Hearing of this, Gillespie borrowed the first weapon that came handy, a lance from a native cavalry officer, mounted his Arab pony, rode at the tiger, and killed it. Many more stories could readily be given of the prowess of Gillespie, but these four are amply sufficient to testify to the fearlessness of the man. His personal heroism in general and his heroism in particular at the siege of Vellore proved of the last importance in raising our prestige throughout India. For our raj, in the last resort, rests on the men who command, and none could doubt that the new officer of the Eighth was most emphatically a man.

The Vellore incident deserves mention. Gillespie had been appointed commandant of Arcot, where the 19th Light Dragoons were stationed, and had not been there many days when, riding before breakfast, he was met by an officer who reported a mutiny at Vellore, fourteen miles distant. Hastily collecting a troop of the 19th and some native cavalry, he rode off at once, leaving word for the rest of the dragoons with their galloper guns to follow. At Vellore he found that the sepoy troops had massacred the Europeans, and that the survivors of the 69th Foot had spent their ammunition, and were making their last stand. With the aid of a rope Gillespie had himself hoisted into the fort, where he rallied and encouraged the 69th until the arrival of the guns from Arcot. Then the gates were thrown open, and the dragoons rushed in, cutting down over eight hundred of the mutineers. Heroism is fine and resourcefulness is fine, and we can judge the impression that the combination of heroism and resourcefulness left on the native mind.[1] Sergeant Brady of Vellore, when he saw the dust of the advancing horsemen, called out: "If Colonel Gillespie is alive, that is he, and God Almighty has sent him from the West Indies to the East for our deliverance." The spirit that men like Gillespie had infused into our soldiers is evident in the splendid story of the sentry who had been posted at the magazine of Vellore. On the outbreak of the mutiny, an officer, running for bare life, passed the magazine, and advised him to save himself while he could. The sentry's reply was that he had been posted there and there he should remain till properly relieved ; if attacked, he said that he had six rounds of ammunition and intended to sell his life dearly. After Gillespie's suppression of the mutiny, the dead body of the sentry with several dead mutineers lay together. We honour our unknown soldier in Westminster Abbey, yet surely here is an unknown soldier worthy to be had in honour.

In 1808 the regiment took the field under the command of Gillespie. On its arrival at Khoundoghaut, it was found that the Sikhs had submitted, and it consequently returned to Cawnpore. Early in the year 1809[2] the Sikhs began to give trouble, and Gillespie commanded the horse artillery and cavalry attached to Major-General St. Leger's army, which assembled between the rivers Jumna and Sutlej. In April Sir Charles Metcalfe established peace, and the troops returned to cantonments at Ludhiana, on the left bank of the Sutlej. In January, 1809, to the heartfelt regret of the regiment, Gillespie was removed to the 25th Light Dragoons. The officers forwarded a memorial to the Duke of York, begging the restoration of their lieutenant-colonel to the

---

[1] *Cf.* Gillespie's own account in Cannon, pp. 122-4. Sir Henry Newbolt wrote stirring lines on this episode.

[2] On the uniform of the regiment then *cf. Colburn's United Service Magazine*, 1864, Part II, p. 177.

corps at a future period. The non-commissioned officers and men presented him with a costly sword inscribed "The Gift of the Royal Irish."[1]

In Bundelkhand there were two strongholds, Ajaygerh and Kalinjar, remarkable for their position and importance. They were in the hands of adventurers who had risen to power by the usual methods. It is a mark of the prescience of Lake that so early as 1806 he warned the Government that until both of them were in our hands, it would be impossible to maintain peace in Bundelkhand. Within six years, his warning proved true. On the departure of Lord Wellesley his forward policy had been dropped. Content under the new régime to offer advice to unruly rajas, they came to think that we neither could nor would do more than offer advice. The forts of Ajaygerh and Kalinjar the rajas regarded as impregnable on account of the natural difficulties due to the hills and of the fortifications by which those hill difficulties had been enhanced. Against these rajas a detachment, consisting of a squadron of the regiment and part of the fifty-third regiment, under Colonel Martindell, was despatched. The ascent to the hills was by steep and narrow paths, overhung in many places by projecting rocks, and from the shelter of these the enemy fired upon the slowly advancing troops. The fort of Kalinjar was stormed on the 2nd of February, 1812, and the fierce resistance of the garrison was so overcome by the fury of our stormers that the raja surrendered in the end ; and on the 13th of February the fort of Ajaygerh also surrendered.

The extension of the raj of the British Empire meant the curtailment—in time—of the practice of robbery, private and public. On the grand scale the Pindaris had indulged in the plunder of the native. As their boldness increased, they came to trespass on the boundaries of the British frontier. As the powers of the Maratha princes declined, the Pindaris not infrequently engaged in hostilities against the chief of whom they were the nominal retainers. There is nothing to choose between these marauding bands of central India and the Free Companies of mediaeval Europe or the raids

---

[1] *Cf. Colburn's United Service Magazine*, 1852, Part I, p. 65.

along the Scots border. General rapine was the object of the Pindaris, and inevitably they saw no reason why our rule should be exempt from their incursions. In September, 1812, the regiment took the field against the Pindaris, crossing the Jumna at Allahabad, and marching to Rhamnagger to prevent the assembly of the Pindaris in the neighbourhood of Benares.[1]   For eight months the work of the repression of the Pindaris pursued its course, and in April, 1813, the regiment returned to Cawnpore, marching towards the end of the year to Meerut in order to relieve the 24th Light Dragoons. The lieutenant-colonel appointed on the 13th of August, 1813, was the Hon. Henry Westenra.

From central India the corps turned to the far north in 1814, when the Eighth under the command of Lieutenant-Colonel Westenra turned their attention to the hardy mountaineers of Nepal.[2]   These Gurkhas were a disciplined force drilled and equipped in European fashion. They had subdued the highlands just as we had subdued the lowlands beside them. There was a border between the two every whit as debatable as the Scots border had ever been. In 1814 the Nepalese officers on the frontier encroached upon the lands of men under our raj. These officers seized two small districts, and Lord Hastings peremptorily demanded their evacuation. On the receipt of evasive replies, he re-occupied the districts by a detachment of troops before whom the Gurkhas quietly retired. On the withdrawal of these troops a party of Gurkhas attacked the post at Bhotwal, massacring twenty men. For the Nepalese had quite persuaded themselves that the English could never penetrate into the mountains of Nepal.

Napoleon used to say that an insurmountable obstacle was one invariably surmounted, and so the Nepalese, to their cost, were destined to find out. Lord Hastings undertook an expedition

[1] On an old jacket of the Eighth in 1811, *cf. the Journal of the Society of Army Historical Research*, Vol. I, p. 25, where Major Parkyn describes it. He also notes the chief points of difference between Light Dragoon and Lancer jackets.

[2] On the Marquess of Hastings and the Nepal War of 1814–16, *cf.* Lieut.-Col. Noel's article in *The United Service Magazine*, Vol. 46 (N.S.), p. 648.

into the interior of the great hill ranges surrounding India. It was the first of these expeditions in which the Anglo-Indian government has ever since—at intervals—been engaged. The frontier which was to be the scene of the war stretched a distance of about six hundred miles, and the enemy had possession of all the passes leading into the highlands. There was the difficulty of moving large bodies of troops in so rugged a country, of providing them with supplies where the soil was so unproductive, and of preserving communications with the lowlands, communications always liable to interruption by the enemy and by the deadly miasma which render the forests on the skirts of the hills quite impassable during part of the year. In the autumn of 1814 it was determined to organise thirty thousand men in four divisions under the command of Major-General R. R. Gillespie. Four separate divisions were formed, which were to ascend the hills at as many places, as soon as the rains had sufficiently subsided to allow of their forward movement.

A squadron of the Eighth under Brevet Major Brutton was attached to the division commanded by Gillespie himself. His division was assembled at Saharanpur on the 18th of October. His orders were to clear the passage of the Dehra Doon, or valley of Dehra, by the end of October, and to be ready to co-operate with the movements to be carried out before the 1st of November by the western division under Major-General Ochterlony.[1] On the 19th of October the advance, commanded by Lieutenant-Colonel Carpenter, proceeded by the Timli pass into the valley of the Doon. Three days later, Lieutenant-Colonel Mawby followed with the main body, and occupied the town of Dehra. As we advanced, the Gurkhas fell back on Kalunga, a small fort about five miles from Dehra at the top of a steep detached hill, six hundred feet high, covered with jungle. The summit was a table-land above half a mile in length; and at the further extremity stood the fort, a stone quadrangular building of no great extent, but enlarged and strengthened by stockades. Six hundred Gurkhas, under the intrepid Balbhadra Sing, formed its garrison.

[1] *I.O., Home Series, Miscellaneous,* 515, f. 58.

Mawby summoned the garrison to surrender. The letter was delivered to Balbhadra Sing late at night; and he observed that it was not his habit to carry on a correspondence at such an unseasonable hour, but that he should shortly pay the writer a visit in his camp. With infinite labour Mawby mounted guns up the hill, and constructed a battery. He found, however, the position too strong for him, and accordingly informed Gillespie of the state of affairs. Gillespie moved forward with the remainder of his force, and surveyed the enemy's position on the 28th. Moved by his promise to Ochterlony that he would be ready to co-operate with him by the 1st of November, Gillespie determined on an assault. Heavy guns were brought up, a battery erected, and preparations were made to carry the fort by storm.

On the 31st of October, 1814, the troops had been distributed in four columns of attack and a reserve of which the dismounted squadron of the regiment formed part. Three of the columns, having to make a circuit of some distance over very rugged ground, marched before daybreak, but had not reached their destination at 8 a.m., when the signal-gun was fired.[1] They did not hear it. In the meantime the garrison made a sortie, which was repelled by the remaining column. General Gillespie, thinking that the retreating column might be followed into their own entrenchment by a brisk and vigorous pursuit, ordered the column, together with the reserve and a troop of the Eighth, to hasten forward and carry the place by escalade. The troops advanced steadily to the foot of the wall to find that Balbhadra Sing, besides manning the ramparts, had placed a gun in an outwork protecting the gateway in such a fashion as to enfilade the wall upon that side. In spite of the gallantry of the troops, the fire from the gun beat down upon them before the ladders could be raised, and destroyed their leading files. Foiled in the attempt to scale the wall, which had sustained no damage from the previous fire of the battery, the men attempted to force the outwork and carry the gate. They were received with such a heavy fire, and suffered so severely, that it was found necessary to draw them off to the shelter of some huts at a slight distance from the fort.

[1] *Nepal Papers*, p. 439.

General Gillespie, together with Lieutenant-Colonel Westenra, left the batteries and walked to the huts sheltered by the stockade. Here they found the troops much shaken by their reverse. Gillespie, irritated by the repulse which had been sustained, persisted in renewing the attempt, declaring aloud his determination to carry the fort or lose his life. Accordingly he placed himself at the head of three fresh companies of the 53rd regiment and of the dragoons, and led them again towards the gate of the fort. Two 6-pounder guns were brought up from the plateau and run up to within twenty-five yards of the gate. These guns were gallantly served, and under their fire the fresh attack was launched. When within range of the Gurkha matchlocks, the men of the 53rd hung back. Lieutenant Kennedy, a scion of the house of Cultra, was beside Gillespie, who called out, "Now, Kennedy, for the honour of County Down." The General, in advance of the line, called on the men to follow him; and, while waving his sword to encourage them to come on, he was shot through the heart, and immediately expired. Abandoning the attack, under the cover of Captain Campbell's detachment our force withdrew. Gillespie was buried at Meerut, and it is curious to reflect that within a stone's throw of his grave the Mutiny broke out in 1857. If the fearless Gillespie had been alive in 1857, or a man of his dauntless temperament, would that mutiny not have been quelled as the mutiny at Vellore had been? His death stirred the nation, and a monument carved by Chantrey forms his memorial in St. Paul's Cathedral, the parish church of the British Empire.

On the 10th of November, 1814, Lord Moira wrote from Lucknow to Lord Bathurst:

> The task is painful which I have to perform in communicating the Death of Major General Gillespie. The loss of an Officer who had distinguished himself so much not only by his Gallantry but by his eminent Services would in any case be matter of deep regret. In this instance our concern must be augmented by his having fallen in an unsuccessful attack. The good fortune which had attended him in former desperate enterprizes induced him to believe, I fear, that the

Storm of the Fortress of Kalunga might be achieved by the same daring valor and readiness of resource whereby he had on other occasions triumphed over obstacles apparently insuperable.

The Assault, in which he was killed at the foot of the Rampart, involved, as I conceive, no possibility of success ; otherwise the courage of the Soldiers would have carried the Plan notwithstanding the determined resistance of the Garrison.

A Detachment of the R: Irish Light Dragoons, who volunteered their Services to lead the Attack on foot, behaved with extraordinary firmness. I enclose to your Lordship a Return of the loss sustained by the King's troops. That of the Company's Forces added would make the total about Two Hundred and Fifty. Colonel Mawby who succeeded to the Command of the Division is waiting for Battering Cannon, on the arrival of which he will renew operations against the Fort.[1]

Daring as the deeds at the storming were, it is no surprise to find that Sergeant-Major John Mawdsley was recommended, in consequence of his gallantry on this occasion, for a commission. Among the wounded were Lieutenant-Colonel the Hon. Henry Westenra, Major Brutton, Lieutenants Heyman and Taylor, and Cornet Macdonald, the last of whom died from the effects of his wound. Out of the company of one hundred, three rank and file were killed ; four sergeants, one trumpeter, and forty-nine rank and file were wounded ; and one private was missing.[2] On the 24th of November a battery of 18-pounders was constructed, a breach effected, and an unsuccessful assault took place. A bombardment was the plan now tried, and within three days the commandant abandoned the fortress of Kalunga.[3] After its fall the squadron rejoined the regiment at Meerut. While the Nepal war had lasted, the regiment had formed part of the army of observation, assembled at Delhi, in order to maintain the Maratha chiefs in wholesome awe. A letter Sir John Floyd wrote from Cheltenham to the Earl of Liverpool on the 6th of September

[1] *C.O.*, 77/34.   [2] *Nepal Papers*, pp. 460, 490.
[3] *I.O., Home Series, Miscellaneous*, 515, f. 90.

throws not a little light on the path to promotion for a soldier of fortune :

My Lord

The advancement of many military Men, and particularly that of my gallant Friend Lord Harris, for the capture of Seringapatam, and the importunities of several Officers who served with me, and who consider their reputation in some degree connected with mine, impell me to the painfull task of speaking of myself, and of requesting Your Lordship will be pleased to submit my name to His Royal Highness the Prince Regent, humbly soliciting Your Lordship's Recommendation for such mark of favour as my Services may be thought to claim.

Not to trouble Your Lordship with the uninteresting detail of a meer military Life I beg to be allowed to mention some leading facts.

I was appointed Cornet in Elliott's Light Dragoons by His Late Majesty in 1760, and immediately served abroad with my Regiment at the Battle of Emsdorf in that Year. My military education was under the late Earl of Pembroke, and the first Lord Heathfield, who honoured me with their particular notice and protection.

In 1780 I was appointed Lieut. Colonel to a Regiment of Light Cavalry, now the 19th, and went with it to India, where I formed it, and led it, and where it acquired considerable Reputation, and it was the first Corps of His Majesty's Cavalry that was sent to that Country.

The command of the Cavalry of the East India Company was conferred on me. A system of Horsemanship and of Discipline was introduced by me, and it was successfully led by me in the Field.

I was second in Command at the final capture, and destruction of the Works of Pondicherry, under General Braithwaite, and the extinction of the French Interest in India.

In 1790 I was detached by General Medows to the River Bowarrie, bordering on the Mysore Country, with three Regiments of Cavalry, one of which was His Majesty's 19th Dragoons, and four Battalions of Infantry, one of which was His Majesty's 36 Regiment—Here, at Sattimungulum,[1] I was assaild by Tippoo's whole Army, commanded by himself, and, after a Fight of two Days and two Nights, beat him off with heavy loss, and was hail'd as the Preserver of the Carnatic.

[1] Satyamangalam.

I served under Marquis Cornwallis in his operations at Bangalore and at Seringapatam, when Tippoo was humbled, and the limits of his Country reduced.

In 1799 I was second in Command under General Harris at the capture of Seringapatam during the supreme Government of Marquis Wellesley, and received the personal thanks of that Governor General, with His Lordships offer to serve me whether my views were for Honour, or Emolument.

On my return to England in 1800, after about 19 years absence the Earl of Buckinghamshire, under whose Government I had served in India, was pleased to name me for the Command in Egypt, and I was actually proceeding there, but on the Receipt of Lord Hutchinson's Letter it was most judiciously continued in his able hands.

At this time His Majesty was most graciously pleased to express His approbation of my Services by giving me the first Regiment of Cavalry that became vacant.

I served on the Staff in Ireland about twelve years, and was, for a considerable time, in command of the Forces there.

In 1813 His Royal Highness the Prince Regent was most graciously pleased to confer on me the Government of Gravesend and Tilbury Fort.

Being entirely a Soldier of Fortune my property is on the most moderate scale for the provision of my Family, and is founded on my share of Seringapatam Prize, about £14,000—and on my military Income.

If your Lordship finds in the circumstances I have related fair grounds of recommendation to His Royal Highness the Prince Regent for the Honour I solicit, I request you will be pleased to name me to the Prince Regent accordingly.[1]

He was created a baronet in 1816, though we feel by no means assured that this is what Floyd coveted. His son, the second baronet, served in the Peninsula, and one of his daughters married Sir Robert Peel, the second baronet, and the other General Sir Joseph Fuller, G.C.H.

In 1815 the regiment was attached to the army of Major-General Dyson Marshall, and was present in February, 1817, at the siege

[1] *Add. MSS.*, 38262, f. 57.

of Hatras. A few of the great Talukdars of the Doab had been permitted to retain many of the privileges which the most considerable of their order had usurped during times of anarchy. By silent consent of the Company the Talukdars exercised supreme judicial authority within their own estates, regulated their own police, kept up large bodies of military followers, and converted their houses of residence into fortresses if not so formidable as Kalunga, yet into places of serious strength. Of these petty chieftains, one of the most considerable was Dayaram, Talukdar of a number of villages in the Doab, in the district of Aligarh. His residence was at the fort adjacent to the walled town of Hatras. The fort was of the usual construction, built of mud, or rather of sun-baked clay, having walls of great height and thickness, with towers at the angles, mounting a number of guns, and defended by a very broad and deep ditch. The town also was protected by a wall and ditch. The force kept up by the Dayaram was about eight thousand strong, of which three thousand five hundred were horse.

Talukdars had sheltered criminals, and had permitted robbers to fix their headquarters in their territories on condition of sharing in the spoil. Now Dayaram was a Talukdar, and the Government required him as a proof of the sincerity of his profession of allegiance to disband his troops and, above all, to dismantle his fortress. Profuse in promise, he was slow in performance. The troops employed against him marched from the several military stations of Cawnpore, Muttra and Meerut. They consisted of the 8th and 24th Light Dragoons, the 3rd and 7th Native Cavalry, the 1st and 2nd Rohilla Horse and Rocket Troop, the 14th and 87th Regiments, and of native infantry the 2nd battalion of the 1st, the 1st battalion of the 11th, the 2nd battalion of the 12th, the 2nd battalion of the 15th, the 2nd battalion of the 25th, the 21st battalion of the 29th, and the 2nd Grenadier battalion. By the 23rd of February, 1817, a practical breach was effected in the walls of the town, but, warned by the experience of Kalunga, the garrison avoided a storm, and evacuated the place the following morning. On the 2nd of March a shell exploded the powder magazine.   Convinced of the futility of further resistance, Dayaram escaped at midnight with a small body of retainers.   The out-picquets of the Eighth met them, and a sharp encounter took place. The retainers, armed with back and breast-plates and gauntlets of steel, gave quite as good as they got.   One of them severely wounded Lieutenant Van Courtland in single combat.   The capture of Hatras proved highly significant.   For it secured the ready submission of other refractory landholders.

On the termination of hostilities with Dayaram the Royal Irish returned to Meerut in March, 1817.   In October it took the field once more against the Pindaris, forming part of the right division of the army under Major-General Donkin.   Lord Hastings resolved on the suppression of the predatory system of the Pindaris, and the Bengal forces were accordingly arrayed in four principal divisions.   By the 9th of November, Donkin advanced to Dholpur, on the Chambal, where he threatened Sindia and Amir Khan equally.   Shut in between this division and the centre, the former chieftain was forced to throw down his arms.   Taking with him a light division, Donkin advanced by forced marches to Kalana on the western Sindh.   Early on the 17th of December the cavalry came up with a body of retreating Pindaris, and immediately dispersed them.[1]   There were other harassing marches against the Pindaris, the Peshwa and the Marathas.   In the end the power of the Pindaris and the Marathas was completely crushed.[2]   The three leading families so often opposed to us—Sindia, Holkar and the Bhonsala—definitely were bound over to keep the peace of India.   The campaign against the Marathas had been age-long : that against the Pindaris had been only three months.   Order replaced disorder, and henceforth the Maratha States were shut up within carefully demarcated limits.

On the conclusion of this their last campaign in India, the Royal Irish returned to its station in Meerut in 1818.[3]   On the death of General Sir John Floyd, the colonelcy of the regiment was given

---

[1] *I.O., Home Series, Miscellaneous*, 89, for the movements of Donkin's troops. *Cf. Add. MSS.*, 23755.

[2] *Cf. The Calcutta Government Gazette*, January 8, 1818.   [3] *Add. MSS.*, 23755.

GENERAL SIR BANASTRE TARLETON, BT., G.C.B.

to Lieutenant-General Sir Banastre Tarleton, Baronet, G.C.B., from the Twenty-first Light Dragoons, on the 15th of January, 1818. Appointed a cornet in the First Dragoon Guards in 1775, he obtained leave to accompany Lord Cornwallis to North America. He served with the army under Sir Henry Clinton in the attack on Charleston in 1776, and was present at the capture of New York, the Battle of the White Plains, the capture of Fort Washington and of Fort Lee. In July, 1777, he commanded the advanced guard of the patrol under Colonel Harcourt, which on the 13th of December made a successful dash and captured the American general, Lee, who, reconnoitring three miles away from his army, had stopped with his escort for breakfast at a farmhouse. Tarleton's merits led to his rapid advancement, and he was promoted to be captain in Harcourt's horse and appointed a brigade major of cavalry.

Tarleton took part in the Battle of Brandywine and the capture of Germantown and Philadelphia. He was engaged in the various expeditions from New York, and was singled out by Clinton for the arduous post of lieutenant-colonel commandant of the British legion. A force originally of light infantry was changed to a mixed force of cavalry and light infantry, and from the colour of its facings was known as Tarleton's Green Horse. By a skilful movement he surprised three regiments of the enemy's cavalry at Bigging Bridge in 1780, and was thus able to horse his legion. With his light troops he scoured the country, cutting off communications efficiently. A born cavalry leader every whit as much as Sir John Floyd, Tarleton completed Cornwallis's victory of Camden by a charge of horse and pursuit of twenty miles. He was present when our men made so poor a stand at Cowpens in 1781. When all appeared lost Tarleton, with characteristic spirit, assembled a party of his troopers with fourteen officers. Leading in a final charge against Washington's horse, he repulsed them, retaking our baggage, and cutting to pieces the detachment of the enemy who had taken possession of it. Eagerly at Guildford he attacked the main body of the Americans, thrice the strength of our men, and put them to flight, losing part of his right hand.

He was promoted lieutenant-colonel in June, 1781. In July he rendered good service in the victory gained against Lafayette and Wayne at Jamestown.

On his return home after the fall of Yorktown, he was tempted to earn parliamentary honours. Readily adapting himself to all classes, he was returned for Liverpool free of expense at the head of the poll. In the House of Commons he uniformly voted with the opposition. The Tories set up as a rival candidate in 1796 his own brother John, whom he easily defeated. From 1783 to 1788 he was on half-pay as lieutenant-colonel. He lived for some years with "Perdita" (Mary Robinson), after she had broken off her connection with the Prince of Wales, with whom he was on intimate terms. He published, probably with her assistance, in 1787, his *History of the Campaigns of* 1780 *and* 1781 *in the Southern Provinces of North America.* The book describes the operations with ability. Like most books, it also describes the character of the author, and it writes him down as filled with both vanity and ingratitude. His vanity gave him away just as much as his uncalled-for attack on Cornwallis, who had so often bestowed cordial commendation on him. The portrait he thus painted of himself is not nearly so pleasing as the noble full-length Sir Joshua Reynolds did of him.

Promoted to be colonel in 1790, Tarleton attained the rank of major-general in 1794, of lieutenant-general in 1801, and of general in 1812. At the close of 1798 he was sent to Portugal, but, not liking the limited scope of the work offered him, he obtained his recall. He was appointed colonel of the Durham Fencibles in 1799, of the 22nd Light Dragoons in 1801, and in the following year of the 21st Light Dragoons. In 1803 he commanded the Cork district, and then the Severn district for six years. The usual governorships fell his way. In 1808 he was appointed governor of Berwick and Holy Island. He was then transferred to the colonelcy of the Eighth in 1818. On the enlargement of the Order of the Bath in 1815, it was limited to officers who had distinguished themselves after 1803. Resenting the injustice thus done him, he made a protest to Earl Bathurst, forwarding a statement of his services. Like so many protests, it was ineffectual at the time. Later, like so many protests, it was effectual. For in truth all does come to him who knows how to wait. In 1818 he was created a baronet and in 1820 he received the knight grand cross of the Bath. Few regiments can boast in succession of two such great cavalry leaders as Sir John Floyd and Sir Banastre Tarleton. Fame the latter won in North America, the former in India.

The 11th Light Dragoons at Cawnpore lost one hundred men in June, 1820, from cholera, that broke out with alarming suddenness. The Government ordered their relief by the Royal Irish one year previous to the original intention, and accordingly our regiment set out for Cawnpore in November, 1820. Sir Banastre Tarleton received orders issued on the 20th of August, 1822, that his regiment was to be armed, clothed, and equipped as hussars, and that the lace of the regiment, which up to then had been gold, should be changed to silver.[1] The gold lace, then, appeared at the review Major-General Gabriel Martin Dell held at Cawnpore on the 3rd of May, 1822, when Major G. R. Deare was in command. In the inspecting returns we read :

> The Regiment has been under the command of Major G. R. Deare since last inspection, who is unremitting in his attention to the discipline, field exercises, and internal management of the corps. He has served His Majesty upwards of 25 years, and is a zealous, active and intelligent officer ; and these qualities are conspicuous in the management of the Regiment under his command.

> The high state of the discipline of the Regiment, in all its branches, clearly shews that the Commanding Officer and Captains have paid due attention to the instruction of the Subaltern Officers who are remarkably attentive to their duty, and are promising young men. The Captains are well acquainted with the interior economy of their troops and competent to command them in any situation. Unanimity and good understanding prevails in the corps, and the officers afford the Commanding Officer that support which he is entitled to require of them.

[1] *W.O., General Orders and Circular Letters,* f. 95.

The Adjutant, the Quartermaster, and the Paymaster are fully competent to the duties of their several situations : the Books consigned to their care are kept with accuracy and regularity and the smart and soldier-like appearance of the Regiment in the field speaks fully to the merits of the Adjutant.

The Troop Quartermasters and Troop Serjeant Majors are fully equal to the duties required of them and are attentive to and understand all the interior economy of their Troops.   It also appears that they are honest in their various transactions, and discharge their duty with fidelity.

The Non-Commissioned Officers are well acquainted with their duty, smart and intelligent, and are in possession of a copy of the Abstract of the Rules and Regulations respecting the Drill and Field Exercises prescribed by His Majesty's Regulations, with the exception of 13 Books wanting to complete, which have never been applied for from England.

The Trumpeters are perfect in their soundings.

The Musicians are limited to the Regulations, play in correct time and the whole are trained to, and fit for the ranks.

The Privates are a fine body of men, but few under the proper standard ; their health is generally good, and but few deaths : the men are clean and smart in their persons and clothes, the number in the ranks corresponds exactly with the returns : they are well drilled, attentive and respectful, and well behaved men.   No man is kept on the strength of the Regiment who is not clothed or who does not do his duty as a soldier.

The interior economy of the troops is duly attended to, and the conduct of the men in question orderly, and but few of them guilty of crimes requiring the extreme alternative of corporal punishment.

The officers mess together, and the Regimental Mess is extremely well regulated, and established on such a system of economy as to enable the subalterns to live at it.

Particular attention is paid to the messing of the men ; the provisions consumed by them are furnished by the Commissariat who contract for it.   The bread is good, but complaints have been made of the badness of the meat, and some which I saw during my last inspection was so very bad that I ordered it to be destroyed.

The Regimental Books, Records and Troop books are kept according to the Established Regulations : the latter are signed and witnessed by an officer monthly ; each soldier having in his possession a small book containing a statement of accounts and clothing agreeable to orders from the Horse Guards. The Captains or officers commanding troops settle in person with the men.

The men are provided with requisite necessaries by officers commanding troops and on reasonable terms.[1]

Here the inspecting return breaks off to investigate the financial claims of Private Creak, of Captain Johnson's troop; of John McCann, of Captain Williams's troop; and of Private Keen, of Captain Scott's company. There were no recruits since the last inspection, nor was it proposed to discharge any men. According to the inspecting return, "the horses of the Regiment are well trained, and in very good condition, and of sufficient size and strength. The forage is of good quality and issued with regularity, under due superintendence of an officer from each troop."[1]

Major-General Dell pronounced that in the field exercises the formation of the regiment is according to the regulations. Moreover, "the various formations are made with correctness, and a proper degree of celerity. The troops work well together and the movements are performed with precision. The officers, non-commissioned officers, and men, are graceful horsemen, and understand the management of their horses, and expert in the use of their swords."[1]

No irregularity appears to have occurred in the proceedings of the Courts Martial. The sentences seem proportioned to the crimes, and corporal punishment had not frequently occurred. The hospital is conducted conformably to the regulations, though its situation leaves somewhat to be desired, as it is too near the barracks and the regimental bazaar, and is not sufficiently airy. Few are sick, and their sickness is of a trivial nature. The assistant surgeon, William Browne, is, we learn, "kind, attentive and humane. The Vaccine inoculation is introduced annually."[1]

[1] *Inspection Returns and Confidential Reports*, Half Year, 1822.

The Veterinary Surgeon, W. S. Rickwood, is fully competent, the farriers are expert in their business, and a proportion of the men in each troop is sufficiently instructed in farriery to shoe horses in an emergency.

The clothing, appointments, and accoutrements of the officers and men are strictly according to the regulations, and are in excellent condition. "The arms are in a serviceable state with the exception of some carbines and rifles whose locks are defective from the springs being weak and unserviceable, and cannot be replaced or properly tempered in this country. . . . The Regimental School is conducted by Serjeant Curwen and Mrs. Jones, who are attentive and competent to the duties of their respective situations. The Chaplain's certificate of progress made by the scholars accompanies this.

"The Chaplain attends the sick in Hospital.

"There is no regular Church. Divine service is performed alternately at the Church Bungalow and Barracks on the right of the Cavalry lines, by the Rev. Mr. Williams.

"The men are practised firing ball at various distances."[1]

Enumerating the documents accompanying his return, Major-General Dell concludes it with these emphatic words: "Having fully and faithfully to the best of my judgement reported without reserve the state of His Majesty's 8th or King's Royal Irish Dragoons, I have only to add my opinion that I do not believe there is a more efficient corps in His Majesty's service." Some of the details in the return are interesting. There were 282 English, 192 Irish, 7 Scots, and 3 foreigners present. Of these 484 men, three were over six feet two, seven over six feet, nine over five feet eleven, and twenty-seven over five feet ten. There were 8 with the service of 25 years, 30 of 20 years, 27 of 18 years, 56 of 14 years, 99 of 12 years, 82 of 10 years, 75 of 9 years, 57 of 8 years, 32 of 7 years, 9 of 6 years, 4 of 5 years, 3 of 4 years, and 2 of 3 years. Of course all served for an unlimited period.

In age, 4 were over 50, 4 over 45, 34 over 40, 56 over 35, 157 over 30, 195 over 25, 28 over 20, 3 over 18, and 3 under 18.

[1] *Inspection Returns and Confidential Reports*, Half Year, 1822.

After service for twenty years in India, the regiment received orders for home in August, 1822, leaving such men behind as cared to extend their time in the country. Accordingly, 280 men and 616 horses were transferred to the 16th Lancers, the corps relieving the regiment. Before leaving Cawnpore, Major-General Thomas acted as inspecting officer, issuing the following in division orders on the 14th of September, 1822:

The review this morning, of the Eighth, or King's Royal Irish Regiment of Light Dragoons, afforded Major-General Thomas the highest satisfaction ; in fact, a mingled sensation of pleasure and admiration, deriving its source from the interesting spectacle of a corps of European cavalry, which, after a service of twenty years in India, under all the disadvantages of climate and tropical sun, appeared to vie with any corps of the same description that the major-general had ever seen in Europe ; exhibiting practical proof that in point of freshness, in vigour, and in all the powerful energies of that branch of an army, in a familiar intimacy with and display of the most masterly manœuvres, together with the numerous minor attentions of the best disciplined corps, the Eighth Light Dragoons stand, in all, eminently conspicuous.

The major-general is sorry that the departure of this noble corps for England will debar him the opportunity of seeing it at the half-yearly inspection, when it would have been in his power to do them this justice in his confidential reports to the Horse Guards, and in which he could not speak too highly of the officers as well as the men.

Proud may Major Deare and his officers be of such a corps. To Major Deare in particular, their commanding officer, who accompanied them originally from Europe, and who must have had so long a share in their discipline, it must be a subject of self gratulation and delight.

But the major-general feels it would be unjust to limit his praise of the Eighth Light Dragoons, to their merits in a military point of view ; what will be no less appreciated, is the estimation in which their moral and social virtues have been held by all classes of people, as well by the natives of this country as by their own countrymen of Europe, evinced by the former in various affectionate and affecting instances of good will and kindness towards them wherever stationed.

The major-general takes this opportunity of bidding farewell to the regiment. Although he has not had the good fortune to be often at the same station with the Eighth, or personally acquainted with many of them, he saw enough in the party that Major Deare had with him on service at Callinger,[1] to be perfectly satisfied that the regiment at large will ever be an honour to the British army ; and he is quite sure that he has the united voice of the Cawnpore community with him in expressing his and their regret, at the loss of their society, and in wishing them a prosperous voyage to Europe, with health and happiness in whatever part of the world they may be destined to serve.

According to Canon Ainger, the motto of contributors to the Dictionary of National Biography was "No flowers, by request." At first blush we feel tempted to think that with the desire of saying nice things for the last time, Major-General Thomas disregarded the spirit of an injunction like Canon Ainger's. For fear this may be the impression of the reader we have been careful to give the confidential report of Major-General Dell for May, 1822, when he expressed sentiments just as favourable as those Major-General Thomas published in his division orders.

The Viceroy, Lord Hastings, endorsed the opinions of Major-Generals Dell and Thomas, for in his general orders of the 6th of December he stated :

On the occasion of the approaching departure of His Majesty's Eighth, or King's Royal Irish Light Dragoons from India, the Most Noble the Governor-General in Council feels himself called upon, and eagerly answers the call, to express the high sense entertained by Government of the eminently valuable services of the regiment during a period of twenty years in this country.

Their career has been marked by everything which can distinguish a corps. A decided spirit of energy has always illustrated their conduct in the field, where they have invariably exhibited to their fellow soldiers an example peculiarly worthy of imitation. A cordial unanimity has likewise subsisted between the officers and men of the regiment and their brethren of the Honourable Company's service, who doubtless

[1] Kalinjar.

will long cherish the remembrance of a corps, as much distinguished for their social qualities and orderly conduct, as for that high principle of military feeling which has so decidedly marked the character of the King's Royal Irish Light Dragoons.[1]

As we bring this chapter to a close, and as we read the opinion of Viceroy and Generals on the campaigns of the Eighth against the Gurkhas, we must express our regret that on its battle honours the word "Nepal" does not occur. With the possible exception of the two campaigns of 1846 and 1849 against the Sikhs, it entailed the hardest fighting we have ever experienced in India, yet no recognition of such splendid service was forthcoming.

[1] *Bengal G.O.*, Vol. 3, January to December, 1822.

Chapter IX

The Long Peace

THE King's Royal Irish Hussars sailed on board the *Dorsetshire*, East Indiaman, on the 11th of January, 1823, and did not land at Gravesend till the 5th of May following. On arrival the regiment received Sir Banastre Tarleton's letter of the 20th of August, 1822, informing its members that they were to be equipped as "Hussars." In accordance with this letter they received their appropriate clothing early in 1824. The dress and the undress jackets were to be, like other regiments of Hussars, all blue.[1] By circular letters of the 11th of June and of the 19th of July, 1823, the uniforms were all to be really uniform.[2] These new regulations were enforced, for a letter of the 19th of July, 1824, sharply called the attention of Lieutenant-Colonel Westenra to the fact that the manner of putting on lace deviated from the patterns.[3]

In 1823 the regiment had been quartered at Norwich and Ipswich. Major-General Lord Edward Somerset had inspected the regiment at Ipswich in October, 1823, and he also inspected it at Romford on the 26th of June, 1824. There were 270 effective men in it, with 12 wanting to complete establishment. Out of 270 men no less than 238 were in Ireland. Sir Henry Floyd, we learn, had been in command for six months; Major Deare for about a fortnight; and Lieutenant-Colonel Westenra from the 9th of May last. Floyd had left the regiment on promotion; but, we learn, during the time he had the command no very satisfactory progress appears to have been made in the formation of the troops. Not only had there been a change in the commanding officer, but there were no riding master and, till lately, no efficient adjutant. "The Discipline does not seem to be very well regulated;

---

[1] *W.O.*, 3/400. There is no reference to changes in arms.
[2] *Letter Book*, 2.38, *W.O.*, 7, f. 7, f. 10.   [3] *W.O.*, 3/405.

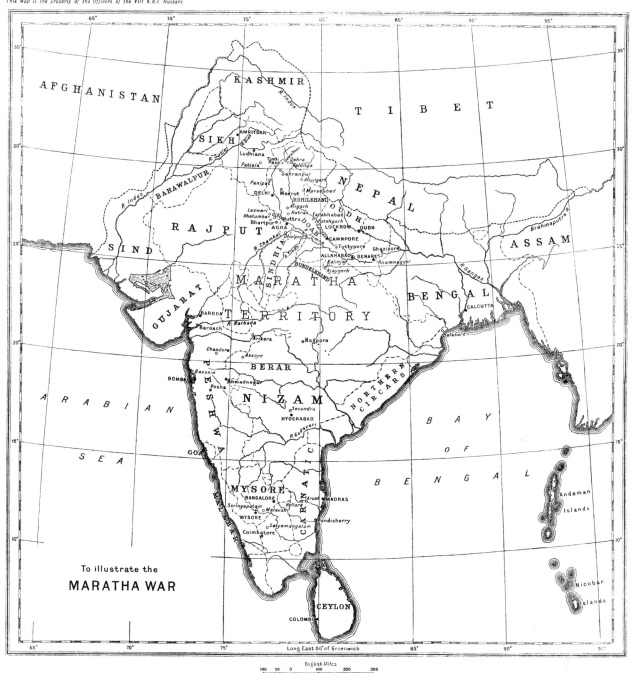

To illustrate the

MARATHA WAR

English Miles
100 50 0   100   200   300

and as yet the training and instruction of the officers and men in the Field Exercise have made but little progress. . . . The Captains who are present appear to be competent to the command of their troops, but the unformed state of the Regiment does not admit of their exercising them. Many of the subalterns present with the corps are young, or newly appointed, and it is impossible as yet to judge of their acquirements. . . . In the unformed state of the Regiment there has been no opportunity of judging of the merits of the different officers. The Commanding Officer states that he is satisfied with the support which he receives from them, and that unanimity and good understanding prevail in the corps. . . . The Privates are a stout, good body of men, mostly young, and of the proper standard. The men have been principally enlisted since the return of the Regiment from India, have, as yet, made but little progress in their drill. Their conduct in quarters has not been perfectly orderly ; several irregularities have occurred, especially instances of men being out of Barracks at night. . . . The Recruits have joined since the last inspection ; of whom one is a boy enlisted by authority of the Commander-in-Chief. The others are promising young men ; and their training is in progress. The Horses, which have been all recruited within the last year, are rather of a mixed description, and not uniformly good, but as they are young much improvement may be expected in their appearance. They are in good condition, but their training is not very completed."[1]

There are no complaints, except indeed by Lord Edward Somerset. He does, however, allow that "due attention is paid to the messing. The officers mess together, and the Regimental Mess is well conducted on such a system of economy as enables the subaltern officers to belong to it. Such of the Serjeants as are unmarried mess together. The meat and bread have been furnished by contract, and have been of good quality. Other articles have been supplied according to Regulation. The average price of bread has been $5\frac{1}{2}$d. per loaf, and of meat $4\frac{3}{4}$d. per lb. The forage has been of good quality, and been issued with regularity under a due superintendence of officers. . . . The Hospital in the

---

[1] *Inspection Returns*, first half year, 1824, No. 160.

Barrack Yard is well situated, and the wards are airy and clean,"[1] surely unusual in the days before Florence Nightingale. The vaccine inoculation is regularly practised.

Lieutenant-Colonel the Hon. Henry Westenra, who entered the cavalry service in 1794, was promoted from the Twelfth to the Eighth Light Dragoons as major, on the 26th of May, 1808, and promoted lieutenant-colonel on the 13th of August, 1813. He saw service in India, for instance, at Kalunga, and he retired from the army on the 28th of October, 1824, and was succeeded in the command by Lieutenant-Colonel Lord George William Russell. The inspection return furnished by Lord Edward Somerset is not exactly creditable to Westenra, and it is not difficult to draw the conclusion that it hastened his retirement, especially as the reviewing general noted that "Lieut. Col. Westenra, who assumed the command on the 9th of May, is an officer of long standing in the service, but does not appear to possess much energy or activity."[1] "Buts" are usually pretty serious, and this "but" is more serious than most.

Lord George William Russell was a distinguished soldier who had taken part in the expedition to Copenhagen, and had been present at the Battles of Talavera and Barossa, and was on the staff of the Duke of Wellington at Vittoria, Orthes, and Toulouse. During his command of the Eighth, he strongly advocated a revision of the cavalry regulations, which were those drawn up by Saldern, and translated by Dundas in the latter part of the eighteenth century. He wrote several times to Wellington on the subject, and sent him a paper in favour of formation in rank entire, resting his argument partly on his experience in the Peninsula. The Duke replied on the 31st of July, 1826 : "I cannot tell you with what satisfaction I have read it, and how entirely I agree in every word of it. . . . I considered our cavalry so inferior to that of the French from want of order, although I consider one squadron a match for two French squadrons, that I should not have liked to see four British squadrons opposed to four French."[2]

[1] *Inspection Returns*, first half year, 1824, No. 160.
[2] *Wellington Despatches, Supplementary*, XIV, pp. 714, 723, and 3rd Series, III, p. 353.

On the 14th of March, 1825, an official letter was written to Sir Banastre Tarleton, stating:

"That the 8th or King's Royal Irish Regiment of Hussars be permitted to retain on its Standards the Badge of the Harp and Crown with the Motto 'Pristinae Virtutis Memores.'

"That it be also permitted to bear on its Standards and Appointments the Word 'Leswaree,' in commemoration of the distinguished Conduct of the Corps during the Battle fought near Laswaree on the 1st of November, 1803.

Also

"That the Regiment be permitted to bear on its Standards and Appointments, the Word 'Hindoostan,' as a lasting Testimony of the exemplary Conduct of the Corps during the period of its Service in India from 1802 to 1822."[1]

Sir Banastre Tarleton was notified on the 25th of March that these distinctions had been awarded to his regiment.[2] The regiment was quartered at Dorchester and Christchurch in 1824; at Hounslow and Hampton Court in 1825; and at Brighton and Canterbury in 1826.

That Lord George William Russell had carried out the reforms he had at heart in part in his regiment is sufficiently obvious in the inspection return of Sir Hussey Vivian made at Hounslow Barracks on the 8th of August, 1825. His general observations are: "In reporting on the state of this Regt. and referring to the state in which judging from the Orders of Major General Lord Edward Somerset in October last it was found by that Officer, I feel that I owe it to Lt. Col. Lord Wm. Russell and to the Officers and N.C. Officers of the Regt. to state that the great improvement that must have taken place in every respect is such as to assure me of the utmost Attention having on their part been paid to their Duties and I have no doubt whatever that by a continuance of such

---

[1] *W.O., General Orders and Circular Letters.*

[2] " Hindoostan" is a battle honour of the Leicesters, the Worcesters, the Oxford Light Infantry, the Highland Light Infantry, the Seaforth Highlanders, and the West Riding Regiment. *Cf.* Norman, pp. 214–7.

2 B*

a zealous discharge of their duty, the 8th Hussars will very shortly become a remarkably fine Regiment."[1]

At Brighton on the 6th of May, 1826, Sir Hussey Vivian again reviewed the regiment. The report reaches the old standard set, say, in that of Major-General Dell, and there is little doubt that the change was mainly due to the real hard work of the lieutenant-colonel, Lord William Russell, ably seconded by Majors Badcock and Craufurd. The number of effective officers and men was 284 and of horses 253. The privates are "remarkably good."[2] The horses are for the most part "remarkably good."[2] In field exercises and movements the regiment moves "with great steadiness . . . but not with great celerity." The arms, with the exception of some thin swords, are in a serviceable state. The clothing, accoutrements, and appointments are all in good condition, except the pouches. The new stable jacket is not exactly in conformity to the sealed pattern, but is exactly like what was previously in wear. This difference consists in the circumstance that the new jacket has a narrow braid on the seam behind such as has for many years been worn by the Hussar Regiments, whereas the sealed pattern is perfectly plain.

Though considerable pains have been taken to instruct all the old officers in all their duties, yet many of the young ones require instruction. Sir Hussey Vivian's general observations are: "It is with the greatest possible satisfaction that I have to make the most favourable report of this Regiment the state and condition of which in every respect does the highest credit to the Commanding and other Officers, the Non Commissioned Officers and men. The improvement that has taken place within the last six months is very great indeed, and unless much dispersed, which might be highly injurious to a Corps composed of such young soldiers, this Regiment will, I have no doubt, in another year be one of the most efficient in His Majesty's Service."[2]

After the absence of a quarter of a century the regiment proceeded to Ireland, and was quartered at Dundalk in 1827, Newbridge in 1828, Dublin in 1829, and Longford in 1830. In

[1] *W.O.*, 27/165.   [2] *Inspection Returns, Confidential Reports,* first half year, 1826, *W.O.*, No. 27.

November, 1828, Lieutenant-Colonel Lord William Russell retired on half-pay from the regiment for which he had accomplished so much, and was succeeded by Lieutenant-Colonel the Hon. George Berkeley Molyneux, a young man of twenty-eight who did remarkable work with the regiment.

After a short stay of four years the regiment left Ireland in June, 1831, and was stationed at Manchester, Newcastle in 1832, and Gloucester in May, 1833. Major-General Sir Charles Dalbiac inspected the regiment at Manchester on the 11th and 12th of July, 1831, and his general observations are: "I consider it highly creditable to Lieut. Colonel Molyneux and to the Regiment at large, that the 8th Hussars after having been dispersed, and very actively employed in the disturbed Districts in Ireland, should have been found, upon their arrival in this Country to be in a state of efficiency at least equal to that of any Regiment, which has been brought under my Inspection.

"I regret having to report that Instances have not been wanting, wherein Serjeants without any positive Crime, irregularity or neglect of Duty, have failed to uphold their authority, with that degree of firmness, of steadiness and self pride, which is indispensable to the maintenance of wholesome Discipline. The consequence has been that there have been corresponding Instances on the part of the men, of a want of due respect, and of obedience towards the Non commissioned Officers. I did not fail to caution the Serjeants assembled, that if Lieut. Colonel Molyneux, at my next Inspection of the Corps, was not enabled to report more favourably with respect to their general Deportment, and manner in carrying on their Command, it would become my Duty to bring the matter under the especial Consideration of the General Commanding in Chief."[1]

The "twenties" in Ireland were marked by agrarian troubles just as the "thirties" in England were marked by political troubles due to the desire for the reform of Parliament. It is plain that the serjeants of the regiment took the counsel of Sir Charles Dalbiac to heart, for there were many more Courts Martial due more to

[1] *W.O.*, 27/209.

the frequency of trial than to the seriousness of crime.   In fifteen months there were 24 District, 2 Detachment, and 22 Regimental Courts Martial.   On his next inspection at Newcastle on the 22nd and the 23rd of October, 1832, Sir Charles Dalbiac was able to report: "I consider the 8th Hussars to be a most excellent and most efficient Corps.   The men and Horses are of a very desirable Description—the Appointments of the Corps in the best state and condition—the interior economy is extremely to my satisfaction.

"I have been gratified by an assurance from Major General Sir Henry Bouverie, that upon every occasion where Troops of the 8. Hussars have been employed by him for the suppression or for the prevention of Tumult, since this Corps came under his Command, the Conduct of the Officers, Non Commissioned Officers and men have met with his entire approbation, and that he has never known more zeal, activity or intelligence displayed upon such occasions by any Corps than by the 8th Hussars.

"I have received similar reports of the good Conduct of the Troops of the 8th Hussars from Magistrates and others under whom they have been placed for the suppression or the prevention of Riot in the Counties of Durham and Northumberland."[1]

On the death of that first-class cavalry leader, Sir Banastre Tarleton, the vacancy was filled on the 1st of February, 1833, by the appointment of Lieutenant-General Sir William[2] Keir Grant, K.C.B., G.C.H.   Gazetted to a cornetcy in the 15th King's Light Dragoons, now the 15th Hussars, he became lieutenant in 1793, and accompanied part of his regiment to Flanders, where he fought at Famars, Valenciennes, and elsewhere in the disastrous campaigns of 1793–4.   He distinguished himself personally in April, 1794, when a squadron of his regiment saved the Prince of Schwartzenberg from the enemy's hussars during a reconnaissance, and he was present at Villiers-en-Couche in April, 1794.   Promoted to a troop in the 6th Dragoon Guards, he served in Germany in 1795 and in Ireland in 1798.   In the latter year Grant received permission from George III to wear the large gold medal given by Francis II in commemoration of the action at Villiers-en-Couche.   Only nine

---

[1] *W.O.*, 27/217.   [2] Grant's first name was originally simply Keir.

of these medals were struck, one being given to each of the eight British officers present, and the ninth placed in the Imperial Museum, Vienna. These officers were also made knights of the military order of Maria Theresa, which, as in the case of other foreign orders previous to 1814, carried with it the rank of knight-bachelor in England and other countries. It also gave the wearer the rank of baron in Austria. The truth was that the charge of two squadrons of the 15th Hussars and two of the Andrew Leopold Hussars saved the Holy Roman Emperor from capture at the hands of the French.

Grant joined the Russian and Austrian armies in Italy early in 1799, and served in the campaigns of 1799 and 1800–1. He was present at the Battles of Novi, Rivoli, Mondovi, and Sanliano; he served in the gunboats at the siege of Genoa, and in several actions in the mountains of Genoa. He was present at the Battle of Marengo and the sieges of Alessandria, Sanaval, Tortona, Cunio, Savona, and Genoa. In 1800 Grant was appointed colonel of the 22nd Light Dragoons, but unfortunately for him he landed in Egypt after the cessation of hostilities in 1801. While on half-pay he was aide-de-camp to the Prince of Wales and afterwards to Lord Moira. In 1810 he commanded the advance of Major-General St. Leger's force on the Sutlej. In the same year he was promoted colonel, and a major-general in 1813, when he commanded a small force of cavalry and grenadiers sent against Amir Khan, a noted Pathan freebooter, in 1814. The next year he was made commander-in-chief and second member of council in the island of Java, a position he held until the island was restored to the Dutch after the peace. In 1817 he commanded the Guzerat field force, part of the army of the Deccan, in the operations against the Pindaris. In February, 1819, he successfully led a force against the Sawunt Warree State, and he did the same in March against the raja of Cutch, defeating the foe and capturing the hill fortress of Bhooj. In October, 1819, the Bombay government despatched him with a strong armament for the suppression of piracy in the Persian Gulf. He specially directed his attack against the Joasmi, a tribe of maritime Arabs of the sect of Wahabees or followers of the Arab religious reformer, Abd-ul-Wahab (Bestower of Blessings). The treaties he signed with the vanquished provided for the entire suppression of piracy in the Gulf. For his services he received the thanks of the governor-general in council and the Persian decoration of the Lion and Sun. He was made K.C.B. in 1822, lieutenant-general in 1825, G.C.H. in 1835, colonel of the 2nd Royal North British Dragoons (Scots Greys), and general in 1841.

On the 12th of June, 1833, Sir Keir Grant inspected the regiment, and expressed his gratification with everything he had seen, noting especially the excellent state of discipline. In 1834 the regiment removed from Gloucester to Coventry, and to Hounslow in 1835. In 1834 guidons were discontinued.[1] By the 1st of January, 1835, the six troops had named twelve representatives who now formed the St. Patrick's Fund.[2] The governor of this fund was the colonel, the trustees were the lieutenant-colonel and the senior major, and the treasurers were Messrs. Cox & Co. The capital was £1800 invested in 3 per cent. Consols. This interest of £54 together with about 220 monthly subscriptions, reckoned to produce £132 per annum, furnished an income of £186. Donations, as they were called, were awarded to subscribers on their becoming non-effective. Men of twenty-four years' service and invalids who had subscribed one year received twelve shillings annually, subscribers for two years twenty-five shillings, subscribers for three years thirty-eight shillings, ranging upwards to subscribers of twenty-three years in receipt of £22 1s., those of twenty-four years in receipt of £25, and of twenty-five years in receipt of £25 12s.

In his third inspection of the regiment at Hounslow on the 15th of June, 1835, Sir Charles Dalbiac stated: "I have to report in very favourable terms upon the State and Condition of the 8th (K.R.I.) Hussars, upon its field discipline, and its general equipment. The only exception to its perfect efficiency is a somewhat more than ordinary number of old and worn out Horses, which should be

[1] *The Standards and Colours of the Army*, p. 206.
[2] *W.O.*, 27/342. Bound up with the *Inspection Returns* of 1845.

parted with as soon as Circumstances will permit. In every other respect there cannot be a more efficient Corps than the 8th Hussars.

"Having had occasion in Confidential Report of last year to animadvert in strong terms upon the increase of Crime and Punishment, which had taken place in this regiment, I have now the satisfaction to bring to the notice of the General Commanding in Chief, that the Number of Courts Martial and of Defaulters in general has very materially diminished, and with some few exceptions amongst the Privates I consider the 8th Hussars to be a well conducted Corps."[1]

In May, 1836, the regiment left Hounslow for Dublin, and was stationed there to October, 1837, when it removed to Newbridge. In 1838 it returned to Dublin, and afterwards proceeded to Dundalk. In August, 1839, the regiment set out for Leeds.

On the removal of Sir William Keir Grant to the Scots Greys, the new commanding officer was Lieutenant-General Sir Joseph Straton, K.C.H., who was appointed on the 24th of August, 1839. Joseph Muter, later Straton, entered the army as cornet in the 2nd Dragoon Guards in 1794, becoming lieutenant in 1795, and captain of a troop in the 13th Light Dragoons in 1797. In 1804 and 1805 he studied in the Royal Military College, High Wycombe, obtaining a first-class diploma. He was then appointed to the staff of the Duke of Gloucester, receiving the rank of lieutenant-colonel in 1808. In February, 1810, he embarked for Portugal with his regiment, serving three campaigns in the Peninsula. His conduct in command of the 13th Light Dragoons at Arroyo de Molinos in 1811 earned him mention in the despatches of Sir Rowland Hill. In 1813 he was raised to the rank of lieutenant-colonel of the Sixth, or Inniskilling, Dragoons, and of colonel in 1814. He commanded the Inniskillings at the Battle of Waterloo, and on the fall of Sir William Ponsonby the command of the brigade, consisting of the 1st, 2nd and 6th Dragoons, fell to him. In his despatch the Duke of Wellington singled out this brigade as having particularly distinguished itself. Towards the close of the battle Colonel Muter was wounded and his horse received two

---

[1] *W.O.*, 27/246, *Inspection Return.*

wounds.   He received a Waterloo medal, the C.B., a very high distinction, the fourth class of the Order of St. Wladimir of Russia, and was appointed Knight Commander of the Royal Hanoverian Guelphic Order.   He was promoted to the rank of major-general in 1825, and to that of lieutenant-general in 1838.   On succeeding to the property of his aunt, Miss Straton, at Kirkside, near Montrose, he assumed the name of Straton.   He was nominated to the colonelcy of the Eighth in 1839, and removed to the Sixth, or Inniskilling, Dragoons in 1840.

Major-General Sir J. W. Sleigh inspected the regiment at Leeds on the 19th of September, 1839.   His general observations are: "I have found the 8th Hussars in a very efficient state highly creditable to Lieut. Colonel Molyneux, the Regiment was a neat compact body of men, well mounted and what I should expect a Regiment of Hussars to be; the external System is good, the School well conducted with much attention from the Commg. Officer. The Officers are well mounted with much esprit de Corps, and the conduct of the men appears exceedingly good.

"Major Wodehouse in the temporary command is well qualified for the situation he stands in, appears well acquainted with the system and internal arrangements of his Regt.

"I had no opportunity of seeing the Regt. out, there being no ground but the parade in marching order was every thing I could wish.

"Courts Martial have decreased, entries in the defaulters book are less by 44, and the list of offenders upon the whole is less by 38 than at the last Inspection.

"I consider the Adjutant and Riding Master as being both particularly good.

"The Regiment is not well put up, crowded in upon the 7th Drag. Guards and Horse Artillery without the full use of a Riding House, no School Room, or Mess House for the Officers, who consequently are deprived of the Mess allowance.   On every consideration it is adviseable that the Regiment should be sent to a Barrack where the Corps may establish its own Hd. Quarters, at present they can do nothing."[1]

[1] *W.O., 27/284, Inspection Returns.*

On the 14th of March, 1840, Sir Joseph Straton was notified that the dress was to be changed from red to blue by 1842.[1] In May, 1840, the regiment left Leeds for Norwich. Major-General Sleigh again inspected it at Harwich on the 17th of October, 1840. In his general observations he states that "the excellent state in which I have found this Regiment throughout, proves the unremitting zeal and constant superintendence of their Commanding Officer—to the Honble. Lieut: Colonel Molyneux my best commendation is due, and I should fail in my duty did I not bring to the particular notice of the General Commanding in Chief the high order he has his Corps in, and the perfect knowledge Lt. Colonel Molyneux appears to possess of every Man and Horse under his charge.

"There is a considerable increase in the number of Defaulters, as well as of offenders generally since the last inspection but there is a difference of 8 months in the period and as the increase in that time of Courts Martial is only three I can safely pronounce the conduct of the Regiment generally to be favourable.

"Two of the Troops are in debt above £10 caused by Desertion but not of any extent."[2]

Sir J. W. Sleigh had a new colonel for this inspection, for Sir Joseph Straton had removed to the Inniskilling Dragoons, and was succeeded by Major-General Philip Philpot on the 30th of April, 1840. Ensign in the Seventy-sixth Foot in 1787, he was lieutenant in 1788, and captain in 1797. For thirteen years he served with the Seventy-sixth, sharing in its brilliant achievements in India. In 1800 he exchanged to the Twenty-seventh, afterwards the Twenty-fourth, Light Dragoons; and served with it when it acquired the honour of bearing the Elephant, with the word Hindoostan, on its guidons and appointments. He was major in the Twenty-fourth Light Dragoons in 1807 and lieutenant-colonel in 1811. On the return of his regiment to England, it was disbanded, and he was placed on half-pay in 1818. He was promoted to the rank of colonel in 1821 and to that of major-general

---

[1] *W.O., General Orders, Circulars, Letters, etc.*, June, 1839—December, 1851.
[2] *W.O., 27/299, Inspection Returns.*

in 1830. In 1840 he was nominated colonel of the Eighth, and in 1841 he was promoted to the rank of lieutenant-general.

In May, 1841, the regiment left Norwich for the Hulme Barracks, Manchester. In August, 1841, Lieutenant-Colonel the Hon. G. B. Molyneux died, and was buried with military honours at Manchester. Unusual sorrow was felt for his loss, and Lord Hill and Sir Charles Napier eloquently testified to the worth of his services.[1] He was succeeded by Lieutenant-Colonel James McCall, the major of the regiment. Major-General Sir J. W. Sleigh, Inspector-General of Cavalry, made yet another inspection at Manchester on the 25th of September, 1841, stating that "I have found the Regiment in the same excellent state in which I was enabled to speak so favourably of it on my last Inspection, evidently caused by the system established by their late lamented Commdg. Officer.

"Lt. Col. McCall shews great zeal and anxiety for the welfare of the Regiment, and I have no doubt will follow the example that has been set by his late Commanding Officer, he appears qualified to do so in every respect and justly feels a pride in succeeding to the Command of so efficient a Corps as the 8th Hussars are."

In April, 1842, the regiment was quartered at Hounslow and Hampton Court. Major-General the Hon. E. Lygon inspected it at Hounslow Barracks on the 2nd of August, 1842, pronouncing that his inspection was "highly satisfactory. Lieut. Colonel McCall is most zealous and active in his dutie, and maintains his Regiment in the best order.

"The Regiment made a fine appearance in the Field, manœuvering with precision and proper celerity.

"I saw the Officers ride in the School, their performance was most creditable to the instruction they had received, as well as to their own marked attention.

"Courts-Martial are not numerous. The Offences on the Defaulters Book are of a light description, and have been judiciously dealt with."[2]

[1] *Regimental Records*, 1693–1899, pp. 28–9, for the testimonies of Lord Hill and Sir C. J. Napier to the value of the services of Lieut.-Col. Molyneux.

[2] *W.O.*, 27/314, *Inspection Returns*.

In May, 1843, the regiment marched to York, detaching one squadron to Newcastle-on-Tyne, another to Leeds, and a troop to Bradford. On the death of Lieutenant-General Philpot in March, 1843, Lieutenant-General Sir John Brown, K.C.H., succeeded him on the 4th of April, 1843. Lygon made his second inspection at York on the 2nd of September, 1843, when he found "all the Head Quarters of this Regiment in good order. Lieut. Colonel McCall very active in his command. . . .

"Court Martials have increased, as also have Entries in the Defaulters Book. Crimes, generally, of a light nature."[1]

Sir John Brown paid a visit to the headquarters of the regiment at the latter end of July, 1843, and remained almost a fortnight. During this time he inspected the regiment in all its details and saw it in review order. On occasion after occasion he took the opportunity of signifying his gratification with the appearance and the discipline of the corps and his sense of the honour of being placed by "Her Majesty" at its head.[2]

In June, 1844, the regiment embarked at Liverpool in three divisions for Dundalk. Detachments were sent to Belfast and Charlemont in aid of the civil power. The "forties" were the time when Daniel O'Connell was agitating for the repeal of the Union, and Ireland was filled with repeal and anti-repeal movements. Nor can we omit the fact that the year 1846 witnessed the terrible famine. It was indeed, as Lord John Russell expressed it, a famine of the thirteenth century with a nineteenth century population. Behind the movements of the regiment we have to bear in mind the forces then agitating Ireland. It marched from Dundalk to Dublin at the latter end of September, 1844, to do duty in the garrison of Dublin, the headquarters and one squadron arriving in Portobello Barracks. Twice Major-General Wyndham inspected it, first in October, 1844, and secondly in May, 1845, and each time he expressed his approbation of the state of the regiment. It remained in Dublin until September, 1845, when it marched to Longford, detaching two troops to Athlone, one each to Mohill and Clone, and one to Dunmore. Leaving Longford in May, 1846,

---

[1] *W.O.*, 27/323, *Inspection Returns.* [2] *Records of the 8th*, p. 43.

it marched to Cahir, detaching two troops to Limerick and one to Clonmel.

The Duke of Cambridge inspected the regiment at Cahir on the 24th of October, 1846, and his general observations run thus:

"Three troops of the 8th Hussars are at present at Head Quarters, a Squadron is at Limerick and one troop at Dungarvan. I inspected most minutely the Head Quarters under Lt. Colonel McCall and am exceedingly pleased with every thing I have seen and with the manner in which the Lt. Colonel commands this very beautiful regiment. They are a very fine body of men, well mounted and I consider them in a very high state of efficiency both as to discipline and in every other respect, as a proof of which I need only mention that there has been but *one Court Martial* since last Inspection. I saw the officers and men ride and was perfectly satisfied with every thing I saw in the Riding School. The Recruits and Young Horses joined since last inspection are very good. The weekly charge for messing each Officer is about £2 8s. 1d."[1]

Up to 1847 enlistment in the army had been for life; but now short service of ten or twelve years was introduced, with the choice of joining for twenty-one years. On the 19th of February, 1847, Major F. G. Shewell succeeded to the lieutenant-colonelcy of the regiment, vacant by the retirement of Lieutenant-Colonel McCall. It marched from Cahir and arrived at Ballincollig in September, 1847, detaching two troops to Cork, one to Bandon and one to Fermoy. Leaving the Cork district it arrived in Newbridge in July, 1848, detaching a squadron to Dublin and a troop to Kilkenny.

The year 1848 is memorable for the political activities of young men over the whole of the western half of Europe. There were "Young French," "Young German," "Young Italian" movements, and there was a "Young Ireland" movement. The last made as little appeal to Ulster as it made to O'Connell. In 1848 it attained prominence through the literary efforts of a brilliant set of men who wrote in *The Nation*. Among these men were Thomas Davis,

[1] *W.O.*, 27/353.

the real leader, Sir Gavan Duffy, Smith O'Brien, and John Mitchel. In their ranks were such true poets as Davis himself and Mangan, Ferguson and MacCarthy. As in the 1798 Rebellion many of the leaders were Protestants, so it was now in the Young Ireland party. One of his friends found Lord Plunket perusing the columns of *The Nation*. He asked the Lord Chancellor what was the tone of the new journal, and Plunket answered with perfect truth, "Wolfe Tone."

A troop of the regiment, on its march from Cork to Newbridge, received orders to join a flying column at Ballingarry under the command of Major-General McDonald to aid in pursuit of the Young Irelanders who had broken out into rebellion. For six weeks it continued in the performance of this duty, and the rebellion, which was never formidable, collapsed. This troop them joined headquarters at Newbridge. Under the command of Lieutenant-Colonel Shewell the regiment marched from Newbridge to the Royal Barracks, Dublin, for the purpose of doing duty during the memorable first visit of Queen Victoria and Prince Albert to Ireland in August, 1849.

At Newbridge the Duke of Cambridge inspected the regiment on the 5th of November, 1849, and he was again able to say: "The 8th Royal Irish Hussars continue concentrated at Newbridge with the exception of one Troop detached to Carlow. This Regiment continues to be in a very creditable and efficient state and is remarkably well commanded by Lt. Colonel Shewell who I look upon as a most intelligent Cavalry Officer. The Officers appear to me to be particularly well acquainted with the Interior Economy of their several troops. The Regiment is well drilled, the men look clean and soldierlike, the horses are good and altogether the Corps is fit for any duty that may be required of it."[1]

After nearly six years of service in Ireland the Eighth embarked at Dublin in three divisions, landing at Liverpool, and proceeded to Brighton in May, 1850, detaching one troop to Dorchester and another to Trowbridge. At Brighton Major-General Brotherton inspected the regiment, and he simply said of it that "it is in

---

[1] *W.O.*, 27/387.

excellent order. I had no fault to find except with the riding of some of the officers."[1] It left Brighton and arrived at Hampton Court in April, 1851, detaching four troops in billets to the town of Hounslow. Major-General Brotherton, Inspector-General of Cavalry, again inspected it at Hounslow on the 6th of August, 1851, and his general observations recorded that "this regiment is well commanded and is in excellent order."[2] Clearly Lieutenant-Colonel Shewell was continuing the fine work of a splendid officer like Molyneux.

In May, 1852, the regiment left Hounslow, and proceeded to Nottingham, detaching a squadron to Sheffield, a troop to Mansfield and another to Loughborough. At Nottingham the Duke of Cambridge made another inspection of the regiment on the 16th of August, 1852. He recorded: ". . . I saw this Regiment in the field all together on Hounslow heath and have inspected since the Hd. Qrs. at Nottingham. I consider the 8th Hussars to be in excellent order in every respect. The drill of the Regiment was all I could wish, the general appearance of the Corps is perfect, the horses excellent and in the best condition. The Officers a most gentlemanlike set of men and well instructed and zealous; the interior economy is properly attended to and the riding from not having been as good as I could wish, improved to such an extent, that I would compliment the Regiment upon it. The best riders I have seen this year in the School are certainly those of this Regiment. Lt. Colonel Shewell is a most conscientious and good Officer of whom I entertain the highest opinion and he is especially well supported by all his Officers. The state of the Regiment reflects the *greatest credit* on the Lt. Colonel."[3]

The Duke of Wellington died on the 14th of October, 1852, and he certainly takes rank after Marlborough as the second greatest soldier we have produced. A squadron of the regiment and the band formed part of the funeral procession when his remains were laid to rest in St. Paul's Cathedral.

In June, 1853, the Royal Irish received orders to practise tent pitching preparatory to going into camp on Chobham Common,

[1] *W.O.*, 27/398.   [2] *W.O.*, 27/408.   [3] *W.O.*, 27/418.

and formed part of a second encampment under the command of Lieutenant-General Seaton. The weather proved so vile that the ground turned into a swamp, and the men were constantly employed in draining the water from the tents and the temporary stables. On the sixth day after arrival a change for the better fortunately occurred, and then field days generally took place four or five days in each week of the nine weeks of the encampment. On its break up the Eighth marched off the ground and proceeded *en route* to Dorchester, detaching a squadron to Exeter and another to Trowbridge. The Duke of Cambridge inspected the regiment at Dorchester on the 3rd of October, 1853, and he stated: ". . . I have Inspected the two former portions of the Regiment and do not think that either as to men or horses they are at all the worse for their recent exposure. The health of the men is most satisfactory, the condition of the horses is excellent. This is a nice Regiment and in very good order, and fit for work in every respect. The Regiment is admirably mounted, the Officers are good and well instructed in all their duties, and a gentlemanlike set of men, the men are a smart body of soldiers, well drilled and ride very well. I regret to say that some serious cases of insubordination have recently occurred, for which it is difficult to account in so well organised a Regiment, but I think there is no blame attached to anybody, but that they are isolated cases of loss of temper, which are much to be regretted and of which I trust there will be no recurrence. I thought it right to speak strongly to the Regiment on the subject, and hope this will have a good effect. I have a very good opinion of Lt. Colonel Shewell as a Commanding Officer and think him extremely anxious and most attentive to his duties."[1] In a note appended to his report the Duke of Cambridge expresses doubts on the judiciousness with which some exercised their authority.

[1] *W.O.*, 27/428.

PRINTED BY
W. HEFFER AND SONS LTD.
CAMBRIDGE, ENGLAND.